Feminist Lives

Feminist Lives

Women, Feelings, and the Self in Post-War Britain

LYNN ABRAMS

OXFORD
UNIVERSITY PRESS

OXFORD
UNIVERSITY PRESS

Great Clarendon Street, Oxford, OX2 6DP,
United Kingdom

Oxford University Press is a department of the University of Oxford.
It furthers the University's objective of excellence in research, scholarship,
and education by publishing worldwide. Oxford is a registered trade mark of
Oxford University Press in the UK and in certain other countries

Published in the United States of America by Oxford University Press
198 Madison Avenue, New York, NY 10016, United States of America

British Library Cataloguing in Publication Data
Data available

Library of Congress Control Number: 2023936658

ISBN 978-0-19-289699-5

DOI: 10.1093/oso/9780192896995.001.0001

Printed and bound in the UK by
Clays Ltd, Elcograf S.p.A.

Preface and Acknowledgments

In 2002 I wrote a book called *The Making of Modern Woman*, an expansive survey that was European in its geographic scope and stretched from the French Revolution to the end of the First World War. It argued that the model of the modern woman we recognize today was produced by a confluence of ideas, events, and experiences that had their origins in the European Enlightenment which provided women with the language and ambition to imagine and strive for a different kind of life. This book is very different. It focuses on Britain and one cohort of women born in the long 1940s. Yet, in many ways, *Feminist Lives* is the child of *Making*, intellectually and historiographically. The women who feature in this study are the descendants, only two or three generations removed, of the women who forged a new kind of womanhood at the turn of the nineteenth century. Their lives are framed by choices that were fought for decades earlier; the constraints on fulfilling their dreams would be recognizable to their great-grandmothers. The feminist lives recounted in this book are then the product of generations of women who argued and debated for change so that women could have the same opportunities as men, equality in education and the workplace, the freedom to express themselves. The post-war generation pushed the door open wider in their desire to live with more freedom and options than their foremothers had done.

Whereas the *Making of Modern Woman* predominantly told the story of the collective experience of women from a distance, using a wide-angle lens, *Feminist Lives* is a study in close-up, focusing on the individual life in relation to the wider community of women. It was important to attempt to do justice to the variety and depth of the stories entrusted to me so I have tried to give these voices the space to breathe, to acknowledge their richness and complexity. The quid pro quo, however, is that the book cannot represent an entire generation. But I hope that my interviewees will at least recognize how elements of their accounts gesture towards the bigger narrative with its themes of generational change, emotional revolution, feminist agency, and the visibility of women's experience.

My local book group and inhabitants of my small Scottish village of Doune provided the starting point for this work, supplemented by interviews with other women drawn from friendship networks and contacts made via national women's organizations. They provided insightful, reflective, and evocative material which went on to inform the themes around which the book pivots. In a sense they were the progenitors of this study; their honest accounts persuaded me that there was a collective story to be told, coalescing around the ways in which the self was made and re-made across the life course. As one interviewee put it, 'I have had many womanhoods'. Although most of them appear under pseudonyms they will doubtless recognize themselves in stories featuring their love of clothes, their propensity to travel, the ups and downs of relationships, the pleasure and value of involvement in women's organizations. Fulsome thanks are owed to all of you who entrusted me with your life stories. You are all within these pages somewhere.

I would also like to acknowledge the work undertaken by previous and current generations of social and feminist researchers who have collected oral history interviews and other forms of personal testimony and made it freely available to the community of scholars via the UK Data Archive. Collections of material dating from the 1960s through to the 2000s provided both contemporaneous and retrospective accounts of women's lives, enhancing and deepening the arguments that could be made. And mention here should also be made of the memory stories gathered and deposited by women's organizations. It remains vital to record women's histories as the process of recovery can only take place if they have a presence in the archive.

This book has been a long time in the making, interrupted by periods of heavy responsibility in the workplace followed by the Covid-19 pandemic. The School of Humanities and especially the community of historians at the University of Glasgow have been generous with leave and the support that facilitates it. My friends in the Centre for Gender History—the best kind of emotional community—have constituted a productive intellectual and social environment. I have benefited immeasurably from being part of this invigorating and empathetic feminist network. In particular Maud Bracke, Tanya Cheadle, Mairi Hamilton, Penny Morris, Alexandra Shepard, Christine Whyte, and Valerie Wright have been there for critical commentary, encouragement, friendship, and coffee and cake when needed.

Every book is indebted to the labour of others and this is no exception. Linda Fleming, Jade Halbert, Eoin O'Cearnaigh, and Valerie Wright conducted some of the research and contributed their own insights to the benefit of my thinking. Ben Boswell-Jones, Jessica Cross, Deborah Hackett, and Charlie Lynch transcribed my oral history interviews. Caitriona Beaumont, Callum Brown, Sarah Crook, Amanda Gavin, Jade Halbert, Carla Pascoe-Leahy, Alexandra Shepard, and Hannah Yoken read chapters and offered insightful and helpful comments and the book benefited from the input from participants at lectures, seminars, and conferences at Cambridge, Glasgow, Keele, Melbourne, Newcastle, Nottingham, Oxford (supported by a TORCH Fellowship), the Royal Historical Society, Toronto, and Wellington. Helen McCarthy provided generous and searching comments on the final manuscript. I received help from archivists at the University of Essex, the Institute of Education at University College London, the National Survey of Health and Development team at the Medical Research Council, BBC Written Archives Centre, Norfolk Record Office, National Library of Scotland, the Wellcome Collection Archives, and the Women's Library. And thank you to the owners of the illustrations who provided them gratis. Cathryn Steele and Karen Morgan at OUP have shepherded this work through the production process and Matthew Cotton championed it from the start. David Overson and Simon Barratt built me a beautiful study in which to write. My brother Kevin Abrams bore a huge share of responsibility as the pandemic severed me from family members. Callum Brown always believed in the project and my ability to complete it, chivvied me along when I flagged, and read the whole thing with the critical eye of a fellow historian and as my best friend. If there are errors, despite all of that, they are my responsibility.

Earlier versions of some of the ideas presented here have been published as: 'The Self and Self-Help: Women Pursuing Autonomy in Post-war Britain', *Transactions of the Royal Historical Society* 29 (2019), pp.201–221; 'Heroes of Their Own Life Stories: Narrating the Female Self in the Feminist Age', *Cultural and Social History* 16:2 (2019), pp.205–224; 'Liberating the Female Self: Epiphanies, Conflict and Coherence in the Life Stories of Post-War British Women', *Social History* 39:1 (2014), pp.14–35.

Contents

List of Illustrations

Abbreviations

BBC	British Broadcasting Corporation
CAB	Citizens' Advice Bureau
CND	Campaign for Nuclear Disarmament
MAMA	Meet-a-Mum Association
MRC	Medical Research Council
NCT	National Childbirth Trust
NCW	National Council of Women
NHR	National Housewives Register
NSHD	National Survey of Health and Development
NWR	National Women's Register
OU	Open University
PPA	Pre-school Playgroups Association
TWG	Townswomen's Guild
u3a	University of the Third Age
VSO	Voluntary Service Overseas
WAM	Working Association of Mothers
WEA	Workers' Education Association
WI	Women's Institute
WLM	Women's Liberation Movement

1
Revolution of the Self

Introduction

Could women be feminist without feminism? Could they foster feminist activism without a movement or an ideology? Could they recraft ways of being female without a plan? *Feminist Lives* adopts a woman-centred approach to understand how women charted a new way of being female in the three decades before the Women's Liberation Movement.[1] Focusing on the so-called 'transition' or 'breakthrough' generation of women who were born in the long 1940s and who grew to maturity in the 1950s, 1960s, and 1970s, the argument here is that this generation of women developed the aspirational model of womanhood that then emerged after 1970 as the norm amongst women in the Global North. *Feminist Lives* seeks to fill 'the feminist history gap', countering a narrative that has for too long neglected and sometimes falsely lampooned this generation of women as fusty and failing, and as just not feminist enough. Using women's voices as the book's evidential and emotional core as they describe themselves, their lives, and their place in the British post-war landscape between 1945 and 1970, this book analyses the modes by which women constructed a modern self, built upon new ways of living and being.

The experiences of women like Anne sit at the heart of this version of post-war British feminist history. Born in 1947, she grew up in a comfortable though not especially well-off family in a university town in southern England. After failing the selective Eleven-Plus examination and attending a secondary modern school which had conventional gendered expectations for its girl students, she ceased education at 16 and found work as a laboratory assistant, the first of several jobs in an era of full employment. But work was not Anne's priority; men took up most of her attention in a culture of parties, drugs, and casual sexual relationships. Although this was the era when the oral contraceptive pill became available to single women, Anne adopted a natural approach to her body. When she became pregnant she was able to access a legal abortion under the NHS, but after another unwanted pregnancy and another abortion she carried her third pregnancy to term and had her first child at the age of 24 out of wedlock with a

[1] Betty Jerman, *The Lively-Minded Women: The First Twenty Years of the National Housewives Register* (London: Heinemann, 1981); Mary Ingham, *Now We Are Thirty: Women of the Breakthrough Generation* (London: Eyre Methuen, 1981).

Feminist Lives: Women, Feelings, and the Self in Post-War Britain. Lynn Abrams, Oxford University Press.
 DOI: 10.1093/oso/9780192896995.003.0001

partner who refused to take either financial or caring responsibility. The welfare state came to her aid, providing her with a council house and financial support. Anne never married—unusual for her cohort—and had two more children, only picking up work again piecemeal when they went to school. As a young, single parent living on a council estate, her life course was determined by her caring responsibilities but the emerging self-help culture of the 1970s did provide respite, enlightenment, and social contact. Anne variously attended a Gestalt group, a women's self-defence class, and the local branch of the National Childbirth Trust. The local Women's Centre offered a place where 'you could go and read or just be'.[2]

Anne described her life as having no pathway. As a young woman she participated in the permissive hippy culture but, in her words, became trapped by motherhood. As an older woman Anne pondered on a life story which, in so many ways, paralleled that of her mother's and yet which, in crucial other ways, was characterized by freedoms unheard of amongst her mother's generation. At the age of 17 Anne 'felt on the edge of stuff... These were the sex and drugs and rock and roll times. No path to follow but wondrous things to see.'[3] There seemed to be what she described as a 'dislocation between generations'. Anne had, at one stage, hated her mother for what she represented, an emotion that drove her headlong into a different kind of life, but later on, informed by her own experiences of motherhood and parenting, she reached a better understanding of her mother.

Anne was not typical of her generation. None of the women featured in this study can claim to be representative. But the life stories Anne and all the other women who speak to us in this book chose to tell are revealing, not just because of the experiences recalled and recounted which add to our knowledge of women's lives in this period, but because of the meanings attached to those experiences. The women who came of age in the decades following the end of the Second World War, who grew up on the eve of the emergence of the Women's Liberation Movement, and who have been described variously as the breakthrough, transition or welfare-state generation, were better educated and had more sexual and personal freedoms than their mothers; they witnessed the steady expansion of opportunities to work, to travel, and to be oneself.[4] And part of that opening up of the public and civic landscape for women was a willingness to narrate their lives as individuals with a legitimate claim to a place in the historical record. Women of this generation, those born roughly between 1938 and 1950, are able to tell their life stories with themselves at the centre, as the heroes rather than the bystanders. They understand that they are the women referred to when

[2] Interview with Anne. [3] Personal correspondence with Anne.

[4] Jerman, *Lively-Minded Women*; Ingham, *Now We Are Thirty*; Eve Worth, *The Welfare-State Generation. Women, Agency and Class in Britain since 1945* (London: Bloomsbury, 2021).

historians write about the massive social changes of those decades: it was they who wore the mini-skirts, who made it to college and university, who had sex before marriage, who limited their families, who went back to work when their children had grown, and who expected more of their relationships, albeit some had to wait longer than others.[5] And in talking about their lives on the record they further contribute to the creation of a collective biography of a generation that sees itself as treading a new path.

The historical shifts and revolutions experienced and enacted by this generation are now the subject of major interpretations of the late twentieth century. Clothing, mobility, sexuality, the expressive and emotional turns, radical politics, the relationship between work and family, between self and family and the individual and the state, all feature women who recognize their part in the story because they *were* a part of it. Now in their seventies and eighties, they are both primary sources and historical actors. Through oral history interviews and other forms of personal testimony brought forth in a confessional culture that legitimizes first person accounts, they provide retrospective versions of lives lived through a period of almost unprecedented opportunity.

Feminist Lives pivots around the stories of individual women who have narrated—in oral histories, in published autobiography and other forms of personal testimony—narratives which reflect upon generation, gender and change in this formative era. This book argues that until the 1950s, there was no widespread and socially acceptable idea of the autonomous woman. Some of course blazed a trail, performing models of womanhood incorporating careers and family and for some, unconventional love lives, but they were in the minority.[6] Most women's lives had been destined by society's rather rigid expectations regarding marriage and motherhood. Most women were constrained by limited educational opportunity and narrow economic prospects as well as conservative social attitudes towards the body and sex. Their self-fulfilment was deemed to be tied to their social role—as wife, mother, homemaker. After scores of decades in roughly the same state, young women's opportunities rapidly changed. Though hitherto somewhat derided by those who formed the later Women's Liberation Movement, the autonomous female self of late modernity was fashioned first amongst this post-war generation. They were the first to benefit in significant numbers from the democratization of secondary education and the expansion of higher

[5] I have used both 'generation' and 'cohort' to describe this group of women. Whilst cohort is a more accurate description of a group defined by their dates of birth, there is a case to be made for describing this group as a generation, framed by their shared responses to social change, not least because many of them regard themselves as belonging to a defined generation, distinct from that of their mothers and the generation of their daughters.

[6] See D.J. Taylor, *The Lost Girls: Love, War and Literature, 1939–51* (London: Constable, 2019); Rachel Cooke, *Her Brilliant Career. Ten Extraordinary Women of the Fifties* (London: Virago, 2014).

education and they had rising expectations.[7] They were also the beneficiaries of post-war welfare reform, housing improvement, and technological change, and felt a widening acceptance of women's economic autonomy and a gradual loosening of moral constraints upon them. They fought for and achieved power over their own bodies through fertility control, abortion, new freedoms in sexual life, and a refashioning of relationships and domestic and family structures.[8] They established new patterns of working and new ways of seeing themselves.[9] This was a time of personal transformation for many, characterized by the embrace of opportunity, independence, and autonomy. In contrast with the lives of their mothers' generation which were shaped by institutional impediments and expectations of service, subservience, self-sacrifice, and self-control, their daughters made the journey from 'home-makers' to 'self-makers'—albeit not without struggle and not all at the same pace. This book will focus on this pivotal moment in the twentieth century for women's experience and women's subjectivity. It argues that women, individually and collectively, were agents of change in their own lives. And that change occurred because women were liberated from the emotional limitations experienced by those who preceded them. Feelings were legitimately expressed in the post-war decades and women made their feelings visible to themselves and to one another, a process that turbo-charged action. That action was the key to self-realization and fulfilment.

Feminist Lives is a study in close-up. The focus is primarily on individual women and their interpretations of what happened to them set in a wider landscape. Their understanding of those experiences, both contemporaneously and in retrospect, provide the starting point, an approach 'from the bottom up' which takes seriously women's opinions on what was important and which assigns meaning to everyday acts. Women's narratives determine the critical points and themes which may challenge some of the interpretations previously identified by historians. The everyday achieves more prominence than the themes that commonly feature in characterizations of this period such as sexuality,

[7] Carole Dyhouse, *No Distinction of Sex: Women in British Universities, 1870–1939* (London: UCL Press, 1995); Peter Mandler, *The Crisis of the Meritocracy. Britain's Transition to Mass Education since the Second World War* (Oxford: Oxford University Press, 2020).

[8] Hera Cook, *The Long Sexual Revolution: English Women, Sex and Contraception 1800–1975* (Oxford: Oxford University Press, 2004); Zoe Strimpel, *Seeking Love in Modern Britain: Gender, Dating and the Rise of the 'Single'* (London: Bloomsbury, 2020); Callum G. Brown, *Religion and The Demographic Revolution: Women and Secularisation in Canada, Ireland, UK and USA since the 1960s* (London: Boydell, 2012); Claire Langhamer, *The English in Love: the Intimate Story of an Emotional Revolution* (Oxford: Oxford University Press, 2014); Marcus Collins, *Modern Love: An Intimate History of Men and women in Twentieth Century Britain* (London: Atlantic Books, 2003).

[9] Helen McCarthy, *Double Lives: a History of Working Motherhood* (London: Bloomsbury, 2020); McCarthy, 'Women, Marriage and Paid Work in Post-War Britain', *Women's History Review* 26:1 (2017), pp.46–61; Eve Worth and Laura Paterson, '"How is She Going to Manage with the Children": Organisational Labour, Working and Mothering in Britain c.1960–1990', *Past and Present*, Supplement 15 (2021), pp.318–43; Dolly SmithWilson, 'A New Look at the Affluent Worker: The Good Working Mother in Post-War Britain', *Twentieth Century British History* 26:3 (2015), pp.424–49.

permissiveness, alternative lifestyles, radical politics, and activism.[10] Oral history in particular has become a methodological mainstay of social history, still throwing up material that would be difficult if not impossible to find in written sources.[11] It is here that we uncover the meaning of the banal to counter the contemporary and historical preference for the spectacular. But the interrogation of narratives for the meaning those narrators ascribe to experience permits the historian to critically consider the applicability of universal themes and overarching frameworks, especially as they apply to women's experience.

This is an episode that we might understand as women's liberation's pre-history, of that generation of women who generally frame their life stories within a feminist or liberationist discourse of equality and opportunity but for whom feminism, in its ideological and activist guises, was like a shadow in the background of their lives. The text of this book burrows into that outlook and the rhetoric they used. This is the feminist generation in an era of British history which was shaped by feminism in terms of a growing acceptance of the basic tenets of gender equality. Many amongst this generation did engage in forms of activity not explicitly defined as feminist or not explicitly part of the Women's Liberation Movement but certainly with the objective of improving their own lives and those of women more widely. Organizations such as the National Housewives Register, the Pre-School Playgroup movement, and the National Childbirth Trust addressed the tensions between motherhood and career, being a wife and being a professional, being a person and a woman, and offered women a place to nurture themselves, to develop networks of like-minded women and to grow. Involvement in childcare provision, community activism, and campaigning issues such as the plight of single mothers, post-natal depression and peace were all signs of a generation of women pursuing a path of independent thinking and personal autonomy. These are the kinds of thoughts women had and which emerge from the evidence. This book seeks to write in the same register.

The Post-War Landscape

The re-imagining of the self undertaken by women since the 1950s is a process that actively, imaginatively, and emotionally intersects with histories of late

[10] For example, Frank Mort, *Capital Affairs: London and the Making of the Permissive Society* (2010); Celia Hughes, *Young Lives on the Left: Sixties Activism and the Liberation of the Self* (Manchester: Manchester University Press, 2015); Jonathan Green, *All Dressed Up: The Sixties and the Counterculture* (London, Pimlico, 1999).

[11] Studies that focus on sex and sexuality are the clearest examples. For instance, Hannah Charnock, 'Girlhood, Sexuality and Identity in England, 1950–1980', PhD thesis, University of Exeter, 2017; J. Hockey, V. Robinson, and A. Meah, *Cross-Generational Investigation of the Making of Heterosexual Relationships, 1912–2003*. Colchester, Essex: UK Data Archive, October 2005. SN: 5190, http://dx.doi.org/10.5255/UKDA-SN-5190-1 [hereafter UKDA SN 5190].

twentieth-century Britain on a number of fronts. The overarching vectors of post-war reconstruction followed by the key components of 'modern Britain' are well known. The rejection of organized religion, especially by women, and particularly its moral stance on matters concerning sex, improvements in the building blocks of everyday life from the built environment and especially housing to wider affluence and being able to participate in the consumer revolution, the impact and experience of migration, the reform of education, especially comprehensivization and the expansion of higher education, changes in work organization and practices and the revolution in popular culture.[12] Taking a different tack, studies of this generation through the prism of the welfare state, motherhood, childcare, and the labour market have emphasized the need to document and understand women's experiences in order to assess the impacts of policy, ideology, and provision.[13] In so doing they demonstrate that women's experience did not align with that of men. Social class and gendered role expectations, and policies and structures that did not dismantle these, continued to shape women's decisions and opportunities. The poor provision of childcare in the 1960s and 1970s is a prime example. And despite major reforms to social provision—the establishment of the NHS, the 1944 Education Act and 1945 Education (Scotland) Act, and the provision of council housing—which in theory and in ambition improved the opportunities and wellbeing for girls and women, it is now clear that the welfare state 'could be both a liberation and a constraint' when looked at over the long term.[14] General claims about educational opportunity and social mobility have been overstated. Women's mobility patterns do not mirror those of men's in terms of experience, opportunity and timing, and this is particularly true of working-class women who were destined for the factory or Woolworths rather than a career or higher education when they left school and who seized the opportunities denied them at 15 later in life.[15] And when extending the story beyond the 1970s, even those women who had benefited from the growth of job opportunities in the fields of health and welfare were negatively affected by de-professionalization.[16]

[12] The literature on the social history of post-war Britain is extensive. Some key works relevant to this study include: Callum G. Brown, *The Death of Christian Britain: Understanding Secularisation 1800–2000* (London: Routledge, 2001); Becky E. Conekin, Frank Mort, and Chris Waters (Eds), *Moments of Modernity? Reconstructing Britain 1945–1964* (London: Rivers Oram, 1999); Jon Lawrence, *Me, Me, Me: The Search for Community in Post-War England* (Oxford: Oxford University Press, 2019); Clair Wills, *Lovers and Strangers: An Immigrant History of Post-war Britain* (London: Penguin, 2017); David Kynaston, *Modernity Britain. Book One: Opening the Box 1957–59* (London: Bloomsbury, 2013); David Kynaston, *Modernity Britain. Book Two: A Shake of the Dice 1959–62* (London: Bloomsbury, 2014).

[13] Worth, *Welfare State Generation*; McCarthy, *Double Lives*; Laura Paterson, 'Women and Paid Work in Industrial Britain', PhD thesis, University of Dundee, 2014.

[14] Worth, *Welfare State Generation*, p.161.

[15] Selina Todd, *The People: The Rise and Fall of the Working Class* (London: John Murray, 2014), pp.225–6 and *passim*.

[16] Peter Mandler, 'Educating the Nation III: Social Mobility', *Transactions of the Royal Historical Society* 26 (2016) pp.1–23; Steph Lawler, 'Getting Out and Getting Away: Women's Narratives of Class Mobility', *Feminist Review* 63:1 (1999), pp.3–24; Worth, *Welfare State*, pp.127–31.

The experiences of women from non-white and non-Christian communities encountered another layer of discrimination on the grounds of race and religion as well as, for some, obstacles to personal autonomy within their own families and cultures.

Alongside the material account of the twentieth century, there is a parallel version in which a new concept of the self operates as the primary lens through which change is interpreted.[17] New ways of understanding the self in relation to the world, influenced by the psychological sciences permeating popular culture in the post-war decades, were manifested in the ways in which people lived their lives and also in modes of self-expression.[18] Increasingly people sought out opportunities for individual growth and self-development, what Steedman describes as the 'valorization of the self', through education, work and intimate relationships; self-fulfilment meant acting on feelings rather than sublimating desires to social expectations.[19] And while relatively few people came into direct contact with the new psychological sciences, from the 1960s their influence pervaded the social realm in the domains of health, education, and social and economic life as well as at the level of the everyday, from women's magazines with their relationship advice to didactic literature on childcare and marriage. The 'psychological subjects' of Thomson's analysis embrace the broad insights of the psy-sciences which, in his words, 'provided a language and topography of self' eroding the culture of deference and emotional restraint, enabling individuals to harness something within themselves in the pursuit of self-realization.[20]

These two versions of post-war Britain, the material and the psychological, have still to be conjoined in a sustained way. The revolution in the ways in which the self could be expressed and understood features in histories of activism amongst the radical left, feminists and campaigners for gay rights, demonstrating how individual subjectivity and collective experience could be the impetus for change, but it is less visible elsewhere.[21] In histories of education, of changes in the built environment and even of the revolution in sexual ethics and behaviour, attention to how individuals' self-understanding was both instrumental in the changes and impacted by them, remains underdeveloped. And yet self-expression

[17] See Mathew Thomson, *Psychological Subjects: Identity, Culture and Health in Twentieth Century Britain* (Oxford: Oxford University Press, 2006).

[18] See Chris Waters, 'Disorders of the Mind, Disorders of the Body Social' in Conekin et al. (Eds), *Moments of Modernity*, pp.13–51.

[19] Carolyn Steedman, 'Writing the Self: the End of the Scholarship Girl' in Jim McGuigan (Ed.), *Cultural Methodologies* (London: Sage, 1997), pp.106–25.

[20] Thomson, *Psychological Subjects*, p.8; Hera Cook, 'From Controlling Emotion to Expressing Feelings in Mid-Twentieth-Century England', *Journal of Social History* 47:3 (2014), pp.627–46.

[21] See Hughes, *Young Lives*; Jonathan Moss, *Women, Workplace Protest and Political Identity in England, 1968–1985* (Manchester: Manchester University Press, 2019); Lucy Robinson, *Gay Men and the Left in Post-War Britain: How the Personal Got Political* (Manchester: Manchester University Press, 2007).

and opportunities for self-fulfilment pervaded all areas of everyday life in post-war Britain, from the music club to the workplace, the boutique to the bedroom, the housing estate to the classroom.[22] Moreover, the liberation of the self was well underway before women's liberation activists made social and political change contingent upon new feminist subjectivities. The testimony featured in this book provides experiential and emotional accounts of social change as it manifested in everyday life. The biographical turn in historical writing enables us to understand subjective responses to material and discursive changes concerning the management of bodies and minds, the contours of personal relationships, the reach of the state, the impact of technology, the reform of education, the structure of the labour market, and the landscapes of social and geographical mobility. It also identifies where women themselves effected those changes. *Feminist Lives* provides the first sustained interrogation of the ways in which new selves were formed through these processes and in turn how the processes of change were driven, in part, by new ways of being amongst this generation of women.

Where there has been a deeper consideration of where new modes of selfhood were formed in relation to post-war social and political change is in relation to activism in radical and left politics including feminism. Highly dependent on memoirs and oral testimony from 'those who were there', studies of these milieux have yielded important methodological and historical understandings of the interplay between emotion, memory, and subjectivity in a context of collective action.[23] As studies of Sixties and Seventies activism—both left-wing politics and feminism—demonstrate, the self was being consciously constructed at the time in new spaces (such as universities, feminist and radical bookshops, squats, the Workers Education Association, anti-racism groups), through new practices (such as newsletter production, banner and placard-making, consciousness-raising) *and* it came to be reconstructed in retrospective narratives about that time.[24] This is a group which self-consciously, then and now, aligned beliefs with

[22] Steedman, 'Writing the Self'; Lynn Abrams, Barry Hazley, Ade Kearns, and Valerie Wright, *Glasgow: High Rise Homes, Estates and Communities* (London: Routledge, 2020), especially pp.36–65; Judith Attfield, *Bringing Modernity Home. Writings on Popular Design and Material Culture* (Manchester: Manchester University Press, 2007); Penny Tinkler, 'Are You Really Living?' If Not, 'Get With It!', *Cultural and Social History*, 11:4 (2014), pp. 597–619.

[23] Hughes, *Young Lives*; Luisa Passerini, *Autobiography of a Generation: Italy 1968* (Middletown, CT: Wesleyan University Press, 1996); Robert Gildea, Mark James, and Annette Warring (Eds), *Europe's 1968: Voices of Revolt* (Oxford: Oxford University Press, 2013); Sheila Rowbotham, *Promise of a Dream: Remembering the Sixties* (London: Allen Lane, 2000); Sheila Rowbotham, *Daring to Hope: My Life in the 1970s* (London: Verso, 2021).

[24] Hughes, *Young Lives* cites one respondent using the interview to reclaim 'a legitimate space for his past and present revolutionary selves', p.286. See also Lucy Delap, 'Feminist Bookshops, Reading Cultures and the Women's Liberation Movement in Great Britain, c.1974–2000', *History Workshop Journal* 81 (2016), pp.171–96; Emily Flaherty, 'The Women's Liberation Movement in Britain 1968–1984: Locality and organisation in feminist politics', PhD, University of Glasgow, 2017; Daniel Renshaw, 'The Violent Frontline: Space, Ethnicity and Confronting the State in Edwardian Spitalfields and 1980s Brixton', *Contemporary British History* 32 (2018), pp.231–52.

identity. Their political consciousness and their active involvement drive a self-narrative that positions their political awakening as a pivotal moment—a rupture—which frames everything that happened afterwards and which helps to interpret experiences prior to the awakening.[25] 'I met people and read books that gave names to these things that said, there are such things as patriarchy, there is sexism, there is oppression', explained a feminist activist. 'So it gave me the language and the kind of framework to understand what all these kind of amorphous feelings and anger and resentment were about.'[26]

Those whose self-identity is framed by their political or activist past, have a common language and set of cultural reference points—an epistemology—comprising key texts, significant campaigns, or events that bind the individual into a collective narrative.[27] They are visible to one another. These narratives are shaped by memories, networks, and friendships originating in the 1960s, 1970s, and 1980s and which continue to sustain a shared culture, summed up in the sentiment expressed by one former Trotskyist some decades later on her involvement with an Occupy protest: 'they are my people'.[28] In their life narratives individuals translate lived experience into a distinctive genre often serving to shore up a myth of collective experience and as testimonials to a belief in a set of fundamental principles which have the purpose of reaffirming the narrator's self-identification and sustaining the discursive narrative for posterity. Moreover, those involved in activist groups tend to associate doing, and especially collective action, with conferring identity or selfhood. Hughes describes the activist 'scene' or subculture amongst the new left which combined the personal and political. Commitment to a political cause was conjoined with new styles of relationship and forms of living. The mutual reinforcement of these two parts of the self expresses itself in a rather self-referential narrative which makes connections within the group or movement but rarely beyond it, and a sense of self that had difficulty situating itself in the present.[29] These narratives can be exclusive, denying those who did not share in the practices the possibility of belonging to the same narrative community.

What has been missing from existing accounts of women's lives in this period is a recognition that new selves could be discovered and new ways of being could be experienced alongside or within conventional social structures such as marriage and family rather than in opposition to them. Beyond the spaces we think of

[25] On the notion of rupture in feminist narratives see Passerini, *Autobiography* and Maud Anne Bracke, *Women and the Reinvention of the Political. Feminism in Italy, 1968–1983* (London: Routledge, 2014), p.24 and p.209.

[26] Glasgow Women's Library: Witness at Scottish Women's Liberation Movement Workshop (transcript), Edinburgh 2009.

[27] See Margaretta Jolly, *Sisterhood and After: An Oral History of the UK Women's Liberation Movement, 1968–Present* (Oxford: Oxford University Press, 2019), pp.35–9. On the importance of the written word for the formation of a collective consciousness see Phillida Bunkle, 'The 1944 Education Act and Second Wave Feminism', *Women's History Review* 25:5 (2016), pp.791–811.

[28] Cited in Hughes, *Young Lives*, p.287.

[29] Hughes, *Young Lives*, p.287.

as the radical alternatives to stifling suburban immobility, women were striving to carve out ways of being that offered a more gradual route to self-fulfilment and a quieter mode of self-expression. As Cohen has argued, change can come about quietly, gradually, and behind closed doors as conventional social mores were stretched.[30] This book argues that women in Britain in this era reimagined the concept of the modern female life course which was more complex, fluid, and multi-faceted than had been experienced hitherto. The fact that the majority married and pursued what looked like conventional lifestyles belies the psycho-dramas which accompanied this. Moving in with a boyfriend, leaving young children in a playgroup, attending a coffee morning or yoga class, returning to college, taking a part-time job: these are part-and-parcel of post-war women's lives which, incrementally, paved the way for a new model of the female life course in which all of these unspectacular activities were normalized.

The tendency in the literature to privilege activism over quiet, quotidian self-transformation echoes the condescension of those who have regarded women's self-help activism as lacking the thoroughgoing political critique that was to be developed by women's liberation in the early 1970s and thus not sufficiently radical to be considered part of the post-war feminist narrative.[31] Self-help or 'do-it-yourself' initiatives as they were dubbed, which addressed concerns around childbirth, motherhood, childcare, and the isolation of housewives, have been seen as reinforcing rather than overturning the subordination of women and thus not integral to dominant contemporary and historical narratives of post-war womanhood and especially of feminism.[32] The result is that organizations that addressed the tension between women's maternal and domestic roles on the one hand and self-expression and self-development on the other hand have, so far, not been integrated into interpretations of post-war change.[33] Studies of the less oppositional spaces which, since the inter-war years, had offered women opportunities to grow as critical citizens such as the traditional women's organizations such as the Women's Institute, Townswomen's Guild and Mothers' Union, political parties, and NGOs, have shown how they could enable women's agency in a public and private sense, promoting 'active citizenship' whilst offering members personal fulfilment without challenging normative expectations of gender roles.[34]

[30] Deborah Cohen, *Family Secrets: The Things we Tried to Hide* (London: Penguin, 2014), pp.xv–xvi.

[31] This approach is adopted by Elizabeth Wilson in *Only Halfway to Paradise: Women in Post-war Britain: 1945–68* (London: Tavistock Publications, 1980) and Anna Coote and Beatrix Campbell, *Sweet Freedom. The Struggle for Women's Liberation* (London: Picador, 1982).

[32] It was Mary Stott, editor of the Guardian's women's page between 1957 and 1972 who described the self-help groups as 'do-it-yourself' organizations. Both terms will be used here. Mary Stott (Ed.), *Women Talking: An Anthology from the Guardian Women's Page 1922–35 1957–71* (London, 1987), p.225.

[33] Lynn Abrams, 'The Self and Self-Help: Women Pursuing Autonomy in Post-War Britain', *Transactions of the Royal Historical Society* 29 (2019), pp.201–21.

[34] Studies include: Caitriona Beaumont, *Housewives and Citizens: Domesticity and the Women's Movement in England, 1928–1964* (Manchester: Manchester University Press, 2013); Sue Innes, 'Constructing Women's Citizenship in the Inter-War Period: the Edinburgh Women's Citizens'

Yet for the post-war generation, such organizations with conventional hierarchies and modes of operation had less appeal than bottom-up, self-organized activism which could bend to women's own interpretation of their needs. As we shall see, though, women's own accounts are emphatic about how personal self-fulfilment and self-realization was often achieved through their involvement in para-feminist activities, voluntary organizations and further and higher education later in life. These actions were not selfish or neutral in their effects. These empathetic communities, whether they be the local National Childbirth Trust group, a Workers' Education Association or keep-fit class, provided spaces for emotional expression rarely present within pre-existing organizations and which, in turn, drove change in individual lives and also the lives of women collectively.[35]

Change, in this woman-centred narrative, occurred stealthily and without much fuss. Organizations dedicated to relieving women's loneliness by meeting in someone's sitting room, drinking coffee and engaging in intelligent discussion were unlikely to ruffle any feathers or attract anything other than benign comment. Notwithstanding the moral panics concerning changes in young people's behavioural codes, at the individual level women—and men—for the most part negotiated their way through life experiences in an incremental rather than revolutionary fashion. This though has translated into the muting of personal stories about these experiences. It is easy to talk about mini-skirts and music for example, because these themes feature prominently in popular representations of the period. But, counterintuitively, it is harder to talk about marriage, motherhood, the everyday. And the absence of a recognizable or publicly acknowledged history of para-feminist activity, that is the activities that went on beyond and around recognizable campaigns concerning women's rights, has had the consequence of silencing those narratives that have been labelled 'not feminist enough'.[36] The magnetism of the Women's Liberation Movement for historians and in popular representations of this period leaves rather cloudy what was happening to the women who matured between c.1957 and c.1975 for whom feminism was something yet to happen or in the background, or a bit scary or something that other people did.[37]

Association', *Women's History Review* 13:4 (2004), pp.621–47; Pamela Graves, *Labour Women: Women in British Working-Class Politics, 1918–1939* (Cambridge: Cambridge University Press, 1994); Pat Thane, 'The Women of the British Labour Party and Feminism, 1906–1945', in H.Smith (Ed.), *British Feminism in the Twentieth Century* (Aldershot: Edward Elgar, 1990), pp.124–43.

[35] See, for example, Katrine-Louise Mosely, 'Slimming One's Way to a Better Self? Weight Loss Clubs and Women in Britain, 1967–1990', *Twentieth Century British History* 31:4 (2020), pp.427–53; Eilidh Macrae, '*Exercise in the Female Life-Cycle in Britain, 1930–1970* (Basingstoke: Palgrave, 2016).

[36] Lynn Abrams, 'Talking About Feminism: Reconciling Fragmented Narratives With the Feminist Research Frame', in K. Srigley, S. Zembrzycki, and F. Iacovetta (Eds), *Beyond Women's Words: Feminisms and the Practices of Oral History in the Twenty-First Century* (New York: Routledge, 2019), pp.81–94.

[37] Mary Ingham argues that the majority of women were too busy for women's liberation and that the 'real concerns of the women's movement were inaccessible to ordinary housewives' and the message was too radical 'for women to relate it to their own problems'. Ingham, *Now We Are Thirty*, p.132, p.138, and p.140.

The long 1960s has, understandably, acted as a flame attracting historians who see this period as marking a 'moment of modernity', not least in terms of subjective expression, whether that be through sexual activity, left-politics, or popular culture.[38] More recently, however, historians have identified the relative affluence of the mid-century decades as fuelling the liberationist demands of the 1960s and 1970s, arguing for a relatively long period in which change was effected and encompassing women born in the inter-war decades as well as their daughters. Lawrence, drawing on 'ordinary people's thoughts and feelings' to chart attitudes towards community since the end of the Second World War, identifies a shared commitment to progress across the post-war decades, only weakened in the 1970s and 1980s. Langhamer situates the origins of the emotional revolution in the 1920s and highlights a 50-year period until the 1970s as a hiatus, a moment of modernity encompassing new ways of conceiving of and enacting the self, primarily through new forms of intimacy. And Selina Todd charts the rise and fall of working-class fortunes from 1910 to the 1970s, arguing for a step-change after the Second World War in respect of the realization of aspiration.[39] Todd makes a case for the importance of attending to the working lives of girls and women since the inter-war decades in explanations of social, political, and economic change.[40] This book argues for a sharper break. Personal testimony is crucial in delineating the ways in which those born in the 1940s conceived of and experienced their lives in very different ways from those born just a few years earlier. They lived lives 'utterly at odds' with what they had been socialized to expect.[41] They enacted the rupture located in the long Sixties, encompassing a confluence of social, economic, and cultural changes: secularization, declining fertility, rising educational achievement, growing labour market participation, and changing attitudes to sex and identity.[42] In contemporary and retrospective testimony they are clear that they saw the world through a different lens. They were a group for whom the educational and professional outlook was comparatively bright, enabling them to construct a lifestyle and outlook very different to that experienced by those born in the 1920s and 1930s.

Of course structural changes impacted on women unevenly according to social class in particular, although geography, religion and race and ethnicity also had a bearing. And striving for autonomy within a framework that still contained many structural impediments such as the absence of childcare, wage inequality, and gendered role expectations at home and at work, intensified existing issues like

[38] See Becky Conekin, Frank Mort, and Chris Waters (Eds), *Moments of Modernity: Reconstructing Britain 1945–1964* (London: Rivers Oram, 1999).

[39] Lawrence, *Me, Me, Me*; Claire Langhamer, *The English in Love: The Intimate Story of an Emotional Revolution* (Oxford: Oxford University Press, 2013); Selina Todd, *The People: The Rise and Fall of the Working Class* (London: John Murray, 2014).

[40] Selina Todd, *Young Women, Work and Family 1918–1950* (Oxford: Oxford University Press, 2005).

[41] Ingham, *Now We Are Thirty*, p.18.

[42] Brown, *Religion and the Demographic Revolution.*

the double burden and produced new ones such as marital breakdown. Yet, these women founded lives upon a liberationist practice albeit at different stages of their lives and running at different speeds, but rarely (or at least not consciously) upon liberationist ideology and movements. For one feminist writer, 'They were everywhere, and yet they were nowhere.'[43] This book aims to remedy that situation.

Feminist Encounters

Recovering women's own understandings and justifications of their lives is a feminist enterprise, founded on the need to reclaim women's experiences from the 'muffled' accounts in the written record and charged with the impulse to learn from individual experience in order to discover, understand, and act upon a common condition.[44] Oral history became a 'feminist encounter' with the potential to liberate women's voices and experiences from patriarchal structures, histories, and language.[45] The evidence in this book is drawn overwhelmingly from personal testimony produced in the form of oral history interviews, questionnaire responses, and autobiography. My own oral history interviews were the starting point for the project. They provide the ballast and the illumination of texture and nuance for the interpretation that follows. Twenty-five women, all white and from a variety of social class backgrounds though now predominantly middle class, spoke to me with candour and humour between 2011 and 2021 when they were in their sixties and seventies. The majority now reside in Scotland, some having done so since they were children, others having moved from other parts of the British Isles as adults. Whilst the preponderance of Scottish residents counters the Anglo-centric character of much scholarship in this field, there is little distinctively Scottish in their life stories apart from a different education system. All of the Scotland-based respondents had spent time in England or overseas at some stage in their lives suggesting greater commonality in the experiences of this generation than might be imagined.[46] It was these encounters that most profoundly shaped this book in terms of the topics and turning points. I also met with some

[43] Wilson, *Halfway to Paradise*, p.185.

[44] Jean McCrindle and Sheila Rowbotham, *Dutiful Daughters: Women Talk About their Lives* (London: Viking, 1977), p.9.

[45] Sherna Berger Gluck, 'What's So Special About Women?' in S.H.Armitage with P. Hart and K. Weathermon (Eds), *Women's Oral History* (Lincoln, NE: University of Nebraska Press, 2002), p.5.

[46] The initial interviews were conducted with members of my village book group and others recruited via the village newspaper *The Bridge*. Subsequent interviews were identified via snowballing and contacts made via the National Housewives Register and Pre-School Playgroup archives as well as the National Women's Register of local groups, some of which I attended. I also gave a talk to the National Women's Register online during the pandemic and recruited some additional respondents as a result. The early interviews pivoted around the question of religious and moral change whilst the later ones took a much broader perspective on women's life histories.

of them in informal focus groups over drinks and dinner and a small number read and commented on some of the earlier publications that utilized their testimony as well as sections of this book. Sharing authority with interviewees did not fundamentally alter my interpretations of their narratives; the story presented here is my responsibility alone and they likely take issue with some of my analysis.[47] But if we accept that the oral history interview is a conversation in which both interviewer and respondent are equally present then it is right to continue that conversation beyond the interview itself.

It is important to acknowledge here the intersubjectivities of those encounters. As I have discussed at greater length elsewhere, for this cohort of women in the Global North, who grew to maturity during the 'expressive revolution' of the 1960s and 1970s and who have experienced and become acculturated to the 'confessional culture' of more recent times, the oral history interview is an appropriate, familiar, and in some senses liberating platform for the articulation of the self and beyond that, a self embedded in a bigger story about the progress of women in the post-war era. This is a cohort of women able and willing to turn themselves into narrative subjects.[48] And yet that willingness may have been facilitated by the rapport I established with many of my interviewees, not least those recruited from my book group. My position as a local resident gave me privileged access to these women; I was one of them. And yet as a white, middle-class, feminist academic born a generation later I was not. To paraphrase Ann Oakley, I was outside myself and inside myself; I was the knower and the known.[49] As I consciously reflect on that simultaneous outsider and insider status it seems that I was the greater beneficiary of the encounter. On the other hand, those interview subjects recruited via different channels such as the National Housewives Register and the Pre-School Playgroups Association, who had no prior relationship with me, were keen to recount their experiences to someone with a genuine interest in and some knowledge of those organizations whilst also ranging well beyond the framework of their voluntary activism, recognizing that in order to make sense of a particular moment in their lives they needed to tell their life story.

The personal testimony produced by other researchers, often to provide data for very precise research agendas, presents different perspectives and material and greater analytical challenges, not least because of the distance of the user of the data from the encounter. Not being present in the room and having to rely on transcriptions or summaries of recordings now lost or unavailable, detaches the researcher from the interpersonal dynamics of the interviews but there is still great value in subjecting this material to analysis using the concepts and theories

[47] Michael Frisch, *A Shared Authority. Essays on the Craft and Meaning of Public and Oral History* (New York: SUNY, 1990).

[48] Lynn Abrams, 'Heroes of Their Own Life Stories'.

[49] Ann Oakley, *Experiments in Knowing: Gender and Method in the Social Sciences* (Cambridge: Polity Press, 2000), p.7.

developed by oral historians in the last few decades to illuminate new insights.[50] In addition to my own feminist encounters, which could never map all the terrain covered by this generation, this book utilizes a number of data collections comprising both contemporaneous and retrospective testimony. The earliest were produced in the 1960s, the most recent from projects conducted in the 2000s. They comprise Dennis Marsden's interviews with lone mothers (1965–6); Ray and Jan Pahl's interviews with the wives of managers (1968); Ray Pahl's study of divisions of labour on the Isle of Sheppey (1978–83); Annette Lawson's study of adultery between 1920 and 1983 (1981–3); published extracts from Ann Oakley's interviews for the 'Becoming a Mother' study in the 1970s and the full transcripts of the interviews conducted by Meg Wiggins for the follow up study 'Looking Back on Motherhood' conducted 37 years later in 2012; Jenny Hockey, Victoria Robinson, and Angela Meah's cross-generational study of heterosexual relationships over 80 years (2002–3); Selina Todd and Hilary Young's study of living standards and social identity in the English working class between 1945 and 1970 (2006–8); and Callum Brown's interviews for a study of humanist lives (2009–2016).[51] Full details of these collections can be found in the Bibliography.

Qualitative material was also mined from the longitudinal survey conducted by the National Survey of Health and Development (NSHD) with the 1946 birth cohort. Much of these data are quantitative or constitute short form responses to questionnaires but the material is supplemented by longer written statements by some of the respondents.[52] And various collections of written testimony solicited by women's organizations provided autobiographical accounts focused on participation in those groups. Finally, this rich and very personal material is supplemented by published and unpublished sources ranging from the records of women's groups including the National Housewives' Register (NHR), the Pre-School Playgroups Association (PPA), National Childbirth Trust (NCT), the Working Association of Mothers (WAM), Young Wives, and the National Council of Women (NCW), and printed and broadcast material from the BBC and national and local newspapers and magazines. All of these organizations and media platforms offered women the space to express themselves at a time when the emotional ecology of post-war Britain was beginning to change. Self-expression found many outlets and people were willing to listen.

[50] There is a lively debate about ethics and value of the re-use of qualitative data. See the roundtable on 'Historians; Uses of Archived Material from Sociological Research' in *Twentieth Century British History* 33:3 (2022), especially contributions from John Goldthorpe, Jon Lawrence, and Mike Savage.

[51] With the exception of Oakley's original study and Brown's interviews, all of these data collections can be accessed via the UK Data Archive. Selections from Oakley's and Brown's interviews are published in Ann Oakley, *Becoming a Mother* (London: Pelican, 1979); Callum G. Brown, *Becoming Atheist: Humanism and the Secular West* (London: Bloomsbury, 2017).

[52] Medical Research Council, National Survey of Health and Development: 1946 birth cohort study. MRC NSHD 1946–2005 Data. MRC Unit for Lifelong Health and Ageing at UCL. http://dx.doi.org/10.5522/NSHD/Q101

The voices of non-white women do feature in these studies albeit they are relatively few and women from Britain's Afro-Caribbean community have a greater presence in the archives than south Asian women.[53] The source material that does exist indicates to me that there are both a number of common features shared by women of all races and ethnicities, but also some marked differences, primarily the result of structural racism and cultural and religious distinctiveness that shaped the lives of women of Black and Asian descent in Britain. The commonalities can be seen, for example, in young women's rejection of the models of womanhood they see their mothers representing, the enjoyment of the new freedoms of post-war culture and in the very similar forms of self-help that emerged from both predominantly white and predominantly black communities in the 1960s and 1970s.[54] The differences are harder to do justice to in this study on account of the sheer diversity of the Black experience and the relative lack of Black women's voices in existing collections of personal testimony. So while *Feminist Lives* is predominantly a book about white women, we should not presume that the arguments and conclusions are excluding of Black women who were also seeking ways to liberate the self from the traditional models of womanhood prevalent in their communities.[55] As Manjit, a Kenyan-Asian girl, remarked: 'I don't care what people think I'm like. I don't want to be like everybody else. I think differently from my family already.'[56]

My analytical approach to the texts mined for this study is to intuitively lean in to their literary or poetic nature. By attending not just to what narrators said but how they said it, I have drawn on the theoretical frameworks developed by oral historians and feminist scholars which enable the historian to dig beneath the words uttered to excavate their meaning.[57] I demonstrate how these women were a critical generation to self-consciously understand that they were experiencing

[53] For example, Beverley Bryan, Stella Dadzie, and Suzanne Scafe, *Heart of the Race: Black Women's Lives in Britain* (London, Verso, 2018); Tracey Reynolds, *Caribbean Mothers. Identity and Experience in the UK* (London, Tufnell Press, 2005); Mary Chamberlain, *Narratives of Exile and Return* (London, Routledge, 2017); Sue Sharpe, *'Just Like a Girl': How Girls Learn to Be Women* (Harmondsworth: Penguin, 1976), Chapter 8: 'Black girls in Britain'. On south Asian women see Amrit Wilson, *Finding a Voice. Asian Women in Britain* (London: Daraja Press, 2018).

[54] See Sharpe, *'Just Like a Girl'*, pp.229–98; Clair Wills, *Lovers and Strangers. An Immigrant History of Post-war Britain* (London: Penguin, 2017), pp.311–15; Jessica White, 'Black Women's Groups, Life Narratives, and the Construction of the Self in Late Twentieth Century Britain', *The Historical Journal* 65:3 (2021), pp.1–21.

[55] An example is the teacher Beryl Gilroy whose autobiography *Black Teacher* (London: Faber & Faber, 2021) narrates her journey from British Guiana to suburban Britain, becoming one of Britain's first Black headteachers.

[56] Manjit cited in Sharpe, *Just Like a Girl*, p.280.

[57] This comprises a vast body of literature summarized in Abrams, *Oral History Theory* (London: Routledge, 2016) but foremost amongst them are: Penny Summerfield, 'Dis/composing the Subject: Intersubjectivities in Oral History', in T. Cosslett, C. Lury, and P. Summerfield (Eds), *Feminism and Autobiography* (London: Routledge, 2000); Charlotte Linde, *Life Stories: The Creation of Coherence* (Oxford, 1983); Julie Cruikshank, *The Social Life of Stories: Narrative and Knowledge in the Yukon Territory* (Lincoln, NE: University of Nebrasca Press, 2000). Personal Narratives Group (Eds), *Interpreting Women's Lives: Feminist Theory and Personal Narratives* (Bloomington, IN: 1989). S.B. Gluck and D. Patai

change, both at the time and in retrospect. They experienced profound identity shifts as they grasped the opportunities available to them in the spheres of education, work and personal life, and their self-narratives are key to accessing the nature of the liberation experienced by this cohort of women. Moreover, they are also the first generation to be prepared to reveal the self so candidly in published autobiographical accounts and in oral history interviews, often in remarkably self-analytical fashion.[58] The autobiographical injunction to write and speak about the self is well manifested in this group of women who understand that the person we are is the story we tell about our self.

Spaces for the Self

The archive is patriarchal. Its suppositions and assumptions, its privileging of some accounts over others, and its subordination of the private, domestic and everyday to public histories, means that it is necessary to excavate women's voices from the research imperatives created by patriarchal systems of knowledge.[59] In order to do this we need to apply the methodological understandings and concepts developed by feminist research and in particular, feminist oral history practice, so that we identify the inequalities in power, the intersubjectivity, and the agency grasped by those women who had few other avenues to express themselves so authentically. When we do this we find that the archive is a repository of feminist accounts, of women speaking out about their feelings, their hopes and disappointments, sometimes through mouths and pens of others, always mediated by interviewers, transcribers and summarizers, questionnaire compilers and data managers.

Life history narratives produced in an oral history interview perhaps offer the most multi-layered material for analysis largely because they incorporate reflexivity and intersubjectivity. Reflexivity by the subject involves the reflection on past experiences from the perspective of the present, creating a distinction between the narrating self and the protagonist or the self at the centre of the story.[60] This is a distinctive feature of the retrospective narrative which is produced in an intersubjective context whereby the story told is the outcome of a three-way conversation: between the narrator and herself, between the narrator and the interviewer,

(Eds), *Women's Words: The Feminist Practice of Oral History* (London, 1991); Srigley, Zembrzycki, and Iacovetta, *Beyond Women's Words.*

[58] The marker for feminist autobiographical writing in this vein is Jill Ker Conway, *The Road from Coorain* (New York: Vintage, 1989).

[59] See Jane Hamlett, 'Mothering in the Archives: Care and the Creation of Family Papers and Photographs in Twentieth Century Southern England', *Past & Present*, 246 Supplement 15 (2020), pp.186–214.

[60] Abrams, *Oral History Theory*, pp.39–40.

and between the narrator and cultural discourses of the present and the past.[61] In the interviews conducted in the early 2000s for Hockey, Robinson, and Meah's study of personal and family relationships across the life course, the women demonstrated the facility to negotiate with their past, presenting themselves as agents with the power to bring a particular vision of their relationship history into being.[62] In contemporaneous accounts that reflexivity can be especially revealing. Some of the managers' wives interviewed in the 1960s for the Pahls' study offered up a conversation with themselves in the presence of the interviewer as they pondered on the meaning of their lives as they were being lived. Mrs Ash who said she didn't like to analyse herself, nonetheless commented: 'I don't quite know where I'm going or what I'm going to do with myself.'[63]

Approaching oral history narratives by acknowledging the various elements in play contributes towards a richer appreciation of women's own interpretations of their life experiences. While discursive representations are important in helping us to paint a picture of the ways in which girls and women were portrayed through various media, and are undoubtedly salient in helping to frame narrative versions of the self, I do not exclude the possibility that women can own their life stories in ways that disrupt dominant or commonly held versions of the past without necessarily becoming 'discomposed'.[64] It follows that I am wary of necessarily ascribing agency to women who are able to align their memory stories with those dominant representations. Indeed, some groups are excluded from the dominant narratives which tend to privilege white experiences or interpretations and give little space to the complexity of non-white narratives. Composure—the idea that one tells a life story with which one is comfortable—can be reached without that alignment and indeed may be essential if the authentic self is to be owned and revealed independent of dominant discursive tropes. And discomposure—generally understood as the effect of being unable to present a coherent narrative either to the interviewer or to the self—might be considered to be a more authentic account and convey greater meaning. When a narrator struggles to piece together an episode or explain—to the interviewer or indeed herself—why she took a particular path we may obtain greater insight into what those decisions meant at the time and in retrospect than if she had presented a smooth account.

Few women of this generation explicitly aligned their experience with dominant or public interpretations of this period although most could anchor some of

[61] Abrams, *Oral History Theory*, pp.58–9.

[62] Jenny Hockey, Angela Meah, Victoria Robinson, *Mundane Heterosexualities: from Theory to Practice* (London: Palgrave Macmillan, 2007), pp.52–61.

[63] Pahl, R. (2018). *Managers and their Wives: A Study of Career and Family Relationships in the Middle Class, 1965–1967*. [data collection]. UK Data Service. SN: 853296 [hereafter UKDA, SN 853296]: Interview with Mrs Ash.

[64] Penny Summerfield, 'Culture and Composure: Creating Narratives of the Gendered Self in Oral History Interviews', *Cultural and Social History* 1:1 (2004), pp.65–93.

their experiences in some of its more well-known elements. The tropes that have had most purchase include: the young woman 'prompted by educational opportunity' or a 'desire for freedom' leaving provincial life for London; the woman who benefited from the opening up of opportunities and spaces, including the freedom to have sex without reproduction; the woman who was both socially and spatially mobile; all creating a picture of increasing personal freedom, self-assertiveness, and self-expression.[65] However, in contrast to the dominant popular representations of the 'long Sixties' which tend to characterize the period as 'permissive' or 'swinging', personal accounts reference a broader landscape of experience: the widening of educational opportunities for girls, the shifting attitudes to intimate relationships and to premarital sex, the cultural freedoms expressed in new ways of dressing and having fun and the new terrain of working motherhood. Yet in acknowledging the opening up of a more unfettered landscape, these testimonies also recognize and recall the constraints: gendered expectations at school and discrimination in the workplace, of being daughters, mothers, and wives. Those constraints are even more evident in feminist literature from the 1960s. Margaret Drabble, Penelope Mortimer, and Doris Lessing all penned novels featuring female protagonists experiencing the very same frustrations, resentments, and predicaments as real women in British society at that time: unmarried motherhood, loneliness in marriage, unplanned pregnancy, and so on.[66] These representations act as a counterpoint to the optimistic, emancipatory narrative that can be inferred from popular representations of the Sixties in particular.[67] Increasing freedoms are juxtaposed against an understanding that these were almost always checked by enduring social attitudes to women's behaviour and roles, more especially amongst working-class women. So sexual freedoms were countered by the fear or reality of an unplanned pregnancy; the freedom to advance one's education could be limited by the continuation of gendered expectations regarding appropriate jobs for women; the desire to return to the labour market after children could be stymied by uncooperative husbands or the absence of childcare.

Historians who have interviewed women across the socio-economic spectrum (albeit predominantly white) have noticed a common propensity to frame their

[65] D.J. Taylor cited in Stephen Brooke, '"Slumming" in Swinging London?', *Cultural and Social History* 9:3 (2012), pp.429–49, here p.430. See also Anthony Giddens, *The Transformation of Intimacy* (Princeton, NJ: Stanford University Press, 1992), p.27 on 'plastic sexuality' disentangled from reproduction and the making of a modern female subjectivity.

[66] Examples include: Margaret Drabble, *The Millstone* (London: Weidenfeld & Nicolson, 1965); Penelope Mortimer, *The Pumpkin Eater* (Harmondsworth: Penguin, 1962); Doris Lessing, *The Golden Notebook* (London: Simon & Schuster, 1962); Lynn Reid Banks, *The L-Shaped Room* (London: Chatto & Windus, 1960). See also Celia Brayfield, *Rebel Writers. The Accidental Feminists* (London: Bloomsbury, 2019).

[67] For example, Jenni Diski, *The Sixties* (London: Profile Books, 2009); Virginia Nicholson, *How Was it for You? Women, Sex, Love and Power in the 1960s* (London: Penguin, 2019).

life story within a discourse or, to use socio-linguist Charlotte Linde's term, 'coherence system' of gender equality. I have described this distinct genre of women's oral history as a feminography, a narrative in which we hear women owning their voices and the stories those voices tell. These are narratives which do not depend on men for their agency. By placing their own desires and decisions at the centre of the narrative these women are drawing on the possibilities unleashed by the expressive revolution of their youth and the feminist critiques of their middle years. Feminist discourses on gender equality, self-determination, and self-realization have created a discursive space for these life stories and have enabled some women to tell life histories in which they set the agenda, privileging their own interpretations of events and experiences and becoming 'heroes of their own life stories'.[68]

Offering a counterpoint to retrospective oral histories produced in a confessional culture is the vast array of contemporaneous material elicited via questionnaires and interviews in the heyday of qualitative social science research in the 1960s and 1970s.[69] Two studies in particular have afforded rich qualitative narrative material from women for this book. The 'Managers and their Wives' project conducted by Jan and Ray Pahl—an investigation of the career and family patterns of the mobile managerial classes—was conducted between 1965 and 1968. As well as questionnaires with both parties to the marriages focusing on men's career mobility—both social and spatial—and its impact on family life, the study incorporated lengthy interviews with 16 of the 86 couples, separately and together.[70] The interviews with the wives were designed to 'form a general picture of her ideas about herself and how these had changed over a considerable period in her life' and to gather 'detailed, factual accounts' of her everyday life.[71] The interviews were not recorded; the interviewer took detailed notes, 'recording factual information in note form but keeping verbatim records of opinions and ideas'.[72] The notes were then dictated and typed up forming lengthy 'transcripts' containing a combination of the interviewer's observations on the home environment and the demeanour of the interviewees, as well as her 'own feelings about particular interviews' alongside reported speech.[73] With the women's age range of between 47 and 30 in 1968, this study provides insights into the perspectives and

[68] Abrams, 'Heroes'; Florence Sutcliffe-Braithwaite and Nathalie Tomlinson, 'Vernacular Discourses of Gender Equality in the Post-war British Working Class', *Past & Present* 254, Issue 1 (2022), pp.277–313.

[69] On the interview as claimed by social science research see Mike Savage, *Identities and Social Change in Britain since 1940: The Politics of Method* (Oxford: Oxford University Press, 2010), pp.165–7.

[70] The study was published as J.M and R.E.Pahl, *Managers and Their Wives: A Study of Career and Family Relationships in the Middle Class* (Harmondsworth: Penguin, 1971). The original data and study materials can be consulted at the UK Data Archive, University of Essex: Study Number 853296.

[71] The interviews were conducted by Marie Corbin. See her account, 'Problems and procedures of interviewing' in Pahl and Pahl, *Managers*, Appendix 3, p.290. See also Appendix 2, 'Interviewer's check list of topics, themes and questions for personal interviews'.

[72] Corbin in Pahl and Pahl, *Managers*, p.297.

[73] Pahl and Pahl, *Managers*, p.297.

experiences of two groups: those of the inter-war generation, brought up in an era of self-control and regulation of the self, and the younger transition generation who had been more acculturated to self-expression.[74] Although for all of the women the interview was an unfamiliar and in some cases a disconcerting experience, the encounter 'opened a floodgate', eliciting 'detailed accounts of grievances, dissatisfactions and frustrations', seemingly mirroring the increasing propensity amongst the younger generation to cast off conventional reserve and engage in a degree of self-revelation.[75] The fact that afterwards many referred to the interview's 'therapeutic value' and compared it to time spent 'on the psychiatrist's couch' indicates at least a familiarity with the new ways of understanding and expressing the self, what Nikolas Rose describes as a 'psychologization of experience'.[76]

Pahl was one of a number of social researchers who embraced the interview as a legitimate methodology providing 'access to the social' through intense focus on individual stories.[77] Around the same time another social scientist, Dennis Marsden, interviewed 116 women in Colchester and Huddersfield for his research on poverty and the fatherless family, producing very singular accounts from women of their lives as lone mothers dependent on national assistance.[78] Unlike Pahl, Marsden personally conducted the interviews, writing down factual data during the interview and only afterwards 'recording on tape for transcription the mother's description of her experiences, as far as possible in the words she had used'.[79] The resulting 'transcripts' contain his observations of the women's material, social, and psychological worlds, their living conditions, physical appearance, and demeanour, and one must assume, an approximation of the words spoken.[80] For Marsden the interview was a means of accessing a kind of 'emotional truth' from a small sample which captured a moment in time.[81]

Both Marsden and Pahl were criticized by feminists who regarded their published work as insufficiently attentive to gender inequalities, both in respect of the methodology and the findings. Marsden recalled that he 'was a bit miffed later on

[74] The oldest was born in 1921 and the youngest in 1937.

[75] Pahl and Pahl, *Managers*, pp.291–2.

[76] Pahl and Pahl, *Managers*, p. 300; Nikolas Rose, 'Assembling the Modern Self', in Roy Porter, *Rewriting the Self: Histories from the Middle Ages to the Present* (London: Routledge, 1992), p.232.

[77] Savage, *Identities*, p.174. In an interview Dennis Marsden described his approach as working from the bottom-up, using the interviews as the starting point for the book and visualized it through the people he met. https://www.youtube.com/watch?v=DJcIZ2OXEWs

[78] I have focused on 25 women in Marsden's sample, those who were single mothers and who were born in the long 1940s. He also interviewed women who were divorced, separated, and widowed. UKDA, SN 5072.

[79] Dennis Marsden, *Mothers' Alone: Poverty and the Fatherless Family* (London: Allen Lane, 1969), p.10. Marsden expounded on his interview methodology in Paul Thompson, Ken Plummer, and Neli Demireva, *Pioneering Social Research* (Policy Press, online, 2021), pp.146–7.

[80] UKDA, SN 5072: User Document: Mothers Alone.

[81] Savage, *Identities*, pp.180–1. For an interview with Ray Pahl in which he talks about the different layers of the interview process and the importance of the qualitative interview see: https://www.youtube.com/watch?v=rQ6xicFNrEE&list=PLaz84-tXzx3lcWvpRFtkwUOhnwTvZJ5gr&index=5.

when the Women's Movement started, in the early seventies, claiming that only women could interview women, and all that Feminist research bollocks'. For him, the justification was in the women who wrote to him saying, '"You've absolutely caught my story". You know, that *Mothers Alone* had illuminated their life.'[82] Similarly, Ray Pahl received 'quite an amount of considerable aggressive flak from the growing feminist movement' for making the assumption that managers were men.[83] The criticisms were understandable at the time but in retrospect, after revisiting the original interview material with the benefit of the range of analytical frameworks provided by oral history theory, these encounters are of value for the granularity of detail of the women's personal circumstances and social worlds as well as the authenticity of their responses despite their hesitancy or inability sometimes to present themselves as coherent narrative subjects. Yet, even those who felt uncomfortable revealing their innermost feelings were familiar with the 'topology of the self'. 'I don't like telling you all my private business…it's like that play…by Pirandello, naked, I feel naked after I've spoken to you' admitted one of Marsden's respondents.[84] When Marsden describes his discomfort with the 'distortions' created by the interview, especially women's 'tendency to restructure past and current experience, each in terms of the other, in too coherent a way' he is inadvertently acknowledging the realities of their non-narrative lives.[85]

Although in very different circumstances, neither the managers' wives nor the lone mothers were practised narrators, offering a contrast with interviews conducted more recently and produced in a culture which encourages, even expects, self-narration. The lone mothers of Marsden's study explain their lives in a rather matter-of-fact way. As far as we can tell, they often inhabited the interview space. They may have lacked material resources and cultural capital and could be inarticulate, but their determination and resilience and sense of pride existed as a not so subtle rebuke to the interviewer's assumptions. These women were the very opposite of what Savage describes as the middle class 'quintessential autonomous and reflexive individuals of contemporary capitalism' who came to dominate accounts of social change in the 1960s and 1970s.[86] And while some amongst the managers' wives found it easier to report on how they thought their husbands saw them than how they saw themselves, the interview opened up a space that many of the interviewees grew into. Mrs Graveney, interviewed by Marie Corbin, when asked what sort of person she saw herself as, initially remarked: 'Bloody horrible. Or at least that's what my husband thinks. I suppose I'm a middle-aged woman

[82] Marsden cited in Savage, *Identities*, p.184. Original interview at https://www.youtube.com/channel/UCmK1mj5dCq0XuCWI7DVKx2w.

[83] Interview with Ray Pahl: https://www.youtube.com/watch?v=vqogIc3N-6M&list=PLaz84-tXzx3lcWvpRFtkwUOhnwTvZJ5gr&index=6.

[84] Marsden, D., *Mothers Alone: Poverty and the Fatherless Family, 1955–1966* [computer file]. Colchester, Essex: UK Data Archive [distributor], February 2005. SN: 5072 [hereafter UKDA, SN 5072]. Interview with Miss Cross (024).

[85] Marsden, *Mothers' Alone*, p.10.

[86] Savage, *Identities*, p.235.

who tries to keep going. I find it difficult to answer this. I'm really such an ordinary person.' But through the course of the interview Mrs Graveney became more confident, admitting she felt resentful of her husband and his work: 'I feel now that I want a life of my own.'[87] These interviews are revelatory in their ability to let the reader in to an intimate place—the self-identity of ordinary women who we would otherwise never have met.

Feminism and Subjectivity

One contemporary criticism of these kinds of study was that the interview practices were guided by dominant social science method which privileged objectivity as a means of collecting reliable data. Ann Oakley described the 'depersonalized' approach to interviewing, a 'masculinist mechanistic attitude', that 'was incommensurate with the practice of feminist social science' and urged practitioners to accept the existence of emotions and a sociology of feelings in the name of scientific rationality.[88] Oakley, along with Hannah Gavron, followed in the footsteps of a pioneering generation of women researchers such as Viola Klein, Alva Myrdal, Judith Hubback, Pearl Jephcott, and Joan Maizels who practised the mantra 'the personal is political' in their work on women, work, and families and who privileged women's perspectives on their situation.[89] The women interviewed by Oakley and Gavron for their research on the female role, were actively encouraged to articulate their feelings in their own words, creating what has been described as an archive of feeling.[90] And deviating from the ethnographic practice of Pahl, Marsden and others whose data contained copious editorializing and subjective interventions in the text such as observations on interviewees' homes or appearance, feminist researchers adopted new modes of working. Oakley's proposition that interviews incorporate elements of a 'transition to friendship',

[87] UKDA, SN: 853296: Interview with Mrs Graveney, pp.3–4.

[88] Ann Oakley, 'Interviewing women: A contradiction in terms?' in H. Roberts (Ed.), *Doing Feminist Research.* (London: Routledge and Kegan Paul, 1981), p.251 and Oakley, 'Interviewing Women Again: Power, Time and the Gift', *Sociology* 50:1 (2015), pp.195–213, here 196.

[89] The volume of work by these women is extensive. For example: A. Myrdal and V. Klein, *Women's Two Roles* (London: Routledge, 1968); Pearl Jephcott, *Married Women Working* (London: Allen and Unwin, 1962); Pearl Jephcott, *Homes in High Flats* (Edinburgh: Oliver & Boyd, 1971); Joan Maizels, *Adolescent Needs and the Transition from School to Work* (London: Athlone Press, 1970); Judith Hubback, *Wives Who Went to College* (London: 1957). See also Helen McCarthy, 'Social Science and married women's employment in post-war Britain', *Past and Present* 233:1 (2016), pp.269–305 in which she argues that these researchers should be regarded as 'important agents in social and cultural histories of gender', p.271. On Pearl Jephcott see Special Issue of *Women's History Review*, 28:5 (2019). Hannah Gavron, *The Captive Wife: Conflicts of Housebound Mothers* (London: Routledge & Kegan Paul, 1966).

[90] This concept has been widely used in feminist and LGBTQ+ studies. For example, Ann Cvetkovich (Ed.), *An Archive of Feelings: Trauma, Sexuality, and Lesbian Public Cultures* (Durham, NC: Duke University Press, 2003).

based on 'shared gender subordination' was widely applauded and taken up by a new generation of qualitative researchers.[91] Feminist social research then created new forms of knowledge about women's lives which took women's interpretations of their experiences seriously and played an important part in reframing public debates on women's role.[92]

Oakley's interviews with 55 women for the 'Becoming a Mother' study in the 1970s (extracts) and those from the follow up study conducted 37 years later (full transcripts) have been utilized for this book as well as the four interviews that feature at length in *Housewife*.[93] Oakley described her interview method as a 'human interaction' which enabled her to place women's experiences in the foreground, because 'I was impressed by the fact that the women said it all much better, and much more clearly and directly, than a sociologist could ever do'.[94] These interviews pay dividends in terms of real-time responses by interviewees to a present state of being. When Oakley and Wiggins undertook the follow up study to 'Becoming a Mother', returning to the original interviewees, it is notable how the respondents were, perhaps unsurprisingly, considerably more expansive and reflective on their experiences of maternity and motherhood. Some were very aware that in the first survey they had responded very much 'in the moment', whereas in the follow-up interview they were able to look back and reflect on a life that was rounder and fuller.[95] Nancy, for example, recounted in the first interview shortly after the birth of her daughter: 'I think it was on the fifth day her crying, her screaming, it just went right through me and I just could not cope...I got hysterical in the end: it was awful, I really hated her and wished to God I'd never had her.'[96] But in the follow-up meeting, Nancy, now aged 63, recognized that although she had actually felt that way at the time, she was now able to put her attitude in perspective:

[91] Oakley, 'Interviewing Women Again', p.196. However, later feminist oral historians were to question whether encouraging friendship was the correct approach in an encounter containing power differentials. Ray Pahl's close relationship with a couple who participated in his Sheppey project over many years, stands as a reminder of the perils of such a position. See Jane Elliott and Jon Lawrence, 'Narrative, Time and Intimacy in Social Research: Linda and Jim Revisited' in Graham Crow and Jamie Ellis (Eds), *Revisiting Divisions of Labour. The Impacts and Legacies of a Modern Sociological Classic* (Manchester: Manchester University Press, 2017), pp.189–204.

[92] McCarthy, 'Social Science', p.303. Oakley subsequently revisited her stance in Oakley, *Experiments in Knowing*.

[93] Oakley interviewed 55 women four times each between 1974 and 1979 for her longitudinal study on new motherhood. The interview material was reproduced in extract form in Ann Oakley, *Becoming a Mother* (London, Pelican, 1979). Forty women were interviewed for *Housewife* but only four of these feature in the book. Ann Oakley, *Housewife* (Harmondsworth: Penguin, 1974).

[94] Oakley, *Here to Maternity: Becoming a Mother* (Harmondsworth: Penguin, 1986), p.2.

[95] The original interviews conducted on average 6 and 26 weeks before the birth and 5 and 20 weeks afterwards. Oakley, *Here to Maternity*, p.4.

[96] Nancy in Oakley, *Here to Maternity*, pp.125–6.

> I look back on it now and think 'Well for God's sake, Nancy, cut yourself some slack', you know?...I've had a chance to redeem myself...I'm a survivor, I am a survivor, and I've only realized in the last 10 years quite how tough I am, and I'm glad. If I hadn't had all these shitty experiences they wouldn't have made me the person I am, would they?[97]

Utilizing testimony produced contemporaneously, or close to the experiences being recounted, contrasts with and complements the retrospective data gathered from the oral history interviews. The example of Nancy demonstrates how she responded almost viscerally to her baby's incessant crying—her feelings about her baby were expressed authentically being so close to the experience. Her retrospective memory of that time, however, is more measured when considered against the background of her subsequent life experiences. This may seem like an obvious point to make, but the existence of this unusual study where we can juxtapose the narratives about an experience gathered at different points in the same woman's lifetime opens the door to thinking further about how different versions of the self might be revealed through personal testimony across the life course.

The contemporaneous perspective is also accessible from the data gathered at regular intervals by a longitudinal cohort study—the NSHD—which sampled around 5362 women and men born in the UK in March 1946.[98] They were then followed up using detailed questionnaires 24 times addressing home environment, social adjustment, educational attainment, adult life choices, and health and wellbeing, though within these broad themes a raft of data was gathered on hobbies and leisure activities, reading habits, religion, and later on residential and marital status, earnings, social activities, and attitudes to class and politics.[99] However, it was not until the subjects reached the age of 13 that they completed the questionnaires themselves; prior to this the data was gathered from parents and teachers. The questionnaires are highly structured and offer limited opportunities for respondents to shape the story of their life course in creative or personal ways, yet some of the later ones in the 1960s and early 1970s when the

[97] Oakley, 'Interviewing Women Again', pp.205–6.

[98] MRC National Survey of Health and Development. https://www.nshd.mrc.ac.uk. All the members of the National Survey were born in one week (3–9 March) in 1946. They form a stratified sample of all births in that week to mothers living throughout Britain, 2815 male and 2547 female children being initially included in the follow-up sample. Helen Pearson, *The Life Project* (Harmondsworth: Penguin, 2016).

[99] For a summary of the NSHD's key aims, the policy problems it sought to address, and the kinds of data it collected during its first five decades, see Wadsworth, M., Kuh, D., Richards, M., and Hardy, R. (2005) 'Cohort Profile: The 1946 National Birth Cohort (MRC National Survey of Health and Development)', *International Journal of Epidemiology* 35:1 (2005), pp.49–54. See also https://www.nshd.mrc.ac.uk/ for a description of the method of data collection.

respondents were in their twenties, did include an open question in which he or she was asked to write about anything important that had happened to them in the previous year.[100] While most left this blank, some seized the opportunity to write quite extensively about their lives, compensating for the tick box approach of the questionnaire. This book draws on a randomized sample of 50 women from this study, along with some additional data gathered from those among the cohort who attended university and those termed 'persistent job changers' as well as the quantitative data generated from the whole study.[101]

There may appear to be little 'space for the self' in this kind of material.[102] In contrast with the oral history narratives or even the social survey data described above, these life stories are assembled from discrete snapshots in time, requiring concrete answers to questions designed to elicit quantifiable data, often through multiple choice answers. The National Survey of Health and Development had little interest in the perspectives and experiences of individual survey members, but in the broad patterns derived from the accumulation of cohort data.[103] And researchers who use these 'archives' rarely move beyond the coded data in order to discern broad patterns across the cohort.[104] Yet longitudinal studies like this can be used to reassemble biographies, albeit incomplete and disjointed, and they can offer us a perspective on lives as they unfolded in time as well as over time. Lacking the coherence and reflexivity of the oral history interview, nonetheless these cohort studies can let us get to know an individual via a 'qualitative reworking' of the material. This means looking beyond the coded data at a meta or cohort level and attending to the information provided by survey members across the life course of each individual.[105] This approach proffers the researcher with a kind of ante-life history narrative, a version of a life as it happened with none of the gaps and swerves and chance events smoothed over or explained, in contrast with the retrospective account.

[100] The blank questionnaires can be viewed at: https://skylark.ucl.ac.uk.

[101] A random sample of 50 women was selected by the NSHD team. I then accessed the questionnaires relating to the 50 on microfiche. The study continued beyond the last available questionnaire in 1972 but this data was not available to me. The questionnaire templates can be viewed at https://skylark.ucl.ac.uk/NSHD/doku.php?id=mrepo:questionnaires. The searchable metadata for the whole study can be accessed via the Skylark interface https://skylark.ucl.ac.uk/Skylark. Qualitative material was also mined from the Student Study Transcripts (1965) and the Persistent Job Changers' Survey (1968), both available from the MRC. The British birth cohort studies require researchers to maintain confidentiality and anonymity of panel members. The individuals in the sample of 50 have been given pseudonyms in the text and are identifiable only by the sample number in the footnotes.

[102] Alison Light, *A Radical Romance: A Memoir of Love, Grief and Consolation* (London: Fig Tree, 2019). p.12.

[103] See E. Ramsden, 'Surveying the Meritocracy: The Problems of Intelligence and Mobility in the Studies of the Population Investigation Committee', *Studies in History and Philosophy of Biological and Biomedical Sciences* 47 (2014), pp.130–41, here 137.

[104] Some of the qualitative material offered up by survey members, especially that provided in answers to open questions, was never coded as data.

[105] Penny Tinkler, Resto Cruz, Laura Fenton, 'Recomposing Persons: Scavenging and Storytelling in a Birth Cohort Archive, *History of the Human Sciences* 34:3/4 (2021), pp.266–89.

The Emotional Self

One of the historian's challenges is how to connect to the experiences of these women whose lives appear to us episodically or in fragments. I contend that we can do this by attending to the feelings they convey, whether spoken contemporaneously or retrospectively. This book focuses on the experience (rather than representation) of this generation of women and the ways in which they narrate and make sense of that experience. As such it is an emotional history. Retrospective accounts of a life almost inevitably bring forth a range of feelings which can shape the narrative offered in interview. Exuberance and joy exist side-by-side with more complicated and deeply held feelings about life experiences which translate into expressive narratives. On the other hand, contemporaneous accounts may capture a person's feelings in the very moment of encounter, allowing the historian access to an emotional self that is impossible to recreate in retrospect.[106]

Emotions, though, have a history. Love, grief, anger, shame, pride, joy—the gamut of emotions must be understood within emotional ecologies or landscapes which shape the ways in which people express their feelings (though it is much harder to know if the feelings themselves are similarly affected). So, in this period, that ecology is characterized by a broad shift from a wartime and post-war stoicism, an 'emotional economy' that valued self-control to maintain morale and national unity, to an emotional expressiveness whereby feelings were regarded as an important means of communication as well as revealing the inner self.[107] For the women whose lives feature in this book, the emotional ecology of British society altered during their lifetimes to privilege self-expression over self-control and thus it is important to attend to the contexts in which they provided their stories.

The interviews conducted in the 1960s and 1970s recorded women at a moment when the outward or public expression of emotion was beginning to be normalized though emotional restraint was still part of the emotional repertoire. We shall see how some of the interviewees used the interview as an outlet for emotions that could not be expressed within the domestic unit or other parts of their lives. By the 2000s, on the other hand, when I carried out oral history interviews for this project, there was less evidence of emotional restraint on the part of interviewees. The late twentieth-century liberation of feelings has freed up narrators to allow their emotions to escape the formal context of an interview. The intersubjectivities of the interview relationship generated a situation in which both parties were comfortable with the outward expression of emotions.

[106] Katie Holmes, 'Does It Matter If He Cried? Recording Emotion and the Australian Generations Oral History Project', *The Oral History Review* 44:1 (2017), pp.56–76.

[107] On the emotions shift in this period see Lucy Noakes, Dying for the Nation: Death, Grief and Bereavement in Second World War Britain. (Manchester: Manchester University Press, 2020), pp.51–68.

An interview practice that seeks to elicit reflection and honest accounts is not designed to promote emotional outpouring, but an easy rapport between the parties and a common understanding of the emotional ecologies of the twenty-first century in the Global North brought forth emotional, embodied responses by respondents using the gamut of expressions from laughter (lots of laughter) to tears. Furthermore, however, the emotions recounted during the interview encounter were used to make sense of the past by narrators. Decisions taken and choices made were explained with reference to feelings whereas previous generations are more likely to refer to expectations and conventions guiding their behaviour and life choices. It is this generational shift in the use of emotions to shape as well as understand and explain the life course that provides the starting point for this book. It was the post-war generation who rejected the stoicism and self-control of their parents' generation and who embraced a new expressive culture in which feelings guided actions.

Emotion is everywhere in the personal testimony utilized in this book. But simply observing it as a phenomenon is not enough. 'What do emotions do?' asks feminist theorist Sara Ahmed.[108] In the context of the social interactions described here, emotional expression signifies meaning for the narrator attached to past experiences and as a social practice in the present. For the listener, emotional expression alerts us that the memory and recounting of an event or an experience is capable of reigniting or producing feelings that have, hitherto perhaps, been buried under the surface. The interview encounter provides the environment for those feelings, or at least some feelings, to be exposed, perhaps for the first time. But the emotion expressed in the remembering and recounting of an experience is a different thing from the emotion brought forth by an event. The former is a practice and has a different origin, impetus, and purpose from the latter.[109]

Why is this important? The history of emotions is a feminist project. The internalization or self-management of emotions by women, often for the sake of others or to conform to societal expectations, is conjoined with traditional negative associations between femininity and emotionality and understandings of the self which depend on rationality rather than emotion. Feminist philosophers and historians have shown us how the command to subordinate emotions works to 'subordinate the feminine and the body'.[110] Thus women have tended to be especially good at regulating their emotional expression on account of the criticism levelled at those who have given full rein to their feelings or indeed because they have learned that 'being emotional' is met with condescension or

[108] Sara Ahmed, *The Cultural Politics of Emotion* (Edinburgh: Edinburgh University Press, 2014), p.4.
[109] Monique Scheer, 'Are Emotions a Kind of Practice? (And is that what makes them have a history)? A Bourdieuean Approach to Studying Emotion', *History and Theory* 51 (2012), pp.193–220.
[110] Ahmed, *Cultural Politics of Emotion*, p.3.

incomprehension. This is especially the case in health domains such as mental health and menopause, where women were often prescribed anti-depressives to dampen down their emotions. There are of course some domains in which women's emotion is accepted and even required. Emotional work in the family, at least until the 1960s, was the prerogative, even the duty of women, especially relating to care.[111] Such 'emotional labour' has also been observed in the workplace where women in particular have been required to manage their emotions appropriate to certain occupations.[112]

But emotional rejection of the domestic and caring role or indeed emotional responses to social and political inequalities in the domestic sphere have often been criticized.[113] Women were admonished to accept their role and to suppress any feelings of resentment or lost opportunity. However, by the mid-1960s the culture prevalent in Britain of self-restraint gradually gave way to a culture in which public expression of feelings by women (initially to one another) became an effective means of gaining sympathy and creating social networks or emotional communities.[114] The value of emotional stoicism which had been deployed to avoid destabilization and discomposure on an individual, community and national level in the 1940s and 1950s, gave way to a realization amongst the post-war generation that the expression of emotion was necessary and liberating and generative of new communalities of feeling. Emotion then, was reclaimed by women, as constitutive of the self, amongst not only those active in women's liberation who owned and celebrated their emotions in the service of the feminist project but many others who acknowledged their feelings to further their emotional and practical needs. Emotion was mobilized to reclaim the self.

For participants in women's liberation in the early 1970s, this idea of emotion as practice was most clearly manifested in consciousness-raising whereby women were urged to access their emotions in order to know and understand themselves and thus their position in a patriarchal society.[115] For Sheila Rowbotham the connection between consciousness and structural oppression was self-evident: 'If the external situation subdues us', she wrote in 1971, 'it is our consciousness that contains us.'[116] As Sarah Crook describes in the context of feminist mental health activism, 'the feminist project therefore necessitated an examination of women's

[111] See John Gillis, *A World of Their Own Making: A History of Myth and Ritual in Family Life* (Oxford: Oxford University Press, 1997), p.215 and *passim*.

[112] See Agnes Arnold-Foster and Alison Moulds (Eds), *Feelings and Work in Modern History: Emotional Labour and Emotions About Labour* (London: Bloomsbury, 2022), p.4. Also Claire Langhamer, 'Feelings, Women and Work in the Long 1950s', *Women's History Review* 26:1 (2017), pp.77–92.

[113] An example might be women's failure to conform to normative models of mothering.

[114] Barbara H. Rosenwein, *Emotional Communities in the Early Middle Ages* (Ithaca, NY: Cornell University Press, 2006).

[115] Scheer, 'Are Emotions a Kind of Practice?'; Ahmed, *Cultural Politics of Emotion*, p.8.

[116] Sheila Rowbotham, 'Women's Liberation and the New Politics', *Mayday Manifesto*, 2:6 (1971), p. 2.

consciousness, the excavation of the structures that regulated and labelled women's emotions'.[117] Emotion in this context became power. As women began to be able to speak about 'me', they were able to connect the personal with the political.[118] Rowbotham described how this happened when formerly isolated women came together: 'private hurts found collective expression in the small women's liberation groups. Feelings of inadequacy, and the all-consuming rage that left a sullen exhaustion in its wake, were not simply *relieved* by being communicated. Startling realizations arose from the fusion of energy that could result.'[119] But it was not only those involved in women's liberation who used their feelings to drive change in their lives. This book features numerous examples of women who rejected the stoicism of their parents' generation and acted upon how they felt rather than what was expected of them.

Ahmed posits that feminism is an emotional response to the world. I argue that emotion is a feminist response to the world. The post-war generation of women liberated their feelings, took them seriously, made them visible, and acted upon them in all realms of life, not just those areas where emotions might be expected to play a part such as intimate relationships. They felt the difference. And in so doing they constituted a new kind of self, a self for which emotions are essential rather than peripheral, things to think, work and act with, rather than to suppress.[120]

The Expressive Self

The narratives of the self which provide the primary material for this book were produced against a backdrop of the 'expressive revolution'. This portmanteau term encompasses the rise of individualism, secularization, and a range of counter-cultural values and lifestyles, many of which began to be incorporated into the mainstream from the early 1960s.[121] It manifested in a sustained shift in the management of feelings whereby emotional needs and desires were acknowledged and acted upon rather than being sublimated to social convention and obligation. And it was accompanied by the 'confessional habitus', constituted by the rise and democratization of the psychological sciences since the 1960s incorporating not only psychology and psychotherapy but a range of

[117] Sarah Crook, 'The Women's Liberation Movement, Activism and Therapy at the Grassroots, 1968–1985', *Women's History Review* 27:7 (2018), pp.1152–68, here p.1152.

[118] Crook, 'Women's Liberation Movement', p.1152.

[119] Rowbotham, *Daring to Hope*, p.16.

[120] This is the opposite of the Socratic position on the self where emotions are peripheral rather than essential—see Kristjan Kristjansson, *The Self and its Emotions* (Cambridge: Cambridge University Press, 2010), p.70.

[121] The term 'expressive revolution' was coined by Talcott Parsons in 1975 in the context of religion and elaborated by Bernice Martin in *A Sociology of Contemporary Cultural Change* (Oxford, 1981), for the 1960s.

counselling and therapeutic practices designed to locate, heal, and liberate the self from oppressive structures and bonds of authority, including patriarchy. Talking, self-examination, and self-understanding were privileged over self-denial and self-control.[122] The expressive revolution also gave rise to modern confessional culture, whereby the private individual participates in a public culture of self-divulgence or revelation, what Anthony Giddens described as 'the reflexive project of the self'.[123] Today this is often via modern broadcast, print or online media. Self-narration in the form of oral history interviews and other autobiographical forms is another element of the expressive revolution and the quest for authenticity. For this generation of women that quest is still an active work in progress in many more domains focused around expressive individualism from new age spirituality to mindfulness and body practices such as yoga focused on self-care, wellbeing, and self-expression.

All of these features of the expressive revolution incorporate what philosopher Charles Taylor has termed the quest for the authentic self. For Taylor this took the form of a clash between the pursuit of personal happiness and self-fulfilment and the strictures of religious discipline and the emphasis on self-control, particularly with regard to sex and relationships.[124] But the search for or cultivation of the authentic self was undertaken in a wide range of contexts, most clearly in the 1960s counter-culture and radical and political movements. For some women involved in the Women's Liberation Movement, the practice of consciousness raising—a sharing of personal experiences within a group in order to better understand and then challenge their oppression—was a critical element of this new emphasis on self-expression and self-understanding. For Black women, their involvement in activism via Black women's centres and groups was a means of bolstering a positive sense of self to counter the sexist and racist narratives of black womanhood circulating in society.[125] But these practices in the quest for the authentic self—a self that aspired to not being constrained by traditional authority, but rather sought autonomy and self-determination especially in matters of personal morality and decisions regarding relationships, the body and belief—permeated everyday life and were not limited to those who explicitly sought out opportunities for self-understanding. The self could be realized in everyday practices as much as in the new ideological and social spaces.

The selves that form the core of this book are also modern in the sense that they were formed in a period when the old model of selfhood characterized by self-control and sublimation of needs and desires was gradually replaced by a new

[122] Chloe Taylor, *The Culture of Confession from Augustine to Foucault: A Genealogy of the 'Confessing Animal'* (New York: Routledge, 2008).

[123] Anthony Giddens, *Modernity and Self-Identity. Self and Society in the Late Modern Age* (Cambridge: Polity, 1991).

[124] Charles Taylor, *A Secular Age* (Princeton, NJ: Harvard University Press, 2007), pp.492–3.

[125] Jessica White, 'Black Women's Groups'.

model characterized by self-discovery and the striving for self-fulfilment or self-actualization, the latter a concept coined by Abraham Maslow referring to the final stage in an individual's growth or 'hierarchy of needs'.[126] As Langhamer puts it, 'self-actualization was increasingly more highly privileged than social obligation'.[127] Whereas social obligation required the subordination of selfish needs, self-actualization, the state of reaching one's highest potential, appeared to privilege individualistic striving. However, as feminist philosophers have argued, for women the self is not a free-standing autonomous being but a relational one.[128] Self-actualization is achieved through meaningful social relations with others. Moreover, feminist oral historians have long identified the tendency of women to position themselves relationally rather than individually, acknowledging the networks of family, kin, friends, and others who constitute their social world and hence their self-understanding.[129]

However, while historians have written about the self-actualizing currents of the 'expressive revolution' of the 1960s, when the liberationist movements of that era offered women and men the space to self-fashion taking in everything from sexual choices to clothing and music, these are generally understood to be achieved through oppositional behaviour or self-examination.[130] This book, however, argues that self-actualization for women was a lifelong process often experienced alongside and within conventional roles. Indeed, it was this generation who actively sought to realize autonomy through the everyday, in the ways they dressed and behaved as teenagers, in their relationships, when they became mothers, in the workplace. This was, as often as not, an autonomy that was dependent upon mutually constitutive social connections, especially with other women. And it was nurtured by many women in self-help organizations relating to children, education, and the home.

[126] Rose, 'Assembling the Modern Self'; Nikolas Rose, *Governing the Soul: The Shaping of the Private Self* (London: Routledge, 1989); M. Shapira, *The War Inside: Psychoanalysis, Total War, and the Making of the* Democratic Self in Post-war Britain (Cambridge: Cambridge University Press, 2013); Abraham Maslow, 'A Theory of Human Motivation', *Psychological Review* 50 (1943), pp. 370–96 and Abraham Maslow, *Towards a Psychology of Being* (New York: 1968).

[127] Claire Langhamer, 'Love, Selfhood and Authenticity in Post-War Britain', *Cultural and Social History* 9:2 (2012), pp.277–97, here p.280.

[128] C. Mackenzie and N. Stoljar (Eds), *Relational Autonomy: Feminist Perspectives on Autonomy, Agency and the Social Self* (Oxford: Oxford University Press, 2000).

[129] Abrams, *Oral History Theory*, pp.38–44. See also Mary Chamberlain, 'The Global Self: Narratives of Caribbean Migrant Women', in Tess Coslett, Celia Lury, and Penny Summerfield (Eds), *Feminism and Autobiography: Texts, Theories, Methods* (London, 2000), pp. 154–66; White, 'Black Women's Groups'.

[130] Martin, *Sociology of Contemporary Cultural Change*. For a discussion of how this impacted on women's narratives of the period see Abrams, 'Heroes'. For an exception to the tendency to see women's autonomy and self-expression as mutually dependent see Dolly Smith Wilson, 'A New Look at the Affluent Worker: the Good Working Mother in Post-War Britain', *Twentieth Century British History* 17:2 (2006), pp.206–29.

Feminist Lives

Feminist Lives tells the story of women's subjectivity across the life course amongst a generation who, in pursuing self-fulfilment rather than self-sacrifice, effected a rupture in conceptions of womanhood. In the chapters that follow we consider what it meant and how it felt to negotiate a new liberated self, how it was experienced at the time and remembered in retrospect. The book describes how women, as individuals and collectively, responded to the encouragement to pursue self-fulfilment, often quietly and with little fuss, and considers the material and emotive outcomes for women of all social classes and parts of the British Isles. It is thus a history of the generation of women who grew up and matured in the post-war decades who charted new ways of being. In the first part of the book (Chapters 2 to 5), we focus primarily on personal relationships and self identity. We journey with them as they separate themselves from their mothers' generation, through the uncertainties of the teenage years and young adulthood, the years of relative freedom, and experimentation with relationships before 'settling down'. The second half (Chapters 6 to 8) addresses the hopes, expectations, and realities of married life, the negotiations made as wives and mothers, and the steps taken towards self-fulfilment and self-actualization. The role of collective feminist action outside and pre-figuring the Women's Liberation Movement via the do-it-yourself or self-help organizations such as the Pre-School Playgroups Association and the National Housewives Register is critical to understanding how this generation of women effected change for and in themselves leading, for some, to changes of direction and an understanding that self-care was an essential component of being a fulfilled woman. At the heart of the change embodied and enacted by this generation is their willingness to explore and express their feelings amongst one another. In being open about how they felt, in making their feelings visible, women brought about change for themselves as individuals and as a collective. The feminist lives recounted in this book are the lives of women who, for the most part, had no formal affiliation to avowedly feminist organizations. Feelings were the difference.

2
Mothers and Daughters

Introduction

> My mother really was a more powerful influence in my life than anything the church said or was. She had been to the same boarding school, got a place at Oxford, but war had broken out and she had gone back to join her parents in south India on the outbreak of war and had married at nineteen and had always bitterly regretted the loss of her university education. And this actually turned her into a not terribly happy person and I sometimes felt I was in the front line in terms of—I mean she really minded that I had freedoms that she hadn't had because she'd married so young and been catapulted into Calcutta...she was envious of my freedom, certainly in the Sixties, and so you know when I, you know, I did embrace that sense of freedom...it wasn't with a sense of 'oh dear what would the church say about anything I'm doing,' it was my mother.[1]

Caroline's reflection on her mother's disappointment at a life unfulfilled encapsulates the gap between the generations and, for some, the tensions that could arise when the younger generation began to grasp opportunities denied to their parents, and their mothers in particular. The mothers' generation had been steeped in duty, self-sacrifice, and self-control—at least in terms of their public persona—they had been commended for their emotional stoicism during the war years, and urged to put family before self.[2] These women born in the inter-war years postponed or compromised self-fulfilment, often at the expense of their own self-identity and sometimes manifest in resentment of the ways in which their daughters acted on feelings rather than expectations. But although those women had been socialized at home, in school, and in church to manage their expectations and to fulfil their duty as wives, mothers, and homemakers, they could still struggle to reconcile their desire for self-fulfilment with the constraints of the immediate post-war decades.[3] By the 1960s some were beginning to recast their

[1] Interview with Caroline. [2] See Noakes, *Dying for the Nation*, pp.51–68.

[3] Lynn Abrams, 'Mothers and Daughters: Negotiating the Discourse on the "Good Woman" in 1950s and 1960s Britain' in N. Christie and M. Gauvreau (Eds), *The Sixties and Beyond: Dechristianisation in North America and Western Europe, 1945–2000* (Toronto: University of Toronto Press, 2013), pp.60–83.

Feminist Lives: Women, Feelings, and the Self in Post-War Britain. Lynn Abrams, Oxford University Press.
 DOI: 10.1093/oso/9780192896995.003.0002

lives as their children flew the nest and they had the time to consider what came next.

This chapter addresses the generational shift constituted by a material and psychosocial change from 'home-making' to 'self-making' but also an expressive change from self-restraint or accepting one's lot to self-expression or acting on feelings. That shift has often been characterized as conflict as girls pushed at the boundaries of what their mothers believed to be appropriate, acceptable or respectable, and mothers attempted to hold the line, to impose their standards of behaviour in the face of unstoppable social change, even when they themselves were questioning the very standards they tried to impose on their daughters.[4] But the story is more complex. Relationships between mothers and daughters in this period were more nuanced and evolutionary. Most parents in the post-war years had aspirations for their children to do better than themselves, to have a better education, a more comfortable and prosperous life, a contented and supportive marriage. Girls were encouraged to take advantage of the educational opportunities their parents had not had, to undertake post-secondary education or training leading to a job in a white-collar or professional occupation and to make a love-match. In the process of watching their daughters begin this journey, mothers began to see the limits of their own lives whilst searching for fulfilment or self-actualization through activities beyond the home. As their daughters were growing up, their mothers began to reassess their priorities and some glimpsed their own future in their daughters' aspirations.

However, the theme of conflict facilitates a certain kind of life story amongst the post-war generation—women who seek to position their model of self as a departure from that represented by their mothers.[5] Mothers' stories, as Lawler has argued, are too often effaced in daughters' accounts of the emergence of the 'feminist self' in which the mother is constituted as 'other'.[6] Daughters' rejection of the self-sacrifice and morality of their mothers—both as their own mothers and as representatives of a generation—provides the explanation, justification and perhaps a convenient foil for their search for and embrace of a new kind of womanhood. Sheila Rowbotham, a prominent documenter of the British women's movement, explicitly links her own and her fellow feminists' journey with a

[4] For example, the doctor and Labour politician Edith Summerskill discussed all sorts of issues including sexual relationships with her daughter through her letters—accepting attitudes were changing to pre-marital sex but reminding her daughter of the consequences for women in terms of social stigma and the difficulties of lone motherhood. Edith Summerskill, *Letters to my Daughter* (London: Heinemann, 1957) pp.126–30.

[5] See Ingham, *Now we are Thirty*, pp.21–38.

[6] Lawler, *Mothering the Self*, p.16. A similar process is observed by Margaretta Jolly in respect of the oral history interviews with WLM activists. *Sisterhood and After*, p.61. The amnesiac tendency within feminism has wider application. See Luisa Passerini, 'A Memory for Women's History: Problems of Method and Interpretation', *Social Science History* 16:4 (1992), pp.669–92; Victoria Browne, 'Backlash, Repetition, Untimeliness: The Temporal Dynamics of Feminist Politics', *Hypatia* 28:4 (2013), pp.905–20.

voyage away from their mothers' generation. 'Determined not to follow the patterns set by our mothers in being women, we wanted to relate differently to men but there were no received assumptions about how this might be.'[7] Some years earlier she concluded: 'Finding ourselves *being* women in new ways, many of us were precipitated into conceiving alternative means of *becoming* women.'[8] For some this process of becoming was recounted as gradual, for others abrupt. And it encompassed both the conscious rejection of some beliefs and standards cleaved to by their mothers—including religious or ethical ones—and steps towards a different lifestyle and set of values. 'I like to live a life of my own', commented Valerie, a young West Indian woman in the early 1970s. 'There ain't no rules saying that you must wash the dishes and clean.'[9] The post-war generation were beginning to develop that sense of independent selfhood so characteristic of the late modern West and which has been described as predicated upon access to fulfilling or well-paid work, financial independence, time and space for oneself, and a sense of ownership of one's body—all things that conflicted with the traditional discourse on ideal womanhood, an ideal their mothers had sacrificed a good deal to adhere to.

And yet in rejecting much of what they stood for, daughters often failed to see that their mothers too were striving to find space for the self, albeit within more prescribed boundaries. Without doubting the daughters' accounts of conflict over practices and ideals, this chapter first turns attention to the women born in the inter-war years who so often became the brunt of their daughters' frustration, anger, and disappointment. Examination of the mothers' contemporaneous testimony articulated in diaries and interviews and indirectly in fictional writing, suggests continuities across the generations sitting alongside conflict. This helps us to better interpret the daughters' accounts. Those continuities, not surprisingly, pivot around the issues of work versus family, self-fulfilment versus self-sacrifice. These can be categorized as structural and ideological issues whereas the points of conflict for many of the daughters concerned individual choice—over clothes, relationships, and motherhood.

In what follows we focus first on the mothers' generation in order to appreciate their self-understanding at a time of significant cultural and social change, as well as their hopes and aspirations for their daughters. Accounts produced by the post-war generation tend to emphasize the experiential and emotional differences between their lives and those of their mothers in order to lend coherence to a life story within a liberationist framework. Such accounts often require the identification of a schism, or epiphany, to explain the rejection of their mothers'

[7] Rowbotham, *Promise of a Dream*, p.10.

[8] Rowbotham, *Threads through Time: Writings on History and Autobiography* (London: Penguin, 1999), p.4.

[9] 'Valerie' cited in Sharpe, *Just Like a Girl*, pp.245–6.

understanding of how a woman should be. Yet, when we can access mothers' subjective accounts, whose stories were much less likely to be elicited than those of their daughters, a more sympathetic and rounded and sometimes more conflicted picture of these women emerges. The personal testimony of the mothers illustrates their day-to-day and metaphysical struggles as they sought to excavate the self from a primary role as wife or mother, carer or homemaker. I argue that although the conflict between the generations was, in many cases, very real, the daughters' narration of that conflict many years later served a purpose in their own version of their life story. Interrogating how the mothers saw themselves reveals that they too experienced psychic turmoil struggling to align their inner and outer lives, their needs and desires with the material and ideological changes characterizing everyday life in post-war Britain.

The second part of the chapter discusses parental aspirations for their daughters and shows how mothers' own conflicts over their role and their self-identity influenced the ways in which they imagined their daughters' futures. While daughters may have seen their mothers as primarily housewives, they did not appreciate the psychological conflicts that were hidden from view. Finally, we address the ways in which the daughters responded to what their mothers represented, considering the points of tension—over lifestyles and relationships—and how they manifested in mother-daughter relationships at the very moment girls were beginning to make their own decisions about how they ran their lives.

Mothers: Self-sacrifice to Self-realization

Laura, born in 1917 in a northern English town, was the daughter of a post-office accountant and a nursery-school teacher.[10] She was educated at a prestigious girls' day school and in 1936 went to Cambridge University to study English where she met her future husband, also a Cambridge student. They both graduated in 1939, she with a double first, and they immediately got engaged whereupon her fiancé joined the army and was sent to India for five years. Laura initially stayed on at Cambridge to carry out research funded by a studentship that she was the first woman to hold. They married in May 1945. Thereafter Laura became an army wife, spending a lot of time on her own with three young children, but alongside this conventional role she worked. For several decades she was an English literature examiner as well as an examiner and recruiter for the civil service, and in the 1950s she was employed in a government role that entailed extensive travel around the country. And she was a writer. Her first novel was published in 1946 followed by another eight through the following three decades.

[10] To preserve anonymity, Laura is a pseudonym and details of her publications have been withheld.

Her most successful is tellingly set in Cambridge, the location of her happiest and most fulfilling years. Yet Laura never had a formal or permanent role in academic life and her work was undertaken on a piecemeal basis alongside the demands of family life.

For this woman, the possibility of an academic career and self-fulfilment through a satisfying job had been sacrificed to the expectations and demands of family life and her husband's profession. Maintaining a literary life was her way of retaining a sense of self that rested upon her academic years at Cambridge and that was distinct from her role as a wife and mother. Laura was a prolific writer, penning regular letters to her husband when he was stationed away from the family home. She maintained a diary which offers a view of the day-to-day tasks and preoccupations of a middle-class woman who enjoyed literature and the arts, nice clothes, and good food, jaunts to London and a busy social life through the years of post-war austerity, rationing, three young children, and the challenges of her husband's career and his occasional depressive episodes.[11] Her examining work maintained contact with her beloved Cambridge—though a visit there for an examiners' meeting in 1947 was described as 'rather heart-breaking'—and brought much-needed income into a household which employed several staff at various times: a housekeeper, gardener, and nanny.[12] The examining work was flexible of course, and could be fitted in around the daily tasks, albeit with the assistance of paid help. One Sunday in 1955, Laura's diary entry records:

> a morning of cooking and cake-making and vacuum cleaning while [nanny] walked the children in the park… After lunch I marked desperately the last 20 of my scripts – in determination to finish by tea which I did by 5. Then translated into a mother again and read 'Alice Through the Looking Glass' till [son] demanded 'Journey into Space'. The evening was spent reading marks to [husband] and tidying up marks and getting things ready for my trip to S. Wales tomorrow.[13]

The visit to Wales for her work for the government's Political and Economic Planning Department was only possible with paid help at home but, in turn, this employment facilitated Laura's lifestyle, including her writing which was squeezed in around the other activities she needed for personal enjoyment and fulfilment. On jaunts to London she went to cocktail parties, the theatre and films, and shopped at Harrods; the store allowed customers to run an account to be paid up once a year which suited the couple's unpredictable financial circumstances.

[11] I am indebted to Laura's daughter for allowing me access to her mother's archive which includes her diaries from 1947–1955 and letters to her husband between the 1940s and 1960s.

[12] Laura's Diary, 4 Feb. 1947. In Sept 1946 she was employed by the civil service to mark 450 essays at 2/- each. Letter from Laura to husband, 29 Sept 1946.

[13] Laura's Diary, 9 June 1955.

In between, she worked away on her novels, often in the evenings when her husband was away: 'I drank my solitary glass of sherry and got down good and hard to my novel. A little creative work makes me feel so much better' she confided to her diary in 1947.[14] Her fictional writing, along with her wider cultural life, represented the core of her self, the bit that had been shaped at Cambridge and which she was desperate to hold on to against the tide of family obligations. One Sunday in 1949, after a chaotic day described as 'one of those occasions when it would be heaven not to have to cope with [the children] for a while', she settled down and 'finished [latest novel], which is quite devastating, surprising and incredible. To think that 3 years work is over.'[15] Over the next few days her husband assisted her in preparing the manuscript, 'checking it over', and a few days later they delivered it to the typing agency in London.[16]

Laura's struggle to preserve a part of her creative self amidst the tide of everyday life was, of course, a common theme for writers from 1900 to 1960, from Virginia Woolf to Penelope Mortimer. But it is important to draw attention to it here because the othering of their mothers by daughters who seek to write liberationist accounts of their own lives tends to diminish the psychic conflicts experienced by a generation who are often portrayed as conforming to self-sacrificial models of womanhood. Laura rarely comments explicitly on that internal struggle, but in 1946 she reported to her husband the view of her brother who told her that 'a) I was not so well-informed about current affairs and politics as I used to be b) my face was setting into a permanent anxious worried look c) I took life too seriously.' 'O dear, o dear' she asked, 'can this be the effect of fish queues and washing nappies?'[17] And some months later, as she was beginning to carve out a life for herself that combined homemaking, children and her own need for activity for both income and creative fulfilment, she articulated a feeling that was to become commonplace in the 1960s and 1970s amongst her daughter's generation:

> Seized with doubt today about my careerless life – a husband and son should be satisfying but I feel my energies could be better used than in scrubbing pans, washing nappies, planning points [rations] etc – or is that a stupid, egotistic view? Here is England crying out for labour, and I sit snug in my detached backwater. But examining and writing novels should be enough. [Husband] and I had a long talk about it.[18]

The feeling that she was not able to live a fulfilling life continued to niggle away. In 1949, after two years living apart from her husband and now with two young

[14] Laura's Diary, 19 Feb. 1947. [15] Laura's Diary, 13 Feb. 1949.
[16] Laura's Diary, 18 Feb. 1949. The novel was rejected by the publisher four months later.
[17] Letter from Laura to husband, 11 Nov. 1946.
[18] Laura's Diary, 28 Feb. 1947.

children, she let off steam to him, expressing resentment at having lost a career as an academic without the recompense of a 'normal' family life:

> Since marrying you, I have worked damned hard and it doesn't seem to have profited us much. Now I see nothing for the months ahead but more hard work of my own with the children and house until 7pm – and then my own work, and the sight of you for weekends. I know that it isn't any better for you, that you are lonely and fed up and depressed, but at least you are doing a job and getting on with your career and in comparative comfort... When I left Cambridge in 1947 and came to [small town] I remember thinking on my last day there, that I was sad to be giving up my life there, but ready to be a proper wife, to help with your career, to entertain your friends, to take part in your sort of life. Through living at [small town], I have always lived on the fringe of your life and had no really satisfactory substitute for my own. People may say that I have the children. I have indeed, but sarcasm apart, obviously they come first, and I suppose I must just make up my mind to be satisfied with them and my life with them.[19]

It is only because we have her personal papers that we are privileged to read Laura's feelings about her situation. The inner turmoil she felt able to express to her husband in private correspondence and in her personal diary could not have been vocalized in public without attracting criticism. As a military wife Laura was alone more than many of her married peers, though there were many such divided families in the fading years of empire in the 1940s and 1950s.[20] She was also conscious that she too could be 'posted', 'rolled around with rocks and stones as it were', a metaphor that perhaps expressed her feelings about having little control over her destiny in more ways than just the fact of having to move house regularly.[21] In fact she moved less frequently than some army wives, unwilling to compromise on housing and willing to trade separation from her husband for domestic comfort and possibly the time to devote to her own pursuits. But Laura had little choice except to roll with the rocks whilst carving out what we might now describe as a portfolio career. While her three children were young she continued the examining and writing which could be fitted around her other commitments and social engagements, but in the 1970s when all three children had left home, she worked in the education sector as a school governor and sat on the governing council of an educational charity until the 1990s.[22] This return to paid

[19] Letter from Laura to husband, 20 Oct. 1949.

[20] For another example of separation which features a woman who was more content to fulfil a domestic role see Lynn Abrams, 'A Wartime Family Romance: Narratives of Masculinity and Intimacy during World War Two', in L. Abrams and E. Ewan (Eds), *Nine Centuries of Man: Masculinities in Scottish History* (Edinburgh: Edinburgh University Press 2017), pp.160–79.

[21] Laura's Diary, 23 March 1955. They moved 25 times between 1947 and 2001.

[22] Laura's curriculum vitae.

or voluntary work in later years was a common pattern that was also followed by the next generation of women in the 1980s.[23]

Laura's accounts of herself are a mixture of the banal and the insightful, the self-pitying and the exuberant. They are a far cry from the model housewife or the lady of leisure so castigated by the critics of a certain kind of domesticity, and her lifestyle bears little relation to the stereotype of the Fifties housewife.[24] Neither does she fit the alternative image of the exceptional woman who made a career for herself despite the obstacles.[25] Rather, Laura encapsulates the compromises made by women of her generation, whose choices were constrained materially, structurally, and ideologically but whose voices we rarely hear. Examining and writing were permissible and possible work because they could be managed around her responsibilities to the home. Being able to afford paid help freed up time, not just for her writing but for leisure, whether that be sitting in front of the fire with a novel or the latest edition of *Vogue*, gadding about in London, seeing the latest films, drinking cocktails, dining at smart restaurants or spending time with her husband. Cambridge had formed her in terms of her tastes, interests and friends, and was a long way from her more humble background. But, despite being one of the smartest students in her year, it could not shape her destiny except as a rather mythological place in her fictional writing. In one novel, the protagonist Frances is similarly torn between expectations and ambition. On the casual offer of marriage from a friend at Cambridge she turns him down citing her career. 'Bed maybe, but not the yoke' she responds to his provocative put down of 'I thought all you girls were just raving for the yoke'. But her next remark is perhaps even more telling: 'The shades of our mothers drive us on; we must be career women for their sakes.'[26] Frances and Laura were both, it seems, avenging their mothers' fate.

The sense of self, albeit multi-faceted, is clearly articulated in Laura's confessional writing. The woman who finds 'queuing to eat, like queuing for a public lavatory... damaging to human dignity'; who observes the 'sweaty waitresses' and the 'drunken porter' in her 'awful hotel' in Liverpool; and who enjoys shopping at Harrods and Fortnum and Mason and Dior fashions, at the same time still hankered after a job in Cambridge and enjoyed sherry with the Principal of Newnham. She acknowledged that her work allowed her to be someone else: on a visit to Cambridge in 1965 she enjoyed being 'flattered and teased' by the younger examiners 'which made me feel better' before 'tomorrow thankfully I whizz back

[23] See Worth, *Welfare State Generation*, pp.142–8.

[24] See Virginia Nicholson, *Perfect Wives in Ideal Homes. The Story of Women in the 1950s* (London, Viking, 2015), pp.290–1.

[25] Such extraordinary women are depicted in Cooke, *Her Brilliant Career: Ten Extraordinary Women of the Fifties* (London: Virago, 2013). Cooke admits the women she chooses were exceptional, while at the same time she claims that the 1950s were more liberatory than is often portrayed. See pp.xxxii–vii.

[26] Details withheld to preserve anonymity.

to quite another self'.[27] But her relationship with her eldest daughter Suzanna was sometimes fraught, especially when that daughter began to live her life according to her own moral compass with a sense of freedom Laura had never enjoyed. Laura set much store by the performance of outward respectability, perhaps on account of her journey from a lower middle-class family to the elite academic world of Cambridge. This performance manifested most strikingly at one particular moment of crisis in her daughter's life. Suzanna recalled that when she became pregnant out of wedlock, 'my mother said that if I had the baby then my father would have to leave the army, and it would ruin his career. And she'd never be able to hold her head up again etc., etc.' Suzanna had an abortion, a decision supported by her parents 'as long as it was legal'. But when she returned home 'the only thing [my mother] *ever* said to me about it: she said two things. One was that I was not to tell anyone. Ever. Which is not a good thing, really. And the other thing was, she said: 'you don't know how lucky you are.'[28]

Nor was that the end of it. Suzanna later discovered from her mother's diary that she too had had an abortion some 20 years earlier. There is little in Laura's diary account of that time that indicates how she felt about either her own pregnancy or the abortion. Laura self-described as a stoic, and, while abortion was available to those with money and connections, it was hardly a common topic of conversation in polite circles.[29] In the three weeks between fainting after a hot bath 'which rather confirms all my suspicions' and the procedure in a nursing home, her diary records the usual round of social occasions, visits to the theatre, shopping and working, interspersed by consultations with doctors and specialists.[30] Only once did she record an emotional response to the situation. On telling her friend 'about the things she was so horrified that I cried for the first time'. But later that day, upon being told by a London doctor that she should not have the baby given her medical history (her last pregnancy had been difficult) she 'went back, considerably light-heartened', so much so that she was able to enjoy the latest Terence Rattigan play with her husband and 'an enormous supper in Gennaro's'.[31] A week or so later, confirmation of the diagnosis was followed by another theatre visit to see 'The Glass Menagerie'.[32] When the date of the termination finally arrived, she spent the morning in Cambridge in the University Library and doing a spot of shopping before reaching her nursing home at tea

[27] Letter, Laura to husband, 29 July 1965. [28] Interview with Suzanna.

[29] Laura, 'My Marriage'. Rachel Cooke comments that by the 1950s abortion was not taboo and cites Penelope Mortimer's 1958 novel *Daddy's Gone-a-Hunting* (1958) which features a mother helping her daughter to arrange a termination. But even in this fictionalized account, the act itself is rarely spoken of directly. Cooke, in *Her Brilliant Career*, p.xxvii.

[30] Laura's Diary, 21 Sept. 1947.

[31] Laura's Diary, 30 Sept. 1948. The availability of abortion was governed by the 1929 Infant Life Preservation Act which only provided a defence where it could proven that causing the death of the child was 'done in good faith for the purpose only of preserving the life of the mother'. Legal access to abortion was introduced, under certain conditions, in the 1967 Abortion Act.

[32] Laura's Diary, 9 Oct. 1947.

time. Only then did Laura commit her feelings to paper: 'I feel curiously cold about it all – cold with doubt and the beginnings of remorse – feeling that perhaps I should have risked it, whatever the authorities said.'[33]

Remembering that Laura had told Suzanna to keep her abortion secret, there was remarkable diary candour about her own and she told at least two friends.[34] And her husband popped in and out with grapes and flowers, whereas she admonished her daughter for asking a friend to accompany her when she went through the same experience, in this case far from home. As Suzanna recalled of her own experience: 'I er, minded, you know? And people didn't know anything really about counselling, or sort of helping you deal with something like that... But I had very supportive friends... And completely ignored my mother's desire for me not to tell anyone.' But when she told her mother that a friend had offered to accompany her, 'my mother said: "Have you got no *pride*?" She didn't use the word pride, but used the word "amour-propre". And obviously [she] thought this was something I had to do on my own, and so I did.'[35]

The contrast is striking. Suzanna was open about needing the support of friends and about her emotional response to the situation. Her willingness to break the silence about a situation her mother regarded as a moral and social taboo was a sign of Suzanna's own liberation from a way of thinking and behaving that maintained feelings of shame and guilt.[36] Laura, on the other hand, narrated her experience of terminating a pregnancy as if she were a member of the audience at one of the plays she enjoyed so much. The *dramatis personae* of the nursing home have leading roles in her drama: the Irish nurses with pleasant voices and 'willing Irish ways', a pregnant girl who 'screamed at every pain' and an old woman whose death she described in considerable detail—'the final last expelling breath – the eerie hiss of the departing soul'.[37] 'I hated it all', she wrote, 'and made a tearful fuss.' As a writer, this focus on the awfulness of the nursing home may have been her way of repressing her feelings about the termination. Alternatively it suggests a reluctance to engage with her reproductive role in contrast with the exuberance with which she recounts her more public persona. And herein lies the conflict at the core of Laura's self-identity which she then projected onto Suzanna, whose openness about feelings endowed her with the third generation's bravura for feminism of the second wave.

Finding the Real Me

We are fortunate to be able to reconstruct the subjectivity of Laura. Her public profile as a novelist, albeit not especially well known, and her copious private and

33 Laura's Diary, 12 Oct. 1947.

34 Laura's Diary, 17 Oct. 1947.

35 Interview with Suzanna.

36 See Cohen, *Family Secrets*, p.xxi.

37 Laura's Diary, 15 Oct. 1948.

public writing offer the historian privileged access to a self, articulated through fictional and autobiographical accounts. Such fulsome contemporaneous expressions of self-identity from women are rather thin on the ground for this generation. One source are the diaries elicited from women by Mass-Observation that Hinton characterizes as 'individual struggles for personal autonomy'.[38] He reads, in women's documenting of their lives, 'stratagems' to negotiate greater authority in the home and the social world and status in the public one.[39] Amongst the generation born in the inter-war decades, these stratagems were real but often piecemeal and constrained by patriarchal structures and attitudes that limited advancement, both in the domestic and public spheres.

Bertha Walton was married to a teacher and in the 1930s relieved her boredom by teaching adult education. She found excitement and relief from the home during the war when she became a factory inspector and union activist. In these roles, argues Hinton, 'personal growth and political activism went hand in hand'.[40] But in peacetime she looked to labour politics for an outlet for her intellectual energy and quickly realized its limitations for a woman: 'all raffles and money raising, no politics, all elderly'.[41] Bertha Walton had a brief taste of the life she wanted during the war years but her effort to achieve greater autonomy through civic engagement after the war was stymied by the dead weight of old structures and attitudes. Whereas Laura had found a flexible and accommodating space in which to enact her creative and academic self—examining existed on the margins of academia and both this and her novel writing could be undertaken at home—Bertha's efforts to carve out a role for herself butted up against an entrenched institution. She and her husband eventually adopted a child who, in Hinton's words, 'seems to have become her life'.[42] As we have seen, Laura's children were important to her but they were never her whole life.

Of course the limitations on women of this generation were both structural and attitudinal, external and internal, and always overlain by social class. We see Laura struggling with internal voices telling her that she *should* be satisfied and there was nothing to disabuse her of this, whereas 20 years later such feelings found echoes amongst women's peers and they did something about it (as we will explore in Chapter 6). Laura was unusual in holding down a job, a writing career and being married with a family.[43] Although it was theoretically possible for a married woman to return to paid work in the 1950s and 1960s—the remaining marriage bars had been lifted in the 1940s with a few exceptions—the route back to work was far from easy, even when children had reached school age. Laura was very fortunate to be able to employ help in the home. Married women of this generation with some post-secondary training or qualifications were more likely

[38] Hinton, *Nine Wartime Lives*, p.7.
[39] Hinton, *Nine Wartime Lives*, pp.6–7.
[40] Hinton, *Nine Wartime Lives*, p.196.
[41] Hinton, *Nine Wartime Lives*, p.188.
[42] Hinton, *Nine Wartime Lives*, p.189.
[43] Writing was one of the few modes of work that could be carried out by women with family responsibilities. See Cooke, *Her Brilliant Career*, pp.xx–xxi.

to consider taking a job outside the home than those with no such education. Amongst one sample of middle-class married women academically surveyed in 1967, half had no plans for work outside the home, but of those with two or more years training three-quarters were working or planned to do so.[44] The alternative to paid employment for those who did not need the additional income and who wished to expand their horizons beyond the home was voluntary work or participation in civic or religious organizations such as the National Council of Women, Young Wives and other church-based groups, the Women's Institute and so on.

Bertha Walton and Laura strived to extricate the self from being buried in the home and family. They saw themselves as more than a wife or mother and Laura endeavoured to hold on to the freedoms of a woman unencumbered with family responsibilities. Were they unusual? The sociologist Ray Pahl succeeded in delving more deeply than most into women's sense of self and discovered a group of women who revealed a range of opinions and identities across a spectrum from the 'home-centred', who were primarily devoted to their husband and children, to the 'more gregarious', who sought a life beyond the family.[45] However, only 13 of the 86 women who completed his questionnaire were in paid employment and only three of those were working full time.[46] The majority saw their role as 'creating a comfortable home' and 'being a companion to their husband'.[47]

It was the in-depth interview with sixteen of these women married to managers that delved into the women's self-identity.[48] When asked questions such as 'What sort of person do you see yourself as?' and 'Do you think you have been, or will be, a different person at different times in your life?', many of the women experienced difficulties articulating responses.[49] Indeed the interviewer admitted that 'to arrive at a "hierarchy of role identities" or "self-conceptions at appropriate stages of the life-cycle"... was frequently unproductive'.[50] Unlike those born just a decade or so later, these women had not been exposed to the 'expressive revolution' and tended to regard such questions as 'too introspective' or simply too challenging to respond to. Some said that they didn't spend much time thinking about themselves.[51] And yet, partly because of their life-stage—the majority were beginning to think about what they would do once the children were less dependent—they used the interview to begin to rehearse what a new kind of self might be. Mrs Eastwell (born 1937) was unusual in having been to university but was one of several respondents who described themselves as 'ordinary'. She was not a home or family-focused person and as a result admitted that: 'One of my problems in life is that I don't have any idea of what sort of person I am... I have a feeling inside that I am capable of great things but I've never decided what they were.'[52] Marriage and children did not satisfy her and she had not enjoyed her

[44] Pahl and Pahl, *Managers*, pp.131–2.
[45] Pahl and Pahl, *Managers*, p.113.
[46] Pahl and Pahl, *Managers*, p.127
[47] Pahl and Pahl, *Managers*, p.115.
[48] Pahl and Pahl, *Managers*, p.290.
[49] Pahl and Pahl, *Managers*, Appendix 2, pp.279–80.
[50] Pahl and Pahl, *Managers*, Appendix 3, p.290.
[51] Pahl and Pahl, *Managers*, p.291.
[52] UKDA, SN 853296: Interview with Mrs Eastwell, p.1.

career as a secretary. Mrs Eastwell lacked a 'schema of understanding' to explain her predicament.[53] In not identifying primarily as a wife, mother or homemaker nor wanting a career, she occupied a kind of limbo, waiting for the children to grow up, hoping it will 'not be too late when she's forty-five to become more independent and concentrate on "finding the real me".' She resented the fact 'that people can find nothing else to talk to her about except children, and she thinks they regard her as a Moron and she finds it insulting that they think the only basis of communication with her is as a mother'.[54] Her narrative, like her identity, lacked an anchor. Mrs Eastwell found it 'insulting' that other people could only relate to her in her maternal role but she recognized that her present situation offered no other basis for communication.[55]

All of the women in this age band were torn between the expectations of duty to husband and family and the knowledge that there were new horizons opening up for women if only they could get there. While they almost all accepted their role as support to their husbands as they pursued their career ambitions, most were now beginning to reassess and, in some cases, fight for the right to some degree of independence. Mrs Ash (born 1926), who was attending classes in the daytime in order to gain a place at teacher training college, stated that she had never resented her husband's career: 'I take it for granted.' But after more than 20 years of marriage she admitted that she felt a 'misfit': 'I don't quite know where I'm going or what I'm going to do with myself.'[56] Mrs Ash was lucky in that her husband was supportive of her desire to find an outlet for her ambitions, but Mrs Manston (born 1933) noted that her husband 'was not keen' on her returning to work and told her she could only undertake her college course if 'she was not out of the home when the children were in it'.[57] She described how her husband expressed his irritation by getting out the Hoover when he felt she was not paying enough attention to the house.[58] The men in this study, at least as portrayed by their wives, had conservative attitudes to gender roles within the marriage. 'He likes me to be ready to be whatever he wants me to be' remarked one, though she followed this up with: 'I'm not really good at this unfortunately.'[59]

In these interviews with the wives of managers we can hear clearly the women's sense of being on the cusp of change but not quite knowing how to make the transition from home-maker to something else. This was a generation, married between 1945 and 1955, who struck a bargain with their husbands and themselves. They married ambitious men whose career progression tended to be

[53] Lawler, *Mothering the Self*, p.14.
[54] UKDA, SN: 853296: Interview with Mrs Eastwell, p.27.
[55] UKDA, SN 853296: Interview with Mrs Eastwell, p.27.
[56] UKDA, SN 853296: Interview with Mrs Ash, pp.1–2.
[57] UKDA, SN 853296: Interview with Mrs Manston, p.9.
[58] UKDA, SN 853296: Interview with Mrs Manston, p.9.
[59] UKDA, SN 853296: Interview with Mrs Olantigh, pp.2–3.

dependent on geographical mobility. As managers their earnings were sufficient to support a family, to buy their own home and furnish it comfortably. Their wives understood that in the short term it was their role—if not their duty—to support their husband. Mrs Graveney (born c.1924) was one of the oldest of the study group. She left school at 14 and worked as a shop assistant and in a factory before she married. Mrs Graveney originally presented herself as fulfilling a traditional domestic role, sacrificing herself to her husband and family. 'If a man studies for years to better himself', she wrote, 'his wife *must* be prepared to move with him.' In the written questionnaire Mrs Graveney made the effort to expand beyond the multiple-choice answers to explicate how she saw herself in her relationship with her husband:

> Bringing up my daughter in this way. Running a large house, and being the type of wife who will listen to her husband's problems (even though he thinks mine are non existance (sic)) and making helpful suggestions. This is my life at present. My daughter and my husband are the most important people in my life. My daughter and husband lead full lives and my life is looking after them and making sure everything is at their fingertips.[60]

Mrs Graveney lived a busy life. She attended Spanish, Bridge and swimming classes in the daytime (her husband, she said, would object to evening classes), hosted coffee mornings, and ran a large house. Before they moved to their present town she had been president of her Woman's Institute branch and was extremely active in the community: she started a meals-on-wheels service and sat on committees for cervical cancer screening, blood transfusion, and the parish hall.[61] But she had no financial independence. Her husband gave her an allowance: 'I like her to have her economic independence, even if it's only three pounds a month, as it was when we started, but at least she can call it her own.'[62] Now, at 44 in 1966, she was unsatisfied and resentful and she articulated these emotions when given the opportunity in a face-to-face interview just a few months after submitting the questionnaire.

> I've been married for 23 years, now, during which time my husband's wishes, the house and A. my daughter have always come first, and I have been there to do anything and everything, and I feel now that I want a life of my own. This is why I'm going to these classes. I want to extend myself…I feel it very deeply, and though I have been content with the home and looking after my daughter and husband and I still want to do that, it's not enough for me now…His work has

[60] UKDA, SN 853296: Questionnaire from Mrs Graveney, p.8.
[61] UKDA, SN 853296: Interview with Mrs Graveney, p.10.
[62] UKDA, SN 853296: Interview with Mr Graveney, p.24.

> always come first and we're pushed very much in the background. I suppose this is just a little rebellion inside of me. I feel we've lost communication and can't converse together anymore...he lives for his work...But after all these years I've had enough of it.[63]

Mrs Graveney was materially comfortable but unhappy. She tried hard to conform to the expectations of the wife of a successful manager. She was a good hostess and always tried to 'look nice when we go out, without being too extreme'.[64] But she felt trapped in a marriage in which her husband treated her like 'his possession', objected to her attending evening classes and regarded sex as a duty.[65] She had never been sexually satisfied but was now resigned: 'If you want something for twenty-three years and not get it, it's time to give it up.'[66] The marriage bargain had delivered Mrs Graveney a child whom she adored and material comforts—they lived in a 'pseudo-Georgian house' and had two cars—but the bargain now seemed like a raw deal. She was wrestling with herself as she tried to express her feelings about a domestic situation that left her feeling unvalued and unsatisfied. Objectively Mrs Graveney had few options: she had no educational qualifications and it seems unlikely that she would have considered separation from her husband despite describing her marriage as 'a complete failure'.[67] So she tried to carve out a life and focused on her daughter who, if she married, 'more than anything else I'd like him to treat her as a human being, not as a possession'.[68]

Mrs Lenham (born c.1933) who was 10 years younger than Mrs Graveney, was already beginning to wonder about her future. She had left school at 14 and worked predominantly in hairdressing until she had her first child, remarking that she was 'quite content and happy with my lot' despite admitting that 'there have been times in the past when my husband has come home tired, tense and very irritable that I have wondered if his job was worth it all'. She explained that she had 'come to know when he can't stand the children's chatter and so [I] keep them away from him until he has had time to unwind from his day's work'. But ultimately Mrs Lenham justified these irritations because 'he loves his job...so if it suits him it suits me'.[69] Like Mrs Graveney, she could see beyond the walls of her three-bedroomed semi with its new Bendix washing machine. She craved more independence. 'I have spasms of thinking I will go back to work...I hate having to ask my husband for extra money and I often wish I had some of my own.'[70]

[63] UKDA, SN 853296: Interview with Mrs Graveney, p.4.

[64] UKDA, SN 853296: Interview with Mrs Graveney, p.3.

[65] UKDA, SN 853296: Interview with Mrs Graveney, pp.9–10. This is not the only instance of a husband who refused to let his wife go out in evenings. See also interview with Mrs Olantigh, p.8.

[66] UKDA, SN 853296: Interview with Mrs Graveney, p.9.

[67] UKDA, SN 853296: Interview with Mr and Mrs Graveney together, p.28.

[68] UKDA, SN 853296: Interview with Mrs Graveney, p.6.

[69] UKDA, SN 853296: Questionnaire from Mrs Lenham, p. 5.

[70] UKDA, SN 853296: Interview with Mrs Lenham, p.3.

She initially suggested that the obstacle was her husband: 'My husband wouldn't let me go to work now even if I want to' though shortly after this statement she expressed her own misgivings about returning to work while the children were still at home, despite knowing 'some married women who went to work', reflecting a widespread social and political discourse of the time.[71] Unlike Mrs Graveney, though, this woman's marriage seemed to be on firmer foundations, with Mr Lenham expressing his willingness to do anything, even give up his job, for his family.

These cases illustrate the tensions already being felt by some married women well before their daughters encountered the conflicting demands of home, work, and self a decade or so later. Women like Mrs Graveney and Mrs Lenham were living in the borderlands between a more traditional, duty-led, family-focused, and self-sacrificing model of womanhood and a model in which self-fulfilment, self-actualization, and independence played a part. In some cases it seems likely that the interview with the female researcher was the first time they had openly articulated their feelings about their lives. And it was difficult for some of these women to put themselves first. Even those who did work outside the home were conflicted. Most believed that staying at home while the children were young was non-negotiable. Mrs Patrick (born 1934), who admitted she got depressed 'sitting around here doing nothing', was undertaking nursing training, in part as it was a job she could fit around the children's needs.[72] Like most others, however, her general view on mothers working was 'that you shouldn't do it if the kids are neglected or they have to be looked after by anybody else'.[73] Mrs Petham (born 1927), one of the few wives in this survey who did have a job as a part-time secretary two days a week, recognized that while her boss thought her 'very capable', her husband 'thinks she is very slack in the home' and only came round to the idea of her working 'as long as it didn't make any difference to the house and home'.[74] While the sacrifice of their own need for self-fulfilment to service their children and husbands is not surprising, what is notable here is the women's desire for paid work not for financial reasons but for personal satisfaction and social contact. 'I have got more to do for the next thirty years than cleaning a home' stated 35-year-old Mrs Manston who was studying to be a primary school teacher.[75]

These contemporaneous interviews encouraged women to articulate how they felt about themselves and their lives at the very moment they were experiencing the tensions between duty and autonomy, self-sacrifice, and self-fulfilment. But without a common framework for interpreting their predicament, they struggled

[71] UKDA, SN 853296: Interview with Mrs Lenham, p.4.
[72] UKDA, SN 853296: Interview with Mrs Patrick, p.2.
[73] UKDA, SN 853296: Interview with Mrs Patrick, p.3.
[74] UKDA, SN 853296: Interview with Mrs Petham, p.2, p.5.
[75] UKDA, SN 853296: Interview with Mrs Manston, p.9.

to understand or explain themselves. 'I suppose really I'm a bit of a vegetable', remarked Mrs Dover (born 1934) who had been a professional dancer before working as a telephonist until she had a child; 'there's not really much to me'.[76] Women were still expected to find their primary identity as wives and mothers, homemakers and carers, but once they reached their 30s and 40s they were beginning to look for something else despite some husbands' expectations that there was no need for them to lift a finger when their wives were at home. Mr Dover pulled his weight in the house when his wife had a job but he said 'Now I feel that she has nothing else to do but look after the house and me and our daughter'.[77] Mrs Herne (born 1935), despite having three children with another on the way, was said to frequently suffer 'from a feeling of doing nothing and has to convince herself that having four happy children is an achievement'.[78] This sentiment was commonplace as we saw Laura uttering very similar doubts despite holding down a job and writing published fiction. Several acknowledged that they feared becoming a 'cabbage' with only the home and children and social chit-chat to fill the time. Mrs Ash felt 'at a loose end' and was beginning to 'feel conscious of change' as her children left home.[79] In contrast, one of the minority of wives who had a professional life of their own complained about a recent move for her husband's career which placed a 'fantastic toll on my own professional time exerted by choosing furnishings etc.'.[80] This couple eventually divorced.

The detailed accounts given by this group of women provide a glimpse into their psychic struggles as they wrestled with how to envisage their present and their future. Emotions that had been suppressed or perhaps expressed indirectly through medical complaints, were given the space to breathe in an interview with a stranger.[81] Listening to the daughters' generation, however, one might gain a very different impression of women stuck in their role as dutiful wife and mother, subordinating their needs and desires to those of the family and not having the ambition to change. The MP Harriet Harman, whose mother had practiced law before she married, at which point she consigned her barrister's clothes to the dressing-up box, rebelled against 'the lives our mothers ended up leading'.[82] Anne, from a very different background, remarked that she 'wasn't gonna do what my mum did. I remember hating her when I was 13…I definitely did not like the vision that I saw of her ironing and washing up.'[83] For Anne her mother

[76] UKDA, SN 853296: Interview with Mrs Dover, p.1.

[77] UKDA, SN 853296: Interview with Mr Dover, p.20.

[78] UKDA, SN 853296: Interview with Mrs Herne, p.7.

[79] UKDA, SN 853296: Interview with Mrs Ash, p.2.

[80] UKDA, SN 853296: Questionnaire with respondent, 65/20.

[81] Edith Summerskill remarks in her capacity as a doctor in 1955–6 on women presenting to her with 'complaints of a rather trivial nature' that can't be 'dismissed by reference to the menopause' and ascribing this to loneliness though also lack of sexual satisfaction. *Letters to my Daughter*, pp.173–4.

[82] Harriet Harman, *A Woman's Work* (London: Penguin 2018), p.3.

[83] Interview with Anne.

represented all that she didn't want to be but, as the managers' wives illustrate, outward role fulfilment often hid complicated feelings about women's sense of their identity and value. In the interviews the managers' wives found a space to express their emotions about their marriages, their unfulfilled potential, their lack of direction in life, but at the same time the pull of duty to family, the power of messages about women's primary role, and the practical obstacles to forging a new path in the absence of childcare, supportive husbands, qualifications, a car or labour-saving appliances, meant that 'finding the real me' could be almost insurmountable.[84] Their feelings about their role were not all that different from those their daughters would feel 20 years later. The difference is not only that the younger generation had generally received a better education than their mothers and may have begun a career before becoming a full-time homemaker, but that they talked about how they felt and did something about it. We shall see precisely how in later chapters of this book.

Having spent years servicing their husbands' career ambitions, acknowledging and then acting on their feelings was hard for these women. Some only managed to do this later in life. Caroline's mother, who we met at the start of this chapter, was one of the first students at one of the new universities in the 1960s. This woman had missed out on her place to study at Oxford when war broke out. She married at 19 and according to her daughter 'had always bitterly regretted the loss of her university education'. But once her children had left home 'she was there on the doorstep the first day as one of the first three mature students. She got a first, she got a job there, so that was the happiest period of her life because she was an intellectual and had been terribly thwarted before that.'[85] The mothers' generation were constrained by the expectations of social class and the necessity of publicly conforming to the notion of the good woman: by dressing for dinner, by attending church, by being perceived by others to be a good wife and mother, by fulfilling social and familial expectations. They recognized this and knew that they were sometimes unhappy and unfulfilled because of it. Some realized, with a shock, that they had built their married lives on shaky foundations. Deborah's mother was, in her daughter's words, 'a person who, before my father came home in the evening, she would go upstairs and change and put make-up on for the dinner, for the evening's dinner, you know. And she would wear make-up during the day and she couldn't understand why some other women in the village didn't.'[86] But in the late 1970s her mother's world came crashing down when Deborah's father 'ran out of money', put their big family home up for sale, and put a deposit on a new house—'a box'—without telling his wife. It 'absolutely shocked her to the core'.[87] Divorce was not an option for Deborah's mother—she had no

[84] UKDA, SN 853296: Interview with Mrs Eastwell, p.3. [85] Interview with Caroline.
[86] Interview with Deborah. [87] Interview with Deborah.

private means and in any case a divorce would have undermined her performance of respectability in their social world.

Some women were very aware that this self-respect had held back their own ambitions. Others acknowledged their internal struggles to maintain a 'balance' between their desire for greater fulfilment and societal demands that they devote themselves to the family. Laura continued to muse on the struggle between the domestic and the world in her fiction. Frances, the graduate in her novel set in Cambridge, reflects on the 20 years since she left the dreaming spires and 10 years since she married. As a young wife and mother she had peered 'incredulously over the rim of her domestic and material world' to her best friend's freedom 'where one could come and go, eat or not eat, wash up or not, at will, without the great machine one was involved with creaking and groaning behind'. But she came to understand that she need not always be a prisoner of 'the machine'. 'When Frances was able to raise her eyes more continuously to other horizons than that bounded by the house, the spectacle was suddenly different.'[88] And yet, she continues to be niggled by unfulfilled ambition. At the end of the novel, in a conversation with her old friend who chose a career over marriage, she speaks not only for herself but for others of her generation who were unable to resolve the eternal struggle. Marriage and the 'warm bosom of the family' was what she 'chose and should be grateful for' but the absence of a career still hurt enough for her to tell herself that she 'should not perhaps have cared for an academic life'.[89] Her wartime job had been interesting but not satisfying in the way she imagined an academic career would have been. For Frances the character and for Laura the author, there were only compromises and mitigations. It is clear that the tensions between duty and autonomy were already being felt for this pre-war generation and those who succeeded in bucking expectations were relatively few.[90] They recognized there were other ways of being, albeit difficult to achieve without spousal consent and financial resources or state support. They did, however, aspire for their daughters to have the choices denied to them.

Aspirations and Expectations

We have seen how women of the inter-war generation experienced conflict between their perceived duty to their husbands and family and their desire to engage in independent interests and pursuits. This included paid work, challenging dominant representations of them as the last representatives of a particular model of womanhood. How then did these feelings translate, if at all, to their ambitions for their daughters? Parents in the 1950s and 1960s were aspirational

[88] Details withheld to protect anonymity. [89] Details withheld to protect anonymity.

[90] The women featured in Cooke's *Her Brilliant Career* fall into the exceptional category.

for their children and saw the education reforms of these decades as instrumental in opening up new opportunities.[91] The 1944 Education Act (the Butler Act in England and Wales) which made secondary education compulsory and free has been seen as transformative, though most especially in its selective agenda. The introduction of the eleven-plus examination, which purportedly distinguished the academically inclined children suited to a grammar school education from the rest who were destined for a secondary modern, looms large in accounts of this period with grammar schools being seen as preferable by the majority of parents. It is certainly the case that in the post-war years, prior to comprehensivization in secondary education, the majority of mothers of all social classes questioned in the National Survey for Health and Development's longitudinal survey of the cohort born in 1946 had aspirations for their daughters at age 10 that exceeded their own educational achievement. Only 19 per cent of the mothers in the survey had an education beyond primary level—unsurprising for a generation educated before the 1944 Act—and yet 63 per cent identified a grammar school education as the most desirable for their daughters compared with 59 per cent for their sons.[92] By the time this cohort of children moved up to secondary school, however, only 23 per cent of girls and 22 per cent of boys in this study met their parents' wishes, with the majority attending either the old secondary moderns or the new comprehensive schools.[93] Fifty-seven per cent of girls left secondary school in 1961 with sub-'O'-level qualifications.[94] Yet despite the evident gap between aspiration and achievement, when surveyed 40 or so years later, 89 per cent of girls judged that their opportunities were better than their parents suggesting that they had achieved superior or more satisfying work or were better off.[95] When asked to reflect on their work opportunities only 17 per cent judged them to be 'very limited'.[96]

Education statistics only tell one part of the story. A closer analysis of my random sample of 50 individuals surveyed by the NSHD amplifies but also revises this general picture. The majority of parents—33 of the 50 in my sample—stated a preference for grammar school for their daughter, but of those girls only 16 actually passed the eleven-plus and attended a grammar, aligning with general trends

[91] Peter Mandler, 'Educating the Nation I: schools', *Transactions of the Royal Historical Society* Sixth series, 24 (2014), pp. 5–28, here pp.13–15. https://sesc.hist.cam.ac.uk/wp-content/uploads/2018/09/Briefing-Paper-Parents.pdf.

[92] MRC, NSHD: https://skylark.ucl.ac.uk/Skylark, dataset MOW56. doi: 10.5522/NSHD/Q101.

[93] MRC, NSHD: https://skylark.ucl.ac.uk/Skylark, dataset SCHT62 (Type of school at 15/16 England only). For Scotland see SCHS61. In 1957 the grammar school population was 50.6% male 49.4% female. https://sesc.hist.cam.ac.uk/wp-content/uploads/2018/06/Briefing-paper-Gender.pdf p.3.

[94] MRC, NSHD: https://skylark.ucl.ac.uk/Skylark, dataset RY7656 (Highest level of education).

[95] MRC, NSHD: https://skylark.ucl.ac.uk/Skylark, dataset JOPA 1961 and WKOP89 (Have you had the opportunity to do what you wanted in your working life?).

[96] MRC, NSHD: https://skylark.ucl.ac.uk/Skylark, dataset WKOP89. Only 11% of men reported their work opportunities as being 'very limited'.

which saw many lower middle and upper working-class parents frustrated.[97] The vast majority amongst this sample left school at 15 or 16; only one continued on to university and four more attended teacher training college. Three of the five who reached tertiary education had middle-class backgrounds. And the first jobs of these girls were remarkably similar whichever type of school they attended: shop assistant, factory work, shorthand typist, hairdresser, waitress, and clerk in a variety of office situations.[98]

Working-class girls who attended grammar school did not, on the whole, reap the supposed benefits of a more academic education to the same degree as their male counterparts. Though they were more likely to enter a clerical job than secondary modern leavers this was more the consequence of changes in the labour market.[99] When asked their opinions on the survey-children's ability to progress to tertiary education in 1961, teachers showed minimal difference between their assessment of boys and girls: 47 per cent of boys were considered suitable for university or technical college compared with 44 per cent of girls.[100] But girls made their own choices and sometimes resisted the entreaties of teachers and Youth Employment Officers to make the most of their abilities. Take Stella from a working-class family—a case that illustrates how parental aspiration and a grammar school education did not guarantee the outcome. Stella was brought up in a council house by a religious family. Her mother, a housewife, expressed the preference for grammar for her daughter and as a hard worker at her primary she achieved this. At the age of 13 she had the ambition to be a primary school teacher and a teaching career was recommended by her school. But in 1962, when she was 16 and against the expectations of her parents and her teachers, she left stating she was 'Fed up with school' and took a shorthand-typing course at a private college which led to a job as a clerk at the local magistrate's office, a job the school considered was 'well below her potential'.[101] At the age of 22 she was still directionless: 'When I left school I had no idea what I wanted to do. I did not know of the opportunities available other than secretarial colleges and this type of work did not appeal to me. Even now I'm applying to several colleges for details of courses in computer work and electronic data processing but don't really know what would suit me most.'[102]

Parents may have expressed aspirational ambitions for their daughters in the context of a changing educational landscape in the 1950s and 1960s, but their attitudes (and especially mothers') towards their daughters' futures were often

[97] Mandler, 'Educating the Nation I', p.14; Todd, *The People*, p.219.

[98] MRC, NSHD: Sample of 50 women.

[99] Todd, *The People*, pp.227–34; Worth, *Welfare State Generation*, pp.35–6.

[100] MRC, NSHD: https://skylark.ucl.ac.uk/Skylark, dataset FEAB (Teacher's opinion as to child's ability for further education, 1961).

[101] MRC, NSHD: Sample 44. School questionnaire 1962.

[102] MRC, NSHD: Sample 44. Postal questionnaire 1968.

ambivalent. They reflected not only their frustrations and what they saw as the reality for adult women but also a more rounded attitude to their children's futures. This was a generation of parents who adopted a child-centred approach to family life, facilitated in part by greater affluence. It incorporated a significant change in child-rearing practices that placed emphasis on meeting more than just children's physical needs.[103] The Dovers from the Managers survey were very worried about having to educate their only child at boarding school because Mr Dover was in the military and might be sent abroad: 'All we've got is a daughter, and we don't want to leave her.'[104] The Olantighs emphasized how they invested in their children's cultural education by 'talking to them about topical events', visiting historic sites and museums and the public library' in contrast with their parents' generation who adopted a more laissez-faire attitude to their children's upbringing and were not aware of children's 'intellectual needs'.[105]

The majority, however, expected their daughters to place marriage before career. In 1968, the managers' wives were asked to comment on the kind of education they wanted for their daughters and sons and in respect of their daughters, the kind of job they expected them to do and the sort of person they would like them to marry. Their answers revealed the ongoing conflicts in the mothers' sense of themselves discussed in the previous section and their uncertainties about what the world offered girls and women.[106] While they were aspirational for their daughters to achieve happiness, this was primarily through marriage to 'a wide awake person' in Mrs Herne's words, or for Mrs Graveney, someone who 'treats her as a human being'.[107] Their hopes that their daughters would find happiness and contentment and space to grow within their intimate relationships often reflected their own experiences. Mrs Graveney's marriage had left her feeling resentful, unfulfilled, and taken for granted. Her only daughter was the focus of her attention and understandably she wanted her to have what she had not: a good education (Mrs Graveney had left school at 14), a rewarding job and a marriage based on companionship:

> I'd like her to see things as they really are, and not as she wants to see them, and that if she has got anything in her at all that she'll not waste it, and make the most of her life. I'm not interested in what job she has as long as it's what she wants and she is not wasting herself. I'd like her to marry probably someone who was of the same degree of intelligence and education, that is, University, if she goes on so that they have something in common...As for her happiness...

[103] Mathew Thomson, *Lost Freedom: The Landscape of the Child and the British Post-war Settlement* (Oxford: Oxford University Press, 2013).

[104] UKDA, SN 853296: Interview with Mrs Dover, p.20.

[105] Pahl and Pahl, *Managers*, pp.211–12.

[106] Pahl and Pahl, *Managers*, p.280.

[107] UKDA, SN 853296: Interview with Mrs Herne, p.5; Interview with Mrs Graveney, p.6.

> Firstly it would be her chosen profession, and then her marriage, which should be more important than her other activities.[108]

In contrast with her husband who 'thinks that if a grammar school was good enough for him, therefore it's good enough for her', Mrs Graveney aspired to a private education for her daughter, seeing this as a stepping-stone to university and a very different kind of life to the one she had had.

Mrs Graveney was channelling her own frustration and understanding of what underpinned that into ambition for her only daughter. But in this small survey of middle-class women, mothers more commonly expressed some ambiguity about the value of post-secondary education for their daughters. This in part reflected their own experiences and their perception of social reality. Mrs Lenham's aspirations for her daughter—that she would attend a good secondary school (not a comprehensive) and university 'if she had the brains'—seemed in part to be guided by Mrs Lenham's desire for her daughter to marry a well-educated person and for her to mix with like-minded people. Like many other middle-class families, the Lenhams were prepared to explore ways of protecting their daughter from having to attend the local comprehensive school. This usually meant paying for private education.[109] Her son, on the other hand, was expected to attend a selective i.e. grammar school 'and then he would go to university'.[110] Mrs Eastwell had been to university herself, but perhaps because her work life had been as a secretary, she doubted the value of this level of study unless 'they are brilliant and academically inclined'. In respect of her daughter, she remarked that 'unless attitudes to married women change, an academic university education is a waste of time. She would rather they had a sort of *cordon bleu* training and to be good housekeepers. "If you are going to do it you might as well do it well."'[111] Similarly, while Mrs Frith would like her daughter 'to be intelligent and make an interesting career for herself', she thought domestic science training would be 'invaluable help later on'; clearly she did not envisage her daughter putting her career before her marriage. She recognized that university carried 'social standing' but only because 'someone in that line might be rather nice' as a husband for her daughter.[112] This couple had paid for a private education for their son.[113] Mrs Manston's own experience at teacher training college as a mature student where she had encountered prejudice from the lecturers against married women indicates that there were still obstacles to overcome.[114] The view was still quite widespread that a

[108] UKDA, SN 853296: Interview with Mrs Graveney, p.6.
[109] Worth, *Welfare State Generation*, p.29.
[110] UKDA, SN 853296: Interview with Mrs Lenham, p.8.
[111] UKDA, SN 853296: Interview with Mrs Eastwell, p.5.
[112] UKDA, SN 853296: Interview with Mrs Frith, p.5.
[113] UKDA, SN 853296: Interview with Mr Frith, p.18.
[114] UKDA, SN 853296: Interview with Mrs Manston, p.11.

university education was wasted on girls and that teacher training was more suitable given the likelihood that their career would play second place to marriage. In 1965, a female student at Oxford who had studied at a co-educational grammar school reported that the view of teachers was that 'the boys should go to university. It wasn't a place for girls.' And a female student at Leicester believed that girls lacked ambition and drive, thinking 'Oh well if we don't pass well we will get married'.[115]

Mothers' attitudes to their daughters' futures were also shaped by the broader context. The reform of secondary education and the expansion of higher education was creating more opportunities for girls to continue their education. And the growing economy opened up more varied job opportunities. But wider attitudes to the value of that education were lagging behind the changes, in part reflecting the realities of the gendered labour market. When mothers expressed their desire for their daughters to find their primary happiness in their marriage, they believed they were being realistic, often unable to envisage what a different kind of life might look like. Janice Galloway's mother, who had been 'a servant, a mill worker, a bus conductress, a cleaner, a dinner-lady in that order' was keen for her clever daughter to become a teacher but faced with the complexities of the journey to get there for a working-class family she wondered whether a job at Boots the Chemist might be 'nicer'.[116] This was the bind the mothers found themselves in; they knew there was an alternative to the pattern their own lives had taken but they were unable to lead by example and had no tangible means of showing their daughters how to achieve it.[117]

What Daughters Thought

The life choices of daughters in the late 1950s and 1960s were made in a context of rapidly changing social mores. The expansion of educational and career opportunities, and the shifting expectations of girls who aspired to new lifestyles and life courses, prioritized their own desires rather than those of society or family. Just as the transition generation of women were reaching their late teens, as they were beginning to be given greater freedoms from family discipline and being asked to make life decisions about education and careers, the culture around them was changing. For some, this was an anxious time. Ann Auchterlonie who

[115] MRC, NSHD: Student Study transcripts: XIX Oxford 18 May 1965: 259/70: History, Lady Margaret Hall; XIV Leicester 75–9 1965.

[116] Janice Galloway, *All Made Up* (London: Granta, 2012), p.124.

[117] For a discussion of mothers' influences on daughters attending university and evidence that shows graduate status conferred fewer social and economic advantages on women than men see Carol Dyhouse, 'Graduates, Mothers and Graduate Mothers: Family Investment in Higher Education in Twentieth-Century England', *Gender and Education* 14:4 (2002), pp.325–36, here p.332.

was brought up in a religious family in Dundee, described in detail the tensions she experienced between her parents' expectations and her own rather unformed desires and ambitions at the age of 16, her concern coming through in her broken narrative:

> I think I was, at that stage rebelling against some of the expectations of how, you know, that you would just get married and have—I mean I have to say that when I left school that Thursday morning, my mother and father were devastated because they wanted me to go to university, and so they were very disappointed that I did, that I did that. But then having not stayed on at university they didn't quite know what I would end up doing but really would have been quite anxious. My mother was anxious to see me settled down then although my father was much more, you know, 'fulfil your potential' etc. It's difficult to actually—I can rem...I think I, these were very confused years for me, I didn't want what I could see happening around me, where people [were] getting engaged and getting married, and I didn't feel that was what I wanted, and I think the whole jazz thing was part of that. Trying to break out of some, some of that but then not quite knowing—And I very much regretted having left school and not going to university, I used to have dreams about it, and dream I was back at school and I was finishing and going—So it was a very confused time. I would, I dearly wanted to travel, I dearly wanted to pack up and go, but I was 16 by the time my parents told me I was adopted, and they had put it off until then because my mother was afraid that once I was told I would turn my back on them, and so there was a lot of emotional pressure not to travel, not to go. I mean I had looked at the Civil Service, I looked at doing the Civil Service exams with a view to not working locally with the Civil Service and looked at that, and actually even considered joining the WRAF, the Women's Royal Air Force at one point, though people just fall about laughing at the idea of me being anything that's rule-bound, but you know, so, it wouldn't have suited me, but, I had this...I really wanted—There was a strong desire to escape from what I was doing, but couldn't really find a way of doing that and ultimately I met my husband and I was married at 22.[118]

The hopes that Ann's parents had for their daughter appeared contradictory. Her mother wanted to see her 'settled', her father wanted her to fulfil her academic potential: 'He would have wanted me to go to university, he always said "marriage is a choice that women make but you don't have to get married, and, you know, but you should have a career that's your own as marriage might not work out for

[118] Interview with Ann Auchterlonie (Humanist Lives Collection).

you and you know... whatever." So he was very much about women being independent and having a career.'[119]

But as we have seen already, parents were as caught in the contradictions and changes of the time as were their daughters, recognizing change was afoot for girls and welcoming that as well as holding on to the certainties that had characterized their own lives. Harriet Harman's parents encouraged their four daughters to 'be educated and independent' but at the same time they were expected to 'find a good husband'. 'We sisters grew up with mixed messages' she writes, understanding that the life their mother had lived was not to be theirs but having no blueprint for a life that combined a career with marriage and family.[120] Liz Heron knew she wanted 'life to be different' as she detected a growing gap between her home life and her aspirations. In her autobiographical writing she recalls her father telling her 'With education, the world is your oyster', but her mother's image of her daughter was to be her carer in her old age.[121] Marriage or 'settling down' represented financial and emotional security and a kind of certainty; higher education and a career were uncharted waters. Life decisions in this period so often required women to make choices which 'challenged the dominant "moral litmus test"'.[122] These choices encompassed a construction of a self that prioritized individual choice, the fulfilment of potential and the pursuance of self-development across many different spheres from dress to intimate relationships and choice of career.

Ann Auchterlonie found the negotiation of this terrain difficult without anyone who could give her a strong steer. She was not unusual, especially amongst working-class girls who were being encouraged by teachers and careers advisors to stay in education, to train for a career but who had little or no idea of what direction to take and were enjoying the freedoms offered on the cultural scene. Ann had become 'disenchanted' with school and left suddenly before taking her exams at age 17 to work as a research assistant with the local newspaper. She only realized her academic potential when, much later, she returned to college to resume her education and got to university at the age of 34, a common pattern amongst her generation and social class.[123] She had been brought up in a church-going family, and found escape in music, travelling around with a jazz band. The enjoyment that could be had engaging in popular culture and the attraction of a wage trumped consideration of longer-term career plans in many girls' minds.

[119] Interview with Ann Auchterlonie. [120] Harman, *Woman's Work*, p.4.

[121] Liz Heron, *Truth, Dare or Promise: Girls Growing Up in the Fifties* (London: Virago, 1985), pp.167–8.

[122] Sarah F. Browne, 'Women, Religion and the Turn to Feminism. Experiences of Women's Liberation Activists in Britain in the Seventies' in Christie and Gauvreau (Eds), *The Sixties and Beyond*, p.86.

[123] Interview with Ann Auchterlonie.

Anne H. was another such directionless teenager in the 1960s: 'I just remember—I had no vision. I had no vision of myself. I mean, I really say, I was kind of wide-eyed and legless most of the time. Like, you know, I said earlier—I didn't have a pathway to follow.'[124] She was not unusual. In 1962, when she was 16 and still living with her parents in a new town near London, Brenda's Youth Employment Officer was disparaging of her lack of interest in her future, remarking that she 'gave the impression that the very idea of a "career" had not penetrated this young lady's mind and that, no matter what its nature, her job would be of little interest or importance compared with her romantic conception of the "real" world & world of boy friends, dates, hair-dos and glamour outfits'.[125] Audrey, who had expressed her desire at 15 to work as a travel agent, left school with no job to go to. She quickly found work as a comptometer operator in a local firm, much to the dismay of her Youth Employment Officer who believed the girl had left school earlier than she should have done owing to 'conflict at school, parents' wishes, friends having left school' and the offer of a job requiring minimum training.[126]

The girls charting a path away from their mothers' values were finding new ways of becoming women, but the process might smash their parents' dreams for them. Social status and ethnic background often determined the manner and outcome. Working-class girls grasped the opportunity to earn their own wage and participate in the revolution in popular culture; they acted on their desires: 'there were just a lot of things I wanted to do' commented Shirley who, on looking back, regretted not persisting with her desire to work with computers. 'I wanted more clothes, and to go abroad for a holiday and just things that you sort of look forward to.'[127] Conversely the West Indian girls interviewed in the early 1970s by Sue Sharpe were very conscious of the hardships endured by their parents and their desire that their daughters would not have to endure the same poorly paid and low-status jobs. But structural racism in education and the labour market restricted girls' opportunities to meet their expectations.[128] Meanwhile, for girls from more privileged backgrounds, the process of becoming adults may appear less fraught and more protracted as university often provided the space and time for reinvention. Suzanna negotiated her way from a private boarding school for girls to one of Britain's new universities in the 1960s, and thereafter to a career in teaching, a story which was punctuated by critical moments when she chose her own path to independent selfhood against her mother's expectations and values. In attending a new plate-glass university instead of Oxford or Cambridge,

[124] Interview and personal correspondence with Anne H.

[125] MRC, NSHD: Sample 36—Youth Employment Office questionnaire 1962.

[126] MRC, NSHD: Sample 01—Pupil questionnaire 1961 and Youth Employment Office questionnaire 1962.

[127] MRC, NSHD: The Persistent Job Changers Survey, 1968, 095–046.

[128] Sharpe, *Just Like a Girl*, pp.249–61.

Suzanna started to chart a life course determined by her own choices. She changed her name upon arriving at university: 'I mean, I'd given myself a new identity. I'd *shed* my private school. I could be friends with whoever was there.'[129] But the dislocation from the values held by parents could be costly. The new freedoms pursued by Suzanna's generation were not unconditional. Suzanna's life experiences and the ways she chose to deal with them, as we will see later in this book, led her to develop a moral system to live by which was not in thrall to the respectability test set by her mother, but along the way mother and daughter found themselves taking positions which brought them into conflict. Suzanna's mother and middle-class women like her, performed a version of womanhood that was governed by the expectations of social class and the necessity of publicly conforming to the notion of the good woman. Anne described her parents as having 'come out of all that stricture and regimen of the wartime and having to do the right thing at the right time'. When she started to rebel—staying out late at parties, hitch-hiking and graduating to drugs, casual relationships, and unplanned pregnancies—she became dislocated from her parents who could not relate to her lifestyle. It was only much later in life that Anne realized that she was more like her mother than she cared to admit. Both focused their lives on home-making and child rearing, only Anne did it alone, without a man.[130]

Conclusions

In 1977 the feminist Nancy Friday's *My Mother My Self*, an exploration of the mother-daughter relationship, provided an inspiration for some feminists who welcomed her argument that women were brought up to conform to an ideal of womanhood that was socially prescribed. She understood that her own mother was a victim of a model of womanhood that constrained, not only her choices, but her ability to express her feelings about those choices. Had she been able to express her 'angers, disillusionments, fears of failure, rage', Friday would have been able to understand her mother and, in turn, better know herself.[131] Thus her mother's inability to speak openly about how she felt about her role trapped them both. Women of Friday's generation had to acknowledge their identity as separate from their mother if they were to live independent and fulfilling lives in the realms of love, sex, and work.

As the historian Carolyn Steedman observed so acutely, her own childhood was shaped by her mother's longing and her response to the world when the

[129] Interview with Suzanna. [130] Interview with Anne.

[131] Nancy Friday, *My Mother Myself: The Daughter's Search for Identity* (orig. 1977. London: Harper Collins, 1994), pp.47–8.

things she wanted so badly were withheld from her.[132] Steedman's personal and historical account of the mother-daughter relationship points up the importance of the stories we tell about ourselves and others. Frequently, the stories told by the daughters' generation portray mothers as representatives of an outmoded and passive model of womanhood which provides a 'schema of understanding', a framework for producing coherence in their own accounts. The self-sacrifice and the stoicism of the older generation are regularly interpreted as proxies for feelings (or the absence of feelings) by women seeking to tell a liberationist narrative rather than as learned and socially prescribed behaviour. The post-war generation held the conviction that the human agent was 'free, self-made and authentic' and so they may have interpreted their mothers' actions as choices rather than responses to external realities and social expectations.[133] This chapter has demonstrated that often the mothers' generation recognized and sometimes railed against the constraints that determined their choices, just as Steedman's mother did in her response to the unfairness she perceived as limiting her own life. But while they were not always content with the cards they had been dealt, options for change were limited which may help explain why their aspirations for their daughters were often equivocal.

Caroline's account of her mother's envy of her daughter's opportunities opened this chapter. It concludes with Caroline's memory of a single incident which epitomized her mother's disappointment that her own life chances had been truncated, that she had not been able to live the life she would have chosen for herself.

> I mean the stupid little story but I remember once going to church in [small town] wearing red stockings as a teenager and getting a completely out of proportion row about this, how ashamed every single person in the congregation would be of me, and even at 16 or whatever I was, I realized this wasn't about the red stockings at all, it was about her. And similarly later on with having boyfriends and so on, these were things she—I mean she only once ever openly said 'oh I really do envy you the chance of doing that' but any, any sort of sense of guilt or not behaving in a way I'd been brought up not to behave overtook erm was because I felt either her disapproval or her envy...It sounds absolutely terrible, I was terribly fond of her and sympathized with all these aspirations.[134]

Feminist accounts which efface the subjectivity of mothers serve the purpose of validating the narrator's version which needs an other. Caroline, however, by the time she undertook her own life review in her seventies, understood her mother's envy, echoing Steedman's observation that 'what my mother lacked, I was given'.[135]

[132] Carolyn Steedman, *Landscape for a Good Woman* (London: Virago, 1986).
[133] Hughes, *Young Lives*, p.3.
[134] Interview with Caroline.
[135] Steedman, *Landscape*, p.122.

Anne who, as a young woman, rejected everything her mother stood for, also came to accept and understand her mother as someone who was the product of her age. In her life history Anne admitted that she deliberately provoked her mother at times:

> I mean, my mother used to come around with, erm, birthday cakes and bedding and helpful things like that, but, you know, she'd sit there with her knitting, quite po-faced and didn't know quite what to do or how to be. I could see it. And my kids were crawling around the floor with no nappies on... And in a way, I see that as—I did then, I think—it was a kind of—'Yes, this is a better way to do it, mother. I don't want your criticism.' Er, that's how I felt. I knew I was gonna be criticized, but she didn't actually ever say anything.[136]

But in retrospect Anne admitted that her life had followed her mother's path 'without the accolades of the marriage' because 'I would not be somebody's help-mate, you know?'

Anne's account encapsulates the material, attitudinal, and emotional differences between the experiences of the two generations and the subsequent reinterpretation of those experiences by the daughters as they look back on their own journeys away from the lives of their mothers. The conflict, when it occurred, was most evident in the post-war generation's younger years as they started out on the journey of self-discovery, combining rejection of some elements of family and community expectation and the revelation that a different kind of life was possible. 'Women of my generation', writes Liz Heron, 'were the first to have the chance to refuse burdens that just couldn't be borne, to understand that it was possible to refuse them without censure, to realize that if you still couldn't have everything, you could at least make some choices about what you could have.'[137] In the chapters that follow, we investigate those refusals and choices which the post-war generation identify in their personal accounts as significant. These stories are rarely linear or smooth; how could they be when they didn't know where they were going?

[136] Interview with Anne.

[137] Heron, *Truth, Dare, or Promise*, p.168.

3

Fashioning the Self

Introduction

Teenagers in the 1950s and early 1960s dressed like their parents. Betty, who was a student in Glasgow, recalled dressing rather primly and remembered the male students wearing suits and ties. Caroline recalled wearing the second-hand cast-offs of middle-aged women that had been cut down to fit. Lorraine, who left a rural town for Glasgow School of Art in 1959, was eloquent on the city style of the students she encountered on her first visit contrasting with her small-town twin-set look:

> When I went for my interview I nearly died of fright because everybody looked so…I mean coming from [small town]…everybody looked so incredibly knowing and gorgeous and the first person I saw was a boy walking down the steps in an ochre-coloured corduroy suit and I thought this is phenomenal! My goodness, everybody—the boys wore denims. I'd never seen a pair of jeans I think, and you cannot imagine! I was in a pleated skirt and twinset I suppose and flat shoes, and all the boys wore desert boots, a bit like Ugg boots, sort of goldeny things you got from Millets or Army & Navy stores, and they were all…half had beards and the rest had long hair—oh fantastic! And the girls had long hair and they were all, oh, beautiful.[1]

By the early 1960s many girls were making their own clothes, shopping in trendy boutiques and beginning, literally, to fashion an identity for themselves through dress. Lorraine soon abandoned the twinsets: 'I wore black jeans and very large jerseys, preferably black and black polo neck—the Juliette Greco look.' Lorraine was able to convey in interview the excitement of the moment when she understood that she could transform herself as she transitioned from home to art college and dress was part of that. As an art school student she was attuned to the visual—she still is. Glasgow School of Art represented far more than just the opportunity to study; it offered a lifestyle and an identity that she could fashion for herself away from the strictures and expectations of small-town life. As she recalled that first encounter on the art school steps in breathless

[1] Interview with Lorraine.

Feminist Lives: Women, Feelings, and the Self in Post-War Britain. Lynn Abrams, Oxford University Press.
 DOI: 10.1093/oso/9780192896995.003.0003

technicolour, Lorraine conveyed the importance of her realization that she could reinvent herself.

Lorraine reinvented herself in another way, by changing her name when she left home. 'I didn't want my name to be Lydia because Juliette Greco and Jean-Paul Sartre wouldn't be able to say Lydia you see.' And later on, wanting something more exciting than working for a London magazine, she applied to work as a holiday rep with Club Mediterranée before a chance encounter on the Fulham Road saw her joining a man she hardly knew on a camper-van trip around Europe. Although the big adventure ended prematurely and badly and Lorraine realized that her 'adventurous spirit wasn't as big as I thought it was!', she repeatedly used travel to challenge her personal boundaries. When a boyfriend took a job in the Sudan, Lorraine drove across Europe to meet him in Athens and their marriage soon after saw her moving to Khartoum for the first four years of married life.

Lorraine encapsulates many of the characteristics of the transition to modern womanhood of this generation. Her desire to look different and be different was facilitated, in part, by her social class and by three years at art school, a privilege still limited to a minority of girls of her age. Similarly, Sheila Rowbotham recounts in her autobiography of the 1960s the 'reconstruction job' she conducted on herself on leaving her sheltered boarding school which incorporated growing her hair, dressing in beatnik clothes and travelling to France, endeavouring to 'transmogrify into a cross between Juliette Greco and Brigitte Bardot'. On her return to Britain and university she 'would quickly start burying recollections of adolescence, embarrassed by that earlier self, adrift without bearings'.[2] Although Rowbotham's experience of this liminal period in her life was notable for an eventful sojourn in Paris, her attempt to reconstruct the self through self-fashioning and distancing herself spatially and ideologically from the expectations of family and school was not untypical, opening up spaces for a reconfiguration of other aspects of her life.

The period of girls' lives straddling the teenage years and the early twenties, between school and settling down into marriage or a career, is a potent memory store. In life stories these few years are heavy with meaning, yielding moments of epiphany and transformation which are seen by the narrator to define the woman they became. Whereas in interview the childhood years, understandably, are characterized by passivity, on becoming teenagers this generation shifted their narrative register as they recounted the active process of differentiating themselves from their parents' generation. The woman in her sixties or seventies briefly becomes that woman in her teens and early twenties and recognizes, in the telling of stories about this time of relative freedom and opportunity, that it was special. The memories are of course familiar to us, likely accentuated by the regular media

[2] Rowbotham, *Promise of a Dream*, p.42.

representation of young women as archetypes of the Sixties, but this does not diminish their significance.

In some cases women recounted stories of profound awakening, incorporating the questioning and sometimes rejection of the religious and moral certainties of their parents' generation. More commonly, however, the transformation from dependent girl to independent woman is told through the lens of self-fashioning and spatial and educational mobility. Personal appearance mattered as it became the easiest way girls could inhabit different selves, be it the fashionable bopper in a mini-skirt or the wannabee Juliette Greco dressed in sophisticated black. Mobility mattered too. Succeeding in education was, for working-class girls, to leave the safety of one's class, one's home and the expectations associated with them, to 'the lure of those promises' of being different, clever, successful.[3] And girls also used travel to distance themselves physically and metaphorically from social expectations and to enable new experiences, even if sometimes they realized, like Lorraine and Sheila Rowbotham, that travel was not necessarily the key to unlocking a new stage of life.

Studies of post-war teenage culture have little to say about the experiences of girls like Lorraine. Until recently they have emphasized teenage rebellion and the moral panics concerning youth cultures, delinquency, gang violence, and sexual precocity, or they have elaborated on the phenomenon of the teenage consumer which saw young people with spending power fuelling the leisure market of the late 1950s and early 1960s. Others paint a picture of the 'Swinging Sixties' with young women as the pin-up girls of the new popular culture.[4] A recent re-evaluation interprets the new expressive culture of this period as a more authentic lifestyle, reflecting teenagers becoming 'agents of change' in their own lives. The teenager in this reading is 'a symbol of meritocracy, affluence and classlessness' who valued authenticity over respectability.[5] She was in touch with and acted on her emotions rather than concerned with social conventions. She was also a beneficiary of the post-war welfare state, notably the reform of secondary education which extended the leaving age to 15 and the expanded provision of council housing providing greater security and comfort for millions. As young girls, writes Liz Heron, 'we had a stronger sense of our possibilities', that there was confidence emanating from the equal provision of education and healthcare, echoing Carolyn Steedman's paeon to orange juice and free school milk as investments in

[3] Valerie Walkerdine, 'Dreams from an Ordinary Childhood', in Heron, *Truth, Dare or Promise*, p.74.

[4] Louise A. Jackson with Angela Bartie, *Policing Youth: Britain 1945–70* (Manchester: Manchester University Press, 2014); David Fowler, *Youth Culture in Modern Britain, c.1920–1970* (Basingstoke: Palgrave, 2008); Pamela Cox, *Gender, Justice and Welfare: Bad Girls in Britain, 1900–1950* (Basingstoke: Palgrave, 2003); Jonathan Green, *All Dressed Up: the Sixties and the Counterculture* (London: Pimlico, 1999).

[5] Selina Todd and Hilary Young, 'Baby-boomers to "Beanstalkers".' See also Andrew August, 'Gender and 1960s Youth Culture: The Rolling Stones and the New Woman', *Contemporary British History* 23:1 (2009), pp.79–100.

the value of young people and, in turn, her understanding that this investment told her 'that she had a "right to exist"'.[6] The possibilities Heron imagined were ill-defined but were to be shaped by a combination of post-war security and affluence, full employment, and cultural change. The stories told by women are not necessarily stories of rebellion or of political awakening but of discovery of the self through everyday practices, enacted by middle and working-class girls alike.

This chapter examines the ways in which the girls of the transition generation explored becoming a woman that didn't look like their mother. Taking fashionable dress as the starting point, but also examining other lifestyle opportunities that became available to young people in the late 1950s and early 1960s, it explores some of the ways in which young women began to express themselves as individuals, how they challenged their own boundaries and how they began to separate themselves from what their mothers represented to them. Self-making encompasses both the mind and the body, the psychological, and the material.[7] While understandings of the modern self tend to focus on the so-called inner self or subjective self, the self that is contained *within* the body, more recent interventions have made the case for considering the 'self in the body'.[8] Modern women, argues Macdonald for the inter-war decades when participation in health and fitness activities became one of the markers of modernity for women, 'had new ways to forge embodied selves', through action and image.[9] By the early 1960s there were new opportunities to do this, forged in the revolution in popular culture. Beatlemania, for instance, the phenomenon whereby adolescent girls screamed and swooned over John, Paul, George, and Ringo, was interpreted by Brian Epstein, the Beatles' manager, as 'self-expression', countering conservative alarm at fans who appeared to be out of control, overcome with 'hysteria'.[10] And there were plenty of young women in the broadcast and print media presenting girls with new ways of being. Models like Jane Asher and Jean Shrimpton, pop stars like Cilla Black and Lulu, actors like Marianne Faithful and Rita Tushingham, and even Christine Keeler and Mandy Rice Davies, appeared to encapsulate the desire for self-expression in the ways they dressed and their glamorous lifestyles, hanging out with pop stars, celebrity photographers, artists, and politicians.[11] And teenagers not only aspired to look like these new women, they were encouraged to think they might follow in their footsteps as 'ordinary' girls like Helen Shapiro and Cathy McGowan made it in the worlds of music and television that

[6] Heron, *Truth, Dare, or Promise*, p.6; Steedman, *Landscape*, p.119.

[7] Charlotte Macdonald, 'Body and Self: Learning to be Modern in 1920s–1930s Britain', *Women's History Review* 22:2 (2013), pp.267–79.

[8] For example, Giddens, *Modernity and Self-Identity*.

[9] Macdonald, 'Body and self', p.275.

[10] Marcus Collins, *The Beatles and Sixties Britain* (Cambridge: Cambridge University Press, 2022), pp.56–7.

[11] Shawn Levy, *Ready, Steady, Go. Swinging London and the Invention of Cool* (London: Fourth Estate, 2002).

were dominated by the young and hip.[12] This appeared to be an egalitarian scene whereby working and middle-class alike could liberate themselves from the 'stuffy conventions', religious hang-ups, and notions of respectability represented by their parents' generation to inhabit a glamorous world of pop music, modelling, and film.[13] McGowan, who had been working as a secretary in the fashion department of *Woman's Own* magazine, was picked in 1963 to present the flagship television programme, 'Ready Steady Go'. She quickly became the archetypal 'girl of the day' with her Mary Quant look, her street talk, and her easy familiarity with the stars of the moment like Donovan and the Beatles.[14] The presence of these women in popular culture projected a desirable image for others to aspire to, but also an attitude that Shelagh Delaney encapsulated in her play *A Taste of Honey*: a desire for love and adventure rather than the conventional future of marriage and motherhood.[15]

The intersection of identity, dress, and mobility in autobiographical narratives has been remarked upon in other contexts, encapsulating a 're-negotiation of the self' through social and spatial movement as well as adopting new dress styles.[16] Self-making thus becomes a process enacted in, through and on the physical body as well as, and in parallel with, the mind. The self is something made (and remade) through the actions of doing as well as being and thinking and of necessity was an active process of self-discovery and contestation with conventional models of behaviour. For some this was manifested in changing one's name, dressing in fashionable and self-chosen clothes, moving away from home and travelling. For others it was a harder journey of self-discovery encompassing the rejection of family and community expectations and the realization that a different kind of life was possible. The walking away from an engagement, the decision to take a job overseas, the freedom of university, rejection of religion, embrace of one's sexuality: such life decisions enabled many women of this generation to 'liberate' themselves in their teenage years and early twenties from many of the constraints that hobbled previous generations of women in terms of self-description and self-presentation.[17] Young women began to question the discourse of respectability, self-sacrifice and service which told them that freedom and choice came with a condition—to be a good girl or a good woman. Seizing the freedom to

[12] Bill Osgerby, *Youth in Britain since 1945* (Oxford: Blackwell, 1998), pp.53–5.

[13] See Todd, *The People*, pp.236–46. This egalitarianism extended to men too. Michael Caine, David Bailey and others found opportunities to reinvent themselves amidst Sixties culture.

[14] https://en.wikipedia.org/wiki/Cathy_McGowan_(presenter).

[15] Selina Todd, *Tastes of Honey. The Making of Shelagh Delaney and a Cultural Revolution* (London: Chatto & Windus, 2019), p.3.

[16] R. Wallis, 'Self-telling, Identity and Dress in Lifestyle Migration Memoirs', *Area* 51 (2019), pp.736–42, here p.737.

[17] Callum G. Brown, *The Death of Christian Britain: Understanding Secularisation 1800–2000*, 2nd ed. (London: Routledge, 2009), pp.191–2; On the implications of women's rejection of religion in this period see Brown, *Religion and the Demographic Revolution*.

dress and travel as one pleased was the start of a journey away from home-making and towards self-making.[18]

Following this injunction to consider both the physical and the psychological, the outward and inward processes of self-discovery and invention, this chapter discusses a number of ways in which this cohort of women sought to do this. Embracing modern fashions was the most visible route to experimenting with new identities, but dressing according to one's own choices was accompanied by other inward and outward actions which are recalled in autobiographical accounts as moments of epiphany or transformation.[19] The shift from the 'mini-mum' or twin-set look to short skirts and shiny coats was significant at the time and in retrospective accounts, but for many women, speaking about clothes can be a deceptively easy way of talking about something else as well. Clothes-talk can establish safe or common ground but at the same time it conveys more than an aesthetic choice. Changing the name she wanted to be known by was, likewise, a sign that a young woman was beginning to fashion an identity independent of her family. Mobility, encompassing moving away from home to for study or work and overseas travel, exposed women to different cultures and alternative lifestyles and permitted them to escape, albeit temporarily, the constraints of their families and communities and to imagine a different future.

Dedicated Followers of Fashion

Just as their mothers had embraced the 'new look' in the 1950s after years of war-time austerity, their daughters grasped the opportunity to dress themselves in the new styles and fabrics to distinguish themselves sartorially from their mothers' generation and to become part of something new. This was the era of man-made and artificial fabrics as well as looser and more casual styles available to everyone, whatever their social class. The mini-skirt is often regarded as the apogee of the 1960s 'look', used as shorthand for 'the Sixties' and for hip-ness. 'The Sixties mini', proclaimed the designer Mary Quant who is often credited with its invention, 'was the most self-indulgent, optimistic "look at me, isn't life wonderful" fashion ever devised. It expressed the Sixties, the emancipation of women, the Pill and rock "n" roll...It was the beginning of women's lib.'[20] Yet hemlines had been rising to above the knee since the late 1950s and women's clothing was already becoming easier and more fun to wear in brighter colours and new, cheaper, and easy-care fabrics. It was simple and relatively cheap to alter one's image.

[18] Abrams, 'Mothers and Daughters'.

[19] On the concept of epiphanies in life narratives see Abrams, 'Liberating the Female Self'.

[20] V&A https://www.vam.ac.uk/articles/the-miniskirt-myth?gclid=CjwKCAjwssD0BRBIEiwA-JP5rLXxMszEpWrKDCp4kwAEnfebNR7i-AKTpIcANVYnJ7_3Lm8510doDBoCy4MQAvD_BwE (accessed 10 February 2023).

Dress in this period and for this cohort of women was a marker of generational but also attitudinal distinction. It operated, as Elizabeth Wilson pointed out, as 'connective tissue', enabling women to perform an identity, albeit that identity may have been quite fragile, and allowing them to identify as part of a group.[21] In interview the new fashionable styles of the early 1960s were vividly remembered, oftentimes marking a transition point from passive girlhood to the more active teenage years and early womanhood. Caroline, Lorraine, Sandra, and Suzanna shared their very similar detailed memories of being made to wear hand-me-downs in their teens that resembled their mothers' clothes and the importance of free choice when they left home:

> Caroline: a little dressmaker with a mouthful of pins who used to make their clothes and she was dragooned into making mine and they were horrible prickly tweed suits.
>
> Suzanna: what I remember was going to [a friend's] mother who had a room in her house where people had handed in hand-me-downs which she sold on.
>
> Caroline: yes and you and I were dressed as 50-year-old women.
>
> Suzanna: dressed in hand-me-downs and they were indescribable, and you didn't have any choice. I mean, that was just what you were given to wear and be pleased.
>
> Lorraine: you can see why when we became students we all wore other things [...]
>
> Caroline: it's an easy way of saying I've changed, I'm doing something different.
>
> Suzanna: but also, I mean if we were all students we were all on grants so we had our own money for the first time.
>
> Lorraine: we didn't shop a lot, we didn't shop like people seem to shop nowadays.
>
> Suzanna: oh no... but we had choices that we could make instead of our parents making them you know [...]
>
> Sandra: what do you remember as gorgeous?
>
> Lorraine: Och one of the frightful dresses... I do remember borrowing a dress when I was at art school actually and it was pink, sort of thick linen. I thought it was divine [laughs from all] and I had a pair of long black gloves [more laughter]. It was a killer. I just <u>loved</u> that dress [...]
>
> Caroline: it was the feeling of being able to do your own thing, I think I must have been incredibly naïve, I just couldn't believe that I could actually wear what I liked.[22]

[21] Elizabeth Wilson, *Adorned in Dreams: Fashion and Modernity* (London: I.B.Taurus, 2009), p.12.
[22] Focus Group (Caroline, Suzanna, Lorraine, Sandra).

This exchange between four friends in their seventies encapsulates the importance of self-fashioning to their teenage selves and demonstrates how, more than half a century later, it is memories of clothes and what they represented in terms of independence and free choice that still resonate. The tendency of teenage girls in the 1950s and early 1960s to be dressed as smaller versions of their mothers is a common theme of life narratives which seek to identify moments or events signifying the emergence of an autonomous self. Carole was able to remember in detail the 'costume' she was bought on the cusp of her teenage years: 'I was very proud of it, it was a greeny skirt and a little green jacket and little shoes with little heels, called kitten heels. I thought I was absolutely the bees-knees but this was bought, it wasn't made. So yes, it was really boring, horrible, it was... basically it was adult clothes cut down.'[23] And Deborah still recalled her humiliation at her school Christmas party when her mother sent her in a home-made dress 'which was blue velvet smocked and a little angora bolero from a pattern out of *Woman's Weekly* and I was laughed at by everybody'.[24] Caroline was one of many who recalled rather painful memories of her identity being smothered in tweeds which prefaced a more positive account of emerging as a young woman in her own right:

> Well I mean all my friends, our mothers chose our clothes till we were about sixteen and I don't know anybody else of my age that that didn't happen to... I don't think teenagers existed as a sartorially different kettle-of-fish from anybody else... But then going to university and having a little pocket money which you could actually, you could go to C&A and buy something, a mini skirt, and I cut my hair, you know I had plaits, and instantly tried to look exactly like Twiggy.[25]

The abrupt shift from school uniform to what Pam described as the 'mini-mum' look of the late 1950s with no concession to the teenage years, was endured by countless young women of her generation. But quite soon Pam discovered, through her older sister, a new way to dress:

> you went straight from school uniforms, and your Sunday kilt and stuff into, er, you got a suit like your mother's and gloves and a hat and that must have been about 15 or 16, I can't remember, but you went instantly... there was nothing in between... school uniform, and a kilt and Clark's sandals to being a mini-mother and that was it, and these thick sort of lisle stockings with seams up the back, and oh, first heels, ok, oh, that was trauma, that was it really. Then gradually that must have been about, that was late 1950s I got my costume and the gloves, and the gloves and the shoes matched, was that right? The gloves and the

[23] Interview with Carole. [24] Interview with Deborah. [25] Interview with Caroline.

> shoes matched and the hat and the bag matched, or the scarf and bag matched, yes.
>
> *Interviewer: Lovely*
>
> Oh very much so, yes, so if you had black shoes and black gloves, then the bag could be different, and anyway…and your little handbag, your little queenie handbag.
>
> *Interviewer: So when did you begin to realize that there were other things to wear?*
>
> Pam: That was '63-ish, '62/'63-ish, and then, very suddenly, my sister was in to shiny black, shiny purple coats and big hoop earrings, and then suddenly I was in to white boots but it must have been about '66/'67 I think.[26]

The sudden revolution in dress was only the most visible manifestation of a more fundamental revolution in attitudes and lifestyle. In 1963 the magazine *Modern Woman*, a publication focusing on home-making and house-crafts and targeted at middle and lower-middle class women, featured a design for a 'quick-make shift' dress, reflecting the fashion for less structured clothing. Readers could write in to request the pattern to sew at home. Despite the loose silhouette of the new fashion-forward design, readers of this magazine were advised that 'midriff and hips must be trim and slender'; a long-line corselette manufactured by Gossard was recommended to achieve the slimline look.[27] Yet, just two years later, Mary Quant brought out her new brand of underwear called Q-Form—a range of bras, panties, and girdles using the new Lycra fabric and marketed as sexy and enabling. Its sex appeal, which for Quant was the 'number one priority', was emphasized in adverts for the new lingerie:

> What's new? Most everything. But most of all *the look*. Female. And provocatively proud of it. Look. Try on some other bras and pull-ons…you're all garment. Slip on new Q-Form. You're all girl. Feel it too. Twisting, running, jumping. There's nothing there to stop you…And what you don't want to show—doesn't.[28]

This kind of underwear, as well as tights in place of stockings, complemented the shorter skirts and looser garments. They resonated with women's sense of liberation: for Diana, tights were almost as important as the birth control pill.[29]

[26] Interview with Pam. [27] *Modern Woman*, May 1963.

[28] *Nova*, March, 1965: advert for Q-form lingerie; Mary Quant, *Quant by Quant: the Autobiography of Mary Quant* (orig.1966, London: V&A, 2018), p.92.

[29] Interview with Diana. The same point is made by Sylvia Aytoun, 'A Love Hate Relationship with Couture', *Costume* 39:1 (2005), p.120.

The significance of clothes to these women is also signalled by their evident attachment to particular items of clothing.[30] Some could describe individual pieces in some detail and others had kept particularly loved garments. For Deborah it was a suede mini-skirt although several key items in her wardrobe remained fresh in her memory, marking a time in her life when she 'started expressing myself with clothes':

> well yeh mid-teens from late school, well we weren't allowed to take the hems of our skirts up at school, had to be on the knee, yes I'm trying to think when I got this amazing suede mini-skirt which I've still got 'cos it's just fabulous...yes lovely soft suede, it's the one my father said was a pelmet...I was wearing this quite short stuff – must have been a frightful sight. I remember a black and white plastic mac, a Courréges type, and that was very short...I think when I was 13, 14...I can't really remember when I started expressing myself with clothes actually. I had some really short stuff at university...I know when I was going out with T. I had—I was 22, 21/22—I had a pair of black hot-pants, cord hot-pants with a big black suede patch on the back and white tights and Anello and Davide lace-up white boots...yeh cos Anello and Davide were the boot makers, they were in Tottenham Court Road, the theatrical people and I was so proud of them, I must have looked a sight [laughs].[31]

In retrospective accounts, self-fashioning through clothes came to stand in for quite marked changes in lifestyle and outlook. Caroline's reflections on her mother's reaction to her choice of red stockings to attend church, a story recounted at the end of the previous chapter, perfectly encapsulated the striving for individual identity on the part of the young woman. The small act of rebellion or self-expression by the teenage Caroline was recalled some 50 years later as a symbol of the clash between her own and her generation's striving for 'freedom' and her mother's realization that her daughter's life was taking a path free of the constraints she had experienced.

The fashionable clothing that enabled Carole and Caroline, Pam, Lorraine, and Deborah to leave behind the mini-mum look was the product of a confluence of technological and cultural changes encompassing all classes and races. Young South Asian women also participated in this fashion revolution, some abandoning their traditional dress for tighter fitting outfits, even mini-skirts.[32] The invention of new synthetic fibres and mass production of ready-to-wear clothes democratized fashion. And the emergence of a generation of young fashion

[30] Kevin Almond and Elaine Evans, 'A Regional Study of Women's Emotional Attachments to the Consumption and Making of Ordinary Clothing, Drawing on Archives in Leeds, West Yorkshire, 1939–1979', *Costume* 56.1 (2022), pp.74–100.

[31] Interview with Deborah.

[32] Wills, *Lovers and Strangers*, pp.311–21.

designers whose innovative styles encapsulated the new mood and who deployed the new synthetic fabrics, introduced a new aesthetic to women's fashion that was easily copied by untrained designers and eventually mass-manufacturers able to produce inexpensive clothing though often by exploiting female labour including that of migrant women.[33] These were aligned to a much broader series of social changes in the decade from around 1955 to 1965, encompassing greater affluence and consumer power, particularly amongst young women, the emergence of magazines and advertising to feed the demand for new fashions and cosmetics and the appearance of independent boutiques selling a range of fashionable clothes soon to be followed by fashion ranges in the larger clothing stores like C&A. A virtuous circle linking supply and demand enabled young women of all classes and races to fashion identities for themselves, by purchasing or making versions of what they saw in the magazines like *Honey* (founded 1961), *Petticoat* (1966), and *Nova* (1965).[34] Suzanna described this environment, in which clothes were part of a broader social change encompassing music, magazines and the new boutiques, as a far cry from her mother's social world. In interview she described a dress that she still owned, some 50 years later, albeit it was now in the dressing-up box. The dress signified a time in her life when she was developing her own personality and rejecting her mother's values.[35] Around the same time, 1967, Suzanna's mother Laura was writing to her husband of her guilty secret: 'I can hardly bring myself to tell you—bought a Dior suit in MacDonalds—dark blue tweed & very French & unorthodox—very Dior en face.'[36] Suzanna recalled that clothes were a source of conflict with her mother but also that they represented her desire for freedom in dress and in other ways too. Her recall of where she purchased the dress and where she wore it keys her memory into the cultural reference points of the 1960s.

> Yes clothes were an issue and I remember the excitement of Carnaby Street and Biba's and all of that absolutely wonderful, oh yes, just so exciting… And I mean there is one dress that I have in the dressing-up box which I bought in [university town], I went to University, and I bought this dress probably in 1967 and literally it comes to about here and it's completely free flowing, it's got a round

[33] See Sheila Allen and Carol Wolkowitz, *Homeworking: Myths and Realities* (London: Macmillan Education, 1987); Aleena Din, 'British-Pakistani Homeworkers and Activist Campaigns, 1962–2002', *Women's History Review* (online 2022).

[34] *Honey* was established in direct response to Mark Abrams' *The Teenage Consumer* (London: The London Press Exchange, 1959), a demonstration of the potential spending power of the teenage market. Cynthia L. White, *Women's Magazines 1693–1968* (London: Michael Joseph, 1970), p.172.

[35] Alison Guy and Maura Banim, 'Personal Collections: Women's Clothing Use and Identity', *Journal of Gender Studies* 9.3 (2000), pp.313–27; Cheryl Buckley, 'On the Margins: Theorizing the History and Significance of Making and Designing Clothes at Home', *Journal of Design History* 11.2 (1998), pp.151–71.

[36] Letter from Laura to husband, August 1967.

> neck and it's gathered and it just falls and it's entirely synthetic fabric and it's very pretty blues and greens and sort of flowers and things but tiny so you're not really aware of what the pattern is just a lovely colour and there were big bloomer type knickers that you wore with it so for the dancing it didn't matter if the skirt flung out because, I mean I remember wearing it to a dance that Jimi Hendrix played at and it was just wonderful you know, fantastic.[37]

The 1950s and 1960s fashion scene was distinctive for its embrace of synthetic or man-made fabrics such as Terylene, Dacron, Crimplene, Tricel, Bri-Nylon, Vincel, Tricelon, Antron, Celon, and Terlenka, the names symbolizing their modernity.[38] They were easy-care—they could be rinsed out and drip-dried in contrast with the traditional woollen and cotton fabrics—and thus were marketed as ideally suited to both the hard-pressed housewife and the generation who wanted up-to-the-minute fashion that was relatively cheap. They could be found in Marks & Spencer and the fashion boutique.[39] Bri-Nylon, a British product, was marketed not only as the ultimate easy-care fabric but as a marker of the go-ahead woman of the 1960s. Accompanied by images of women skiing and parachuting wearing Bri-Nylon clothing, an advertising campaign centred on the 'BRI-NYLON Breakaway girls' proclaimed: 'They'll be no holding them. Their name will be on every woman's lips from the go-ahead teenagers to the with-it old ladies. See how they shake the fashion world.'[40]

Each new synthetic fabric was sold as the ultimate in modern textile design and advertising language was directed to this new generation of women who didn't speak or dress like their mothers. Take Terylene, which was promoted by Simplicity patterns in *Petticoat* in 1967 for its smock dress:

> Simplicity itself this 'Terylene'. Nothing complicated here. 'Terylene'/cotton just isn't. Dead simple smock. Dead easy to make. And the 'Terylene'/cotton removes all that crushing labour. Fab! Wild colours. Won't go drear. Won't go all skimpy when it's washed either. Tough stuff this 'Terylene'.[41]

The synthetic fabrics suited the new generation of designers, both in terms of the properties of the textiles (light, floaty, colourful, non-crease) and the innovation of the fabrics which translated easily into modern and sometimes futuristic designs. PVC (polyvinyl chloride) became Quant's signature fabric in the early

[37] Interview with Suzanna.

[38] Rachel Worth, 'Fashioning the Clothing Product: Technology and Design at Marks & Spencer', *Textile History* 30:2 (1999), pp.234–50; Rachel Worth, *Fashioning for the People: A History of Clothing at Marks & Spencer* (Oxford: Berg, 2007), pp.53–5.

[39] Jade Halbert, 'Just like the King's Road, Only Nearer: Scotland's Boutique Bonanza', *Costume* 56:1 (2022), pp.101–24.

[40] *Drapers' Record*, 11 Sept. 1965.

[41] *Petticoat*, 12 March 1967.

1960s. Her 'wet collection' of plastic raincoats—shiny, short, and in 'Peter Pan colours'—launched in 1963, featured on the front cover of *Vogue* and was soon being worn by celebrities like Cynthia Lennon.[42] All sectors of the fashion industry—fibre producers, designers, and advertisers—keyed-in to the modern aesthetic. Terlenka, for example, was dubbed the 'space age fibre' which was 'light years ahead of anything on earth'.[43] And in an advert for PVC macs with the brand name Astramac, the manufacturer Wethergay positioned its product firmly within the modern space era with both the image and the words conjuring up a brave new world that women could be part of albeit dressed in a shiny, plastic mac:

> Astramac goes space-ace-star-shiny-bang-bang
> Astramac makes wet days jet-days-go-days-glow-days
> Astramac makes drizzle birds, sizzle birds, gin-fizzle birds
> In fiz-whizz-sky-bright-fly-high heaven colour
> With rap-snap-ding-dongh-super-shine
> Get rev girl- 3-2-1 zero girl – get Astramac. Tomorrow.[44]

Designers and consumers celebrated the fakeness of synthetics as a rejection of the conservative and 'unethical' fabrics of the past. The new fabric could also be moulded and shaped in new ways that defied convention and their handling qualities—drip dry, lightweight, non-iron, non-crease, high strength, and cheap—meant they rocket-propelled high street fashion.[45] For women consumers these revolutionary clothes were desirable and symbolized reinvention and rejection of the twinset aesthetic.

Women's magazines were key to this growth in the fashionable ready-to-wear market, featuring up-to-date designs and advertisements and, in turn, stimulating the rag-trade by offering a shop window for new designers and manufacturers. In the early 1960s two new fashion magazines, *Flair* and *Honey*, featured clothes in the medium price range for young women along with lists of stockists. It was the magazines, rather than retail outlets, that very quickly responded to the vast expansion in relatively cheap, ready-to-wear fashion and young women's consumer power. And it was teenagers with their 'High fashion demands' who transformed the rag trade and the journals associated with it.[46] Retailers and publishers prospered in response to the potential spending power of the teenage market, a phenomenon identified by Mark Abrams in his *Teenage Consumer*. Teenagers' rising wages fuelled consumer spending amongst this group which, he argued,

[42] https://www.vam.ac.uk/articles/fashion-unpicked-the-wet-collection-by-mary-quant Susannah Handley, *Nylon: the Manmade Fashion Revolution* (London: Bloomsbury, 1999), p.106.

[43] *Nova*, Oct. 1969. And see https://www.vam.ac.uk/articles/an-introduction-to-1960s-fashion on the space-age aesthetic.

[44] *Petticoat*, 12 March 1967.

[45] Handley, *Nylon*, p.113.

[46] White, *Women's Magazines*, pp.171–2.

almost determined the character and prosperity of some segments of the market such as clothing and cosmetics. He estimated that a fifth of teenagers' uncommitted spending went on clothing and footwear, by far the largest category of expenditure, with middle-class girls committing the most to the purchase of these items.[47]

Although Suzanna, and many other women who recall the excitement of the clothes revolution of this era, name check the most famous boutiques—Biba, Mary Quant, Miss Selfridge—the vast majority of female consumers of the new fashions shopped locally in the new fashion boutiques or department stores which began to open in-store fashion boutiques to attract a younger clientele. Jenni Murray recalled acquiring 'the regulation uniform of the Mary Quant Sixties cheaply from Barnsley market', never able to afford the 'white Courréges boots' she so desired 'and never had the money to take a train to London and go to Biba'.[48] Boutique fashion as a concept began in London's Carnaby Street catering to a male and predominantly homosexual clientele. But as the spending power of young people and especially young women increased, the boutique concept spread to women's ready-to-wear and moved out of London, both to major cities but also smaller towns. These were clothes emporiums stocking the latest fashions and often run by independent and first-time entrepreneurs. In Glasgow, the owner of possibly the first boutique aimed at teenagers in the city, 'Modrock', recognized the untapped spending power of young people who can 'afford a new dress every other week'.[49] 'In Gear' was typical of this trend, opened in 1966 by first-time retailers Anne and Gerald Hirst in the west end of the city, adjacent to the University and the emerging bohemian quarter dubbed Glasgow's Chelsea (see Figure 3.1). It stocked Marion Donaldson designer clothes (Scotland's Mary Quant) in a fun and relaxed atmosphere.[50] Soon, the established department stores cottoned on to the trend and created in-store boutiques such as 'Just In' in Latters and 'The Underground' at Hendersons in Glasgow: 'Just like the King's Road only nearer.'[51] In provincial Scotland women could still get their hands on the latest fashions. Falkirk had 'Go Gal', Hamilton had 'Boutique 263' and in the new town of Cumbernauld there was 'Dip Boutique' established by a local designer.[52]

[47] Abrams, *The Teenage Consumer*, p.9. Middle-class girls were said to spend 24/9d per week on clothing and footwear compared with the 14/6d spent by working-class girls. Abrams, *Teenage Consumer Spending in 1959* (London: The London Press Exchange, 1961), Table 2, p.6.

[48] Jenni Murray, *Memoirs of a Not so Dutiful Daughter* (London: Transworld, 2009), p.101.

[49] Jade Halbert, 'Marion Donaldson and the Business of British Fashion, 1966–1999', PhD thesis, University of Glasgow, 2017, p.191.

[50] Halbert, 'Marion Donaldson', p.193.

[51] Halbert, 'Just like the King's Road', pp.101–2; Halbert, 'Marion Donaldson', p.200.

[52] Halbert, 'Marion Donaldson', p.189; Halbert, 'Just like the King's Road', p.110.

Figure 3.1 In Gear fashion boutique, Glasgow, 1966.

Home-made

Although the new ready-to-wear fashions were desirable, they remained relatively expensive until the advent of the fashion retail chains such as Chelsea Girl (1965) and Miss Selfridge (1966).[53] Amongst these was C&A, a Dutch clothing store, which became known for its ability to produce inexpensive versions of the latest catwalk designs. In 1967 C&A launched a fashion collection designed by Twiggy.[54] Rosemary remembered C&A as cheap for fashions but 'even then they were still expensive... so it did pay to make your own clothes, so we all had sewing machines and we were all sewing away'.[55] Women frequently made or adapted their own clothes, inspired by what they saw in shop windows or magazines. Alexandra Pringle secretly shortened all of her skirts one evening, inspired by photographs of Twiggy.[56] When she reached her teenage years Carole, who grew up in a working-class family in Newcastle, began to make her own clothes, helped by the availability of cheap fabric and simple patterns. Carole could only afford to buy new clothes once she was working: 'We would go in to Newcastle... and go round Selfridges and Lewis's and all these places and look at what there was and they were way out of my means.' But she was handy with a sewing machine so she and her sister would make their own, buying a yard of material from South Shields market, running up a dress—'very short'—and wearing it that night.

> *So you would just run up a little kind of shift thing?*
>
> Carole: It was a little short shift dress, different colour, different material and it would probably cost about ten shillings; probably really raggy & horrible inside but it looked good. So every week I had a new dress on, but home-made. So it was in the days of Twiggy, Mary Quant, black & white. I remember having my fingernails one black, one white, one black, one white... and my hair was cut short, it was cut really short one side and longer at the other and black and white dresses and mini dresses, and miniskirts.[57]

Sheila had been taught to sew by her grandmother which came in handy when she and her sister wanted the new fashions.

> So we were able to run up our own little Butterick patterns on our sewing machines... Mini-skirts, you know, we would copy the latest trends and...

[53] https://en.wikipedia.org/wiki/River_Island; https://www.retailappointment.co.uk/career-advice/company-a-z/companies-k-o/miss-selfridge (accessed 21 January 23).

[54] https://www.c-and-a.com/uk/en/corporate/company/about-ca/history/ (accessed 21 January 23).

[55] Interview with Rosemary.

[56] Alexandra Pringle, 'Chelsea Girl', in Sara Maitland (Ed.), *Very Heaven. Looking Back at the 1960s* (London: Virago, 1988), p.38.

[57] Interview with Carole.

> You would see something in a magazine and think 'well, I could make that', you know, little shift dress, you know, little long black/white boots, false eyelashes—you could run it up on a Thursday and wear it on a Saturday you know.[58]

A home seamstress could always produce a dress much more cheaply than purchasing ready-to-wear. Home sewing has often been regarded as the poor relation to the rise of ready-to-wear in histories of fashion but making by hand has recently been interpreted as a socially empowering activity which drew on women's ingenuity, creativity, and skill.[59] The growth of the paper pattern industry in the 1960s, led by companies such as Butterick/Vogue and Simplicity, enabled anyone with a sewing machine to run up an A-line dress or simple top which achieved the look of some of the leading designers, especially as pattern makers teamed up with leading designers like Mary Quant and Jean Muir.[60] The patterns were used not only by amateur makers but also by some of the new generation of designers who had not had a fashion training. The Glasgow designer Marion Donaldson for instance had attended art school and had no training in tailoring or pattern cutting. Her earliest designs were cut out and sewn together on her kitchen table.[61]

Whereas the white women interviewed for this project used clothes simultaneously to distinguish themselves as individuals from their mothers and to fit in with their peers—here we recall Deborah's embarrassment wearing an ensemble her mother thought suitable to her school party—women of the Black British community it has been argued, used dress to assert their cultural identity albeit adhering to respectable codes. Immigrants, argues Tulloch, were at pains to 'present themselves with pride'.[62] In this reading, style was used to deflect racism in a display of confidence in one's dress. A contemporary observer, the Ghanaian documentary and fashion photographer James Barnor who documented the Black experience in London in the 1960s, likewise saw Black people's use of clothing to communicate their identity as Black and British.[63] Making garments was part of a process of self-styling, undertaken to maintain an aesthetic presence through the wearing of stylish, respectable, well-made clothes.[64] Sewing skills were either passed on within families or girls were apprenticed to dressmakers. Gloria Bennett, a Jamaican living in Doncaster, used her superior dressmaking skills to construct elaborate dresses which she wore in what Tulloch describes as a

[58] Interview with Kathleen.

[59] Barbara Burman, 'Home-sewing and "Fashions for All", 1908–1937', *Costume*, 28:1 (1994), pp.71–80, here pp.71–2.

[60] Joy Spanabel Emery, *A History of the Paper Pattern Industry: The Home Dressmaking Fashion Revolution* (London: Bloomsbury, 2014), p.185.

[61] Halbert, 'Marion Donaldson', p.179.

[62] 'From Windrush to Ms Dynamite: 50 years of black British style', *The Independent*, 5 Oct. 2004.

[63] https://sites.courtauld.ac.uk/documentingfashion/2021/05/18/james-barnor-britain-in-the-1960s/ (accessed 21 January 2023).

[64] Carol Tulloch, 'Style—Fashion—Dress: From Black to Post-Black', *Fashion Theory* 14:3 (2010), pp.273–303, here p.276.

'meticulous presentation of self'. Bennett derived confidence and power from 'the craftmanship of self' emanating from her personal styling.[65] However, Black representation in fashion in the UK in this period was extremely limited. The first Black model to feature on the cover of British Vogue was African-American Donyale Luna, in 1966 but inside the covers Black models were rare.[66] For some, the United States was more influential on style choices as Beryl Gilroy, who arrived as a student in London from Guyana in the1950s recalled: 'My cousins copied styles from True Romances, Ebony, or Jet sent from the U.S. The U.S. had a "black" style.'[67] These tantalizing and partial glimpses of Black women's engagement with fashion are suggestive of a relationship with style at least partly shaped by racial identity but more research is needed to better understand how and to what extent this manifested in young women's clothing practices.

The new fashions—free and easy, modern, and liberated from constraints—stood for a new kind of lifestyle encompassing other kinds of freedoms: to travel, to pursue a career, and liberation from the moral certainties of the previous generation.[68] Wearing the new unstructured clothes made from synthetic fabrics that did not require shaping and supporting undergarments or careful laundry regimes, young women could envisage themselves living a different, freer and more authentic lifestyle—or at least this is the image the advertisers constructed, linking a woman's choice of clothes to other lifestyle choices. Thus, readers of *Nova* in 1965 were told they could travel 'light, pretty and uncrushable' wearing Orlon, the synthetic fabric 'with the look of linen', in this case flying with Air-India.[69] The same issue of this aspirational magazine contained an advert for outerwear in association with Austin motors: 'You can drive an Austin without wearing a Deréta Dandycoat. But then you'd be missing a number of important fashion features, road tested by Deréta for glamour and comfort'. A feature item on holidays contained recommendations for the single girl—'a combination of St Tropez and Kitzbuhel would make a stimulating year'—and the family—'for the winter park the children and get off for a break on your own'.[70] The *Nova* woman was not only fashion conscious, she was mobile.

Ticket to Ride

'Far cry from Carnaby Street…only BUA run non-stop flights….Suggest you pack Tricel'.[71] In 1967 *Nova's* March fashion feature combined Tricel fashions with

[65] Tulloch, *Birth of Cool*, pp.194–6.
[66] https://www.vogue.co.uk/article/donyale-luna-model-vogue (accessed 21 January 2023).
[67] Beryl Gilroy cited in Carol Tulloch, *The Birth of Cool. Style Narratives of the African Diaspora* (London: Bloomsbury, 2021), p.189.
[68] On the intersection between dress, identity, space and place in memoirs see Wallis, 'Self-telling, Place, Identity and Dress'.
[69] *Nova*, March 1965. [70] *Nova*, March 1965. [71] *Nova*, March 1967.

a British Ugandan Airlines promotion. With its photographs of scantily dressed models in exotic locations featuring Mary Quant lipstick and Christian Dior nail varnish, this late-1960s advertisement was something of a departure in its staging and a far cry from the shift dresses and plastic macs of just a few years earlier. The modern woman, so this advertisement implied, could fly to a hot part of the world and still emerge uncreased and fashionable. '5.45 am sighted by giraffes at Chobe stop I wore Tricel all day stop not one crease.'[72] *Nova* appealed to a slightly older and wealthier readership than its sister magazines and thus was a few years ahead of the curve in terms of depicting a carefree and glamorous lifestyle incorporating foreign travel. While advertisements such as this one were primarily aspirational, conjuring up an image of a jet-setting way of life few could ever achieve, overseas travel to less exotic climes was beginning to become more mainstream for work or for a holiday and presented women in their late teens and early twenties with opportunities for escape from the expectations and constraints they experienced at home. Rather few young women in the 1960s had the resources to take off on a holiday overseas, let alone to Africa. But many fantasized about travel within the UK or overseas and some who were looking for excitement, love, work or an escape did take up the growing opportunities to travel abroad.

The late 1950s and early 1960s witnessed 'a proliferation of representations of girls going places' giving the impression, argues Tinkler, that all sorts of girls were mobile.[73] And indeed they were, constituted by teen migration for work, a growth in female students studying at teacher-training colleges and universities away from home, and the rise of holiday and leisure travel within the UK and overseas. Some of that mobility existed in girls' imaginations. The media shaped expectations as much as encouraging actual travel. Yet, while filmic and pictorial representations of mobile women tended to emphasize the growing opportunities for travel for white, middle-class girls, working-class girls, especially those with independent wages, were not excluded from the mobility revolution. Certainly, the dream of travel featured quite prominently in many girls' wishes for their future in 1961 when they were 15.[74] A working-class girl who, at the age of 13 listed knitting and sewing and looking after her pets as her hobbies, two years later dreamed of travelling and living abroad.[75] Another expressed her desire to (1) 'to be able to travel round the world' (2) 'to have a boat of my own' (3) 'to live in South America'. Ten years later she had partially achieved her wanderlust by working in Africa for a year.[76]

[72] *Nova*, March 1967.

[73] Penny Tinkler, 'Going Places or Out of Place? Representations of Mobile Girls and Young Women in Late-1950s and 1960s Britain', *Twentieth Century British History*, 2020, pp.1–26, here p.3.

[74] MRC, NSHD: in answer to a 1961 question 'what are your 3 wishes', working, travelling, and holidaying abroad were frequently mentioned.

[75] MRC, NSHD: Sample 10—Child's questionnaire 1959; Pupil's Questionnaire 1961.

[76] MRC, NSHD: Sample 07—N.F.4 Survey of Mental Ability and Scholastic Achievement 1961; postal questionnaire 1971.

From the early 1960s travel was increasingly associated with the quest for meaning and for some, dropping out of mainstream society, manifested in the Beat poets Merry Pranksters bus trip across the United States in 1964, the Beatles much reported trip to India to visit the Maharishi Mahesh Yogi in 1968 and the hitchhiking and backpacking youth of the later 1960s.[77] Youth travel has often been understood as a rite of passage, marking the transition to adulthood, separating the young person from home and encompassing adventure and risk and culminating in 'the completion of the self'.[78] Particularly in the 1960s and 70s across North America and Europe, travel in the form of hitchhiking and cheap bus and train travel (the inter-rail scheme was introduced in 1972) came to symbolize the 'coming of age' of young people. The 'rucksack revolution' was a phenomenon in North America and Europe by the early 1960s as young people hit the road—influenced by Jack Kerouac's *On The Road* published in 1957—to seek authentic experiences and find freedom from convention.[79] Anne recalled hitchhiking around Europe with a schoolfriend until their money ran out. Neither remembered contacting their parents 'which now seems very strange behaviour' but then 'it was not even expected'. 'Maybe' she reflected, 'they didn't feel qualified to break into our world which was something nobody understood. Least of all us that were doing it. It was an experience.'[80] For her friend, the trip was taken in the gap between leaving school and starting college. This was not the case for Anne who described herself as having 'an open ended pathway'.

More prosaically, British people were slowly discovering foreign resorts. European destinations were more accessible in the 1960s with the advent of cheaper air travel and the introduction of the package holiday. More than three million British people travelled abroad on holiday in 1960.[81] From the mid-1960s women's magazines contained features and advertisements for foreign holidays. At the top end *Nova* provided information for holidays to destinations from Ireland to Morocco and adverts for Barbados, the Dalmatian Coast, and Mediterranean cruises.[82] But for Suzanna, it was Spain that provided the opportunity for hedonism and self-discovery in the summer of her first year at university.

> And the three of us *hit* the beaches of Spain together, for a month. And had a *wild* time. And the other two girls were sleeping with their boyfriends that they met on the beach, and whatever, and I wasn't, until I met this Frenchman, who

[77] Robert Stone, *Prime Green: Remembering the Sixties* (New York: Harper Collins, 2008); Dominic Sandbrook, *White Heat: A History of Britain in the Swinging Sixties* (London: Little Brown, 2006), pp.231–2.

[78] Linda Mahood, *Thumbing a Ride: Hitchhikers, Hostels and Counterculture in Canada* (Vancouver: UBC Press, 2018), pp.12–13.

[79] Mahood, *Thumbing a Ride*, pp.74–5.

[80] Personal correspondence with Anne.

[81] Dominic Sandbrook, *Never Had it So Good: A History of Britain from Suez to the Beatles* (London: Little Brown, 2005), pp.134–5.

[82] *Nova*, January 1966.

> was absolutely gorgeous, and *wonderful*, and I fell in love with, and we made love. And I was completely taken aback—so was he when he discovered I was a virgin. I mean it was sort of like (gasps).[83]

Suzanna's account is echoed by that of Jenni Murray, though in a Turkish resort where she was spending time with her parents before commencing university. Losing her virginity at 18 to the strains of Jose Feliciano's 'Light My Fire', Jenni relayed the details to her best friend at home.[84] Jenni had finally escaped her mother's moral control by creating a physical and cultural distance between them.

When the magazine *Cosmopolitan* offered its readers regular travel features in the early 1970s they were tailored to the more realistic ambitions of a younger clientele, with the 'Cosmo girl's guide to the summer scene' in 1973 recommending holidays in Majorca, Greece, Morocco, and Tunisia. A year later it featured holidays for single women and details of holiday companies such as Club Dateline and Club Mediterranée which hosted 'meet-each-other-weeks' and activity holidays.[85] Club Mediterranée was founded in 1950 as a not-for-profit package holiday organization with a hedonistic philosophy summed up in its strapline: 'The aim in life is to be happy. The place to be happy is here. And the time to be happy is now.'[86] And for those who wanted to travel but could not afford the high prices of package holidays, there were 'jobs for the girls'—working holidays as au pairs or employed by the growing holiday companies such as Thomson as baby-patrollers or villa hostesses.[87] The *Cosmopolitan* route to overseas adventure via work with a package holiday company was an attractive proposition for some. Lorraine spent a couple of years after art school working for a magazine company in London but 'wanted something more exciting'. A chance encounter on the Fulham Road provided that opportunity:

> I decided to send off a letter to Club Mediterranée to be a tour guide/hostess whatever you call them and I had the letter in my hand walking to the post office in Fulham Road where we had a flat, and we nipped into one of the pubs there for a drink…and there was G. with a chap—'Good grief what are you doing here?' 'I'm just having a drink with M. and M. is about to sail round the world and he is looking for a cook!' So, I set off with M. who was from New Zealand. My poor parents, how did they put up with this? We got as far as…we drove in a VW minibus thing through Amsterdam with G., he was there too, it was the three of us. We drove up through Germany as far as Copenhagen and we had so many rows that finally I left. I hadn't put the syrup away neatly in the little

[83] Interview with Suzanna. [84] Murray, *Memoirs*, pp.116–17.

[85] *Cosmopolitan*, July 1974: 'Go it alone'.

[86] https://www.francetoday.com/culture/club_med_the_story_behind_the_iconic_french_brand/ (accessed 10 February 2023).

[87] *Cosmopolitan*, January 1973.

> cupboard and everything had to be ship shape as otherwise there was no room to travel. I don't know whether I hadn't put the lid on the syrup, or shut the bloody cupboard door, anyway, we opened the cupboard and the syrup had spilt all over the cupboard and he gave me a complete row, such a row and we were quite near the station and I said 'that's it, I'm not going any further, I can't bear this it's ridiculous' and I marched out and got the train home!...I got as far as Copenhagen. I believe M. ended up in jail somewhere, something to do with drugs. Not good.[88]

Lorraine's 'something more exciting' had been quashed by the expectations that she be the little housewife on the big adventure. Julie Walters' account of an over-land car trip from the UK to Istanbul in the summer of 1971 with her boyfriend and another couple, encapsulates this spirit of adventure while also highlighting the potential perils for women who were vulnerable to sexual exploitation in unfamiliar circumstances, in her case in the bowels of a ferry to Corfu. When she was propositioned by one of the crew she used her sea-sickness to deter him. The comedic way in which she recounts the story perhaps downplays the jeopardy in which she found herself, a situation that many other solo travelling women may well have experienced. [89]

The sexual risks of girls' mobility had been the subject of fears since the nineteenth century. But in the 1950s the migration of especially Irish girls to London for work or adventure sparked a panic about sexual exploitation.[90] By the 1960s the focus shifted to 'foreign girls' working in England as au pairs who, it was said, were the victims of 'domestic slavery' though as Tinkler observes, loneliness was a more widespread problem amongst this group.[91] A number of women's organizations were active on behalf of such girls: for example, the National Council of Women campaigned for hostels for girls working away from home and the Women's Fellowship of the Methodist Church in London ran such accommodation although by the 1970s their effort was focused more on support for unmarried mothers.[92] The independence so many sought by moving was hard won, especially for those on poor wages and living in bedsitters for whom 'swinging London' never really materialized.[93] Janine, despite having her dream job as a fashion journalist which required a move from the home counties to London, found living in the city as a single woman stressful. In 1972, at the age of 26,

[88] Interview with Lorraine.
[89] Julie Walters, *That's Another Story. The Autobiography* (London: Weidenfeld & Nicolson, 2008), pp.144–50.
[90] Tinkler, 'Going Places', pp.16–18. See also Julia Laite, *Common Prostitutes and Ordinary Citizens: Commercial Sex in London, 1850–1960* (Basingstoke: Palgrave Macmillan, 2011).
[91] Tinkler, 'Going Places', pp.18–21.
[92] Norfolk Record Office [NRO], SO 226/9: National Council of Women committee meeting, 11 Sept 1963; FC 79/424: Bulletin of the Women's Fellowship of the Methodist Church, Winter 1973.
[93] See the examples in Tinkler, 'Going Places', pp.22–5.

unmarried and living in a flat she reported that 'You work on your nerves. You're up against it all the time... Because I'm not married perhaps I have to look after myself and conflict between the job and boyfriend/social life. I'm a worrier and worry about it.'[94]

In contrast to the moral panic about the sexploitation of young women within the UK, travel for work overseas was represented as an adventure with risk-taking seen as an essential element of self-discovery.[95] Less risky, yet adventurous nonetheless, were the opportunities for work in the Foreign and Commonwealth Office overseas, government aid programmes, and colonial administration.[96] Elizabeth was working as a midwife when she responded to a Department of Overseas Development advert in the *Nursing Times.*

> Well it was because I was in Edinburgh for about six years and the midwives that I worked with were fabulous... But, because I was one of the youngest and they kept saying, 'oh if I only had done so and so when I was younger' and I kept thinking well I don't really want to do this for the rest of my life and not being able to say that I've been somewhere. I might be a good midwife, but I just felt I was in a rut. So I decided I would go off. And in the nursing journals, of course there were some really good jobs advertised and the job I went after was in one Laos... [laughs] My mother she went down with me—it was in the Ministry of Overseas Development—and she went down with me for the interview and they didn't give me the job there, they wanted someone who had had previous experience. So they offered me the job in Sabah, that's north Borneo. And the girl who got the job in Laos, she was in Laos for six months and she was shot by the Vietcong. Your life's mapped out for you.[97]

Elizabeth went on to work in the Solomon Islands in a similar capacity and a few years later, after a break back in the UK, she volunteered to go to Ethiopia during the 1974 famine with the Red Cross. Elizabeth had been, by her own admission, 'sort of a very shy quiet person' so working overseas helped her come out of her shell and gain in confidence. Spurred on by the regrets of the older nurses, Elizabeth grasped the opportunity to travel and experience the world before settling down into marriage back in the UK.

A number of agencies facilitated overseas work and travel such as the Graduate Service Overseas scheme and International Voluntary Service (founded 1931 which became Voluntary Service Overseas, VSO) which provided volunteer

[94] MRC, NSHD: Sample 49—personal questionnaire 1972.

[95] Tinkler, 'Going Places', pp.11–13.

[96] On the FCO's promotion of clerical work overseas as 'exciting' albeit temporary see Helen McCarthy, *Women of the World: the Rise of the Female Diplomat* (London: Bloomsbury, 2014), p.289.

[97] Interview with Elizabeth.

assistance in developing countries.[98] Ruth was attracted to VSO because of its pacifist credentials and was sent to Thailand to teach English in Bangkok, staying for 15 months. It was an experience that changed her thinking about Christianity. Ruth was an evangelical Christian and joined a church in Bangkok but it was run by 'these awful missionaries from the American south, they had such an ignorant and condescending attitude towards Thai civilisation & Buddhism and all that; that really put me off'. She reflected on the experience as something of an epiphany 'which was people aren't necessarily better people because they are Christians and I think that was the first time I had really thought that, and then when I was in Thailand I think I realized that it's cultural like you believe what you've been raised to believe really or what trapped you, if you like as an adolescent'.[99]

VSO also provided women and men with the opportunity to expand their horizons. Founded in Britain in 1958 following the phasing out of National Service and conceived of as a form of post-imperial service for young British elites, it initially recruited people to teach English in Borneo, Ghana, and Nigeria but it soon expanded to many developing countries offering experiences that opened the eyes of the volunteers.[100] The girl we met at the start of this section who had ambitions to travel round the world, spent a year in central Africa in her twenties after a few years teaching. The experience was potentially life-changing: 'Now I realize what poverty really means', she wrote, '& how sickening our petty western materialistic ideals are. Not sure whether I believe in God anymore—this is really worrying me. I feel I would like to marry and have children but not sure if this is just a wanting to escape into a secure backwater!! On the whole this year has been one of finding new values—exciting, challenging, but also frightening.'[101]

Diana had initially applied to VSO but when her application was rejected she found a job with the British Aid Programme. She had trained as an agricultural secretary after school but moved to London to work in the commercial sector where the wages were better and it was there that she spotted an advert from the office of the Crown Agents, a public body which, in the era of decolonization, managed projects in the colonies of the British Empire. At the age of 21 Diana signed up for two and half years in Zambia:

> What I remember, my memories actually were of flying on this lovely black VC10 which touched down in Cairo, that was my first experience of Cairo... and then flying onto Entebbe and arriving at Entebbe something like the middle of the night or early morning, and this fabulous—anyone who knows it will know—the smell of heat—and then flying down to Lusaka so it was a long

[98] https://ivsgb.org/history/ The former is mentioned in Nicholson, *How Was it For You*, p.59.
[99] Interview with Ruth.
[100] Jordanna Bailkin, *The Afterlife of Empire* (Berkeley, CA: University of California Press, 2012), pp.55–94.
[101] MRC, NSHD: Sample 7—personal questionnaire 1971.

> journey. But what was lovely it was a tiny little airport, airstrip, and being met by a government driver...and it was hot and it was sunny and he was black in a Land Rover so there was a touch of the exotics—and then taking me to a government hostel so I was in a secure environment, and all your meals were prepared and there was a whole bunch of people—it was a government hostel to everybody, it was all ex-pats, single, 'cos married people got houses, so single and you met, you know mostly young and that was it, great social life. Didn't have a night in for two and a half years hardly, parties and you know you had enough money.[102]

Diana, like Ruth and Elizabeth, undertook her overseas adventures within safe boundaries and with little reflection of the wider ideological and post-imperial context in which they participated. She was paid well and lived in a safe environment with other government employees. The experience was not life changing but, as she remarked, 'it formulated a lot of my attitudes I suppose. I mean they do say once you've been to Africa you are never the same person again, and that's true.'[103]

Closer to home, Europe was becoming familiar to people through the growth of the package holiday. When Pam was looking for an escape from an imminent marriage and future as a teacher in her own community in the West of Scotland she alighted on an advert for a job in Spain:

> It must have been '68 or '69. I've kind of forgotten—it was the late Sixties. I had to get a teaching job again so I looked in all the...in the *Times Ed.* for a job abroad because I would get out of here and found a fabulous job in the south of Spain teaching in an American school...so I could do that and I got that, and off I went and had a glorious time and that's when I really found boys and men and life.

In recalling her decision to leave behind all that she knew for a job in a country she had never visited and whose language she didn't speak, Pam was clear that this was 'really important'.

Her move to Spain for work opened her eyes to a different kind of life that she hadn't hitherto imagined. She was exposed to 'something totally different' in the architecture, the climate, the food, and the people and realized that 'you could work all around the world, you could do things'. Pam's Spanish adventure was a turning point in her life—'that was when I grew up, yes, yes'—and although she returned home after two years when her mother became seriously ill, this interlude presaged a significant change, encompassing a break with her Catholic friends who 'didn't approve' of her new lifestyle. And in relating this episode Pam

[102] Interview with Diana.

[103] Interview with Diana.

signalled in the register of her voice and her switch to speaking in the first person, that leaving everything that was familiar for a new, albeit temporary, life overseas was a moment of self-discovery.

Conclusions

The writer, teacher, and feminist Alison Fell recounted her teenage years as a story of searching: for an identity and life in which she could be comfortable. At 17, experimentation with clothes and make-up established her rebel credentials. At school dances:

> She opts for the Bad Girl look, in tight red or luminously striped dresses she runs up at home...At last she has heard of Juliette Greco and the Left Bank with its candlelit cellars and existentialists, and so she grows her hair and bleaches it...'Dirty beatniks', her mother snorts, watching her paint black lines round her eyes.

Unlike her older sister—who chose a safe job over continuing her education and joined the church, the ultimate respectability test in lowland Scotland—Alison found an alternative route to self-fulfilment. At art college, in a city miles away from her home town, 'there's no stopping her'. 'Duffle coats and striped college scarves, drainpipes and jazz, bell-bottoms and the Beatles: the last of the Bohemians, the first of the Rock Generation.'[104] Alison's account of resisting the pull of family, community and expectation, finding herself through education and creativity, and crediting her membership of one of the first Women's Liberation groups with saving her 'from a weight of guilt about how badly I fitted into my womanly role' is told through a personal history of the embodied self. Dressing as a Beatnik, travelling for education, work or just for fun, made girls feel different from their older sisters and mothers. By finding new ways of being female, distancing themselves materially and spatially from the old, Alison's generation made a psychic shift which enabled them to imagine new futures no longer shackled to an outmoded construct of femininity.

The stories women tell about clothes and travel are ways of speaking about changes in their self-identity within personal landscapes. Clothes especially mark particular moments which have meaning because of what they represent.[105] Even those who, like Fell, saw education as the key to escaping the world of engagements, marriage and babies, used the image and action of the embodied self to

[104] Alison Fell, 'Rebel With a Cause' in Heron (Ed.), *Truth, Dare or Promise*, pp.22–4.

[105] See Buckley, 'On the Margins', p.168; Carol Tulloch, 'Style—fashion—dress: From black to post-black', *Fashion Theory* 14 (2010), pp.273–303, here p.276.

convey a subjective transformation which is much harder to describe. Lorraine adopted a more French-sounding name at art school; it fit with the identity she wanted to inhabit. And Suzanna distanced herself from her middle-class origins when she got to university. In 1966 she attended a new university rather than Cambridge where her parents had studied.

> I remember standing in the queue to register and two things happened. One, people asked me my name and I said it was Suzanna and they would say yes but what do people call you? and I decided that Suzanna obviously wasn't acceptable so I said Suzie and for most of the 1970s until I met my husband I was called Suzie...So that was the first thing, and the second thing was people said where did you go to school? And I said [elite private school] and then they would go and talk to somebody else [laughs] so sort of like the third person who asked me I said I went to school in [southern town] and that was fine.
>
> *Interviewer: So you kind of recreated yourself.*
>
> I recreated myself and that was, you know I had a wonderful time...I mean, I'd given myself a new identity.[106]

When she returned home the significance of this decision became clear. Suzanna had defined the woman she wanted to be as opposed to the woman her parents thought she should be. 'When someone telephoned and asked to speak to 'Suzie' [her father] responded 'there's no-one called Suzie living here...because it was a cancellation of what they called me.'[107] Changing her name was an act that signified walking away from a particular construction of femininity which ceded control of the body to others. However, as this generation embarked upon intimate relationships the process of acting upon feelings and desires got more complicated.

[106] Interview with Suzanna.

[107] Focus Group Discussion (Suzanna).

4
Intimate Selves

Introduction

In 1969 at the age of 19, Julie Walters abandoned her career as a nurse and moved to Manchester, the first step on the road to an acting career. She cohabited with her boyfriend in a bedsit whilst telling her parents she was living with a friend, reporting that her mother 'might not have been religious but she was of the same generation as Mary Whitehouse'. 'Living in sin', wrote Julie, 'felt like one in the eye for her and her ilk; we were, after all, the "Make Love, Not War" generation.'[1] Julie had lost her virginity to her 'first proper boyfriend' a few months previously, discovering 'sex, in a big way', living the 'permissive age' though concealing it from her parents. Yet, despite her liberated lifestyle, Julie still imagined a conventional outcome to this relationship. The couple decided to get married in 1973. 'Everyone was thrilled; his mother approved and he had bought me a gorgeous antique engagement ring'. But just a few weeks before the wedding, at the age of 23, Julie Walters' desire for self-determination trumped social expectations. She backed out claiming she wasn't ready: 'There's too much of life to do first. I just can't!'[2]

Julie Walters' near miss, sidestepping marriage when the overwhelming majority of her peers were still pledging their troth in their early twenties, is emblematic of the lifestyle change that is usually described as 'the sexual revolution'. Marriage had never been so popular as in the early 1970s and yet, at the same time, Walters' generation enjoyed the comparatively innocent freedoms of the Sixties—liberating fashions, pop culture, and travel—whilst questioning the moral certainties and practices of their parents' generation, quietly and surreptitiously at first but then more openly. Walters and her friends slowly and incrementally charted a new course in personal relationships characterized by the exercise of personal choice and the questioning of the morality and expectations of a previous age. Not every young woman availed herself of this, yet it was this generation that achieved the separation of emotional and sexual intimacy from marriage. This journey was not without conflict or risk; it often involved wrong turnings and was not embarked upon equally by women of all social classes and ethnicities. And as we shall see, nor was the journey entirely about sex. But women in

[1] Walters, *That's Another Story*, p.124.

[2] Walters, *That's Another Story*, p.161.

Feminist Lives: Women, Feelings, and the Self in Post-War Britain. Lynn Abrams, Oxford University Press.
 DOI: 10.1093/oso/9780192896995.003.0004

their late teens and early twenties were seeing new possibilities and making autonomous decisions about intimate relationships, jettisoning behaviour patterns and moral positions held by their parents and, indeed, of generations of their forbears.

This chapter explores how young women of the 1950s and 1960s contemplated, navigated, and recalled heterosexual relationships before marriage.[3] We see how varied women's experiences were, how ambivalent and hesitant they were at times, how change was enacted with little fanfare, and how stress and emotional pain as well as joy feature in their narratives. Yet, shining through, we see a gritty determination to formulate new opportunities, to challenge parental and other restrictions and to redefine, for their own wishes and delight, the nature, number, and framework of relationships. Acting on feelings in the context of intimate relationships was freighted with excitement but also uncertainty and risk. The girls and women who had found new ways of being themselves through dress, travel, popular culture, and wider horizons than their home town, found themselves negotiating the relationship, dating, and courtship scene without a road map. They lacked the support of shared knowledge amongst their peer group about how to conduct heterosexual relationships. Anne described herself as being 'wide-eyed and legless', with no pathway to follow but 'wanting whatever else the world had to offer'. Her experience encapsulated the dilemma of young women who negotiated this era of experimentation without guidance, only knowing they didn't want to be like their parents and wanting to experience freedom. However, using feelings as a guide to action led some women down a route they had been seeking to postpone or avoid: marriage or lone motherhood. Anne discovered that the relationships she embarked upon were one-sided. She described 'meeting males who were taking the freedom of the times, literally, and taking no responsibility for their actions—I was left fuming and pregnant'.[4] And alone. Marriage had not been on her immediate horizon, but she had not expected the irresponsibility she encountered from the men who fathered her children. Anne said:

> So I was *stunned*. I was actually *stunned* by this. When I was pregnant and had this baby and had no support from this guy—I mean, he stayed around, but he kind of—it ended up with him saying, 'Well, I'm gonna take you back to your mother's'—which I was (laughs)—I was absolutely *appalled* by this statement. Back to my mother's?! What are you *talking* about? I'm a mother, you know?

[3] Homosexual relationships featured in a very limited way in my own interviews or in the data collections utilized for this book. For an examination of everyday homosexual intimacy (as opposed to activism) in the post-war decades see Amy Tooth Murphy, 'Reading the lives between the lines: lesbian literature and oral history in post-war Britain', PhD, University of Glasgow, 2012 and Rebecca Jennings, *Tom-Boys and Bachelor Girls. A Lesbian History of Post-War Britain, 1945–71* (Manchester: Manchester University Press, 2007).

[4] Personal correspondence with Anne.

> This is our child! It's like he was gonna hand me back. (Laughs). *Crazy!* (Laughs). Anyway, so that was a period of huge humiliation for me actually, that.[5]

This historical narrative of the shift in the conduct of relationships in the 1960s emphasizes freedom and independence albeit recognizing the risks. Women like Anne, who were finding new ways of being, found that using their feelings as a guide to the conduct of relationships could have unexpected consequences owing to their relative lack of power. The institution of heterosexuality, and the structures and beliefs that maintain it, exist beyond the couple, but, certainly in the mid-twentieth century, despite the appearance of greater freedom, the impact of this intimate revolution on women and men was unequal. At critical points male dominance was maintained and women continued to be channelled into marriage or, as in Anne's case, left to manage alone with their children.[6] In an environment where rules were being rewritten, it was sometimes difficult for women to negotiate them on their own terms. And the gendered power dynamics of heterosexual relationships are especially evident in accounts given by women brought up in working-class communities who had fewer opportunities to escape the observation of family, tended to take less time settling on 'the one' and for whom the consequences of an unplanned pregnancy were stark.

Even several decades on, women's accounts of their relationship histories reproduce the uncertainty and experimentation of that stage of life. But the narratives also challenge depictions of heterosexual relationships that assume women's subordination to men and which take for granted women's capitulation to the myth of romance.[7] Through close attention to retrospective and contemporary accounts, it is clear that women both exercised agency in relations with the opposite sex and claimed it subsequently in interview. They made choices, resisted expectations, and followed their feelings. Shared knowledge around relationships and sex might have been absent but, with the furtiveness and risk involved in sexual encounters, women from all backgrounds did begin to chart a new path through the relationships' minefield, establishing—sometimes painfully—new cultures of intimacy through their own agency.

[5] Interview with Anne.

[6] Victoria Robinson, Jenny Hockey, and Angela Meah, 'What I Used to Do…On My Mother's Settee': Spatial and Emotional Aspects of Heterosexuality in England, *Gender, Place & Culture* 11:3 (2004), pp.417–35, here p.418.

[7] Jenny Hockey, Angela Meah, and Victoria Robinson, *Mundane Heterosexualities: From Theory to Practices* (London: Palgrave Macmillan, 2007), p.45. On the romance myth see Hera Cook, 'Nova 1965–1970: Love, Masculinity and Feminism, But Not As We Know It', in Alana Harris and Tomothy Willen Jones (Eds), *Love and Romance in Britain, 1918–1970* (Basingstoke: Palgrave Macmillan, 2015), p.225–44. Those who question the relationship between the discourse of romantic love and self-fashioning include Stephen Brooke, '"A Certain Amount of Mush": Love, Romance, Celluloid and Wax in the Mid-twentieth Century', in Harris and Willen Jones (Eds), *Love and Romance*, pp.81–99 and Judy Giles, '"You Meet 'em and That's it": Working-class Women's Refusal of Romance Between the Wars in Britain', in Lynne Pearce and Jackie Stacey (eds), *Romance Revisited* (London: Lawrence & Wishart, 1995), pp.279–92.

Histories of Intimacy and Liberation

The period between the late 1950s and early 1970s has been dubbed 'the permissive age' with the 1960s identified as the critical moment when earlier notions of respectability collapsed amidst a revolution in social attitudes and pre-marital heterosexual sex became normalized for the coming-of-age generation.[8] The general claim of permissiveness has recently been subject to challenge however. While most historians accept that change did occur, they have disagreed on its timing and speed.[9] For some it was a gradual decades and even centuries-long process, albeit culminating in the much more radical behavioural changes facilitated by the availability to unmarried women of the oral contraceptive pill in 1968. Others have argued that the heterosexual revolution can be dated more precisely to the 1960s. Before 1960 there was little significant growth in the rate of pre-marital sex (measured by illegitimacy rates) with 1955 marking a high point in sexual restraint, whereas sexual activity outside of marriage grew from the early 1960s, accelerated when doctors were able to prescribe the pill to single women, and became acculturated from the early 1970s when couples began to have children outside wedlock by choice.[10] Notwithstanding the growing frequency of sexual activity before marriage from the early 1960s, marriage remained popular until the early 1970s, with the marriage rate reaching its all-time UK peak then, although there is little certainty (or even academic discussion) about the causes of this interesting late surge of apparent conventionality. Age at marriage continued to decline through the 1960s so that by 1971 men were on average 24 and women just 21 at first marriage. Along with this, however, people's expectations of the marital relationship were changing markedly. Sex had been disentangled from reproduction for some women but it had also been separated from

[8] For example: Dominic Sandbrook, *White Heat:* Arthur Marwick, *History of Britain in the Swinging Sixties* (London: Little Brown, 2006); Arthur Marwick, *The Sixties: Cultural Revolution in Britain, France, Italy and the United States, c.1958–c.1974* (Oxford: Oxford University Press, 1998); Jeffrey Weeks, *The World We Have Won: the Remaking of Erotic and Intimate Life* (London: Routledge, 2007).

[9] For the debate on timing, extent and impetus for change see: Jane Lewis, *Women in Britain since 1945: Family, Work and the State in the Post-war Years* (Oxford: Blackwell, 1992), p.48; Helena Mills, 'Using the Personal to Critique the Popular: Women's Memories of 1960s Youth', *Contemporary British History* 30:4 (2016), pp.463–83; Sandbrook, *White Heat*, pp.452–3; Hugh McLeod, *The Religious Crisis of the 1960s* (Oxford, Oxford University Press, 2007), pp.215–31; Nigel Yates, *Love Now, Pay Later: Sex and Religion in the Fifties and Sixties* (London: SPCK, 2010), pp.78–85; Sam Brewitt Taylor, 'Christianity and the Invention of the Sexual Revolution in Britain, 1963–1967', *Historical Journal* 60:2 (2017), pp.519–46; Hera Cook, *The Long Sexual Revolution. English Women, Sex and Contraception, 1800–1975* (Oxford: Oxford University Press, 2004); Hannah Charnock, 'Girlhood, Sexuality and Identity in England, 1950-1980', PhD, University of Exeter, 2017; Callum G. Brown, 'Sex, Religion, and the Single Woman c.1950–75: The Importance of a "Short" Sexual Revolution to the English Religious Crisis of the Sixties', *Twentieth Century British History*, 22:2 (2011), pp. 189–215; Charlie Lynch, 'Scotland and the Sexual Revolution c. 1957–1975: Religion, Intimacy and Popular Culture', PhD, University of Glasgow, 2019.

[10] Brown, 'Sex, Religion, and the Single Woman'.

marriage as the conjugal relationship was transformed in the imagination and public discourse at least, if not always in reality, into a receptacle for love and mutuality.[11] Also, young pop stars like the members of the Beatles and the Rolling Stones made weddings hip, especially in Registry Offices.[12] So, while there is no doubt that greater permissiveness in sexual and relationship matters was an accelerating feature of the 1960s, the continued popularity of marriage indicates that too great an emphasis by historians on sexual activity can deflect attention away from experimentation and the more fundamental redefinition of the nature of intimate relationships.

This is not a story of sexual emancipation in any simple sense. While more frequent pre-marital sexual activity amongst this generation was a topic of much public comment and concern, so-called sexual liberation was just one aspect of a broader shift in attitudes towards intimate practices in heterosexual and eventually homosexual relationships. Indeed, if we shift the emphasis towards a broader understanding of intimacy that admits of its quotidien nature, the story of this generation's negotiation of the relationship game takes on a more nuanced character, with less focus on sexual intercourse and more on the reworking of personal relationships. Giddens' formulation of a concept of modern intimacy assumes emotional and sexual equality in a relationship with broad implications for the democratizing of interpersonal relations more generally.[13] In the arena of personal life, he writes, 'autonomy means the successful realization of the reflexive project of the self—the condition of relating to others in an egalitarian way'.[14] Whilst Giddens is primarily interested in sex, however, Jamieson's theory of the 'intimacy of the self' as opposed to the 'intimacy of the body' is more helpful in understanding how this generation set about redefining relationships. What she terms 'mutually shared intimacy' or 'disclosing intimacy' is what many young women strived for, a relationship sustained by mutual self-disclosure and 'intense interaction' which facilitated self-fulfilment.[15] When women talk about their intimate relationships it is in this more rounded sense in which sexual activity is only one element.[16]

[11] Marcus Collins, *Modern Love: Personal Relationships in Twentieth-century Britain* (Newark, DE: University of Delaware Press, 2006); Claire Langhamer, *English in Love: The Intimate Story of an Emotional Revolution* (Oxford: Oxford University Press, 2013).

[12] George Harrison married Patti Boyd in Epsom Registry Office in 1966; Paul McCartney married Linda Eastman in Marylebone Registry Office in 1969; Mick Jagger married Bianca Pérez-Mora Macías in 1971 in St Tropez.

[13] Anthony Giddens, *The Transformation of Intimacy: Sexuality, Love, and Eroticism in Modern Societies* (London: Polity, 1993).

[14] Giddens, *Transformation of Intimacy*, p.189.

[15] Lynn Jamieson, *Intimacy: Personal Relationships in Modern Society* (London: Polity, 1997), p.1, 137.

[16] The exception here are the interviews conducted for UKDA SN 5190: *Cross-Generational Investigation of the Making of Heterosexual Relationships, 1912–2003*, which were interested in sexual experiences and practices as part of the wider project. For full details see the project User Guide.

From the weight of first-hand evidence and contemporary criticism from some quarters, there is little doubt that major change in young people's attitudes to relationships was underway during the long Sixties and that it was part and parcel of the cultural revolution that incorporated 'sporting a CND badge, seeing Dylan when he toured in 1964, or wearing black eye liner' in Mary Ingham's words.[17] She might have added the rejection of the romanticized depiction of intimate relationships that had been so pervasive in film and music. But moral shifts are harder to pin down in terms of timing or cause. 'I tried to think back to when it was that I decided to fly in the face of Evelyn Home', continued Ingham. 'When was it that I decided virginity didn't matter that much, that sex wasn't awful and wicked, and that the kind of boy who was hypocritical enough to want sexual experience for himself and still expect to marry a virgin... wouldn't be the kind of boy I wanted to marry?'[18] Ingham's reflection on her personal moral revolution is revealing. She was unable to pinpoint either the moment or the underlying reason for her rejection of the moral certainties associated with the agony aunt who responded to readers' letters to *Woman* magazine for 40 years.[19] She knew that she wanted a relationship founded upon love, a companionate partnership as the 'basis for mutual respect and mutual affection'.[20] She resented her parents' 'puritanical attitudes' towards pre-marital sex, but like all young women of her generation the spectre of an unwanted pregnancy hung over her and her peer group's early relationships with boys and like most of them she anticipated getting married at some point. Indeed marriage for many women was not imagined as a domestic straitjacket but a means to have a sexual relationship without the furtiveness and fear that characterized many liaisons. And for some, marriage was also seen as a route to self-fulfilment and autonomy as well as sometimes the only way of leaving the parental home.

This chapter follows our cohort of women as they began to explore social and intimate relationships in their late teens and early twenties in the gap between leaving school and getting married or finding an alternative life path. It is a story that has largely been told until now either through the lens of sexual activity, or through the prisms of risk and anxiety as new spaces opened up for young people to socialize and girls in particular were represented as in moral danger as they pushed the boundaries. Girls who ventured into the public sphere to visit coffee clubs, suburban dance halls and cinemas, to scream at the Beatles or just to hang about on the street, were objects of concern as their embodied boldness contrasted with their perceived sexual and emotional immaturity.[21] They were

[17] Ingham, *Now We are Thirty*, p.86. [18] Ingham, *Now We are Thirty*, p.87.

[19] Peggy Makins (Evelyn Home) was born in 1916. She took the pen-name Evelyn Home for its comforting and conservative associations (Eve and Home).

[20] Collins, *Modern Love*, p.93. See also Langhamer, *English in Love*.

[21] Louise A. Jackson, 'The Coffee Club Menace: Policing Youth, Leisure and Sexuality in Post-war Manchester', *Cultural and Social History* 5:3 (2008), pp.289–308; David Fowler, *Youth Culture in Modern*

deemed to be at sexual risk in the new conditions of modernity where they were vulnerable to predatory men.[22] The journalist Lynn Barber's schoolgirl affair with the much older Simon, who picked her up in his sleek maroon car while she was waiting for a bus in 1960, is the archetypal case of the supposed vulnerability of young women that caused so much hand wringing, although not by her parents who were keener to see her married than to attend university.[23] But the wider picture, amongst young women ranging across social class, wealth, region, and individual inclination, is more nuanced than this, especially if we focus on what girls actually did rather than what people thought they did and how they judged their actions. Representations of girls' behaviours and discursive or normative codes such as that of romance or danger are poor guides to how young women behaved and interpreted that behaviour.[24] The argument that discourses of romantic love provided an important resource for models of post-war selfhood casts young women as consumers of an idea rather than producers of new relationship models.[25] The story of our generation's attempts to find pleasure in intimacy is a complicated story as we zoom in on individual narratives because, against a backdrop of a sexual and cultural revolution, personal choices were made within local contexts and cultures, informed by community expectations, peer pressure, educational trajectories, social class, race, and the vagaries of luck, love, and misfortune.

Imagining Intimate Futures

In 1956 marriage was the dominant theme for teenage girls asked to write their imagined life story from the perspective of the end of their life: 'Marriage is the accepted future, and is confidently expected' concluded social researcher Thelma Veness in her study of the aspirations and expectations of school leavers; 'No girl has troubles in finding a husband'. In fact when asked what job they envisaged having a few years after leaving school, many women mentioned marriage and a significant percentage—48 per cent of grammar school girls and 39 per cent of those attending secondary modern schools in one town—indicated that they did

Britain c.1920–c.1970: from Ivory Tower to Global Movement—a New History (London: Bloomsbury, 2008), pp.170–4 on criticisms of pop culture, especially the Beatles. See also Collins, *The Beatles*, on those who connected Beatlemania with the 'premature arousal' of adolescent girls' sexuality, pp.57–60.

[22] Janet Fink and Penny Tinkler, 'Teetering on the Edge: Portraits of Innocence, Risk and Young Female Sexualities in 1950s and 1960s British Cinema', *Women's History Review* 26:1 (2017), pp.9–25, here p.14.

[23] Lynn Barber, *An Education* (London: Penguin, 2009).

[24] The significance of codes—of romance especially—is discussed in relation to *Jackie* magazine in Angela McRobbie, *Feminism and Youth Culture* (Basingstoke: Macmillan, 2000), pp.67–117.

[25] Langhamer, 'Love, selfhood and authenticity', p.278.

not expect to work afterwards.[26] The results were not surprising given marriage was seen by these adolescents as a vocation and coterminous with becoming an adult.[27] 'Settling down', a phrase used by many in their life stories, could only be achieved by marrying and establishing a family.[28] Teenage girls in the 1950s and early 1960s thus spent a considerable amount of their spare time pursuing this objective, encouraged by a cultural environment imbued with the rhetoric of romantic love.[29]

Surveys of young women's leisure in the early 1950s discovered they spent much of their spare time either at home undertaking hobbies or chores or enjoying commercial leisure such as the dancing, the cinema, and shopping, often with the aim of meeting boys.[30] In Nottingham around a third of girls surveyed attended the cinema once a week and slightly more went dancing. Esme, at just 15, had belonged to the Girl Guides and Sunday School when she was younger but had 'sprung a passion for dancing' and was described as 'very boy conscious'.[31] Sixteen-year-old Rosie, a factory worker, spent most of her leisure time 'in making contact with the local boys'. Along with her best friend 'They made use of the pictures, of dances and "up the street" for this purpose—all in a discreet and diligent way'. Her main interest was 'the acquisition of a serious boyfriend'.[32] And boyfriends, along with 'dates, hair-dos and glamour outfits' took precedence over work, except for the wages earned to facilitate this lifestyle. 'The very idea of a "career" had not penetrated this young lady's mind' remarked a Youth Employment Officer in 1962 of a 16-year-old girl who was working for a large-scale clothing retailer. '[N]o matter what its nature, her job would be of little interest or importance compared with her romantic conception of the "real" world…This could well have played a decisive part in her choice of occupation, since the large nationally operating firm with whom she works is itself closely identified with the whole pseudo-sophisticated world of the teenager.'[33] Similarly, a girl who left school at 15 to work in a factory despite having been in the top stream at her secondary school, was regarded as lacking in ambition and, implicitly, wasting her opportunities. 'Her first job offered training in needlework but she left this to take her present employment which offered more pay. She did not have the slightest idea of what she was making or helping to produce…All the girl could tell me was that she was drilling holes in metal…Her one aim in life at

[26] Thelma Veness, *School Leavers: Their Aspirations and Expectations* (London: Methuen, 1962), pp.26–7; Table 38 p.175.

[27] Joyce Joseph, 'A Research Note on Attitudes to Work and Marriage of Six Hundred Adolescent Girls', *The British Journal of Sociology* 12:2 (1961), pp.176–83.

[28] Veness, *School Leavers*, p.31.

[29] Penny Tinkler, *Constructing Girlhood: Popular Magazines For Girls Growing Up In England, 1920–1950* (London: Routledge, 1995); Tinkler, '"Are you really living"', pp.598–9.

[30] Pearl Jephcott, *Some Young People* (London: George Allen and Unwin, 1954), Table 5A, p.166.

[31] Jephcott, *Some Young People*, p.45.

[32] Jephcott, *Some Young People*, pp.48–9.

[33] MRC, NSHD: sample 36—Youth Employment questionnaire 1962.

the present time is to get married. She is on piece work at the factory and quite happy in her work.'[34] The girl self-reported that she spent her spare time 'reading, knitting, TV. And courting.' She was married at the age of 20 and at 25 she was a full-time housewife with a daughter.[35]

Amongst this cohort of young women—15 and 16-year-olds in the 1950s—dating, a 'dalliance relationship', graduated to courting, an altogether more serious proposition which meant adhering to 'recognized rules' and abandoning all other leisure activities.[36] Dating could be conducted alongside or within existing friendship networks whilst courting required an exclusive commitment to one person. Elsie was just 18 when she got married having started courting at 15 'from which time she centred her energies on her boy and getting married'. Before she married her leisure time had been spent with her boyfriend on his motor-bike, dancing and walking out, but following marriage her life was far more home centred with her leisure time spent knitting, ironing, washing, mending, and spending time at her mother's as her husband was away.[37] Elsie had achieved her aim but at the cost of her freedom.

Working-class girls often left school as soon as they could. In 1962 82 per cent of girls left school for paid employment compared with 68 per cent of boys; in 1967 the figure for girls had dropped only slightly to 79 per cent.[38] In Gavron's sample of working-class women, 73 per cent had left school at the statutory minimum leaving age and only 19 per cent had gone on to some kind of further training which was likely to be secretarial or nursing training. Few in this cohort attained any kind of skill.[39] While work was plentiful in the 1960s, working-class girls often lacked the support, the resources, the careers' advice or the ambition to undertake further training. It was not uncommon for girls with few qualifications to move from one unskilled job to another. This so-called persistent job changer in 1968, said she desired to be able to afford more clothes and a holiday and was employed in clerical work. She had 'always fancied going into computer programming', but the combination of a lack of careers advice and wanting 'ready cash' meant that 'you sort of postpone things like that'. 'Now of course I'll be getting married soon, you see there is always something that crops up.'[40] For many young women the period between school and marriage was spent, in Pearl Jephcott's words, 'prospecting around, in a mild way, for a husband'.[41] The conflicting discourses of self-reliance and marital destiny characterized these girls' attitudes to

[34] MRC, NSHD: sample 21, employment and training questionnaire 1962.

[35] MRC, NSHD: sample 21, postal questionnaire 1968; postal questionnaire 1977.

[36] Jephcott, *Some Young People*, p.66.

[37] Jephcott, *Some Young People*, p.47.

[38] https://sesc.hist.cam.ac.uk/resources/statistical-tables/.

[39] Gavron, *Captive Wife*, p.119. Amongst the 1946 cohort surveyed by the NSHD in 1964 at age 18, only 13% of girls were in work as apprentices or trainees contrasting with 50% of boys, MRC, NSHD: Skylark JOBTS64 (Training status).

[40] MRC, NSHD: Persistent Job Changers Study, 095–046.

[41] Jephcott, *Some Young People*, p.55.

their futures. 'I don't want too much, I don't want to make it a career' responded one young woman, a secretary who had at one time wanted to be a teacher but who left school at 16. She cavilled against her dependence on her parents, knew that she needed to get 'out into the world' but set her sights on marriage and a family as the route to fulfilment and independence, rightly seeing no other way to achieving this state.[42]

Their equivocation—wanting some independence but rejecting a career for marriage and perhaps a return to the labour market when the children were at school—was not surprising given the mixed messages conveyed through popular culture and the economic realities of a single life. Although the post-war period witnessed increasing interventions to educate girls 'to think independently and to earn [their] own living', girls continued to be caught within 'a claustrophobic and oppressive world of teenage romance' which portrayed marriage as their ultimate destiny and the difficulties of singledom.[43] But there were other more significant push factors. It was only by marrying that a woman could attain her own home.[44] The other factor was sex. As Szreter and Fisher argue, the 'preservation of innocence and modesty' was one element of working-class women's self-identity which, at least until the early 1960s, was contained within the dominant conservatism in attitudes to pre-marital sex.[45] But this veneer of respectability could conceal a rather different reality whereby women prized their innocence but were rather less ignorant than they claimed.[46] Social researchers had found no appreciable difference between middle and working-class levels of pre-marital sex but working-class girls were more likely to marry in the event of an unplanned pregnancy.[47] The girls who dressed in mini-skirts and back-combed their hair into beehives saw marriage as destiny because they understood that pre-marital sex was frowned-upon and risky, especially if they became pregnant. Before the availability of the contraceptive pill for single women, working-class girls could become trapped by their autonomous sexuality; marriage was the only financially viable route to a (respectable) family life.

By the late 1960s however, while marriage remained as popular as ever, attitudes towards it had begun to change amongst this generation. Girls of all social classes were reluctant to give up the freedoms they had enjoyed since leaving school. 'This year seems to have started off quite well and I have just about got over a broken heart (well not that broken) but I now feel better off without him,

42 MRC, NSHD: Persistent Job Changers Study, 208–036.

43 Charnock, 'Girlhood, sexuality and identity', pp.19–20.

44 MRC, NSHD. The personal questionnaire of 1962 when girls were 16 asked 'What else do you want at 25'—Sample 01: ' To be married and have a home of my own, but still working'; Sample 14: 'A home of my own by 25'.

45 Brown, 'Sex, Religion and the Single Woman', p.22.

46 Szreter and Fisher, *Sex Before the Sexual Revolution*, pp.83–91.

47 Michael Schofield, *The Sexual Behaviour of Young People* (London: Longmans, Green & Co., 1965), p.142.

he was rotten to me anyway' reported a shorthand-typist in 1966 when she was 20. She had joined a sailing club and had plans to holiday in Ibiza following a solo trip to Spain the previous year. 'I was a little dubious to start with, but I thoroughly enjoyed myself and kept out of trouble.' Two years later she still placed her social life above finding a permanent partner: 'I do not have a regular boy-friend at the moment, and this does not bother me in the least, except that a man is useful as a partner sometimes, when going out in the evening, either for a drink, or a party.'[48] This woman was unusual in not mentioning marriage; most of her peers were explicit about their desire to marry but at the same time were reluctant to compromise. The rather rueful reflections of a 22-year-old in 1968 encapsulates that sense of ambivalence. She had enjoyed her work as a nurse and had made the most of her spending power and personal freedom: 'I was engaged to be married 2 years ago this month but broke off the engagement the following June. Looking back we had a lot of freedom as students and also were working . . . and I could not be bothered with saving to get married.' Her long-term boyfriend did not want to get married but she felt she was in a rut.[49] Marriage was the means to move on with her life.

Some like Julie Walters and Janet Street-Porter made decisions to delay marriage rather than reject it altogether in order to pursue personal fulfilment. Street-Porter recalled that in 1967 she 'left home at 19, having cancelled my forthcoming wedding to the man I had been engaged to for two years. I moved in with my lover, who I would later marry.' 'I was 20 years old, and Mum and Dad could no longer control what I did, any more than they could control what I wore or how I did my hair.'[50] Both women eventually tied the knot but, in waiting, they created space and time for themselves to experiment with relationships, sometimes involving sex but often not. Rare was the woman whose self-determination triumphed over marriage altogether in this period. The writer Ann Quin who was interviewed by fellow writer Nell Dunn in 1964 was one such:

> I was brought up on this [respect]. I had a great conflict when I was in my teens, I wouldn't give myself to any man unless I got married. If I'd got married I would have got married at nineteen.
>
> Nell Dunn: How did you manage to avoid it?
>
> I think I just realized that it was a whole lot of bloody sort of social system thing and came to realize that I was a person in my own right and I could choose and it didn't come up to that at all.

[48] MRC, NSHD: Sample 42—postal questionnaire 1966; postal questionnaire 1968.

[49] MRC, NSHD: Sample 07—postal questionnaire 1968. She did marry a year or so later and gave up her work on the birth of her first child.

[50] Janet Street-Porter, *Fall Out. A Memoir of Friends Made and Friends Unmade* (London: Headline, 2007), p.7.

Nell Dunn: Do you think it takes a lot of courage to live how you want to live?

I think so yes. A lot of determination.[51]

Choice, of whether or not to marry, might be regarded as a privilege of white girls though we should take care not to over generalize about the experiences of the non-white community characterized by a wide range of religious and cultural traditions. In the case of many young Asian women, family and cultural beliefs concerned with honour, reputation, and respectability, controlled their social interactions with both white and Asian friends and determined their marriage futures. Although marriages were more likely to be semi than fully-arranged in this period, Wilson argues that coercion was still present and girls were merely 'allowed the dignity of pretending that you are doing it of your own free will'.[52] Making a love marriage against the will of the family was to risk losing their support. Nonetheless, personal choice was beginning to make inroads into parental control amongst these groups as young Gujarati women related stories of friends who had run off with white or West Indian men.[53] Inter-racial marriage, whilst not common, had grown in the wake of two forces: post-war migration from the Caribbean and the Commonwealth and the increasing propensity of marriage for love.[54] But those who did follow their hearts were subjected to social stigma and branded as threats to the social and moral order, especially white women who married Black men. Amongst some African Caribbean communities on the other hand, marriage was approached 'with reservations'. Girls wanted to enjoy themselves before being tied down. 'Don't want to get married, at least not yet' was Barbara's view. 'Want to be independent...Be free for a while I guess.'[55] In part this was on account of the struct rules imposed on girls by parents who were fearful of their daughters' getting into trouble and bringing shame on the family. They had also seen their mothers struggling as new immigrants, juggling work and children, often with absent or shadowy husbands and fathers. And in some Black communities the pressure imposed on women by their partners to 'have a baby for me' trapped them when they were left to manage alone.[56]

Personal choice rather than societal expectation and convention did begin to influence women's relationship decisions however, and that balance shifted markedly by the late 1960s. Although marriage was still the ultimate destination for the vast majority of women, the period between leaving school and making a permanent commitment was increasingly a time when girls in their teens and early twenties fashioned selves which did not easily transmogrify into wives, or at least

[51] Nell Dunn, *Talking to Women* (London: Pan, 1966), p.120. Quin committed suicide in 1973.

[52] Wilson, *Finding a Voice*, p.127.

[53] Wilson, *Finding a Voice*, p.126 and pp.131–2.

[54] Clive Webb, 'Special Relationships: Mixed-race Couples in Post-war Britain and the United States', *Women's History Review* 26:1 (2017), pp.110–29, here p.114.

[55] Sharpe, *Just Like a Girl*, pp.246–9.

[56] Bryan, Dadzie and Scafe, *Heart of the Race*, pp.215–18.

not the kinds of wives they perceived their mothers to be or imagined themselves to be. Becoming a person in their own right had been achieved through exploring social and sexual relationships at work, study and leisure; independence, however partial, was not congruent with a traditional marriage relationship. This cohort of women sought out new experiences and began to develop their own views on intimacy. Sheila Rowbotham's reconstruction of the self through self-fashioning and distancing herself from the expectations of family and school encountered in the previous chapter, was not untypical, opening up literal and metaphorical spaces for a reconfiguring of relationships with the opposite sex.[57]

Much has been made in the historical literature of women's claim to and demonstration of respectability in sexual matters 'before the sexual revolution'.[58] But by the 1960s those discourses on respectability were heard and understood by young women but increasingly not listened to as they lived their lives influenced by competing messages emanating from popular culture and, more importantly, their friends whose attitudes and views superseded the warnings of parents.[59] According to Charnock, for women in adolescence and young adulthood in the post-war decades, participation in sexual activity was influenced less by the values of chastity and respectability and far more by notions of emotional integrity and intimacy. As the nice girl ideal gradually began to lose its purchase with this age group they began to reformulate, through trial and error, a way of engaging with the opposite sex that brought both pleasure and autonomy. This meant that for a growing percentage of women, their first experience of intercourse was not within the context of marriage.[60]

Spaces, Experimentation, and Constraint

The practice of developing intimate relationships was experienced on several overlapping levels: moral, embodied, and spatial. The majority of young women, whether they moved away from home to study or work or remained living with their parents during this transitional stage of life, encountered material and

[57] Rowbotham, *Promise of a Dream*, p.42. In *Daring to Hope* she describes these relationships in detail.

[58] Szreter and Fisher, *Sex Before the Sexual Revolution*; Judy Giles, '"Playing Hard to Get": Working-class Women, Sexuality and Respectability in Britain, 1918-40', *Women's History Review* 1:2 (1992), pp.239–55.

[59] The age of majority was lowered to 18 from 21 in 1969 by the Family Law Reform Act in England and the Age of Majority (Scotland) Act. It is unclear how or if this affected young women's experiences of the transition to adulthood.

[60] Charnock, 'Girlhood, sexuality and identity', p.178. According the 1990 National Survey of Sexual Attitudes and Lifestyles, whilst 38.5 per cent of women born between 1931 and 1955 had first intercourse within the context of marriage, only 5.3 per cent of women born between 1956 and 1965 were married when they had penetrative sex for the first time: Kaye Wellings, *Sexual Behaviour in Britain: The National Survey of Sexual Attitudes and Lifestyles* (Harmondsworth: Penguin, 1994), pp.74–5.

psychological constraints on their activities. These took several forms: social policing, lack of privacy, and fear of pregnancy. For working-class girls especially, intimate interactions with the opposite sex were shaped by the spatial environment of their communities. These women had to experiment with relationships in public view, at dances, at the Mecca bingo and other leisure spaces where young women and men met. In one of Glasgow's peripheral estates, a 15-year-old respondent to Pearl Jephcott's study of young people's leisure described how, in the absence of entertainment, 'At night girls and boys just walk about the streets and hope for the best. We just go with the boys and have a carry on. Even then there is too much police about.'[61] Eileen Parr recalled her first kiss at the age of 14 at a barbeque and being questioned by passing police whether their parents knew where they were.[62] And Sadie Innes described what having a good time meant in her working-class community in Yorkshire:

> 'avin' a drink, 'avin' a dance, enjoyin' meself, [...] I mean, an' you could safely get in a car with 'em [.] I was lookin' for a boyfriend, a serious boyfriend, but [...] in the process of it, you know, like, you'd meet lads, they'd [.] you could get in the car with 'em an' you could go an' you could fumble with 'em, you know, 'eavy pettin' or whatever you would want to call it, but the line drew...
>
> Interviewer: Through clothes?
>
> Er, yeah, well, you never got undressed, you'd be in [.] if you got a lad with a car, you see, that was the thing.

When asked whether things might have gone further Sadie explained that it depended on having somewhere to go:

> hey'd 'ave to 'ave a vehicle or you'd 'ave to be somewhere, where you could be on your own, an' people didn't 'ave [.] an' it was a while before you could take anybody 'ome, you know, you couldn't just suddenly start goin' out with a lad, 'e came to your 'ouse an' they left you alone downstairs, that didn't 'appen at that time [.][63]

Such furtive coupling was commonplace as couples pushed the boundaries of what was deemed respectable and acceptable. When Michael Schofield conducted research into the sexual behaviour of young people in 1965 he found that 93 per cent of girls between 15 and 19 in his sample had kissed on a date but only 12 per cent had experienced sexual intercourse, with the incidence of other forms of sexual activity ranging from 72 per cent having taken part in deep or French kissing to

[61] Jephcott, *Time of One's Own*, p.1.

[62] UKDA, SN 5190: Interview with Eileen Parr, p.6.

[63] UKDA, SN 5190: Interview with Sadie Innes, p.11. Schofield's study identified the partner's home as the most frequent location for the first experience of sexual intercourse amongst young people. Schofield, *Sexual Behaviour of Young People*, p.63.

21 per cent who reported close contact of the sex organs without penetration.[64] Lynne Archer described getting 'up to a few things in the caravan that was parked on mum's drive', though 'nothing dangerous', and Eileen Ogden who was sleeping with her boyfriend before they married because 'he was the one' explained how they used to find 'sneaked moments': 'it was like, oh, your mum's out now quick'.[65]

Moving away from home certainly provided, in theory, greater privacy though universities and especially teacher training colleges attempted to police female students' activity with restrictions on visitors to student halls in particular. Jane's physical education college in Eastbourne proscribed male visitors unless the warden had provided written permission 'and she used to walk past and check that nothing was going on in this sitting room that you were entertaining your visitor in'.[66] At St Andrews University the application of *in loco parentis* by the university authorities was applied through the women's hall wardens' control of visiting hours and restricting male students' access to women's rooms.[67] But it also offered young women more time to navigate a mixed-sex environment for those who came from single-sex schools, and a culture that was often more liberal than they were used to. Frances grew up in a middle-class family in the south of England, attending a single-sex grammar school before studying sciences at a university in Scotland. As a student living far from home Frances' relationships at university were romantic, platonic, and conducted largely within the context of her wider social groups. Such relationships were rarely sexual as she explained:

> my close friends just waited. We just...there wasn't the opportunity or we just...I was very immature in many ways certainly in that respect, possibly didn't actually want to, I don't know. Lovely after a dance, kissing by the sea, endlessly and that was it...I mean certainly...amongst my friends it was certainly not...there was no pressure to have done it, or...I really don't think—we didn't talk about it because there wasn't an 'it' to talk about I don't think. It was who you were going out with and whether they were nice or not or whether you were totally besotted or maybe just a little bit, but you know.[68]

Frances' dating experience is fairly typical of her social class in the late 1950s and early 1960s. Not long out of twinsets and just beginning to enjoy university in a city often some distance from home, these women formed mixed social groups with other students to navigate their new environment. Shirley, who moved from a small town in the north of Scotland to Edinburgh to study medicine in the early 1960s lived in digs with five other girls in her first year including two from

[64] Schofield, *Sexual Behaviour of Young People*, p.30.

[65] UKDA, 5190: Interview with Lynne Archer, p.8; Interview with Eileen Ogden, p.8. See Robinson, Hockey and Meah, 'What I Used to Do'.

[66] Interview with Jane.

[67] Lynch, 'Scotland and the sexual revolution', pp.97–100.

[68] Interview with Frances.

England 'who seemed so much more sophisticated than me and worldly wise and grown up'. Her first year there was spent 'just finding your way and getting a sense of values and things' but her social life consisted of dances and the cinema—the more risky behaviours increasingly associated with youth culture were not part of Shirley's world:

> *No*, no that wasn't me, no not at that stage in my life...I don't remember people doing it either, even these very sophisticated English girls in the digs, no, not really. I don't remember them smoking either actually. I certainly did try smoking but I can't think it was at that point but I never particularly liked it actually so I never persisted, and sex, *no*, definitely not, I had, um, yeh, you know you met people at dances but never anything very serious really, no. No, really I was very naïve, really naïve.[69]

Edinburgh in the early 1960s was a conservative city and its ancient university likewise. As late as 1968 the university was convulsed by a public row leading to the resignation of the Rector, Malcolm Muggeridge, over the provision by the University Health Centre of information to students on the contraceptive pill.[70] For students the city offered friendships and fun rather than experimentation and promiscuity. Caroline recalled having an 'immensely social time' as a student: 'there we were aged 19, 20 or something having wonderful parties. I don't know it was a very high-octane part of my life in Edinburgh'. When asked if she and her friends would have cohabited with boyfriends Caroline remarked: 'No, no, I think that would have been felt to be terribly committing and I think that we very much felt that we should be having fun and fun didn't involve moving in with people...we had loads of people with whom you went out to dinner with or to a party with without necessarily going to bed with them.'[71]

On the west coast in Glasgow, Lorraine who attended Glasgow School of Art—more liberal than the other institutions in the city—and lived in an all-female dormitory, described student life as:

> all very scary but immediately it was the life you wanted to lead but it was quite artificial because, you know, when I look back on it, I was 18. Forgive me, I was young, I was a fool, but it was—there was so much Art School that was scary but fun, and Art School dances were always the best fun in a terrifying way. It wasn't pop music then, see, it was traditional jazz at the dances and then after a year of, well—And at the University dances as well, that hollow sound, that echoing noise of a band. I don't know if anyone these days could appreciate the fear as you walk in, that's when you started to smoke to give yourself something,

[69] Interview with Shirley.
[70] See Lynch, 'Scotland and the sexual revolution', pp.72–95.
[71] Interview with Caroline.

> anything, so you don't stand around. Nowadays you probably drink, we didn't drink an awful lot; I did drink, but not much, but smoked and the whole palaver of Zippo lighters, which kind of cigarette you smoked and you had to look cool at all costs, and I'm sure we didn't! We were just so full of nonsense.[72]

Lorraine's breathless account recalled the excitement, anticipation and fear of the new as she negotiated an unfamiliar environment where people remade themselves. Although for her Glasgow was 'not a den of iniquity'—this was a city scarred by industry and poverty and containing little evidence of alternative or more bohemian lifestyles at that time—living and playing in a city miles from the moral certainties of home offered freedom to push the boundaries. When Lorraine moved out of the dormitory and into flat shares she began to experiment with relationships but kept these from her parents. 'I didn't want them to know as they would really disapprove, and there was a general feeling of disapproval, but we were all at it, so, you weren't being condemned for that, but I wouldn't want my parents to know at the time. No, definitely not.'[73]

Lorraine, Caroline, Shirley, and Frances left home to study, finding themselves in spaces conducive to the production of new or different standards of personal morality. Their accounts ooze a sense of fun and self-discovery. University offered the opportunity to push at boundaries. Joan Bakewell who attended Cambridge in the 1950s described arriving there 'eager to make up for lost time', and an atmosphere of pent-up lust and nervous initiation into heterosexual encounters despite the efforts of university authorities to keep women 'safe'.[74] Living in digs liberated men and women from the petty rules and ineffective policing of halls of residence yet Sandra, who also attended Cambridge, recalled a restrained and careful approach to intimacy. Despite being in a serious relationship with the man who was to become her husband, she explained that:

> we didn't live together, and didn't exactly sleep together either, I mean quite close to it but not, so—but I think both of us felt quite happy about that—it was, I mean obviously I had had lots of other boyfriends by then—but quite soon we knew we'd be married so um, so, no, not living together and mostly people were not living together, although certainly they were sleeping together. Lots and lots of my friends were, but most of them weren't I suppose, I mean the people I knew best um in this house that I lived in where I had close friends, I don't think any of them were sleeping together probably.[75]

Unlike women of a later generation for whom sex was something shared, creating a 'social life of sexuality' whereby talking about relationships and sex bound them

[72] Interview with Lorraine. [73] Interview with Lorraine.
[74] Joan Bakewell, *The Centre of the Bed: An Autobiography* (London: Sceptre, 2019), p.104.
[75] Interview with Sandra.

together in an emotional community, for women like Sandra and most others of their generation, sex remained something private.[76] Sandra's uncertainty about whether her friends were sleeping together illustrates the still rather furtive environment for intimacy prevalent in the early 1960s.

Sandra and Lorraine, in different ways, perfectly described the dilemma of their generation who were excited by the opportunity to experiment with their identities including engaging in intimate relationships with men, but who felt conflicted because of the fear of pregnancy and the continued existence of moral and material barriers to pursuing sexual freedom. Lynne Archer who left her rural home for teacher-training college in a nearby town in 1967 at 19 admitted that when the opportunity to sleep with boyfriends arose she thought 'this is what I really, really want to do. But I didn't.' She put her resistance down to 'fear, pregnancy you know, and partly the fact that nice girls didn't.'[77] An unplanned pregnancy was, in Lorraine's words, 'the dread of your life' because of the 'fear of disapproval, all of these things. Fear for yourself—mmm—it wasn't a physical fear, it was entirely the feeling that the public humiliation would have been enormous, absolutely... it was the idea of utter humiliation and you felt you would have ruined your parents' life as well, and you'd never be looked upon in the same way ever again by anybody.'[78] That fear was often justified.

The fragility of the moral carapace was exposed by women who dared to explore youthful intimacy beyond the hand-holding and kissing stage and who were caught out in the cruellest way. Ignorance of birth control or inability to access it—Joan Bakewell was rebuffed when she approached a doctor in the 1950s, years before the pill became available, leaving her to take her chances—meant sexual encounters were freighted with risk.[79] Lorna Sage described how a teenage love affair transitioned to something more serious without her being able to admit to herself that they had 'gone all the way' because 'we *hadn't* had we?'[80] 'What have you done to me?' was Lorna Sage's mother's anguished and angry response to being told her 16-year-old daughter was pregnant in 1959. 'Over and over again. I've spoiled everything, now this house will be a shameful place... I've soiled and insulted her with my promiscuity, my sly, grubby lusts.'[81] Suzanna's mother similarly imputed her daughters' actions would bring shame and ruin in the family on hearing that Suzanna was pregnant at the end of her first year at university in 1967.[82] As we saw in Chapter 2, Suzanna did have an abortion but

[76] Hannah Charnock, 'Teenage Girls, Female Friendship and the Making of the Sexual Revolution in England, 1950–1980', *The Historical Journal* 63:4 (2020), pp.1032–53, p.1034. On privacy see Szreter and Fisher, *Sex before the Sexual Revolution*, pp.348–62.

[77] UKDA, SN 5190: Interview with Lynne Archer, p.10.

[78] Interview with Lorraine.

[79] Bakewell, *Centre of the Bed*, p.109.

[80] Lorna Sage, *Bad Blood: a Memoir* (London: William Morrow & Co,. 2002), p.235.

[81] Sage, *Bad Blood*, p.236.

[82] Interview with Suzanna.

her mother's shame was projected onto her daughter via her desire to maintain secrecy about the whole affair.

Suzanna and Lorna Sage were both lucky and determined, rare examples of women who succeeded in negotiating the sexual wild west on their own terms. Lorna Sage married the father of her child, had a daughter, went on to sit her 'A' levels and gained a place at university. Suzanna returned to her studies at a new university in the late 1960s in a more liberal environment. Just a few years earlier, women who became pregnant during their studies were punished by being expelled.[83] Jane was aware of some fellow college students who were 'experimenting (pause) out of college, probably drugs and sex', but news of any getting pregnant was not widely shared. Those who did were 'ostracized out'.[84] And even at Oxford, where there were 'murmurings of a bohemian culture' and people were 'having sex', the women's halls were still policed 'like convents' and girls were still punished for sexual misdemeanours. A good friend of Rhian's suffered the consequences in contrast with the fate of her boyfriend: although he married her immediately, and they remained in Oxford so that he could finish his degree, she, despite being 'very, very bright .... [was] sent down from one of the women's colleges for getting pregnant'.[85]

Suzanna's experience reveals much about the hypocrisy of attitudes towards unplanned pregnancy and abortion in this period. Her parents, her boyfriend's parents and her university doctor 'all appeared to take the line that this was an inconvenience which should be got rid of'.[86] She was encouraged to have an abortion. There was no discussion of adoption or of keeping the baby, evidence that amongst the middle-classes at least abortion was available privately, albeit covertly. Secrecy was not infrequently the solution to the embarrassment of an unplanned pregnancy in respectable circles. The case of Miss Cross, a young woman who had a grammar school education before leaving at 16 and working for a time before attending art school, highlights in the starkest terms the gap between her own behaviour and the attitudes of her 'straight-laced' parents who sought solutions for the shame their daughter brought upon them when she became pregnant. Her history of casual relationships was recounted by social researcher Dennis Marsden who interviewed her as one of more than 100 'mothers alone' in 1965–6.

> She was first seduced by somebody at the Art school and since then has had intercourse with five different people. Somehow fairly casually...and for such a seemly [sic] shy person she was comparatively promiscuous, the man she'd been with before the father of her baby was a married man 'his wife didn't used to mind she went off with somebody else and he could go off with me whenever

[83] Bakewell, *Centre of the Bed*, p.107. [84] Interview with Jane.
[85] Interview with Rhian. [86] Interview with Suzanna.

> I wanted, in fact when we went off to the seaside for days she would put up sandwiches for us'. 'He packed me in and that did upset me, no it wasn't so much the sex it was I missed him telling me how beautiful I was.' Almost on the rebound she went out for just one night with the baby's father 'he was young and I'd always liked him he was only 22 and he was just married and whenever he saw me in the works he used to wink at me and I used to think I'd like to kiss him, we were working late one night and my lift didn't come to take me home so he offered to take me home and that was the only time I've been out with him, I don't know anything about him, I liked him but perhaps if I'd known more about him I wouldn't have liked him as much.' When she'd been with the married man they used to practise withdrawal and this was what they did the night when she went out with the baby's father, 'we weren't going to tell anybody about it it was just a secret between the two of us'.[87]

Miss Cross gave an unapologetic account of her love affairs, a sign of her generation's more liberal attitude to relationships and sex. But with no access to reliable birth control she became pregnant. Until that point she could engage in casual intimacy; her unplanned pregnancy though brought into view the moral chasm between her generation and that of her parents. As Lorraine had explained, 'we were all at it' but ignorance or studied avoidance of the facts on the part of those who disapproved of this pattern of behaviour protected these women from direct personal moral censure. The censure was only manifested when a pregnancy became known and the sex moved from the private to the public sphere. Miss Cross recounted that her mother 'wanted me to have an abortion [or] to have him adopted, she said I could stop at home if I did that but I didn't want to do that, no I never felt like that'. The family sent her away to live in a caravan while she was pregnant.

> It was very shocking in my family my dad's nearly 70 and my mother's 67 in fact it still is, if any friends come I've got to hide away. I didn't mind about it except for them. I've got a sister but I've not seen her for a year. I don't like her, it was over the baby, she was so shocked and said how could I do it to the mother and father, I've had hardly anything to do with her since.[88]

And even though her parents had visited her and made a fuss of the baby, Miss Cross continued to experience moral judgement from the midwife at the hospital, her former employer at the Co-op who asked her to leave, even passengers on the bus: 'Sometimes in the bus people will look at me when I'm holding the baby and they all look sorry for me and smile.' And she was socially isolated:

[87] UKDA, SN 5072: Interview with Miss Cross (interview 24).
[88] UKDA, SN 5072: Interview with Miss Cross.

> She leads a pretty lonely life on the estate, nobody knows much about her although she doesn't wear a ring, she pretends that her husband is away in Aden and this was the story that the other women had heard but they said there was never a man about and they didn't believe it the site owner still calls her Mrs. She had a friend next door but she fell out because the woman wanted to talk about who the baby's father was then the girl on the other side was Irish 'she kept coming round to say could she borrow a couple of slices of bread for her husband's tea and that sort of thing so I stopped that. I'm not a very outgoing sort of person I don't make friends very easily.'[89]

Miss Cross felt trapped. The freedoms she had taken for granted now signified what she had lost. 'Well I mean you can't just go off where you want to. You can't just hitchhike.' But she thought she might get married in the future.[90]

Miss Cross's dilemma, as a woman who had embraced the new intimate practices of the 1960s but who had fallen foul of the double standards that continued to pertain with regard to women's sexual behaviour, was sidestepped by some of her peers who took different decisions. As we saw in Chapter 2, Suzanna's experience of an unplanned pregnancy and the trauma it occasioned left her, unlike Miss Cross, with choices and a clearer sense of how she could determine her own destiny. Suzanna's attitudes towards intimate relationships were clarified. Accused by her mother of being 'promiscuous' Suzanna rejected her definition, asserting that she had always practised serial monogamy: 'I had a number of relationships. But it was always one after the other . . . that was not my definition of promiscuity.'

Suzanna's decision to take control of her own destiny was not without cost. It involved some painful episodes and some distancing from her parents. Frances' experience—of a number of relationships at university and swift marriage following graduation—was more typical of her cohort of women who attended university in the late 1950s and early 1960s and for whom marriage was less a receptacle for the expression of love and more a practical means to maintaining a sexual relationship when cohabitation was morally unacceptable and sometimes practically impossible. Marriage was still an expectation and, unless one was willing to defy convention, the only acceptable way to set up home with a member of the opposite sex.[91] Joan Bakewell described how she and her boyfriend had been a couple in their third year at university, 'sharing friends, food and Michael's bed.'[92] But when they graduated and moved to London cohabitation was impossible. This was the late 1950s when the weight of convention and the façade of respectability combined to thwart couples' desires live together. A marriage certificate

[89] UKDA, SN 5072: Interview with Miss Cross.

[90] UKDA, SN 5072: Interview with Miss Cross.

[91] See Sarah Aiston, 'A Maternal Identity? The Family Lives of British Women Graduates Pre- and Post-1945', *History of Education* 34:4 (2005), pp.407–26, here p.414.

[92] Bakewell, *Centre of the Bed*, pp.124–5.

was required to rent a flat. So, Bakewell recounts, 'if we were to have a regular and unrestrained sex life we would have to be married'.[93] Margaret Forster likewise married straight after graduating from Oxford at the age of 22: 'If marriage was nothing to us but everything to our mothers, why not just get married.'[94] And beyond the perceived cosmopolitanism of the south, girls like Carole in the north-east were marrying young because living together simply was not what you did, not least for fear of bringing shame upon one's parents, even in 1970:

> I mean obviously they couldn't stop me, I was of age but remember 'age' was 21 in those days and I always had—I suppose I was always frightened of my Mum and Dad, in a way. I always wanted to please them so I didn't—I wouldn't have done something like that, it just wouldn't have entered my head and a lot of my friends were thinking the same way, because most of them got married. I don't really know of many who just went and lived with people. I am sure that people were doing that, and when I read books and…avant-garde people seemed to be doing it all the time but most of my friends didn't.[95]

There is no doubt that girls glimpsed, and sometimes tasted, new models of intimacy which may have included sexual intercourse outwith marriage. But sexual activity was still, for the most part, concealed, not even talked about amongst friends. Respectability still trumped openness in the heterosexual intimacy stakes, with consequences for those women who did get pregnant, not least in terms of their future options.

Choice and Autonomy

When women speak about the lived reality of heterosexual encounters, the power of discursive injunctions is superseded by women's sense of their own agency which, in turn, was a product of them acting on their feelings rather than conforming to what was expected. Pam's experience of breaking off an engagement against her family's expectations was unusual although she stressed her family's acceptance of her decision. She swerved convention and instead chose her own path. Pam was brought up in a predominantly working-class community and was educated by Roman Catholic nuns. In both, the culture emphasized respectability and conformity over independence and autonomy. As Pam reflected:

> [There was] no ambition but you were kept in this very careful restrained Catholic box and did it for another generation and another generation and that's

[93] Bakewell, *Centre of the Bed*, p.125.
[94] Margaret Forster cited in Nicholson, *How Was it For You?*, p.13.
[95] Interview with Carole.

> the lasting impression I have of it...Restricting—how you thought? Yeh, restricting your ambition to be a good Catholic mother, if you couldn't be a good Catholic nun, then you could be a good Catholic mother and that was it really, and if you did go to be a teacher it would just keep you going until you could be a good Catholic mother, and really that was it...No, and different ideas, no, no—there was only one right way and one right thought, and one right way to behave and one right way with your eyes cast down like that.[96]

Pam's upbringing conformed to a model of working-class respectability that prized marriage as a route to security. She had attended the local Catholic primary school, graduated to the girls' convent school, was a student at the Catholic teacher-training college in Glasgow and became a primary school teacher at her old school. She described how the pressure to conform started at college:

> Um, er, oh at college you started, yes; there was actually a great pressure, you've probably heard this before, but there was a great pressure to get a boyfriend and be engaged, a great pressure, great social pressure...if you weren't married by 23, 24 you had a problem, you were on the shelf, or there was something—you know, there was a great social pressure from your contemporaries; a real competitive getting-engaged-ness was quite rife.
>
> *So the other girls in your peer group were doing that were they?*
>
> Yes, uh huh, very much so, it was quite time-consuming in life, a time-consuming thing. I don't know if you were looking for a lifetime partner, but if you were looking for an engagement ring very much so
>
> *Right, which is different isn't it really?*
>
> Yes, absolutely, it's like wanting a baby and realize you'll get a teenager later. It's the same kind of thing—oh, I've got an engagement ring, oh, dear, now I've got a man. There was no, um, no vision of what it meant except that oh you had to get this ring and be a, be a success which is strange...it had great worth, it had great social and yes, personal value just to be.

Pam initially fell into line; she became engaged to a local man in 1968 but called it off shortly before they were due to be married. The married life she could have had was no longer what she wanted, 'realizing there is a world out there and just get away from this'. The breaking-off of the engagement was a catalyst for Pam to hand in her notice and to move to Spain which opened her eyes to a new way of living her life that was not hidebound to convention. On her return to the UK she did marry—'it just sort of happened'—but importantly, marriage this time was on her own terms.

[96] Interview with Pam.

In life and in her interview Pam asserted her agency. Whereas the decision to cancel the engagement was acting on her gut feelings, in her narrative account decades later this moment takes on added significance as it serves to align the present self with the past self. The rejection of that marriage was an act of resistance to dominant discourses and expectations in her community and it serves today to reify her self-presentation as an autonomous woman who made her own choices. Speaking to women about their negotiation of intimate encounters elevates women's agency. They decided how to act guided by how they felt rather than what their parents would say. Audrey, along with several other West Indian girls interviewed about boyfriends, grumbled about her parents assuming that boyfriends meant sex and their daughter ending up 'in a sticky position'. Parents 'don't talk to their kids about this', complained Sharon.[97] Carol Kirk, who grew up in a working-class community in East Yorkshire, described her relationship with her first serious boyfriend as 'equal'; there was no question of him having pressurized her into sleeping with him. Carol recognized that she was unusual amongst her peers in not considering him as a potential marriage partner—'I thought that there was more to life out there than getting married at that time'—and she ended the relationship.[98] Shortly afterwards she met the man who would become her life partner. Speaking about this period of their lives decades later, women like Pam and Carol provide a glimpse of the ways in which their generation began to edge towards what Hockey, Robinson, and Meah describe as 'doing heterosexuality' their way.[99] This meant women making their own choices, exuding a confidence that we tend to ascribe to later generations and resenting their parents' failure to trust them. Retrospective accounts, of course, may tend to exaggerate that agency. Narrators tend to construct versions of the self with which they feel comfortable, one which coheres with the self they inhabit at the time of the interview. For Pam, her Spanish interregnum provided the narrative epiphany which enabled her to achieve narrative coherence. This meant that the passive Catholic schoolgirl became the confident adult, able to jettison the submissive self for the autonomous self. Carol provided an account which appears inconsistent—at one point she admitted she was unusual amongst her peers for not wanting to marry young yet this is precisely what she did—but in her account of their courtship she assigned agency to herself: 'I said if we get engaged we're not going to be engaged for more than a year, so we got married a year after we got engaged.'[100]

A rather more assertive sexuality is also evident amongst some of the accounts given by this generation of women, challenging ideas about women's submissiveness or passivity in heterosexual relations. This was an alternative model for some working-class women, a way of behaving that paralleled young women's

[97] Sharpe, *Just Like a Girl*, p.240. [98] UKDA, SN 5190: Interview with Carol Kirk, p.11.
[99] Hockey, Meah, Robinson, *Mundane Heterosexualities*, p.61.
[100] UKDA, SN 5190: Interview with Carol Kirk, p.13.

confidence in other spheres: in their dress, language and consumption patterns, producing 'an unpredictable, spontaneous, emotionally honest, sexually active young woman'.[101] Eileen Parr grew up with girls who were having sex and talking about it in their mid-teens. She recalled one girl recounting a casual sexual encounter: 'and she said, oh and he come, and it went all over my suspender belt'.[102] At this time Eileen remembered joining in with the laughter but was thinking 'what is she talking about?' Eileen herself was propositioned at 16 by a boy she had met at the wrestling. 'I can remember him saying to me, I would like to make love to you' but she 'wasn't quite sure what making love meant' so she told him she was a virgin and he 'didn't want to know'.[103] She waited until she was 19 to sleep with a man for the first time, the result of 'larking about' with someone she had grown up with followed by sex 'with just a lad I knew on the street, we just had sex, 'cause it was a fun thing to do'.[104] Eileen recounted these experiences in a matter of fact fashion; her decisions determined events. Sex outside marriage was commonplace in her community and once it had happened sex for her 'didn't mean anything at all'. The fear of pain or pregnancy or that somebody would find out had gone and when she met the man who was to become her husband they slept together before they married. As we shall see in Chapter 5, unfortunately for Eileen, her marriage failed caused by her husband's alcoholism and cruelty. Sexual assertiveness was not without risk.

The author Nell Dunn's 1963 semi-fictionalized portrayal of working-class women in *Up the Junction*, placed in Battersea, London, is the epitome, perhaps an exaggeration, of this kind of representation of sexual confidence, featuring the characters Lily, Rube and friends who, in their rough, sexual language and sexualized appearance, are the very opposite of innocence. While *Up the Junction* is a somewhat voyeuristic sexual odyssey through the eyes of a middle-class author, the centrality of sex—talking about it, doing it, and the consequences of it—pervades this portrayal of a working-class community in which women appear the assertive sex but who ultimately pay the price with their bodies.[105] A brash confidence conceals their vulnerability. In a scene in the communal laundry, the women's conversation moves from Rube's loss of a pre-term baby to her latest love interest:

> Getting rid of that kid hasn't half changed me. I don't know what I want anymore…Met a gorgeous bloke last night – the sort of bloke when you see him

[101] Christine Geraghty, 'Women and 60s British Cinema: The Development of the "Darling" Girl', in Robert Murphy (Ed.), *The British Cinema Book* (London, 2001), pp. 101–8, here p.107.

[102] UKDA, SN 5190: Interview with Eileen Parr, p.4.

[103] UKDA, SN 5190: Interview with Eileen Parr, p.5.

[104] UKDA, SN 5190: Interview with Eileen Parr, pp.5–9.

[105] Brooke, 'Slumming in Swinging London'. Dunn wrote in *Poor Cow*: 'Most of what I wrote in Up the Junction I heard; some of it I made up.' Nell Dunn, *Up the Junction* (orig.1963, London: Virago, 2013), p.xi.

> you want to grab hold of him…He kept pressin' himself against me, then his hands began to wander. 'You ain't half hot blooded' he says. I kept takin' them away, then he'd put them back again. 'I can't help being sexy' I says.[106]

and from Sylvie's fear that she might be pregnant to her repelling an assault:

> 'I think I might be carrying' says Sylvie. 'I'm going up to Hastings tomorrer to put down on a bedroom suite'…'I nearly got raped last Sunday, but he was an old bloke and I didn't fancy him, so I didn't let him.'[107]

The sexuality expressed by Rube and Sylvie was, on the one hand, bold and confident; they expressed a model of womanhood that was unashamed of their sexuality and were prepared to use it. This was a world, as Margaret Drabble remarked in the foreword to Dunn's follow-up, *Poor Cow*, the story of 21-year-old Joy, 'where women did not depend on male patronage, where they went their own ways, sexually and financially…a world where women could lead real lives.'[108] Dunn's women were 'cheeky, rebellious, loud-mouthed';[109] and they challenged ideals of domesticity and companionability', illustrated by Johnny's remark to one of the women: 'I guess you're not like those women in the ads what you see giving their husbands a meal, serving it up, and worrying all the time how they're going to get the washing up done. I guess you're more casual, isn't that right?'[110] But this confidence concealed a vulnerability. Being 'casual' carried risks for women which are all too evident in Dunn's creative reportage. The apparent sexual freedom practiced by Rube and Sylvie was more than matched by the freedoms men enjoyed. For all the women's bravado it was they who dealt with the consequences of unwanted attention and unwanted pregnancies. The casualness with which Sylvie threw Rube's premature baby down the toilet 'wrapped in the *Daily Mirror*' underplays the harsh reality of these women's lives. Joy, the heroine of *Poor Cow*, married to a thief and left with a baby to care for when her husband is jailed, understands only too well the paradox of her life. On leaving hospital with her week-old son, the contrast between her situation and the glamour that was widely portrayed in the popular culture of the time, crystallizes as she sits in a café on her own, her husband nowhere to be seen:

> Joy looked at her son. 'What did I go and get landed with him for, I used to be a smart girl?…Outside in the street a young woman passed pushing a pram, a fag hanging from her lip. 'Now I look like that'…Above her head an

[106] Dunn, *Up the Junction*, p.68. [107] Dunn, *Up the Junction*, p.71.
[108] Nell Dunn, *Poor Cow* (orig, 1967, London: Virago, 2013), p.xv.
[109] Dunn, *Poor Cow*, p.xv.
[110] Brooke, 'Slumming in swinging London', p. 441; Dunn, *Up the Junction*, p.49.

> ad with a lot of golden girls in bathing suits read COME ALIVE. YOU'RE IN THE PEPSI GENERATION!
>
> 'Fuck that', she said.[111]

Joy takes her pleasures when she can. Her perspective is short term. On finding some contentment with another man when her husband is in prison she ponders: 'Even if it's only for six months that might be six months of happiness and anyway it's six months of life got through.'[112] And then when Tom is released and begs her to set up home him with him again Joy is pulled between her need for affection and her rejection of domesticity and hankering after the woman she was before she was pregnant.

> I won't stay longer than six months—six months of security is the longest I can stick. I'm not going to stop at home all day. I'll have to go out to work. I'll be a barmaid again then I can dress up and look really smart—you've got to be able to dress up to keep yourself going.[113]

In Joy's world men are unreliable, unfaithful, jealous, and violent. She understands her predicament only too well: what she wants is 'a close intimate life' but in her world the men don't offer that kind of relationship. Yet the alternative, living on her own with her child, would mean 'one room and National Assistance'.[114] She has no choice.

In the London of Nell Dunn and her semi-fictional protagonists, working-class sexuality is the site of pleasure and of pain. Her characters encapsulate the contradictions negotiated by young working-class women in the 1960s. Having enjoyed the freedoms of the single life—the money, the independence, the enjoyment of dressing up to go out, having their hair done, dancing and liasons with men—they begin to understand that relationships come with constraints on their freedom and sometimes risks and dangers. There was little evidence of 'mutual disclosure' or democratic intimacy on display here. Few men were willing to allow their girlfriends or wives the freedoms they had enjoyed before 'settling down', including working outside the home or going out with their friends, and women like Joy found that hard to accept. Eileen Parr accepted her husband's unfaithfulness, alcoholism and cruelty for nearly 30 years before walking out, understanding that although everything she did revolved around him, he never respected her.[115]

The portrayal of the sexualized women of the metropolis, for whom desire is the driving force, underplays the banality, secrecy and sometimes the tragedy of

[111] Dunn, *Poor Cow*, p.2. [112] Dunn, *Poor Cow*, p.27.
[113] Dunn, *Poor Cow*, p.114. [114] Dunn, *Poor Cow*, p.133.
[115] UKDA, SN 5190: Interview with Eileen Parr, p.32.

the lives lived by working-class women who found themselves struggling to survive with a child, little or no support from the father and social isolation. Jan remembered how in her community 'they were talking in quiet tones about the girl across the road who'd had this baby. And I never saw her come out, actually, of her house, she must've stayed in.'[116] The outlook for these women who embodied a sexualized subjectivity was a far cry from the more common representations of London in particular as a 'site of pleasure and autonomy'.[117] There was little autonomy to be had in living in a bed-sit with a baby and surviving on the state although for some this situation was preferable to being married. The consequences of the trend for early marriage coupled with the still common injunction to marry on the occasion of an unplanned pregnancy were often loneliness, boredom and a feeling of entrapment. In Hannah Gavron's research sample, 98 per cent of working-class girls had married before the age of 25 and 33 per cent were teenage brides. Around a third believed they had married too young in retrospect with one saying 'I must have been mad. I didn't have a clue' and another wistfully, 'it's the dancing I miss'.[118] These were not shotgun marriages—only 10 per cent of the working-class women surveyed by Gavron were pregnant before they married—and yet still they keenly felt the gap between their single and married lifestyles.[119] And when children came along working-class mothers felt tied down and isolated.[120] The freedoms these women had experienced in their adolescent years was rudely curtailed.

Some achieved their marriage goal or made the best of it; others found themselves in a far less enviable position as single mothers. The stories gathered from unmarried, separated and deserted mothers by Dennis Marsden in 1965–6 in Huddersfield, a northern industrial town, and Colchester, a southern town with an army barracks, provide unvarnished accounts of financial and emotional deprivation, poverty and pride, and a peek into the consequences of what some would have called 'permissiveness'. The women told of casual and multiple liaisons, relationships with married men, accepting or fatalistic families and past histories characterized by poor or absent parenting. These are not the women of Nell Dunn's Battersea who assertively display their brash sexuality; rather, the single mothers of Colchester and Huddersfield are those who participated, sometimes naively, in the new culture of going out, dressing up, and having fun. Casual sex could be an accepted part of this culture where women no longer resisted the entreaties of men to go a bit further but men held greater power.

Miss Gale, just 17 years old in 1965, had been with her boyfriend for three years when she became pregnant, and remarked that 'she knows lots of other girls

[116] Interview with Jan.
[117] Brooke, 'Slumming in swinging London', p.442.
[118] Gavron, *Captive Wife*, p.65.
[119] Gavron, *Captive Wife*, p.66.
[120] Gavron, *Captive Wife*, p.89.

who became pregnant about the same time'.[121] Nineteen-year-old Miss Black used to go out every night before she had the baby but explained: 'All my mates got pregnant, and then they got married, they either married the father or they married someone else.'[122] This then did not conform to the pattern identified by some historians whereby couples slept together prior to marriage. The women interviewed by Marsden were perceived to be part of the 'explosion' in pre-marital sexual activity of the mid to late 1960s where marriage was not always and sometimes never part of the picture.[123] Miss Black was said to be 'just one of the unfortunate ones in that there had never been any question of marriage, and she wouldn't want to marry the father'. Neither had there been any question of her giving up the baby: 'She'd never thought of adoption, she had no feelings of guilt or shame, and the neighbours certainly didn't ostracize her.'[124] Likewise Miss Gale had decided 'she wouldn't have liked to marry [the father] anyway. She's glad that she didn't. She's going out with somebody else whose (sic) now.'[125]

Amongst those interviewed for this study were a small group of West Indian women who remained unmarried despite having good relations with their children's fathers. Marsden suggested that differences in social structure between the Caribbean and Huddersfield explained this situation. The practice of consensual unions, whereby a woman needed to 'produce a child' for a man to gain the best chance of marriage, may have worked in the West Indies where women were embedded in networks of kin who could care for the children in the event that marriage was not the outcome.[126] But in the UK these women were socially isolated and the men saw no reason to marry the mothers of their children. It was acknowledged within the Black community that many women did bring up their children alone but by the 1980s there was another explanation than that of cultural tradition: 'We do not raise our families in this way because we are superwomen or "sturdy Black bridges"', wrote the authors of *The Heart of the Race*, 'but because we have been compelled to accept this responsibility both historically and because of the internalized sexism of many Black men today.'[127] This analysis from the perspective of those who understood the position of Black women to be historically constituted, exhibits a consciousness of racial subordination that postdated Marsden's study and was not evidently a part of his interviewees' understanding of their predicament. And yet while they stressed their self-reliance, one remarked astutely: 'she would like to be married... everybody prefer to be somebody'.[128]

[121] UKDA, SN 5072: interview with Miss Gale (interview 38).
[122] UKDA, SN 5072: interview with Miss Black (interview 07).
[123] Brown, 'Sex, religion and the single woman', p.24.
[124] UKDA, SN 5072: interview with Miss Black.
[125] UKDA, SN 5072: interview with Miss Gale.
[126] Marsden, *Mothers Alone*, pp.93–4.
[127] Bryan, Dadzie, Scafe, *Heart of the Race*, pp.220–1.
[128] UKDA, SN 5072: interview with Miss Winter (Interview 10).

The majority of single mothers interviewed in Marsden's study convey the overwhelming impression of being unfortunate victims of circumstance: broken families, poverty, and a certain vulnerability in a liberalizing sexual culture. This was perhaps especially the case in Colchester, an army town with a high proportion of rootless single men. The case of Miss Cresswell, an unmarried mother, paints a picture of a girl who was a victim of her upbringing in a poor family with few prospects. In her desire to escape from home she had been engaged to be married at 16 but her mother denied her permission to do so. Marsden's account of his encounter with Miss Cresswell, 'A short square girl with bushy ginger hair, and glasses' provides an insight into her motivations for marriage and the consequences when she was left on her own with a child. While she had enjoyed the pleasures of many girls of her age—'She used to like to go for a drink, only bitter lemons or things like that in the Plough, and this was where she met most of her friends, or in the Casa Prima café'—she became pregnant with a soldier from the garrison who then denied paternity. This young woman was left to fend for herself, living in cramped accommodation with her sister and her four children, then moving in for a while with the baby's father in a condemned building with no electricity. At the time of the interview she had turned out the father, been evicted on account of the landlady discovering she was not married, and ended up in damp rented rooms, relying on National Assistance and the support of friends who were in no better position than she.[129] Not unlike Joy in Dunn's *Poor Cow*, Miss Cresswell understood that the price of the relationship with the baby's father was high.

> He would've stayed with me if I'd let him go off with other girls, but I'm not that sort, he was sex mad... But he was this type, you musn't speak to anybody, he wouldn't let me go round to my dad's, he always said I wasn't going round for the reason I said I was, it was some other reason, and he wouldn't let me speak to any friends or have anybody round to talk, but he could go out.

And while she was preparing to marry her present boyfriend she was equivocal, recognizing that marriage was a compromise for women in her situation:

> Getting married doesn't appeal to me so much now, I feel as though I'd be tied down, where now I'm independent, when you're married, you have to fall in with their wishes. It's just that I would like sometimes someone to lean on, someone to talk to, and if you've got someone to go out with, it's something to look forward to isn't it. Instead of just doing things on your own.[130]

[129] UKDA, SN 5072: interview with Miss Cresswell (interview 023).
[130] UKDA, SN 5072: interview with Miss Cresswell.

Marsden's encounters with these women are characterized by a somewhat judgemental attitude towards their lifestyles and intelligence, yet the accounts they give of their circumstances do offer some insight into the reasons for their predicament. These were not, in the main, women who had been sleeping with a man as a prelude to marriage; nor were they the brash, feisty women of Dunn's Battersea. And their accounts, given to an academic male interviewer in the midst of their everyday situation, surrounded by children, nappies and evidence of their straightened circumstances, possibly brought forth bravado rather than the agency claimed by those offering retrospective accounts of their young selves that were discussed earlier. Marsden's subjects were young women with few prospects who had been misled by men who turned out to be married or who got involved with men who had no intention of marrying them. These women had been left to bring up a child on their own, often with the support of mothers and sisters and they were mostly coping, albeit sometimes living in poor housing with few resources. They had been forced to make their own way without the support of a man and were wary of marriage. Miss Gladwin 'won't ever get married, "Once caught... I know they're not all the same, but you do think like that." '[131] 'I think that getting married for the sake of a baby is unfair to yourself and to the baby (that is unless you love the person)' commented another unmarried mother who was living with her parents while working as a nurse. When she did eventually marry a few years later the relationship lasted just twelve days before she returned to her parents having discovered her husband was 'an alcoholic and a sex pervert'.[132]

This was not the permissive, metropolitan world of the capital; it was the everyday world of poor people with limited resources and few choices. The women interviewed in this study did not feel sorry for themselves. Neither had they been sucked in by romance narratives. They accepted, albeit fatalistically, their situation, drawing on networks of non-judgmental family and friends, and just got on with it.

Conclusions

Intimate relationships were being reimagined and reassessed in this period by women who were just beginning to figure out who they were and who they wanted to be. Women of the post-war generation found more and new spaces and time in which to practice various levels of intimacy with the opposite sex and they were more likely to have sex outside of the context of marriage or engagement than their predecessors, acting on their feelings rather than abiding by the moral codes prescribed by their parents. But negotiating the line between

[131] UKDA, SN 5072: interview with Miss Gladwin (interview 41).

[132] MRC, NSHD: Sample 06—personal questionnaire 1972.

prohibition and permission could be fraught, especially as pre-marital sex remained relatively covert and risky and women didn't share experiences freely. It required women to find in themselves a degree of self-knowledge or confidence to make the right choices. In this domain, autonomy was hard to realize though as we have seen from the very different accounts of Suzanna, Pam and Anne, it was possible to own one's intimate and sexual destiny. Suzanna did so by rejecting her parents' moral values and coming to her own settled understanding of morality. Pam, in walking away from an engagement, rejected dominant cultural expectations for her personal and career destiny. And Anne, who led what many would have described as a promiscuous lifestyle, rejected marriage and, in the end, male partners too when they failed to deliver on their responsibilities to her and their children.

The renegotiation of relationships was hard fought and challenging the patriarchal institution of heterosexuality had to be done through resistance with all the risks and compromises that entailed. The evidence from life histories conducted contemporaneously and in retrospect illustrates that young women, despite their inexperience and perhaps because of their understanding that they wanted something different from relationships than the model represented by their parents, claimed ownership of their bodies.[133] The apparent confidence, albeit concealing a fear of being different, of women like Eileen Parr, who had sex with a boy 'because it was a fun thing to do' and because she wanted to get it over and done with, appears to be a different animal from the intimate practices described by middle-class women, but they are all part of the same story told in different ways. That story is about how feelings—not only of love, indeed rarely of love, but excitement, risk, and curiosity—drove practice and how personal accounts of intimacy and especially sexuality cannot be reduced to the performance of normative discourses. Rather, narrators reveal themselves as sexual agents, aware of and engaging with discourses that were prevalent at the time of their experiences as well as at the time of the interview, yet telling stories that are profoundly individual, emotional, and reflective.[134] Eileen's life history also alerts us to how individual experience and responses to it over time lead to change in how they interpret past relationships. At the time of interview Eileen had a new partner who had given her reason not to trust him. But whereas with her husband she avoided confrontation 'because the alternative is worse than the challenge', now she was willing to stand up for herself, a response that enabled her to re-evaluate her marriage.[135]

[133] See Joanne Bryant and Toni Schofield, 'Feminine Sexual Subjectivities: Bodies, Agency and Life History', *Sexualities* 10:3 (2007), pp.321–40: 'the sexual subject is brought into being as agential and desiring', p.324.

[134] Bryant and Schofield, 'Feminine sexual subjectivities', p.329.

[135] UKDA, SN 5190: interview with Eileen Parr, pp.26–7.

This chapter challenges depictions of heterosexual relationships that assume women's subordination to men and to the romance myths which dominated popular literature. It suggests that the interpersonal domain was not impervious to resistances which, over the long term, heightened women's expectations of what intimate relationships might offer them in terms of self-growth and self-actualization. Inequalities still existed, in particular in women's responsibility for the consequences of an unplanned pregnancy, yet the picture as a whole shows this generation of women exerting their agency, negotiating their way through the relationships' minefield by trial and error, lacking the knowledge-sharing about sex that was to become commonplace amongst teenage girls just a generation or so later. Women did find these early experiments with intimacy as opportunities to discover more about the self in ways that were more emotional and complex than hitherto. Suzanna discovered the hard way, through sexual relationships with men in her late teens and early twenties and having to bear the consequences of unplanned pregnancies, the kind of woman she wanted to be and the kind of life she wanted to live.

For the majority of women of this generation, including Suzanna, marriage was still where adulthood and independence could be properly realized in the context of the companionate love match. Their conception of marriage could nurture the female self rather than suppress it. Yet, while marriage might have been able to deliver 'a guilt-free sex life' and, in the short term, the escape from the parental home and the companionship many women and men desired, it was for most also a default; one way or another most girls imagined they would marry though they hoped that it would be on their own terms.

5
Settling Down

Introduction

Married for 23 years to a successful manager, Mrs Graveney spoke at length in 1968 about a relationship she described as a 'complete failure'.

> I suppose in a way I expected it to be all lovey-dovey and thought it would be a merging of two people, merging their personalities and getting the best out of the relationship. Oh Hell! I thought marriage would give me more happiness than it has, and it's not really given me any happiness, not the marriage itself. I have a nice house, and I can afford things, and I have a nice daughter, and my husband has a nice position, but deep down I have not had the happiness I expected. I suppose this was because we were not compatible from the beginning. It always goes back to this sort of thing of my husband seeing me as one of his other possessions.[1]

Mrs Graveney's disappointment encapsulates a much broader shift in women's expectations of what marriage could offer them in the 1960s. Her notion of a merging of personalities signalled something more modern and much more ambitious than the romantic model we looked at earlier. Although she was a little older than most of the generation at the heart of this book, she had come to understand marriage as a site of self-fulfilment and emotional sustenance achieved with a man. She had found herself trapped in a marriage that revolved around the material provision her husband made but it was not nurturing or stimulating for her. She was frustrated that they had 'lost communication' and bemoaned the fact that he lived for his work. Her statement that 'He is more important than the provision he makes' signalled that she had desired a relationship based on mutuality. 'I'd rather live and be poor and happy, than have position and wealth and have an empty life' summed up her predicament.[2] She wanted 'a life of her own'.

Mrs Graveney's testimony is central to the experiences of many women for whom marriage was a complex and ambivalent experience which had to be negotiated without a community of feeling to aid the navigation. This chapter follows

[1] UKDA, SN 853296: Interview with Mrs Graveney, p.8.
[2] UKDA, SN 853296: Interview with Mrs Graveney, pp.4–5.

Feminist Lives: Women, Feelings, and the Self in Post-War Britain. Lynn Abrams, Oxford University Press.
 DOI: 10.1093/oso/9780192896995.003.0005

our cohort of women as they 'settled down' after some years of post-secondary education, training or work. During that time they had begun to discover who they were—their identity—through employment, study, and relationships used as intimate spaces for self-disclosure and fulfilment. This period of much greater autonomy instigated the gradual loosening of ties with their parents and in some cases with their home communities. And their expectations of marriage had begun to solidify, not as to whether or not they would marry—this was still the expectation of most young women as we saw in the previous chapter—but in respect of the kind of marriage they envisaged. Girls' romantic dreams and conventional outlooks were slowly supplanted by a vision of marriage as a space where the self could be sustained and nurtured.[3] In other words, the romantic myth of marriage in which women were expected to experience fulfilment through family and home life coexisted with, and was gradually overlaid by, a model which emphasized self-actualization and growth. In this model, the marriage relationship was not the sole source of self-fulfilment.[4] The contradiction between these styles of marriage—the one requiring the woman to subordinate her identity to her family, the other allowing for an autonomous albeit relational identity—formed a kind of double helix, the strands co-existing but separate. Women expected marriage to deliver togetherness without requiring them to sacrifice their autonomy.

The 1940s generation was not settling down to replicate the life pattern of their parents. Historians have charted the inexorable rise of the companionate marriage reaching its apogee in the early 1970s when, not coincidentally, marriage attained the peak of its popularity in Britain. The modern marriage was characterized by 'personal freedom, equality of status and mutuality of consideration'.[5] Mutuality, an 'intimate equality' in Collins' words, achieved through mixing of the sexes, shared activities, and shared sexual pleasure, was an aspiration of modern thinkers on intimate relationships but it also found favour amongst those anticipating marriage in the post-war decades.[6] They tended to reject the model of marriage represented by their parents on the grounds of its unequal gender roles and the absence of mutuality. Mrs Dover, interviewed in the late 1960s, described her parents as being 'happy in their own way' but she and her husband had 'a much better man and wife relationship'. Her husband agreed. 'Yes, they [his in-laws] are not so much man and wife, as man and woman, and they go their own ways and are completely different.'[7] By contrast this couple emphasized the trust they had in one another. But mutuality had its limits when tested by the structural inequalities of the labour market, inadequate childcare, and the

[3] See Annette Lawson, *Adultery: An Analysis of Love and Betrayal* (London: Wiley-Blackwell, 1989), p.25.

[4] Lawson, *Adultery*, p.25.

[5] Ronald Fletcher cited in Collins, *Modern Love*, p.168.

[6] Collins, *Modern Love*, pp.93–9.

[7] UKDA, SN 853296: Interview with Mr and Mrs Dover, p.23.

persistence of social attitudes which resisted equality in marriage if it meant women's needs and desires were given equal weight to those of men. Collins' discussion of cases dealt with by Marriage Guidance counsellors identifies how companionship was always an idea in flux and contained contradictions which could result in mutual incomprehension and conflict for some couples.[8] Mutuality did not mean equality and even those couples, and more especially women, who did aspire to a more equal relationship however they defined it, sometimes found it hard to achieve without sacrificing marital harmony or indeed their self-identity.

We shall see in this chapter how the institution of marriage and the relationship that developed within it constituted a pivotal moment in the lives of this generation of women who had begun to chart a new course in personal relationships. Many had trusted and acted on their feelings in deciding on whether to have sex before marriage, to try out a number of partners before they tied the knot. Few had ambitions to be a stereotypical housewife; most continued in employment until a first child came along. With new questions about what they wanted before and within marriage, the institution occupied an increasingly ambiguous place. And the ambiguity centred on imagining and nourishing their self, developing ways it could flourish and grow within a framework that still constrained women's opportunities, especially if they had children. Women placed stress on the need for independence from their parents, upon sex without guilt, a home of one's own, material security, family life, emotional—including sexual—fulfilment and mutuality with a husband through shared interests and activities. The majority did not necessarily see this as creating a contradiction between domesticity and self-actualization. They were modernizing the concept of marriage because, notwithstanding the strength of their desires, for most women there was no alternative to achieving their goals than within marriage. Cohabitation outside marriage had, for most of the men and women of Britain, not been invented by the 1960s or even the 1970s. Social and legal impediments remained too strong. So, being married was the only feasible route to moving on, achieving adult status and getting a degree of independence. Marriage remained the venue for the new woman, and it was there that the post-war generation of women set about reinventing their self in their twenties and thirties.

The proof of that rests in the numbers. No matter that young people were transforming their sex lives, dress, deportment, attitudes to religion and morality; marriage was extremely popular amongst them. This explains the apparent contradiction of marriage reaching in 1969–72 its all-time popularity at the very time that the supposed breakdown in British society was occurring in the form of drugs, nudity, sexual activity with the pill, student rebellion, and the challenge to the establishment. Yet contradiction accurately describes attitudes to marriage at

[8] Collins, *Modern Love*, pp.118–27.

this time. In a survey conducted by the magazine *Nova* in 1969 amongst 100 'intelligent' women, from artists to MPs, the question 'do you agree that social and economic pressures still force women into marriage against their best interests?' produced split responses. Sixty per cent responded no, amongst them the Roman Catholic MP Shirley Williams, the celebrated author Margaret Drabble, and the conservative-leaning pop singer Cilla Black. Yet those who agreed with the proposition included liberal bohemians and the non-religious including actor Lynn Redgrave, authors Penelope Mortimer and Brigid Brophy and fashion designers Jean Muir and Mary Quant.[9] There is no sense here of a common view. And that lack of unanimity perhaps reflects not only the diverse ways of doing marriage in this period but also the knowledge that marriage was being reinvented overwhelmingly by women. Marriage became the site of the women's negotiation, experimentation, and reinvention, a pivotal moment and productive space for them to reformulate the female self for the modern era.

By the mid-1970s, the marriage rate began to slow and divorce became more accessible and thus more widely utilized. In England and Wales 22 per cent of marriages in 1970 did not last beyond the fifteenth anniversary and the overall divorce rate was 4.7 per cent. Just ten years later the rate had grown to 12 per cent.[10] This was a sign that sometimes the negotiation failed, that expectations diverged and for some women the pursuit of selfhood could not be contained within an institution based on interdependence rather than independence. What Lawson calls the 'myth of me', the striving for autonomy and self-development by both partners, tended to involve conflict with other members of the family with the marriage becoming a constraint rather than an enabler.[11] Partnership wasn't straightforward or uncontested. As we shall see in later chapters, marriages were put under strain by changing dynamics relating to assumptions around separate gender roles, especially when men retained their notional position of authority as primary earners outside the home. I argue in this chapter that, although there were many and diverse ways amongst this generation of 'doing' marriage, it was primarily women who effected changes in order that it met their needs for self-fulfilment and development.[12] And because the marriage relationship involved just two people, in many ways insulated from the social world, women often did this work alone. The exclusivity of that relationship meant women lacked a community of feeling, especially in the early years.

[9] *Nova*, January 1969: Survey conducted with 100 women on a variety of topics.

[10] https://www.ons.gov.uk/peoplepopulationandcommunity/birthsdeathsandmarriages/divorce/bulletins/divorcesinenglandandwales/2011-12-08

https://www.graysons.co.uk/advice/divorce-statistics-england-wales-small-rise-couples-divorcing-amid-general-decline/

[11] Lawson, *Adultery*, pp.25–6.

[12] See Drusila Beyfus, *The English Marriage* (Littlehampton: Littlehampton Book Services Ltd, 1968) in which she identifies seven models or ways of being married ranging from the 'the need to be free' to 'the success drive' and 'the sex imperative'.

Evidence from personal testimony gathered both contemporaneously and retrospectively indicates that women could find all kinds of marriage relationships sustaining. Some were content to fulfil the role of wife, mother, and homemaker, at least in the first few years, experiencing togetherness through nest-building and, for most, bringing up children. There were those for whom marriage was a love match and a mutually enriching partnership. Others, however, quickly felt trapped in an institution that was regarded by many feminists as a grave for women's autonomy. For such women, marriage closed down opportunities, engendered a lack of self-confidence and sometimes cut them off from support networks. 'You've made your bed, now lie in it' was an oft-heard aphorism in some working-class communities which isolated those struggling in an unhappy marriage.[13] With such diversity being developed by women of this generation, the dilemma for the individual wife was, in the words of an article in *Nova* in 1966, how 'to live with someone in marital harmony and yet retain one's own identity'.[14] In what follows we focus on just some of the ways of being married through close attention to the experiences of six women: Caroline, Suzanna, Carole, Pam, Eileen, and Sadie. Each of them wrestled with the conflict between the self and marriage albeit at very different points in their marriage pathway. But all of them resolved those conflicts, finding ways of preserving, developing or reclaiming the self, both in real time and in retrospective accounts.

Expectations of Marriage

In 1964 Caroline, a student at the University of Edinburgh, won a magazine talent contest for aspiring journalists and upon graduating she immediately bagged a job on a major newspaper. In London she began to live a high-octane life. She took full advantage of all London had to offer: 'it was the height of the Sixties and I just plunged straight in without a backward look'. Her job on the fringes of Fleet Street 'opened up a whole new professional world' and gave her the opportunity to follow her dream, to be a journalist and writer. After three years in London Caroline left to return to India where she had spent much of her childhood. Unlike some of her contemporaries who did the 'very Sixties kind of thing... you know to travel hippy fashion', she picked up freelance work there and got to know the country before returning to London and journalism once again. Then, after seven years in the workplace she married, gave up her job, and returned to Scotland to settle down into married life just a few miles from where she had spent her teenage years. Recounting this episode in her life in the 2010s, Caroline

[13] Anni Donaldson, 'An oral history of domestic abuse in Scotland, 1945–1992', PhD, University of Strathclyde, 1992.

[14] *Nova*, February 1966: 'Making marriage work'.

reflected with some incredulity upon the way in which the decision was made to jettison her former life.

> And that to me is the extraordinary thing which is different. That it never occurred to either of us to consider for one moment that it would be me who gave up my job. I didn't do it with any resentment. I felt, I was very, very happy in London and loved my job but felt seven years had been enough, I was quite ready for marriage and children and I would've gone anywhere with him, but I think I was earning, I was definitely earning more than he was.
>
> *Did you have the discussion?*
>
> No, no discussion whatsoever [laughs]. We are both now so ashamed of this we can't believe it.
>
> *And did you miss it when you did give it all up?*
>
> No, I think I was so desperately in love that I just loved everything about coming to live in [small town] in a tiny flat. We went to [Africa] the first year we were married for several weeks, probably a couple of months, so it wasn't at all boring. And then I produced [son] fairly quickly—not that quickly—it wasn't for a year and 8 months. But I had never planned to come back to live four miles from [home town]. I really thought I'd shaken the dust of [home town] off my feet forever.[15]

Caroline's story sits at one extreme in this period of the experience of women in this period who married. She had enjoyed several years as an independent career woman after university and was in no hurry to commit to a permanent relationship despite two long affairs: 'I think that would have been felt to be terribly committing and I think that we very much felt that we should be having fun and fun didn't involve moving in with people.' But upon meeting her future husband she and he 'knew that was it and we were engaged within eight weeks and married within three months I think and happy ever after'.[16] Caroline's somewhat guilty admission that she gave up her job (although not her career—she did return to journalism when her children were older) and furthermore, that she and her husband-to-be did not even discuss the possibility of an alternative division of roles in their marriage, indicates that she recognized in retrospect that she was a little out of step with her cohort, the majority of whom stayed in work at least until they became mothers. But the decision itself highlights the confidence of a woman who had surfed the wave of educational and career opportunity and who understood that marriage to the man she loved would bring her emotional fulfilment. Caroline knew her marriage would provide her with sustenance, that it would be a marriage of equals founded on mutuality, enabling both partners to

[15] Interview with Caroline. [16] Interview with Caroline.

grow and thrive. Women like Caroline were taking their time to find a lifetime partner and in that time their expectations for the marriage relationship matured.

In a different vein, in 1969 Jenny, from a skilled working-class Catholic family in the north of England, expressed her views on settling down. Having benefited from a grammar school education and teacher-training college she was now an art teacher and living in a furnished flat. At 23 she would have been aware that most of her contemporaries were engaged or married but she was unwilling to compromise.

> Like most girls I want to get married fairly soon but I'm determined not to marry for security or anything less than because I love the man for himself. Two men have asked me to marry them but I don't really think they wanted me for myself but they wanted someone to look after them and who would fit in with their own image of themselves. The one or two men I am interested in are still involved in their own education and do not want the responsibility of marriage as yet.[17]

The clarity with which this young woman expressed her desire, not only to marry for love but to maintain her self-identity distinct from the role of wife, is striking. It accords with the view of Drusilla Beyfuss, whose study of marriage in England in 1968 identified an 'introspective approach' amongst her younger interviewees, 'in which they analysed their own reactions, emotions and feelings towards the marital tie' in contrast with older couples who accepted matrimony almost without thinking.[18] In Jenny's brief account she also acknowledged the power of social convention; marriage was something that most girls desired and she thought she should too. Shortly after giving this account she spent a year with VSO in Africa. Marriage remained on her horizon but she struggled to accommodate her desire for independence and autonomy with her own, and presumably others', expectations that she would conform to the pattern followed by the vast majority of her peers. 'I feel I would like to marry and have children but not sure if this is just wanting to escape into a secure backwater!! On the whole this year has been one of finding new values—exciting challenging, but also frightening.'[19] Five years later in 1973 she was back living with her parents and still expressing the desire to marry and have children.[20]

The question of whether to marry was resolved by the vast majority of young women in this period in the affirmative. Amongst the 1946 birth cohort study, 85 per cent of women who were married by 1972 had done so by the time

[17] MRC, NSHD: Sample 7—postal questionnaire 1970.
[18] Beyfuss, *The English Marriage*, pp.xii–xiii.
[19] MRC, NSHD: sample 07, postal questionnaire 1971.
[20] MRC, NSHD: sample 07—self rating questionnaire 1972.

they were 23.[21] As we have seen already, marriage was still the most acceptable way of legitimizing a long-term relationship; cohabitation, while on the increase by the late 1960s, tended to be the privilege of the educated, those who had already left home for study or work and who were able to set up home some distance from their parents. Eileen Ogden, who was working as an assistant in a butcher's shop and who married in 1968 aged 19, recalled that she 'wanted to be really daring and just live together, but Andrew [..] I don't think he would, we'd talked about it but neither of us ventured into, d'you know what I mean.'[22] Those who did reject marriage as an institution often did so at the cost of parental approval and support. Maureen related how, when her parents visited the home she shared with her boyfriend, she 'tidied his things away and he went out and I pretended I lived on my own', though she admitted that 'they were masters at closing their eyes to what they didn't want to see'.[23] And when cohabiting couples began to plan for children, marriage was back on the cards.

Amongst middle-class girls, the social and financial pressures to marry quickly were less urgent than amongst their working-class counterparts. In the 1950s, women whose husbands were employed in a non-manual occupation were less likely to be married by the age of 25 than those who married men in manual work—61 per cent compared with around 75 per cent.[24] Having enjoyed the freedom of independent living or the relative comfort of the parental home, they were more likely to wait for the right person to come along. At 22 Sally, who was living at home with her mother while working as a data processor, was engaged to be married. She found her work dull and complained that in the office she 'was treated like a child'. Nonetheless, marriage for her was not an escape. 'I feel that many girls these days get married before they are mentally ready for it. They don't seem to realize that good marriages don't just happen but that you have to work hard at it.'[25] Two years later and married, she was still of the view that marriage was something to be worked at: 'We do not have any family yet & hope not to have any for a few years yet. We both feel we ought to learn to be good husbands and wives before taking on the difficult job of being parents.'[26]

The move towards marriage amongst those who embarked on careers has been described as 'more of a merging of two paths than a takeover bid in a flurry of romantic over expectation'.[27] Romantic marriage expectations seem to have been mostly confined to teenage idealism. Mrs Eastwell who married at 23 admitted to imagining her marriage as 'terribly cosy, mutual admiration, a Garden of Eden,

[21] MRC, NSHD: Skylark MARAG1972—'When were you married?' doi:10.5522/NSHD/Q101.
[22] UKDA, SN 5190: Interview with Eileen Ogden, p.7.
[23] Ingham, *Now We Are Thirty*, p.130.
[24] Rachel M. Pierce, 'Marriage in the Fifties', *The Sociological Review* 11:2 (1963), pp.215–40, here p.217.
[25] MRC, NSHD: sample 26—Health and Employment Questionnaire 1968.
[26] MRC, NSHD: sample 26—postal questionnaire 1970.
[27] Ingham, *Now We Are Thirty*, p.133.

an ever idealistic picture'. It didn't turn out as she envisaged, admitting that she would have liked a husband who was able to show his affection in public: 'I married the wrong person for this.'[28] But looking back on decades of a marriage relationship as opposed to commenting contemporaneously as Mrs Eastwell was doing, women recognized that friendship, mutual interests, and compatibility were more important than love or sexual attraction.[29] When asked how she knew her future husband was 'the one' Carol, who married at 21, sought to rationalize: 'I honestly, I think, I honestly don't think you know that they are the one. I [...] I think that if you're friends first, then it goes along with, and, and [...] I don't know, he was just, he was, he was, he was very, I just think, he had a lovely sense of humour and he always made me laugh.'[30] Lynne had a number of boyfriends when she was at teacher-training college before she met the man who was to become her husband, attracted by his intelligence and the fact that he made an effort, borrowing his parents' car to take her out, meeting her after her theatre rehearsals and taking things slowly.[31] By the early 1970s it was becoming more common for couples to live with one another for a period (and certainly to sleep with one another) before marriage, so that taking the time to find the right partner meant that women had developed an understanding of what marriage would mean. Shirley who married in 1971 after cohabiting for a year recalled that 'I remember being frightened about the finality of marriage, the commitment, losing my freedom. But we did everything together and I knew I couldn't stay unmarried forever. I was 25.'[32] Marriage was seen as almost inevitable, so women needed to reconfigure it not as an ending but as a beginning, a place to continue to grow within a loving, nurturing relationship.

Suzanna's account of her relationship history in the 1960s after she graduated from university epitomizes the kinds of choices women were making and the considerations they weighed up when contemplating long-term commitment. She recounted two very different occasions when she had rejected marriage, vividly demonstrating a degree of self-knowledge and understanding of the kind of relationship that would enable her to thrive and be herself, both at the time and in retrospect. In the first instance she was courted by an older man whom she had met through her parents who 'desperately wanted to marry me'. His wooing of her entailed visits to expensive restaurants, envied by Suzanna's mother who regarded this man as a catch, 'Because I was living the life that she would love to have', but which invoked scorn in Suzanna who, as a university student, was rapidly rejecting her parents' values.

[28] UKDA, SN 853296: Interview with Mrs Eastwell, p.6.

[29] Langhamer, in 'Love, Selfhood and Authenticity', pp.285–90 argues that love was part and parcel of a pragmatic approach to marriage in the 1950s but that it did achieve much greater importance in the 1960s.

[30] UKDA, SN 5190: Interview with Carol Kirk, p.13.

[31] UKDA, SN 5190: Interview with Lynne Archer, p.16.

[32] Interview with Shirley.

> And I'd put him through hell. And I would *challenge* every belief he had. And he kept asking me to marry him... And there was this man, whom I was treating quite sort of contemptuously, who continued to think that I was absolutely wonderful. And I think—the point when I *really* knew I couldn't marry him was when he said at some stage, he was driving me somewhere and there had been an accident and he said: 'Oh, there's been a bit of a poopoo here, hasn't there!' [spoken in a posh accent]. And I thought, I can't marry someone who uses language like that![33]

Suzanna was growing away from her parents and moreover, she was beginning to develop her own understanding of what marriage could be. It was not what this man offered. When he proposed to her at a party—'he sort of got on his knees and asked me to marry him'—she was blunt:

> I said 'look, this is just not going to happen'... And I thought, you know, again, I thought, that's no good. I've got to be able to do what I want to do, I don't want to be sort of schooled in the right way to behave. I mean, in that sense I've always been a rebel. I won't do what's necessarily expected of me.[34]

Suzanna was becoming more certain in her own beliefs about relationships, contrasting her embrace of 'serial monogamy' with her mother's accusations of her promiscuity and rejecting marriage when it would have been the easy solution. When she experienced an unplanned pregnancy a few years later, marriage was on the table once again.

> that occasion was very difficult because as soon as he knew I was pregnant he asked me to marry him and I had one of those, you know those insights where I thought, of all the things in my life I do not want to marry this man. He is not, I may have thought I loved him, I may still have that attachment to him but he is not the sort of person I want to spend the rest of my life with... And it was very interesting because initially I agreed to marry him and even though I had this voice saying you know. And I wrote to my parents saying I was pregnant and I was getting married and he told his parents and I met them and that was horrendously embarrassing and I went to stay with them in this horrid little house—now this is me being a snob. It was a horrid little suburban house and I'd already kind of thought you know at the back of my mind, this is not what I want to happen, and I just said I can't go through with this.

[33] Interview with Suzanna.

[34] Interview with Suzanna.

In the face of her boyfriend's desire for her to have the child Suzanna rejected both marriage and motherhood at this time. Despite social pressure and cultural expectations she listened to her own voice. Marriage for her had to be founded on love and mutual respect which she found a few years later.

Suzanna's account of taking her time to find the right partner, despite parental and social pressures, contrasts with the expectation that working-class girls were expected to 'make a satisfactory marriage and to be reasonably quick about it'.[35] For girls who left school at 15 or 16, in undemanding and poorly paid jobs and still living with their parents, marriage may have appeared attractive. We saw in Chapter 4 how the dating game in some communities was merely a prelude to settling down. In the context of full employment and a housebuilding boom, 'couples didn't see the need to wait'.[36] For some of course, an unplanned pregnancy precipitated an early marriage. Eileen Ogden acknowledged this was the case for some in her social group of young women in their late teens:

> Well, we'd talked about getting married, a lot of our friends were already married, and a lot of them already had babies, they were pregnant when they got married, that was the era of, because the pill and that hadn't really come in then. The pill came in just after we got married, really, and, like contraception. It was very much hit and miss before that. A lot of our friends had already had children and got married, and we didn't.[37]

Marriage for Eileen did not immediately bring the independence she and so many hoped for; the couple lived with her parents for two years—their first child was born there—until they managed to save enough for a deposit on their own house just before their second child was born. This was a common pattern: 'That's what the working classes did' remarked Eileen Parr. 'You stayed with your mum and dad until you got a place of your own.'[38]

But by the mid-1960s even working-class women were taking more time to settle down and they were becoming more choosy. Pam had grown up in a respectable working-class community in the west of Scotland. She was expected to conform to the expectations of her family—'we were quiet people. It never occurred to you that you didn't conform.' She acknowledged the peer pressure to find a husband and marry:

> it was quite time-consuming in life, a time-consuming thing. I don't know if you were looking for a lifetime partner, but if you were looking for an engagement

[35] Jephcott, *Some Young People*, p.66. See also Claire Langhamer, 'Love and Courtship in Mid-twentieth Century England', *The Historical Journal* 50:1 (2007), pp.173–96.

[36] Todd, *The People*, p.172.

[37] UKDA, SN 5190: Interview with Eileen Ogden, p.7.

[38] UKDA, SN 5190: Interview with Eileen Parr, p.13.

> ring very much so...it's like wanting a baby and realizing you'll get a teenager later. It's the same kind of thing – 'oh, I've got an engagement ring, oh, dear, now I've got a man'. There was no, um, no vision of what it meant except that oh you had to get this ring and be a, be a success which is strange.[39]

Pam did find a man—she was engaged for a year—but broke it off shortly before the wedding having realized that it 'wasn't right'. She gave up her job as a primary school teacher and moved to Spain, a critical episode in her life in that it offered up new possibilities:

> Um, that the world wasn't grey and [smalltown-ish] and tied in to—that it was bigger than you had ever been lead to believe and there were people doing the most extra-ordinary things and there were perfectly valid lives, where the only valid lives at home had been respectability and getting married and having children and keeping a clean house; and that was, that was a validity somehow, behaving and not bringing shame on your family. Suddenly these things became just—ok they were quite important, um but frankly [inaudible] things that mattered and um—There were people doing all sorts of weird and just um, but were dead ordinary to them, and 'oh, yes, we can do that'. It was astonishing.

Pam knew when she broke off the engagement that she wanted more than marriage to a local man could offer her. She was already questioning her religion and its moral rules—'I was struggling really hard with being in a Catholic school and having to teach this religion'—but it was the move to another country and the opportunity to live a different kind of life that crystallized her doubts about the conventions she had been brought up with. Pam's determination to step out of the tramlines and shape her life according to her own values was about more than realizing the man to whom she was engaged was not 'the one'.

This generation of women were imagining—and demanding—more of marriage as an enabling period of life, and not just a necessary stepping-stone to adulthood. For some it promised economic and emotional security, a home of one's own and a path to family life. For others the marriage relationship was an expression of emotional intimacy (including sexual intimacy) and provided the opportunity for personal fulfilment, whether that be through home-making, motherhood or mutuality, sometimes described as closeness or togetherness. Although these expectations may not have been new—Langhamer argues that in the 1930s many saw marriage as a 'quest for security and self-determination'—by the 1960s there was a new factor: now most women were not content to equate settling down with settling for the kind of marriage their mothers had.[40]

[39] Interview with Pam.

[40] Langhamer, *English in Love*, p.180.

Rather, they imagined and worked for a relationship they often described as 'close' that allowed them the space to grow the self alongside or in tandem with one's chosen partner.

Togetherness

Togetherness or closeness were common terms used by women and some men of the post-war generation when describing the type of marriage they wanted. They depicted a marriage relationship in which a couple had a common understanding, communicated freely, and were united in a joint endeavour of home-making and child-rearing.[41] When Mr and Mrs Beckham described their relationship as 'close', Mr Beckham explained: 'It means...a complete acceptance, almost like another limb—no sensation of being apart—and everything between two people being completely free.' Mrs Beckham was also keen to expound on her philosophy of marriage: 'I don't believe in talk of perfect marriages. The perfect state between two people is knowing each other and seeing each other as you really are to the best of one's capabilities. It is best if you can understand each other and accept each other's personality and faults.'[42] Closeness was about open communication, shared goals and, in the early years of marriage, joint endeavours often focused on the home. It was mutually shared intimacy in practice. 'I am very happy about married life' reported a woman who had left school at 16 and married at 20. 'I have been fortunate in finding a very understanding and loving husband. We very rarely go out, except to do the weekend shopping, but we are happy as long as we are together. He is the one person, apart from my mother, to whom I can freely talk to.'[43] The early years of marriage, especially before children arrived, are often described as the time when couples who were both earning could practise this closeness, enjoying their joint income, spending it on home-making and joint leisure activities. A nurse who had recently married a policeman recounted their cosy domesticity in terms of a popular television cookery couple: 'Together we enjoy painting and decorating and motoring. We also fancy ourselves as "Fanny and Johnny Craddock" by concocting mad recipes and curries.'[44]

Women marrying in the 1960s had expectations that their marriage would be a partnership. Decades of debate about the contours of the marriage relationship had, by the 1960s, normalized understandings about what constituted the companionate marriage. In the inter-war period, the idea of marriage being

[41] 'Close' was also interpreted as 'more egalitarian' than the marriages of their parents. Pahl and Pahl, *Managers and their Wives*, p.210.

[42] UKDA, SN 853296: Interview with Mr and Mrs Beckham, together—p.22, Mrs Beckham alone p.4.

[43] MRC, NSHD: Sample 22—Health and Employment questionnaire, 1966.

[44] MRC, NSHD: Sample 12—postal questionnaire 1970.

'less an institution than a relationship intended to serve as their primary arena for emotional expression and satisfaction' had been popularized amongst some higher-class couples.[45] By the post-war decades, open communication, the sharing of activities, emotional and sexual intimacy and an emphasis on equality, practised in the context of the growing privatization of family life, was much more widely anticipated, especially by women for whom the family was still the primary focus. A social worker who married in 1964 explained why she was attracted to her husband-to-be. It wasn't sexual attraction but rather 'the most important and overriding fact of any relationship with the opposite sex, particularly one's potential husband is the emotional side…it's the affection, the emotional support and the feeling that one is needed that, to me, is absolutely vital. Far more than a really super lover.'[46]

That emotional closeness was situated, ideologically and materially, in the home. It is important to recognize that nest-building, often prior to starting a family, was for women an important element of cementing that togetherness and many found satisfaction and enjoyment in creating a first home. Mainstream media in the early 1960s still predominantly identified married women as homemakers. BBC television's 1961 'Homemaker of the Year' competition harked back to the Fifties in its focus on domestic skills and qualities as a mother and a citizen. Entrants were asked to complete an extensive questionnaire which asked: 'In a woman's relationship with her husband, it is most important for her to: (a) be a first-rate housekeeper, (b) be attractive in dress and appearance, (c) be an interesting companion, (d) be a good lover.' The 84 who reached the regional finals were invited to attend a domestic economy training establishment where their domestic skills could be assessed. All 84 were visited at home by assessors and the 28 finalists were filmed for a 10-programme series to be shown at 2.45 in the afternoon, presumably timed for when housewives had completed their domestic chores.[47] Homemaker of the year must have seemed incongruous to women of our generation however. The post-war reconfiguration of family life and its corollary, the house-building programme, had facilitated a home life that was more about togetherness than domestic economy. The house-building boom in the two and half decades after 1945 when local authorities, new town corporations and private builders erected more than 2.5 million homes, provided modern residences designed primarily with families in mind. In 1948 owner occupation accounted for only 24 per cent of the homes of the 1946 cohort of children, with 47 per cent in private rented accommodation and another 20 per cent in housing

[45] Collins, *Modern Love*, p.93.

[46] Lawson, A., *Adultery: An Analysis of Love and Betrayal, 1920–1983* [computer file]. Colchester, Essex: UK Data Archive [distributor], November 2004. SN: 4858, http://dx.doi.org/10.5255/UKDA-SN-4858-2 (hereafter UKDA, SN 4858): interview 001.

[47] BBC Written Archives Centre: File Folder: R51/1016/4 Woman's Hour 1961, 'Homemaker feature' including questionnaire and memo from Editor of Women's programmes television, 24.2.1961.

rented from the council.[48] In 1972, when most of our cohort of women had married, 46 per cent either owned or were buying their own home, a figure that had increased to three quarters by 1982 when they were in their thirties.[49] It was this generation that spearheaded the lifestyle change characterized by a home-centred family life.

In 1969, John and Carol, a young married couple from Glasgow, moved from a cramped, unmodernized tenement apartment to a brand-new high-rise flat, beneficiaries of the massive investment in new homes in the city to address the appalling housing conditions that prevailed here after the Second World War. They had started their married life four years earlier, typically living with John's mother before they found a place of their own, a rented flat with a window looking out onto the bins, no hot water, and an outside toilet. When they moved up the housing list and were offered a flat in one of the new high-rises they were delighted. Upon moving to the sixth floor of a new block, a combination of hire-purchase and John's DIY skills enabled them to transform a spartan flat into a space that reflected their aesthetic. Their living-room especially reflected the lifestyle to which they aspired. They saved up for a 'space-age' Orbit three-piece suite with swivel bucket chairs and Carol described how her living room was her pride and joy:

> my living room was, I thought it was gorgeous…and I had a lovely little table that we had our Trimphone on, because we managed to get a 'phone which I had to wait a million years for, it was one of these nice wee Trimphones, and John and I were just reminiscing the other day about our radiogram that we had. It was a long wooden radiogram and that's where you had your LP's and your singles and everything, and that was fabulous…and I thought my house was fabulous, I really did (laughing). Of course I told you about the lamps, you know, the standard lamp, the table lamp and the big ash tray, all matching you know. So that was my house.[50]

Carol and John were part of the post-war promotion of family life facilitated by the provision of better housing (whether for ownership or rent) and the availability and—though at a stretch for many—affordability of consumer goods. The expectation that newly-weds would spend the first years of marriage living with their parents was receding. Carol's enjoyment of her modern home was described as an act of togetherness whereby the young couple participated in creative

[48] MRC, NSHD: Skylark OWN48. doi:10.5522/NSHD/Q101.

[49] MRC, NSHD: Skylark OWN72; OWN 82. doi: 10.5522/NSHD/Q101. Sandbrook gives a figure of 50% home ownership in 1970. *White Heat*, p.78.

[50] Interview with Carol and John conducted for a project on 'Housing, Everyday Life and Wellbeing over the Long Term, c.1950–c.1975', University of Glasgow, 2014–16.

home-making and she—indeed both of them—derived pleasure from recalling the fun they had making a home for themselves.

Whether rented or owner-occupied, having a place a couple could call their own was high on the list of desirables amongst 16-year-old girls who were asked, in 1962, what they wished for apart from a job, and was frequently mentioned in later years by those who had married as a significant event or change in their lives.[51] This is not surprising. For many of the girls of the 1946 birth cohort, a home of their own signified long-term security and was part of the anticipated 'double-gift-wrapped package' comprising marriage and children that was so widely promulgated.[52] The overcrowding, inadequate facilities, lack of privacy and insecurity of tenure that characterized much working-class housing in the 1940s and 1950s also fed the desire for one's own space. A waitress who had grown up in an 'isolated farmhouse with no electricity, gas, bathroom or running hot water' remarked that, although she regarded it as important that she was earning her own living, she expected to be a housewife at 25 and wanted a home of her own.[53] Carol Ann, who featured in a 1967 magazine article querying whether marriage was out of date, was resigned to carrying on working after marriage because 'we'll have to get that bungalow we've set our hearts on somehow'.[54]

For this generation home was now family and leisure-focused, epitomized by the abandonment of older symbols of working-class respectability such as the 'best' room or parlour reserved for special guests and occasions, and by the DIY revolution whereby people could afford to create homes that suited their lifestyles in respect of decoration and spatial organization.[55] With the purchase of carpets and sofas, radiograms and televisions, young couples engaged in what must have seemed to their parents a home-making extravaganza, creating comfortable spaces for their own enjoyment together and with friends. Carol and John in Glasgow usually had a Friday night Chinese takeaway and they often invited friends in—there were no pubs on their 'scheme' or estate—participating in the new trend for home-based entertaining. This was also evident amongst the manual and non-manual workers of Luton interviewed for the 'Affluent Worker Study' who transformed the 'best room' into a family television room while installing 'cocktail bars' and radiograms for their own and others' entertainment.[56]

[51] MRC, NSHD: study member at youth employment office questionnaire 1962, question 11. Postal questionnaire 1970: 'has anything significant happened'.

[52] Ingham, *Now We are Thirty*, p.119.

[53] MRC, NSHD: sample 24—personal questionnaire 1962.

[54] *Nova*, March 1967: 'Bells and a Bungalow'. On working-class women working to afford mortgage payments see Laura Paterson, 'Women and paid work in industrial Britain, c.1945–71', PhD thesis, University of Dundee, 2014, p.237.

[55] Jon Lawrence, *Me, Me, Me*, pp.129–34. Pahl and Pahl in *Managers and their Wives* comment upon middle-class couples with closer relationships spending time together on family focused activities at weekends, p.221.

[56] Lawrence, *Me, Me, Me*, pp.133–4, p.146.

The meanings attached to home life were rapidly changing. John and Carol were typical of young couples beginning to map out a new way of living that prioritized comfort and enjoyment. They had little use for the outward symbols of respectability that had characterized so many working-class neighbourhoods although, as we shall see later, the embrace of the home as the prime signifier of family life brought with it new pressures to maintain higher standards of comfort, pressure that almost always was unequally distributed despite the assistance of technology in the form of vacuum cleaners and washing machines.[57]

Togetherness also found expression in the home-based lifestyles of middle-class families. The Newingtons, a middle-class family living in a detached house with a large garden and two cars, epitomized the 'close' marriage which centred on the home and family life. The couple described the basis of their relationship as 'honesty and friendship' and she described her husband as her best friend. The weekends were spent on family-focused activities: gardening, decorating, taking the dog for a walk with the children, going to the beach and they always had Sunday lunch together. They had their own hobbies—dressmaking for Mrs Newington and a model railway for him—and they were looking forward to when they could spend more time with each other when the children were older. Yet while they were adamant that 'no-one came first' in the family, Mr Newington acknowledged that his wife's primary focus was on making sure that he was 'comfortable'. 'I think she knows I've got to go to the office and keep the job going'; he remarked not altogether sarcastically, 'I get continuous priority at a high level'.[58] The only time this changed was when his wife was pregnant. The Newingtons displayed one kind of marriage which, at the time they were interviewed, apparently met both of their needs. The closeness their relationship engendered was not based on equality but Mrs Newington was largely content: 'From a child, I've never wanted anything but a home and family'. However, she did worry about what she would do when the children had grown, and was thinking about undertaking a teacher training course.[59] She recognized that long term, her home and family might not be sufficient to fulfil her.

A home of one's own, however, was no guarantee of facilitating the togetherness that women anticipated from their marriage. Mrs Herne lived with her manager husband in a modern detached house on a new estate. Before marriage she had been a carpet designer but now she had three children and they and the home were her primary focus, though she did not feel a 'slave to housework'.

[57] Lynn Abrams, Ade Kearns, Barry Hazley, Valerie Wright, *Glasgow: High-Rise Homes, Estates and Communities in the Post-War Period* (London: Routledge, 2020), pp.44–56. On adaptations in new town homes see Judith Attfield, 'Inside Pram Town: A Case Study of Harlow House Interiors, 1951–1961' in Judith Attfield and Pat Kirkham (Eds), *A View from the Interior: Feminism, Women and Design* (London: Women's Press, 1995).

[58] UKDA, SN 853296: Interview with Mr and Mrs Newington, p.28.

[59] UKDA, SN 853296: Interview with Mrs Newington, p.11.

Yet Mrs Herne was disappointed in the way her marriage had turned out. She had 'expected more togetherness... with "cosy evenings and home making" and doing such things as making lampshades and so forth'. She would have liked them to do more 'creative homebuilding' together but 'she does it all herself'.[60] It transpired that the couple spent very little time with one another. Mr Herne was rarely at home, pursuing his hobby of sailing when he wasn't at work.[61] He regarded work as his primary focus whereas she had little choice but to be immersed in the home. It was unsurprising then, that Mrs Herne lacked self confidence, reporting that she 'frequently suffers from a feeling of doing nothing', and was considering returning to work.[62] Mr Herne believed there 'was absolutely no platform of communication between himself and his wife'. The anticipated togetherness through sharing of activities had not transpired and Mrs Herne was not alone in her disappointment.

Other women in this study of aspirational career men and their wives experienced similar disatisfaction with husbands who filled all their spare time working or pursuing sport. Mrs Kingston complained about her workaholic husband to the interviewer who reported: 'She used to fight for his time and supposes it has got a little easier to live with but, being frank, she is not truly reconciled to the situation.'[63] Similarly Mrs Eastwell, who admitted she was not a natural homemaker or mother-figure, complained that 'there is no question of [Mr Eastwell] "letting up", "devoting more time to his family" etc. He is caught in the machine. I wish very often I had married a lesser light, to whom I could be more use, who had some energy left at the end of the day for his wife and children, and who had both time and inclination to put up the odd shelf, paint the odd room etc.'[64] Living in a detached house in the country were the Ickhams with their two children, but the idyllic marriage Mrs Ickham had envisaged had 'not exactly' materialized. She felt isolated in the week and the weekends revolved around her husband's sporting activities: 'If my husband goes off to play hockey and I don't watch then I tend to feel a bit sore. I feel we should spend more time together... I think generally we're probably geared more round my husband at weekends', though she admitted that with small children her freedom was limited especially as she didn't like to leave them with her husband.[65] Togetherness, it transpired, only worked in these marriages when the wives subordinated their needs to those of their husbands.

These women used the interview with the researcher to express their discontent at the lack of togetherness in their marriages, while at the same time

[60] UKDA, SN 853296: Interview with Mrs Herne, p.5.
[61] UKDA, SN 853296: Interview with Mrs Herne, p.21.
[62] UKDA, SN 853296: Interview with Mrs Herne, p.7.
[63] UKDA, SN 853296: Interview with Mrs Kingston, p.10.
[64] UKDA, SN 853296: Questionnaire with Mrs Eastwell, handwritten comments.
[65] UKDA, SN 853296: Interview with Mrs Ickham, p.8.

emphasizing their role as companion and support to their husband and primary carer for the children. While they did not have the language to describe their role in this regard, we would now label this 'emotional labour', a phenomenon described by McCarthy in the case of working graduate wives in the 1960s as encompassing not only the care of children but the 'mothering' of husbands and sometimes their clients.[66] Yet Mrs Eastwell's desire for reciprocity in her marriage is notable here. Her husband was a workaholic, and she was prepared to listen to him when he needed to get something 'off his chest' 'because I love him'. But, she added, 'Men should perform the same service for their wives'.[67] Others were genuinely perplexed as to how to rebalance their marriage. Mrs Kingston saw herself as 'someone to share her husband's relaxation', yet he was 100 per cent involved in his work, seven days a week and evenings. 'I should be very grateful for some knowledgeable advice as to whether it is my duty to encourage this way of life if he is happy, despite the effect on his health, or whether I should fight for some of his time.'[68] Mrs Kingston epitomized the shift in what women wanted from marriage. Her husband's description of their marriage as having 'a lot of team feeling' did not accord with her experience.[69] He didn't consult her on a recent promotion and took over the housework 'when it needed a blitz'. Her marriage was not close enough.

Together but Unequal

Women surrendered more of themselves to the home-making project. Carol, who we met in the previous section, described her marriage to John as a 'great team' and in interview both she and John enjoyed the telling of stories about decorating and furnishing their new flat. But later on John admitted:

> They were happy days, and if I had been a more sensible person they'd have been even more so, but I was pretty irresponsible like most guys of my generation and age…I was probably married about ten years before I realized I was actually married, you know, before it dawned on me…I just carried on as if I was a single guy with the rest of my pals, you know…Carol talked about going out with the kids, but she was the one who done the most of that. I done it occasionally and I have to say the times that I did do it, it was one of these things that it was like the happiest day of my life, you know, and yet I never repeated it often enough.

[66] Helen McCarthy, 'Career, Family and Emotional Work: Graduate Mothers in 1960s Britain', *Past and Present*, 246, Issue Supplement 15 (2020), pp.295–317, here p.297.

[67] UKDA, SN 853296: Questionnaire with Mrs Eastwell.

[68] UKDA, SN 853296: Questionnaire with Mrs Kingston.

[69] UKDA, SN 853296: Interview with Mr Kingston, p.17.

Carol eventually returned to part-time work when their two children went to school but there was no question of John sharing the housework. 'No, no. I can safely say without fear of contradiction...no John didn't. I just went back to work and I was... I was just always the one that did things, I was always, I suppose, a doer.'[70]

The gendered division of labour in respect of housework was and still is often used as an indicator of the degree to which a marriage degrades women. For feminists housework is socially structured and conditioned to be undertaken by women who, as housewives, are treated as economically dependent and thus subordinate to their husbands and in society.[71] It stands out as an enduring area of division in marriages which otherwise emphasize companionship and noted by those who investigated family life in the 1960s and 1970s.[72] It is difficult to generalize about the willingness or otherwise of men to undertake a share of the housework and what that says about women's contentment. When women from across the class spectrum were asked the extent to which their husbands helped with the housework in 1957, fewer than 2 per cent reported them helping 'regularly' and 46 per cent helping 'a bit'.[73] In the next generation, little appears to have changed despite expectations of greater egalitarianism being expressed.[74] One of the managers, Mr Newington who we met earlier describing his marriage as a team, was very frank and unapologetic about the division of labour in his home:

> I do the garden and the car, but very little in the house. I don't cook; I do dry up most weekends and evenings, under protest, but I don't do any housework unless the place is particularly untidy, when I might take out the Hoover... I feel it's a natural and normal sort of division; I don't do anything that's really a woman's province, though I do light the fires which my mother always does in my own home.[75]

Patterns established in the parental home were not easily cast off by the next generation of women. In 1968 a recently married 24-year-old shop assistant wrote about her weekly routine: 'I lead a very simple life on the whole. I get up with my husband at 6.30 to get him off to work. A couple of hours housework before starting of [sic] to work which I start at 9 o'clock & finish at 5.30. Go home to start my husbands tea & start again. We go out most weekends.'[76] A full-time nurse explained that: 'I suppose the way that my husband had been brought up I did

[70] Interview with Carol and John.

[71] See Oakley, *Housewife* for the clearest articulation of this interpretation.

[72] See for instance, Wallace, C.D., Pahl, R.E. (2019). *Social and Political Implications of Household Work Strategies, 1978–1983*. [data collection]. UK Data Service. SN: 4876, http://doi.org/10.5255/UKDA-SN-4876-1

[73] MRC, NSHD: Skylark HFC5057—Help with housework, 1957—doi:10.5522/NSHD/Q101.

[74] Pahl and Pahl, *Managers and their Wives*, p.207.

[75] Pahl and Pahl, *Managers and their Wives*, p.214.

[76] MRC, NSHD: Sample 24—personal questionnaire 1968.

everything you know, it was sort of stop the ironing and clean my shoes. Stop the ironing and make me a cup of tea.'[77]

The adherence to an old normativity around gender roles in the home was likely more pronounced amongst working-class couples though the evidence is somewhat contradictory and impacted by the distribution of paid labour. Hannah Gavron's survey for her study of married women with children in the 1960s indicated that working-class couples were more likely than their middle-class counterparts to share the household tasks and only 8 per cent of working-class men did nothing around the home at all. In fact in her assessment the working-class couples in her study were especially 'family-minded and home-centred'.[78] Likewise sociologist Ferdynand Zweig stated that by the 1960s husbands of the affluent working class had become dutiful 'home-birds', the majority of whom endorsed their wives' equality.[79] Supporting equality is not the same as practising it however. In Pahl and Wilson's study of household work strategies including the domestic division of labour on the Isle of Sheppey in the 1980s, it was concluded that in households characterized by economic insecurity the division of labour was more rigid although case studies of couples offered a more nuanced picture.[80] In the household of Linda and Jim, featuring work precarity, the fulfilment of household needs was shared. Jim 'doesn't think there's any jobs that he won't do because it's women's work'.[81] Conversely, in Wight's study of a mining community in Lanarkshire where a rigid division of labour had been practiced prior to pit closure, unemployed miners resisted any degree of role reversal despite their wives carrying a double burden of paid and domestic work.[82] And in some areas of deprivation in Glasgow the sharing of domestic labour was said to be unknown, leaving young married women to replicate the roles borne by their mothers.[83]

In more affluent homes one might have expected a different picture. Middle-class wives, argued Oakley, had an 'instrumental orientation' to housework, sometimes adopting a 'self-consciously disparaging attitude' to household chores and the label housewife.[84] Yet in the Pahls' study of managers and their wives, the overwhelming majority of wives—90 per cent—attached importance to caring for the house and children, almost half had no plans to take a job outside the home and, for those who were in paid employment, their domestic roles took priority.[85] This meant that those with jobs as well as domestic responsibilities felt the strain.

77 UKDA, SN4858: interview 017.

78 Gavron, *Captive Wife*, pp.93–4.

79 Ferdynand Zweig, *Women's Life and Labour* (London, 1952), p.18.

80 UKDA, SN 4876, User Guide, p.91.

81 Ray Pahl, *Divisions of Labour* (Oxford: Blackwell, 1984), pp.277–310.

82 Daniel Wight, *Workers not Wasters: Masculine Respectability, Consumption and Employment in Central Scotland* (Edinburgh: Edinburgh University Press, 1993), pp.36–9, 199–200.

83 UCL, Institute of Education Archive, Pre-School Playgroup Association Collection (hereafter PLA): PPA 2/28: Scottish Pre-School Playgroups Association, *Playgroups in Areas of Need (1977)*, p.16.

84 Oakley, *Housewife*, p.98.

85 Pahl and Pahl, *Managers*, p.132, Table 5.4, p.130.

Mrs Olantigh was a part-time teacher whose husband did not help with the housework. She described how 'At weekends I'm cleaning, cooking, shopping, or preparing meals and I have no time to do much else'.[86] Contemporaneous evidence indicates some women's acceptance of this state of affairs, at least in the early days of marriage. 'It was a game, playing house' commented Julie who married in 1970. 'But as time went on I did think it was a bit unfair that I did it all while Steve sat down and read the paper.'[87] As married women increasingly returned to the job market, domestic chores became more a matter for negotiation. 'I've got more to do for the next thirty years than just cleaning a home' remarked one woman who was training to be a teacher.[88] This self-conscious rejection of the housewife role was to become more widespread as women grew in their marriages and had the self-confidence to state their wishes at the outset. Rhian was adamant at the very start that her marriage would be an enabling and fulfilling one for her: 'I remembered saying when we were getting married, "if we get married, you know, it's got to be on my terms because I'm not going to stay home and do everything" but he's always been, well, you know what it's like I mean he's said he's prepared to put up with being married to a fierce bad feminist (chuckles).'[89]

Reclaiming the Self

So far this chapter has charted how women strived to find a space for the self within the marriage relationship, often against the weight of expectation, traditional assumptions about gender roles and structural inequalities that militated against change. They effected that change by resisting expectations and exerting choice like Pam and Suzanna, by working on marriage as a partnership like Carole and by openly expressing their needs like Rhian. Later on in their marriages, many amongst this generation returned to paid employment as a means of building back their self-confidence and achieving a sense of fulfilment beyond the family as well as to bring in additional income. We will consider that choice in more detail in Chapter 7. But for some, the nature of the marriage relationship was closed to choice and self-fulfilment by obstructive and abusive husbands.

One such was Eileen Parr who was only able later in life to reclaim a subordinated self through speaking about her experience of being stifled in an unequal and abusive relationship. Eileen grew up in a working-class community and had a number of short-term relationships before she met the man she was to marry at the age of 21 in 1968. Her expectations of marriage were conditioned by the relationships she had observed amongst her family and friends. She did not expect to

[86] Pahl and Pahl, *Managers*, p.135.
[87] Cited in Ingham, *Now We are Thirty*, p.131.
[88] Pahl and Pahl, *Managers*, pp.132–3.
[89] Interview with Rhian.

be looked after; in this community where men often worked away from home, working-class women had a reputation for independence so when she followed her husband to London two weeks after the wedding she was pleasantly surprised: 'he'd got this flat, and I went to see it, and I thought, oh, maybe he's not so bad, you know, he's got me somewhere to live'. In London she quickly found office work but was also responsible for all the housework 'because that's what I expected what I would have to do. I expected I'd have to go out to work and then come home and get the tea ready and do all the housework all on a weekend or whenever.' Describing the division of labour in the marriage in those early months she excavated her feeling of independence from the burden of paid and unpaid work:

> Um, it was, I was too busy, never had a minute, I worked full-time, so I was leaving the house at 8 o'clock in the morning, and didn't get home till like 6 o'clock at night, and then I had a meal to cook, I mean, on a weekend, Saturday was spent all day at the launderette, doing the shopping, cleaning the little flat that we had, changing the bed, and, I just never had the time, I didn't have time to worry about anything, really, it was really good, because it gave me the independence that I'd never had and would never have got if I'd stayed at home.

But if she didn't fulfil the role to her husband's satisfaction there would be a row.

> So, say, like, I'd cooked tea and the pots didn't get washed after tea, and he came home the next day and they still weren't washed, we'd have a row about it... Why hadn't I done it before I went out to work in the morning? But it never occurred to me to say, well, why didn't you fuckin' do it last night before you went to bed? That never occurred to me, it was my fault. Everything that ever happened, in most of our marriage was my fault. I saw it as my fault, 'cause he made me think it was my fault, and that was OK, 'cause that's how women were.[90]

Eileen was talking about her marriage in 2003, two years after she had left her husband and, just as significant, following her return to education to follow a university course in gender studies. She had become aware that her marriage had been unequal and abusive but in telling the story of the relationship and its eventual demise, she reclaimed the autonomy she objectively lacked in the marriage by casting herself as an active agent rather than passive victim. '[From] then on it was, it was my own destiny then, I made my own destiny then, I made what, wherever we lived or whatever we did, it was always me that did it, because I knew, I never trusted him enough to do it for me.'[91] While berating herself for not confronting her husband during their marriage, she explained this to herself and

[90] UKDA, SN 5190: Interview with Eileen Parr, p.12.
[91] UKDA, SN 5190: Interview with Eileen Parr, p.10.

the interviewer by saying: 'because sometimes the reason why, it often hurts more than the fact that they've done it, so you just don't ask do you?'[92] The blatant inequality in Eileen's marriage became even starker when she became pregnant. She explained how, although she would have liked to have remained in London, her husband did not: '"cause that would have meant then that he was a proper husband and father, wouldn't it? Whereas if I came home, there was my mother there and my family and his mother and his family.' Marriage had enabled Eileen to leave the parental home; at the time it was the only way she could attain some degree of independence. She had slim expectations of what marriage would deliver and she stayed with her husband for decades despite repeated incidents that shamed her, adopting what she described as a 'put up or shut up' attitude. She had been conditioned to accept her husband's behaviour and she was offered little support when she sought help. A doctor who treated her when her husband contracted a sexually transmitted disease while she was pregnant told her to disregard her husband's infidelity because he provided financially: 'just look at it as a night out at the pictures for him.'[93] But again, in interview, Eileen reclaimed her agency, an act encapsulated in a vignette in which she took control of her destiny at a point when she was suffering from post-natal depression and her husband was absent:

> and [I was] standing in the phone box waiting for it to ring and it never rung…and walking down the street, there was this bus, I could see this bus, and it's as if it was yesterday, and I could see this bus coming and I said to myself, you've got two choices, you either pull yourself out of this or you throw yourself under that bus…never, ever going to get any worse, I'm going to get better, and I let that bus go past, and that was like a turning point in my life…it was just as if something had lifted, it was a decision that I'd made, I was going to make myself better, and from then on I did. I even went out the next day and got myself a job, and um, I never, and I have never, ever let that get me down again.[94]

It took Eileen more than 30 years to liberate herself from her marriage, both physically and psychologically. One morning 'the strength wasn't there' to live with the hurt her husband caused her.[95] The interview she gave in 2003 revealed a woman who endured a bad marriage because she felt she had no choice: 'you make your bed and you lie on it.'[96] But in speaking about her experiences she came to understand how a relationship could look different and she could make changes. 'I think, as you grow and you mature…you sort of say to yourself, that

[92] UKDA, SN 5190: Interview with Eileen Parr, p.16.
[93] UKDA, SN 5190: Interview with Eileen Parr, p.16.
[94] UKDA, SN 5190: Interview with Eileen Parr, p.14.
[95] UKDA, SN 5190: Interview with Eileen Parr, p.23.
[96] UKDA, SN 5190: Interview with Eileen Parr, p.29.

you're allowed to change your mind, you're allowed to see things differently, and I think that's what happened . . . you've got to see, it doesn't matter how much other people tell you about these things, it's only when you believe them inside that you can actually act upon it.'[97] Eileen understood that only she could enact the change that was needed to free herself from a marriage that bore little relation to the mutually sustaining model of intimacy to which so many aspired.

Sadie Innes' journey is similarly illustrative of how a working-class woman had to strive hard to liberate her self through her marriage. Sadie was unusual amongst her peer group for marrying relatively late, at 26. Her husband worked long hours in a physical job and she carried the double burden of working full time and managing the home: ''e didn't do anything. We didn't have washin' machine . . . and there was meals to cook.'[98] A number of years at home owing to ill-health left Sadie lacking in confidence. 'I felt I was wastin' at home . . . I couldn't get a job, and I felt, you know, I 'ad something to give . . . I mean I was doin the 'ousework an stuff, budgetin and so on, like that, but I felt I shoulda been earnin' money.'[99] She admitted that she would defer to her husband because he was the breadwinner. However, when Sadie did find work as a receptionist she became more assertive and empowered, so much so that the tables had turned in their marriage. Rather touchingly, it was her husband who put the changes into words:

> I was 'er stability, I was 'er rock, or whatever you like to call it, you know, and [.] that, that, at times, was 'ard to keep [.] to be a rock for Sadie an' to do me work, you know, it become a conflict, whereas now, Sadie 'as become 'er own rock, she's probably more stronger than I am at the present moment.[100]

Sadie's marriage allowed her to grow in confidence and independence and when she and her husband were interviewed in 2002 they embraced the partnership model of marriage. Sadie emphasized the importance of being friends before anything else and Frank added: 'we give the best of what we've got to each other into the relationship and the home.'[101]

Conclusions

The women of the transition generation made great changes in the British marriage in the 1960s and 1970s. In something of a contrast with their mothers, they imagined the marriage relationship as a place where they could continue to

[97] UKDA, SN 5190: Interview with Eileen Parr, p.29.
[98] UKDA, SN 5190: Interview with Sadie Innes and Frank Innes, p.21.
[99] UKDA, SN 5190: Interview with Sadie Innes and Frank Innes, p.26.
[100] UKDA, SN 5190: Interview with Sadie Innes and Frank Innes, p.26.
[101] UKDA, SN 5190: Interview with Sadie Innes and Frank Innes, p.26.

develop and grow, where they would find support and friendship in relation to their partner and that the marriage relationship would be mutually sustaining and more equal than their parents' marriages had been. This was the generation that manifested the modern 'emotional standard': the embrace of romantic love as the basis for a mutual, companionate marriage.[102] But in order for this to happen they had to make it happen. And this could take time. After years of exploration and self-fashioning as young women, marriage could be either a caesura or a stepping-stone between one kind of life and another. How women negotiated this step has been described as a conflict between the merger and the seeker within them. Merging implied a gravitation towards the safety and security of marriage whereas seeking manifested in an 'impulse to grasp at life' and to look for opportunities for growth.[103] Typically, women took time to understand what it was that they wanted and needed from their marriage relationship in order to feel content and fulfilled and to find ways of putting themselves first. Marriage didn't come ready-wrapped for this generation. Although the idea of marriage as an honest partnership in which each partner could find satisfaction was widely promulgated, there were many ways of achieving it. In this period it was a negotiated state and continued to be so through the life of the marriage.

In their personal accounts, especially those gathered contemporaneously, women narrators articulate the self in relation to others, primarily their husbands. It is because marriage constrained women's identities, as wives and mothers, homemakers, and housewives, that the women in the Pahls' study of career managers struggled to articulate themselves as individuals at all. Only Eileen Parr, interviewed much later in life for another project, whose marriage was the most unequal of those discussed here, was moved to excavate her autonomous self from a relationship characterized by abuse and the subordination of her interests. There was no self that she could identify in relation to her husband. And she did this only when she was separated and had the self-knowledge and the language to analyse and understand her past.

The majority of women who married in the 1960s found that just being married was not sufficient to fulfil them. The romance that had propelled many into marriage was not sustaining in itself. The emotional revolution that shaped modern marriage since the 1950s according to Langhamer, was increasingly incompatible with social and economic structures and it was predominantly women who experienced the disconnect.[104] They required husbands who communicated with them and who took their feelings seriously. And over time they began to crave more independence once the home-making was accomplished, whether

[102] Tim Willem Jones and Alana Harris, 'Introduction: Historicizing "Modern" Love and Romance' in Harris and Willem Jones (Eds), *Love and Romance in Britain, 1918–1970* (Basingstoke: Palgrave Macmillan, 2015), p.15.

[103] Ingham, *Now We Are Thirty*, p.141. Lawson, *Adultery*, describes this as the 'myth of me'.

[104] Langhamer, *Love and Romance*, p.210.

that was through returning to paid work or learning to drive or taking up interests (or other relationships) external to their marriages. This generation had more or less jettisoned the romantic myth of marriage but not marriage itself. They were in the process of working out the alternative and, in the process, figuring out who they could be having found the domestic self wanting or unfulfilling. In the absence of a community of feeling, this could be hard. It would take those who found women's liberation in the 1970s to provide alternative conceptions of living for a generation who grew up in the expectation of marriage.[105] The autonomy advocated by feminists was not necessarily inimical to marriage but it did, as Collins argues, imply more equality and less intimacy.[106] The transition generation, for the most part, did not reject marriage per se; rather they took action to effect change, to demand more equality, informed by their feelings about the loss of the self they experienced as wives and mothers. The next chapters explore how they did this.

[105] Collins, *Modern Love*, pp.180–205.

[106] Collins, *Modern Love*, p.184.

6
The Expressive Self

Introduction

In 1966, the British blues band The Rolling Stones had a hit with an unlikely song about domestic neurosis. The lyrics of *Mother's Little Helper* describe the resort to tranquillizers—the 'little yellow pill'—by women who complained to their doctors of a variety of symptoms ascribed to the deadening suburban lifestyle. The Stones were famously to be associated in the media with recreational drug use, one feature of the expressive culture of the 1960s, yet this song was very much of its time, reflecting the connection made, in both medical circles and in popular culture, between domestic entrapment and symptoms of mental disturbance, primarily amongst housewives and mothers. Whether it was called 'suburban neurosis', 'domestic stress', or 'nervous trouble', from the mid 1950s the idea that the home and woman's role within it could be the source of mental ill health gained traction across a breadth of media and professional authorities.[1] The 'problem that had no name' identified by Betty Friedan in the context of the United States, and ascribed to the unhappiness produced by an unrealistic and stultifying ideal of femininity, in fact had many names in the UK: everything on a spectrum from the 'wives at home' problem to the more medically inflected 'nervous strain', and the professional psychiatric designations of depression.[2]

Many sections of the female population were said to be affected, from the middle-class educated women who had commenced a career only to encounter loneliness, boredom, and lack of fulfilment at home when they started a family, to the wives of career-oriented husbands such as some of those interviewed for the Pahls' managers' study, and working-class women on new housing estates with limited economic resources and social capital like Sadie and Eileen who we met in Chapter 5. Women of the post-war generation who married and had children in the period between the late 1950s and early 1970s were by no means the first to experience a shock upon becoming full-time housewives and mothers. Neither were they the first to experience mental depression and other affective disorders such as anxiety, stress, and agoraphobia. But they were more likely than

[1] Jill Kirby, *Feeling the Strain. A Cultural History of Stress in Twentieth Century Britain* (Manchester: Manchester University Press, 2019), pp.133–60; Ali Haggett, *Desperate Housewives, Neuroses and the Domestic Environment 1945–1970* (London: Pickering & Chatto, 2012).

[2] Betty Friedan, *The Feminine Mystique* (London: Victor Gollancz, 1963).

Feminist Lives: Women, Feelings, and the Self in Post-War Britain. Lynn Abrams, Oxford University Press.
 DOI: 10.1093/oso/9780192896995.003.0006

generations before them to see themselves in the popular debate about female neurosis, to become the subject of research on the matter and the first to find a way of speaking about their feelings, amongst themselves and in public. Many of them also took action to effect a change in their lives. The emotions women experienced as a result of the expectations and realities of their role as wives and mothers were now more freely communicated, given space to breathe by the loosening of constraints around individual expression, and these feelings ultimately informed ideology and action.

The figure of the unhappy housewife, caught between the demands of family and the desire for personal freedom, plagued with guilt and experiencing a range of emotions from 'the miseries' to anger, anxiety, and depression, is a stereotype promoted and perpetuated between the late 1950s and the early 1970s by the media, by popular and literary culture, and by contemporary academics, professionals, and feminists. This chapter seeks to widen the scope of our understanding of women's emotional states in this period by shifting the focus away from so-called domestic neurosis and the pharmaceutical response to this phenomenon, towards a broader consideration of the causes and expressions of poor mental health and their responses to it amongst middle and working-class women, especially those who had recently married and had young children.[3] It describes the new discursive landscape of emotions that emerged from the late 1950s in Britain and argues that this brought forth a tsunami of speaking about feelings amongst ordinary women, both in public and in private. Finally it argues that although some women may have been so unwell that medical intervention via drugs or talking therapy was deemed necessary, for the vast majority the path to regaining their identity as an expressive individual was via any one of a number of self-help organizations which developed in direct response to women's distress of this period. Although it was to be the Women's Liberation Movement that was to be most closely associated with the critique of gender roles in the family, in fact women had been speaking about and acting on their feelings of entrapment for at least a decade before WLM voiced its demands.[4]

The mid twentieth century in Britain saw a marked change in attitudes to the female self—amongst women themselves, medical professionals, sociologists, popular media commentators, and feminists. The 'unhappy housewife' was widely identified by medics and psychologists as well as popular commentators in the 1950s but, unlike in earlier decades, she was not universally denigrated but rather understood as an expression of the changing realities for women in the post-war decades. Approaches to the problem—medical, therapeutic, self-reform, or

[3] Haggett has comprehensively dealt with the medical and pharmaceutical response to female neurosis in her *Desperate Housewives*, pp.75–103.

[4] BBC radio, Woman's Hour: '50 years since the first WLM conference', https://www.bbc.co.uk/programmes/m000dqyd.

radical structural change—not only varied but were contested. Here we focus on the way in which discussion of and responses to this 'problem' shifted around these poles in the period from the 1950s to the 1970s and how women themselves responded. Ideas for treatment and 'cure' were varied, with the trend to medicalization of the 1950s colliding in the 1960s and 1970s with self-care and self-help initiatives which privileged women's own interpretation of their experience and which endeavoured to build from the ground up, starting from women's material and psychological situations. This chapter traces the key trends of this transition to a new female selfhood. To do this, we listen to women's voices, filtered through medical, media, sociological, and feminist engagement with female 'neurosis' through interviews and questionnaires, as they related their personal experiences of 'the problem' to societal organization and changes in their own lives. A new discourse with multiple scripts emerged, and while some of these scripts were formed in medical and media circles, the very public recognition of the problem generated a new outpouring of self-expression. From this female expressive revolution came proto-feminist organizations offering new spaces in which to articulate and construct deeper, better-imagined vernacular feminisms. Ideas started to cement into transformative opportunities for women, especially in the 1970s. This was the ground-level genesis of a late modern feminism that would reinvent the relationships between women, work, and family.

This is a key moment in post-war women's lives, when they began to service the self rather than—or in tandem with—servicing others. We have seen how this cohort of women, especially those with economic and social capital, were often the first in their family to experience financial and personal independence. They were the first generation of women to benefit from the self-actualizing currents of the 'expressive revolution' of the 1960s when the liberationist movements of that era offered women and men the space to self-fashion and self-direct, incorporating everything from sexual choices to clothing and music.[5] Yet these currents are commonly depicted by scholars as separate from 'traditional' roles and structures such as the heterosexual family and motherhood. Furthermore, the behaviours and beliefs associated with the expressive revolution are usually seen by academics to be achieved through independent or oppositional behaviour, involvement in counter cultures or by self-examination such as consciousness-raising, or psychotherapy.[6] There is little room in this conventional story for married women with children. In part this emphasis is a result of feminist and Marxist rejection of the structures of patriarchy—marriage, domesticity, the traditional family with its gender roles—which were seen as oppressive of women and incapable of

[5] The term 'expressive revolution' was coined by Talcott Parsons in 'Religion in Postindustrial America: The Problem of Secularization', *Social Research* 41:2 (1974), pp.193–225.

[6] Bernice Martin, *A Sociology of Contemporary Cultural Change* (Oxford: Blackwell, 1981). For a discussion of how this impacted on women's narratives of the period see Abrams, 'Heroes of their own life stories'.

nurturing authentic behaviours or new practices of care. Feminists in particular, at least in the early years of the women's movement in the 1970s, while recognizing and problematizing women's emotional distress with its roots in the domestic, sought to channel those feelings into action to challenge patriarchal systems and structures. They continued to see the home and its gender roles contingent upon marriage, home-making and childcare as a site of neurosis for women without acknowledging the need and desire of many women of all social classes for security and self-fulfilment that came with a home of one's own and a family.[7] The feminist critique of the medical response to women's poor mental health—that in prescribing drugs doctors were merely enabling women's adjustment to the patriarchal system that was itself the cause of their symptoms—failed to take seriously most women's desire to maintain their sense of self, their individuality, in the context of family life, not outside it.

Cynthia's Story

Cynthia was a successful journalist on a local newspaper in the early 1960s. Her career came to an abrupt end after having three children in quick succession. As one of few female reporters she had enjoyed the advantages of working in a predominantly male environment and experienced personal and financial independence at a young age. But in the absence of childcare and discouraged by her former editor who, when she requested a part-time role responded by saying 'no, my dear, your place is with the children now', Cynthia quickly became isolated from the world of work, a feeling recalled in a vignette which encapsulated her predicament. 'Oh yes, I have a very distinct memory of a colleague coming to see me, and she had been the Woman's Editor, and had just come back from the Paris Shows, and I was with sort of dribble all down my front (laughing).' Cynthia had 'what anyone else would have called a breakdown' and was prescribed the popular sedative Librium by her doctor, a drug widely used to treat anxiety. She also engaged an au pair to help with three children in nappies. But the key to Cynthia's recovery—both in terms of her mental health and her reclamation of a self that she recognized—was firstly attending a public speaking class at the invitation of a friend. 'And the first thing we did when we got there was deep breathing and relaxation…I came home the first night saying: 'Wow! I feel better than I've felt for ages.' And then a neighbour suggested that she could have a break from her eldest child:

[7] Susie Orbach speaking about the women's therapy centre: Sisterhood and After https://www.bl.uk/sisterhood–and Sarah Crook, 'The Women's Liberation Movement, Activism and Therapy at the Grassroots, 1968–1985', *Women's History Review* 27:7 (2018), pp.1152–68.

> [A]nd I remember that I took him to the playgroup and left him and got home and realized that I'd also left the pushchair with the second one in!...and the third one I was just as poorly when he was three...it was sort of '69 I began to feel better, and he was two coming on to three, and someone said, 'oh, there's a course for Mother Helpers at the Octagon, would you like to go to that?' And so I went along with him, and that was the beginning, really.[8]

While the sedatives took the edge of Cynthia's anxiety, they made her feel 'sort of woolly, and only half with it'. It was self-help and the networks of friends she established that really aided her recovery. The public speaking class was Cynthia's breakthrough moment, but her involvement with the Pre-School Playgroup movement was a critical therapeutic experience which enabled her to travel from 'Depressed mum of three to PG [Play group]/PPA training'. Thereafter she became a local authority social worker and then co-founder of a therapeutic community for women with mental health problems. Cynthia described her experience using some of the classic tropes of the feminography:

> In the first three years as a mother it seemed as if I had lost all status and excitement from my life. I slipped into a depressed state and was prescribed the then 'wonder' pill Librium. But here in the playgroup was a new beginning. I was greeted warmly, made to feel I had something to offer the group and then applauded for my usefulness...Over the next decade I moved on with confidence through further courses, tutor group...and then to a national PPA committee. At home I watched our sons grow with new enthusiasm and was soon involved with Open University in my 'spare' time. This led into a Social Services post as a Playgroups and Childminding Officer covering a third of Norfolk, and then an MA in Social Work.[9]

Cynthia's psychological reaction to the dramatic change in her life, from trainee reporter in an environment in which she detected 'a bit more equality', to stay-at-home mother, was not uncommon albeit at the more serious end of the scale. She had lost the 'labels for the self' to use Barbara Taylor's description.[10] Many young mothers of the 1960s who suddenly found themselves in the house all day with only young children to talk to and with few friends or family in the vicinity, reported a range of symptoms on a spectrum from feeling frustrated, bored, and under-stimulated at one end, to full-blown depression at the other. And whilst the incidence of depression and anxiety amongst women in these decades was

[8] Interview with Cynthia.

[9] IoE, PLA/PPA 6/1 (3): Memories of Playgroups: Cynthia Robinson.

[10] Barbara Taylor, *The Last Asylum. A Memoir of Madness in our Times* (London: Penguin, 2014), p.119.

almost certainly exaggerated by some social scientists and also by feminists who regarded the home as a structural site of oppression, there is no doubt that some women in Cynthia's shoes were momentarily stopped in their tracks by the everyday realities of a domestic life and their temporary loss of identity.

For women like Cynthia, the prescription of an anti-depressant to treat her mental health problem, albeit by a sympathetic doctor, was a sticking plaster, helpful in the short term but not effective in treating the underlying causes. However, involvement in a local woman-centred self-help group provided Cynthia with a stepping-stone to recovery and self-fulfilment. She discovered a fascination with child development and with the structures of engagement facilitated by the playgroup movement whereby participants could graduate from volunteer mother-helper a few hours a week to local committee work and fundraising and eventually training courses leading to greater responsibility within the Pre-School Playgroup organization. Like thousands of other women, Cynthia made social connections and gained new skills and confidence which, in turn, brought about the reclaiming or rediscovery of the self.

Cynthia's openness about her own mental health problems, both at the time and subsequently in writing and in interview, is illustrative of how, in this context, women began to give themselves permission to talk about their feelings. Liberated from the constraints experienced by their mothers' generation who were more likely to suppress their emotions or at least not openly express negative feelings about their role in the home, Cynthia and other women like her were given greater licence by the more open landscape of feeling to share their emotions, with friends and family but also with professionals and they, in turn, were more willing to listen.

Unhappy Housewives

The figure of the unhappy housewife has been a constant in public debate and scholarly research since the 1930s, reaching a peak in the 1960s and early 1970s. In Britain *The Lancet* had been the initial conduit for claims of suburban neurosis by Dr Stephen Taylor in 1938 when he influentially described the rise in the number of 'young women with anxiety states'. The patients, according to Taylor, were bored young (lower middle class) housewives who had moved to the new interwar housing estates: 'Existence in the suburbs is such that the self preserving, race-preserving and herd instincts can be neither adequately satisfied nor sublimated.' The result was pathological anxiety. The causes according to Taylor? Boredom, not enough to do, lack of friends, worries about money and ultimately 'a false set of values'. 'The suburban woman', he announced, 'has made a fetish of the home.' 'The small labour-saving house, the small family and the few friends have left women of the suburbs relatively idle. They have nothing to look forward to, nothing to look up to, and little to live for.'[11] Twenty years later *The Lancet's* editorial argued there was reason to believe that 'the risk of neurotic reactions' had lessened in the new towns owing to improved planning, yet the risk was said to be still present in the plethora of new out-of-town estates. Citing evidence from one 'out-county municipal estate' where the incidence of so-called 'neurotic symptoms' was significantly higher than the expected average, the influential journal announced in 1958: 'Here then is the suburban neurosis presenting itself again' and once more, it was ascribed to the women who 'tended to follow the obsolescent middle-class pattern of social isolation as a standard of respectability'.[12]

Suburban neurosis as a phenomenon then was regarded by doctors and commentators from the 1930s onwards as a 'woman problem' associated with women's relationship with the home. Here was a group of women whose housing conditions had been vastly improved but who failed to thrive because of their isolation, boredom, and lack of meaningful social contact. With the building of new housing estates and new towns across Britain after the war, a number of variables of 'suburban neurosis' were proposed including the 'new town blues', 'high flats neurosis' and 'estate neurosis'. A series of studies demonstrated that Taylor's initial proposition was unfounded—there was no significant increased incidence of GP consultations for minor neurosis in new neighbourhoods with the exception of high flats.[13] Yet some women did find adaptation to their new environment and circumstances difficult, at least in the short term, and some clearly experienced a shock on moving away from established networks (often to follow a husband's employment) and spending the day at home looking after young children as opposed to being in the workplace. Even in leafy Richmond in south London, it was reported that women with young children who moved to new council flats were driven out of their minds by loneliness, the absence of friendly neighbours and nowhere for children to play.[14] The everyday routine of housework and motherhood could be oppressive and stultifying. The writer Penelope Mortimer discovered this after giving birth to her sixth child. 'Instead of the relative freedom of the past four years there were broken nights, nappies, feeds. I was harassed, dull company, trying to write another novel, reluctant even to go to the pub.'[15] A temporary solution was to take 'uppers'—'I felt they supplied something I lacked that other women presumably had', allowing her to work through the night. When it was realized she was not just 'in the dumps', 'it was arranged that I should see a Dr Fieldman', a Freudian psychoanalyst. In her notebook written

[11] Stephen Taylor, 'The Suburban Neurosis', *The Lancet* 231, no.5978 (1938).

[12] R. E. Barrett, 'Suburban Neurosis Up to Date', *The Lancet* 271 no.7017 (1958), p.429.

[13] See for example, S.D. Coleman, *Mental Health and Social Adjustment in a New Town: An Exploratory Study in East Kilbride* (University of Glasgow, 1965).

[14] LSE, Women's Library: 5WAM/1, WAM Newsletter, November 1971, pp.4–5.

[15] Penelope Mortimer, *About Time Too, 1940–1978* (London: Phoenix, 1994), p.52.

contemporaneously in 1956 Mortimer expressed the entrapment she felt, in her body and in her domestic set up:

> A lax umbilical cord goes from this chair along the hall and up the stairs and through the rickety bars of his cot. I feel it and he doesn't…If only one lived in another age, if only everything wasn't imprisoned in this body, belted and covered and clamped and sitting upright in a hard armchair.
>
> After that there's no more to say. I would like to write for hours but there isn't any more, so I'll get up and hobble somewhere, upstairs or down, in my tight skirt; apologize to the children.[16]

Of course Mortimer's frustrations were those of the economically and socially privileged woman who was habituated to self-expression through her writing (and to managing her own time) and who was now tied to the rigid routines of motherhood. For women without Mortimer's advantages, such as those living in high-rise flats, on new social housing estates and in more traditional working-class communities, isolation was often compounded by poverty, poor housing, and absence of amenities in the vicinity as well as rigid gender roles which offered women little relief from the daily round of housework and childcare. One Scottish study conducted in areas of need in 1977 remarked upon the 'enormous' difficulties faced by women 'and all…face them alone inasmuch as their families are usually unable or unwilling to provide any support and the husband or co-habitees feel little or no obligation to the children.'[17] Living in cramped accommodation with no access to respite from young children, and lacking an escape through work or a social life, women in these conditions felt cooped up and anxious.[18]

The commonplace medical response to the presentation of 'neurotic' symptoms by women in this period was prescription of tranquillizing or anti-depressant drugs. From the 1950s, medical professionals were labelling a wide range of symptoms experienced by women as a neurosis. This was accompanied by a widening of definitions of mental disorder to include those on the neurotic spectrum and 'problems of daily living' which had the effect of pathologizing conditions formerly understood as social.[19] The psychiatric profession began to understand certain disorders as socially constructed as opposed to ascribing them to a pre-existing organic pathology which meant that more minor neurotic disorders began to be taken seriously and medicated. In the 1960s a range of affective or mood disorders (such as anxiety, depression but also including OCD, agoraphobia, and bi-polar syndrome) were now more commonly treated with

[16] Mortimer, *About Time Too*, p.55.

[17] IoE, PPA 2/28: Playgroups in Areas of Need Report, 1977.

[18] See Lynn Abrams et al., 'Isolated and Dependent: Women and Children in High Rise Social Housing in Post-War Glasgow', *Women's History Review* 28:5 (2019), pp.794–813.

[19] Haggett, *Desperate Housewives*, p.105.

drugs including tranquillizers or sedatives and antidepressants as pharmaceutical companies began to compete to offer medications in this new lucrative market.[20] GPs, as Cynthia discovered, could be sympathetic to women who approached them for help for a range of disorders and psychological conditions, but were likely to prescribe chemical as opposed to alternative, that is psychiatric or self-help, interventions. Librium and, in the UK, Valium (diazepam), were widely prescribed as anxiety relievers for a range of 'non-specific emotional disorders' and despite some concerns about the extent of prescribing and the potential for dependency, pharmacological treatment of affective disorders was accepted as the norm through the 1960s, especially as alternative psychotherapeutic interventions such as one-to-one therapy were deemed impractical in the primary care environment.[21] By 1970 doctors had issued more than 12 million prescriptions for Librium, Valium, and Mogadon, the majority of them to women.[22]

Beyond the medicalization of women's mental health however, there is another story to tell which centres on the growing recognition and normalization of stress and anxiety as a product of women's everyday life. Women's subjective feelings across a broad spectrum from boredom and frustration to depression and nervous breakdown, became the object of research by social and medical researchers in the 1960s and 1970s, and of interest for the print and broadcast media and women's organizations, in the process creating a new landscape of feeling in which women could place themselves and a language with which they could talk about how they felt.

Talking about Feelings

In 1966 *The Times* newspaper ran an advertisement in *Nova*, the new upmarket magazine marketed at 'the new kind of woman [who] has a wide range of interests, an inquiring mind and an independent outlook'.[23] Headlined, 'When you've only the baby to talk to', the advert was illustrated by a photograph of a fashionably made-up woman holding a crying baby and aimed to appeal to educated young mothers who missed the stimulation of the workplace.

> you sometimes wish it were you going to the office instead of your husband. Not that you're bored exactly, or would want to leave the baby for long. But you miss being with people on your own wavelength. You miss the talk, discussions—even the casual remarks on what's happening, what's new and what isn't... Taking *The Times* everyday can't change this of course, but it *can* help. It *can* give you

[20] Haggett, *Desperate Housewives*, pp.75–103. [21] Haggett, *Desperate Housewives*, p.100.
[22] Crook, 'The Women's Liberation Movement', p.1155.
[23] On the editorial approach of *Nova* see White, *Women's Magazines*, pp.222–4.

> the intellectual stimulation you're missing. It *can* give you the discussions... and it can take you to all the exhibitions, all the shows, all the films, all the sales, with critics who respect your intelligence as much as their own.[24]

The Times cleverly tapped into a popular discourse on the conflicts and dissatisfaction experienced by stay-at-home mothers. The work versus family dilemma had been addressed since the 1950s, especially in relation to college-educated women who, according to graduate mother Judith Hubback, were not given the opportunities to use all their capacities once they gave up a career upon having children. University-educated women were faced with a limited range of occupations with teaching being the most favoured, seen as appropriate to the female sex and accommodating of family life. But even teachers faced discrimination when they tried to return to work after having children.[25] Hubback's *Wives Who Went to College* appeared in 1957 and was the first broadside in the public debate addressing the difficulties faced by college-educated women who wanted family and a satisfying career.[26] Hubback advocated more flexible and part-time opportunities as well as support for those who wanted to refresh or retrain. Her intervention sparked much media interest and responses from women on both sides of the argument, preparing the ground for a broader public discussion about the frustrations of this cohort of women spread across the broadcast and print media.[27]

Hubback wrote about the 'grit of discontent' within educated women who were unable to fulfil their potential in the workplace.[28] That piece of grit worried away at Hubback herself who sought help from psychotherapy for depression.[29] That being unfulfilled could have consequences for women's mental health was beginning to pervade public consciousness. The BBC was alert to women's mental health issues via its 'Can I Help You?' unit and the letters received from the radio programme Woman's Hour 'listeners in distress'. Amongst the 540 letters received in 1960 were those detailing marital problems, post-natal depression, loneliness, and a variety of mental health conditions including agoraphobia.[30] A year later, two years before the publication of Betty Friedan's *The Feminine Mystique,* and

[24] *Nova*, October 1966.

[25] Sarah Aiston, 'A Good Job for a Girl? The Career Biographies of Women Graduates of the University of Liverpool Post-1945', *Twentieth Century British History* 15:4 (2004), pp.361–87, 383.

[26] Judith Hubback, *Wives Who Went to College* (London: 1957). Hubback, a history graduate, anticipated the social scientist Viola Klein's more extensive study of married female graduates by several years. See Helen McCarthy, 'Career, Family and Emotional Work', p.295.

[27] On the reception of Hubback's work see McCarthy, *Double Lives*, pp.261–5.

[28] Hubback, *Wives Who Went to College*, p.79.

[29] Hubback went on to train and practice as a Jungian analyst. Barbara Wharton and Jan Wiener, 'Judith Hubback: Obituary', *The Guardian*, 7 February 2006.

[30] BBC Written Archive Centre: Woman's Hour BBC R51-774-1: 'Listeners in Distress', 1960. A report by the 'Can I help you' unit responded to an enquiry from the National Association of Mental Health concerned about the fate of these letters. On the role of the BBC in raising awareness of postnatal depression in particular see Sarah Crook, *Postnatal Depression in Postwar Britain: Women, Motherhood, and Social Change* (forthcoming).

several years before Gavron's *The Captive Wife*, the journalist and television presenter Elaine Grand hosted a four-part series on BBC afternoon television's *Family Affairs* programme on the subject of 'The Married Woman's Place' addressing issues of loneliness and boredom at home, combining home and full-time work and training for work in middle age.[31] In a follow-up article for *The Observer* provocatively headlined 'Miserable Married Women', Grand claimed that the programmes had attracted a 'flood of letters' from women, with 75 per cent of them (the majority under the age of 35) saying 'yes, we *are* bored and lonely'.[32] And it was claimed that more than 200 women penned letters responding to the articles.[33] One wrote: 'Only those who have been through it can understand the torture and the strain... One's mind goes round and round trying to escape... I have almost lost all hope of feeling normal again... There are many like us, please help us save our reason.'[34] Correspondents told of their feelings of inferiority as housewives, being 'haunted by the sense of wasted time', guilt and 'despair over wasted training and skills'. And the spectre of mental illness was raised. 'I would like to see some figures on the mental disturbance of women who are temperamentally unsuited to an exclusively housebound existence' wrote one. Yet Grand opined that these letters did not come from 'neurotics or hysterics'. Rather, such women were lonely and unfulfilled:

> Bringing up children is *not* always a full time job and though it requires patience, understanding and a good deal of intelligence, it does not stretch the intellectual facilities, and it is these which I find so neglected that in the end I fear they may be totally atrophied. In two or three years my youngest child will join the other three at school but by that time I shall probably be so cabbage like that there will be no hope for me.[35]

Grand had evidently struck a chord. She had tapped a vein of frustration articulated by women who may have experienced further or higher education and had commenced careers only to be 'trapped' in full-time housewifery and motherhood as a result of social expectations and the absence of affordable and accessible childcare. Jessica Mann was typical. Married in 1959 at the age of 21, just a week after graduating from Cambridge (a not uncommon pattern amongst her cohort of female graduates),[36] Jessica reflected on the next few years during which she and her husband had four children:

[31] BBC Programme Index: Radio Times, 'Family Affairs' programme content, 19 January, 26 January, 2 February 1961. https://genome.ch.bbc.co.uk/issues.

[32] 'Miserable married women': *Observer*, 7 May 1961.

[33] 'Miserable married women: Final diagnosis', *The Observer*, 28 May, 1961.

[34] 'Miserable married women', *Observer*, 7 May 1961.

[35] 'Miserable Married Women', *Observer*, 7 May 1961.

[36] Pat Thane, 'Girton graduates: Earning and learning, 1920s–1980s', *Women's History Review* 13:3 (2004), pp.347–61.

> A married woman's life was easier only in the sense that a prisoner's life is easy—difficult choices were made for you... Having achieved exactly what every girl was supposed to long for then, I knew I ought to be satisfied. Instead I was prey to a mixture of undesirable emotions. There was boredom... There was frustration – surely there ought to be something else? And there was shame – why wasn't I happy when I had everything women were supposed to want?[37]

Through the course of the 1960s the theme of the wife and mother suffering from lack of stimulation was a regular topic for journalists in the quality press. *Nova* was typical. It was a magazine that sought to attract a readership who was looking for intelligent debate and which, as one reader put it, 'was about you as an "about to be", or "a bit", independent woman.'[38] *Nova* spoke to the frustrations of women who cavilled against convention and in its associate editor, Alma Birk, it had someone who recognized that between the agony columns of *Woman* and the fashion pages of *Vogue* were thousands of women in desperate straits, for whom marriage was not working out as a story with a happy ending. 'They were educated women stuck at home and they were women who had never realized they had any potential at all. It was to these readers that *Nova* was dedicated, in her own mind.'[39] Typical articles were 'The Marriage Roundabout' in 1965 featuring the case of a young woman trapped at home with young children and frustrated with her lot, and 'Walled in Wives' to mark the publication of Gavron's *Captive Wife* followed by the publication of readers' letters expressing a range of views from those castigating the 'self-pity' of 'neurotic housewives' to those who treated it as a 'call to action'. 'I feel so fed up with my self-absorption' wrote one correspondent.

> However I have done something about me. There was a time when I wept alone on the street with my pram—and I never want to repeat that. I don't know the full solution, but I have some suggestions. Don't let us continue our lonely agonies: it's time people recognized that the enormous number of women in this position indicates something is very wrong somewhere.[40]

A year later an article with the plaintive title, 'Darling please talk to me' featured a fictitious woman who gave up her job upon marriage 'to be the sort of wife his mother had been.'

> I really had the impression that housewives were a dreary little body of ladies who hadn't much initiative and who like to sit at home drinking coffee all day,

[37] Jessica Mann, 'What good old days?', *The Guardian*, 28 April 2012.
[38] Alice Beard, 'Nova Magazine, 1965–1975: a History', PhD thesis, University of London, 2013, p.296.
[39] Linda Grant, *Sexing the Millennium: Political History of the Sexual Revolution* (London: Harper Collins, 1993), p.100.
[40] *Nova*, January 1967: 'Letters'.

> arrange the flowers, read the newspapers and wonder what to do with themselves. Now I know differently and it's very unfair. I don't really resent my role in life, but the burden – it's not really a burden is it? .... He has all the going out and the social and I have all the staying in and the babies... I'm well aware that every day I grow farther away from the original girl I was when Charles met me. [41]

Nova was not alone in documenting the discontent women were experiencing in the home and articulating the feeling so many had of losing sight of the woman they had been before they had children. Indeed, as Moskowitz demonstrates in the American context, women's magazines contributed to the discourse of discontent by acknowledging women's dissatisfaction and normalizing their feelings.[42] Such magazines, she argues, helped to create a tension between a set of domestic ideals and women's frustration at not being able to meet these ideals. In the UK the more conservative women's magazines such as *Woman's Own*, were more likely to feature correspondence in the problem pages regarding 'nerves' and anxiety. While these complaints were rarely explicitly linked to women's role in the home, the simple acknowledgement that women suffered from these complaints and could be treated for them, for the most part with various forms of self care but also with the prescribing of the new psychotropic drugs, was part and parcel of an emerging culture which permitted women to acknowledge their feelings.[43] It was to be *The Guardian* newspaper, however, and its 'Mainly for Women' section under the editorial direction of Mary Stott which became more than a sounding board for women's frustrations. It became a vector in the emergence of women's self help by offering space, not only to those who had an opinion to express on the subject but those who wanted to do something about it. We will return to the place of self help later in this chapter.

Researching Women's Feelings

By the end of the 1960s the emotional restraint that had so dominated British culture until the 1960s began to be relaxed and researchers from the medical and social sciences were beneficiaries. Now people had a language to describe how they felt and the confidence to know they were not alone with their feelings of anxiety, depression, and frustration. In 1972 the National Survey of Health and Development asked its then 26-year-old respondents, whether they experienced

[41] *Nova*, March 1965 and April 1968.

[42] Eva Moskowitz, '"It's Good to Blow Your Top": Women's Magazines and a Discourse of Discontent, 1945–1965', *Journal of Women's History*, 8:3 (1996), pp.66–98.

[43] See Haggett, *Desperate Housewives*, pp.114–16 for analysis of the impact of the print media.

'nervous strain' in their work or in their home and personal life.[44] The survey's interest in mental health was part of a much wider movement across the medical and social sciences at this time to make mental ill health visible in order to make interventions from a variety of professional and social activist standpoints. This was the first time the 1946 birth cohort had been asked in a face-to-face interview to report on their mental health, though respondents also sometimes volunteered information about the state of their mental health in the open comments sections of questionnaires and since the age of 16 visits to a doctor had been recorded and a 'susceptibility to anxiety' was calculated.[45] At this point many of the cohort were married with young children so it is perhaps unsurprising that significantly more women reported experiencing nervous trouble than men: 25 per cent of all women who responded compared with just 12 per cent of men.[46] It seems that the language used by the survey—nervous trouble or strain rather than more medicalized terms—was recognized by respondents and perhaps especially by women, bearing in mind the lower likelihood that men would report or seek medical help for symptoms and women's greater exposure to discourses centring on female mental health in the popular media.[47] When offered the opportunity to elaborate, many women mentioned their 'nerves', a catch-all term that had been commonplace in popular discourse for much of the twentieth century, incorporating a broad range of symptoms, everything from worry and short temperedness to depression and mental illness serious enough to require hospitalization.[48] One woman, a working-class housewife with two young children who had recently moved to a housing estate, reported 'some' nervous strain at home but put it down to 'the children—they start shouting and bawling—get on my nerves'. 'I sit down & have a good "greet" [cry] to myself.'[49]

Just 5 years later they were asked again at age 31 whether they were under strain at home or at work, and again more women than men reported strain at home (30 per cent of women compared with 21 per cent of men reported some or

[44] MRC, NSHD: personal questionnaire A, 1972: 'Would you say in your home and personal life you are under: Severe nervous strain; Some nervous strain; Little or no nervous strain—If severe or some could you say what the main cause is and how it affects you. Q10: have you had any nervous trouble—if so when did it start, what kind of trouble and how did it affect you.'

[45] This was calculated using a neuroticism score (a score of more than 6 on the neuroticism scale of the MPI being regarded as a high score) and one of 'nervous trouble'. A survey member who had consulted a doctor for at least a minor psychological problem between 16 and 26 years was regarded as being 'at risk' on this measure. N. Cherry, 'Women and Work Stress: Evidence from the 1946 Birth Cohort', *Ergonomics* 27 (1984), pp.519–26.

[46] MRC, NSHD: Skylark—NERVRE72. doi: 10.5522/NSHD/Q101

Frequency was higher in numerical terms amongst women in social classes II and III (intermediate and skilled non-manual). Amongst women who were in full-time work, on the other hand, the rate of nervous strain as compared with working men was very similar.

[47] See Haggett, *Desperate Housewives*, pp.108–10 for a discussion of problems with these kinds of surveys.

[48] LSE, Women's Library: 5WAM/2: a study report 'Playspace in Richmond' (1972) cited a number of mothers suffering from 'nerves' and 'tension', p.10.

[49] MRC, NSHD: Sample 34—personal questionnaire 1972.

severe strain). The survey's interest in the incidence and causes of stress continued into the 1980s, though by then the terminology had changed. Respondents were asked in 1982 whether they suffered from 'nervous or emotional trouble or persistent depression'.[50] More women than men answered in the affirmative—17.6 per cent of women and only 8.4 per cent of men. And finally, in 1989 when respondents were asked to look back over their adult life and consider whether nervous or emotional trouble had 'ever stopped you from working or doing domestic chores or having social contacts for a fortnight or longer?' 15 per cent of female respondents replied yes compared with 10 per cent of men and it is notable that the highest percentage of those women who reported in the affirmative belonged to the unskilled—26 per cent—compared with just 6 per cent of professionals.[51]

Only 15 per cent reported more debilitating and long-term mental health problems over the life course, generally following trauma such as miscarriage, death of a child, or breakdown of a marriage. A working-class woman who had left school at 15 and had a number of jobs from machinist to shop assistant before she married in 1967 and had a child, reported in 1968 that although she had a happy marriage: 'When I left work I was very sad and lonely. But I have got over that now.' Four years later she lost a child shortly after the birth and reported 'depression brought on by death of baby'.[52] Similarly a woman who, at 20 years old, was married with a child and living with her in-laws reported being 'very happy about married life' and this continued when they moved to a flat of their own. But in 1971 this woman experienced a miscarriage which precipitated a period of depression, treated by her doctor with 'pills'—'Everything was too much trouble, just couldn't cope'.[53] These findings are supported by Roberts' earlier research in 1964 on 'housebound housewives'—women with agoraphobia—which demonstrated that their phobic anxiety symptoms had been triggered by traumatic events or severe illness. While the majority of patients were described as house-proud and meticulously tidy, there was no suggestion that their domestic role was the cause of their anxiety symptoms.[54]

And the NSHD data tended to show that for the majority of women, marriage, home life, and children tended to bring contentment. It was paid work that caused them stress, countering the popular view that it was entrapment in the home that caused women to develop neuroses. 'I dislike my job intensely', 'Makes my nerves bad—get depressed, makes me irritable'. Yet the small number of women in my

[50] MRC, NSHD, main questionnaire 1982.
[51] MRC, NSHD: Skylark NERV89. doi:10.5522/NSHD/Q101.
[52] MRC, NSHD: Sample 41—personal questionnaire 1968.
[53] MRC, NSHD: Sample 22—personal questionnaires, 1968, 1971. Sample 36 also experienced 3 months depression after miscarriage—postal questionnaire 1972.
[54] A. H. Roberts 'Housebound Housewives: A Follow-Up Study of a Phobic Anxiety State', *British Journal of Psychiatry* 110 no.465 (1964), pp.191–7.

sample who ascribed their nerves to their work cannot, perhaps surprisingly, be seen as an indicative of a larger trend of nervous illness contingent upon more women taking on the double burden of work and family. These two women did not have children and one was single. 'I've had to learn to live with the fact that I don't like my job' reported a librarian who disliked contact with the public. But she traced her 'nervous trouble' to her early twenties: 'Anxiety neurosis—caused by strain of examinations and after that the strain of [illegible] my work.'[55] More commonly women commented on the intensity of work which brought on 'nervous strain'. 'You work on your nerves. You're up against it all the time' commented a journalist who also admitted to a history of anxiety and depression which 'started at 25. Physically and mentally exhausted and I was put on tranquilizers, off work for 3 weeks.' 'I was tearful and depressed and constantly exhausted no matter how much sleep I got and very worked up.'[56]

The language of nervous strain and mental illness was not alien to the women surveyed by the NSHD though they employed vernacular descriptors to articulate their feelings: 'nerves', getting 'worked up' and not able to cope.[57] And their reported symptoms ranged across a spectrum from stomach upsets at the milder end to serious psychiatric illness treated with ECT. This group had become acculturated to reporting on all aspects of their health and lifestyle—the survey was in touch with them almost every year—so it is likely they would have been more open than their peers when asked to respond to questions about their mental health. Moreover, they had grown up with background noise concerning psychiatric problems from mild anxiety and frustration to more serious mental illness to women of their age group. And this was a cohort of women who, if they experienced anxiety or stress, would have seen themselves reflected back in a plethora of media outlets, all of which saw female neurosis as a legitimate talking point.

Feminist researchers also sought to make visible women's distress, though their enquiries were framed by a different agenda to most medics and social scientists, understanding that the language and conceptualization of 'suburban neurosis' misrepresented and misunderstood the symptoms of stress and anxiety articulated by women of all social classes.[58] Following on the heels of Judith Hubback, Alva Myrdal and Viola Klein, and Pearl Jephcott who had already written about the conflicts of home and work, Hannah Gavron's research in the 1960s identified the 'conflicts' of young middle- and working-class women who were caught between emancipatory impulses and gendered expectations and structures pertaining to housework and childcare. Gavron was a young mother herself, and was

[55] MRC, NSHD: Sample 19—personal questionnaire 1972.

[56] MRC, NSHD: Sample 49—personal questionnaire 1972.

[57] The language of coping is much used by Ann Oakley's respondents in *Becoming a Mother*, indicating a sense that they should have been able to manage the demands of new motherhood.

[58] Hera Cook, 'From Controlling Emotion to Expressing Feelings in Mid-Twentieth-Century England', *Journal of Social History* 47:3 (2014), pp.627–46.

'chafing at the restrictions on her free time', 'always rushing in and out of the house in a hurry' as she tried to combine her research on the 'conflicts of house-bound mothers' with being the mother of a child of three and a four-month old baby, albeit she employed a nanny.[59] She showed that all women experienced, to some degree, 'conflict and stress' as a result of the contradictions between societal expectations and women's own desires and aspirations.[60] The strains of poor-quality housing, absence of support networks, and insufficient resources to alleviate these conditions left many young working-class mothers isolated with little meaningful contact with the outside world and looking forward to when they could return to paid work. Middle-class women, while more outward looking and less socially isolated, still expressed dissatisfaction with the 'relentless boredom' and the feeling that their role in the home was not valued.[61] Gavron's study, published posthumously as *The Captive Wife* in 1966 after her suicide the year before, was timely and pioneering. As with so many feminist researchers she pursued a line of enquiry that had its roots in her own experience of refusing to accept the constraints imposed on her as a woman.

Ann Oakley similarly adopted a qualitative approach as a means of giving women the space to articulate their feelings in their own words as opposed to merely recording the supposed symptoms of affective disorders. A few years after Gavron, in 1971 Oakley conducted 40 interviews with housewives in London from which four were used as the focus for her pathbreaking study *Housewife* which provided a historical and contemporary analysis of women's subordination to domesticity. Juliet Warren had been a stay-at-home mother for a year and was still finding the transition difficult. Juliet had been a television production assistant in London, a job she enjoyed and which involved a lot of contact with people. 'Well, I haven't really come to terms with it all yet' was her response when asked what she was doing to get out of the house.[62] Her husband was supportive and she was financially well off; she enjoyed her baby too but she had not come to accept her role as a housewife: 'If I was asked to put my occupation on a form I wouldn't put "housewife", I'd put "mother", I would hate to think of myself just being a housewife. I think that's why I'm so frustrated: I really cannot come to terms with the fact that I am.'[63] The sentiment that one no longer recognized the self or indeed had become invisible was commonplace. 'Measured by the values of a society like ours', commented a woman correspondent to *The Times* in 1961, 'where the real business of life is held to be what people do in their working hours, I'm standing still. I don't exist.'[64]

[59] Jeremy Gavron, *A Woman on the Edge of Time: A Son Investigates His Trailblazing Mother's Young Suicide* (London: Experiment, 2016), pp.122–5.

[60] Gavron, *Captive Wife*, pp.144–5.

[61] Gavron, *Captive Wife*, pp.95–100 (working-class women); p.132 (middle-class women).

[62] Oakley, *Housewife*, p.118.

[63] Oakley, *Housewife*, p.125.

[64] Cited in Gavron, *Captive Wife*, p.132.

While Juliet's experience fits the commonly understood model of the frustrated housewife of this period, another of Oakley's 'housewives'—Sally—described the travails of a working-class wife and mother, trapped in a marriage characterized by traditional gender roles. 'I'm going through a nervous depression at the moment' she reported.[65] Her daily routine comprised cleaning, cooking, and taking care of the children with no help from her husband and fitted around a part-time job. She had little social life and her work, whilst unskilled, provided her with social contact and extra money to supplement the housekeeping. Sally does not conform to the stereotype of the suburban neurotic. Resigned to her lot, she was nevertheless determined to hold on to her identity. 'I think of myself as a housewife, but I don't think of myself as a cabbage.'[66] Bored with the drudgery and monotony of housework and unable to escape her marriage which she described as 'like boss and employee', Sally perhaps had many reasons to be feeling depressed, not least a history of miscarriages and stillbirth. For Oakley, Sally was oppressed as a housewife and she interpreted her reference to seeing her doctor for her 'nerves'—'He could help me, give me some pills'—as the 'conventional psychoanalytical interpretation of a female disorder'.[67] Oakley evidently gave Sally the space to open up about her feelings and to express her conflicted views on her situation. And in this context it is significant that Sally spoke freely about her 'nervous depression' and her 'nerves', using the vernacular to describe her emotions. Oakley's interviews were undertaken at a turning point in British culture when emotional authenticity and the promotion of and search for personal growth was in the ascendant. Her own feminist research practice was part of a wider reaction to the social-scientific method of gathering data and a desire to allow women to speak for themselves. And in producing a book from women's accounts that combined or intermeshed her professional perspective with her personal experience, Oakley was following the first signs of an expressive wave that understood emotions as legitimate and meaningful but expanding that space to include women's voices.[68]

In her extensive and repeated interviews with first-time mothers, Oakley uncovered a spectrum of emotions amongst women who had recently given birth in the mid 1970s including post-partum depression, but they struggled to articulate how they felt in the absence of a framework and language to describe and account for it.[69] Sandy admitted she lacked confidence 'and you're nervous the whole time'. Once she returned home from hospital she 'was pretty depressed those first few days', struggled with managing her daughter's routine and 'started

[65] Oakley, *Housewife*, p.153.

[66] Oakley, *Housewife*, p.153.

[67] Oakley, *Housewife*, p.142.

[68] Oakley, 'Introduction' in *Here to Maternity;* Ann Oakley, *Taking it Like a Woman* (London: Flamingo, 1984) which intertwines autobiography with fiction.

[69] See Carla Pascoe-Leahy, *Becoming a Mother: An Australian History* (Manchester: Manchester University Press, 2023).

to get a bit upset about it all'. 'I haven't taken to motherhood very well, I don't think. I don't know if it's a general feeling.'[70] Maureen spoke with more certainty about her diagnosis: 'But it was terrible. I felt really awful. I've never *ever* felt like that in my life. I thought I was going mad. I thought I was going peculiar... I mean I'd heard about baby blues—I mean postnatal depression...but to feel that bad with it, I don't think I've ever cried so much in all me life.'[71] Some decades later, when re-interviewed about her experience, Maureen told the story of her depression in a very similar way, while emphasizing the support she received from her husband and parents and acknowledging that speaking to Ann Oakley had been helpful 'because...she knew people who'd had similar experiences and it was just nice to have somebody to talk to...I mean if it can help someone else, I think it's very good.'[72]

In facilitating women to talk about motherhood in honest ways, Oakley highlighted the role that mothers played in recognizing the meanings of their unhappiness and the impact on this of a feminist consciousness. Women experiencing some form of postpartum depression, more commonly known as the 'baby blues' at the mild, mood disorder end of the spectrum though postpartum depression and psychosis were the more serious and long-lasting conditions, talked freely to Oakley at a time when public understanding of the condition was poor.[73] In 1960 the National Childbirth Trust (NCT) implemented a new service called 'the friendly ear' whereby three NCT members were available to any new mother, to visit or telephone at any time of the day or night, to combat post-natal depression and 'new-mother loneliness'.[74] But this kind of initiative was rare at a time when the dominant discourses around motherhood found it difficult to acknowledge manifestations of depression.[75] Local support groups were thin on the ground until the 1970s. Following the BBC's airing of Nemone Lethbridge's Play for Today, 'Baby Blues' in 1973 based on her own experiences, the self help group Depressives Associated was established. This was followed in 1979 by the Association for Post-Natal Illness, another self-help group set up by Clare Delpech

[70] Oakley, *Here to Maternity*, pp.141–2.

[71] Oakley, *Here to Maternity*, pp.144.

[72] Wiggins, M. (2013). *Looking back on becoming a mother: Longitudinal perspectives on maternity care and the transition to motherhood.* [data collection]. UK Data Service. SN: 850818, DOI: 10.5255/UKDA-SN-850818 [hereafter SN 850818]: interview with MO37JP.

[73] Oakley, *Here to Maternity*, p.146. Years later Oakley contrasted the medical explanations of post-natal depression with the experiences relayed to her by mothers whereby they were suffering from exhaustion, the shock of motherhood, hospitalization and so on. https://www.socialsciencespace.com/2013/04/podcast-ann-oakley-on-womens-experience-of-childbirth/ (accessed 9 February 2023). See also Ann Oakley, *Women Confined: Towards a Sociology of Childbirth* (Oxford: Wiley-Blackwell, 1979) especially pp.135–66.

[74] Wellcome Trust Archives: NCT PP/GDR/F/12: Box 64—National Childbirth Trust Chairman's Report of the AGM, 19 July 1960.

[75] Lisa Held and Alexandra Rutherford, 'Can't a Mother Sing the Blues? Postpartum Depression and the Construction of Motherhood in Late 20th-Century America', *History of Psychology* 15:2 (2012), pp.107–23, here p.112. See also Angela Davis, *Modern Motherhood. Women and Family in England, 1945–2000* (Manchester: Manchester University Press, 2012), p.104.

who also had experienced postnatal depression, and MAMA, the Meet-a-Mum-Association in the same year.[76] Even the popular term, the 'baby blues', makes scant appearance in the popular press until the 1980s and it was only in this decade that the mother and baby advice literature addressed postnatal depression head on.

In addition to openly discussing their feelings about childbirth and the emotions it brought forth, Oakley's respondents were equally candid about how they felt about being a mother and the ways in which this identity crowded out others. 'I don't really feel like I've got an identity at the moment' said Juliet Morley. 'So I suppose I do feel different, yes. I spend far less time thinking about myself and what I want to do and how I feel.'[77] Former shop assistant Nina Brady remarked: 'I don't feel like I'm a mother...I still have the feeling that I'd like to be at work. I haven't got much to do. I think it's boring if you haven't got a lot to do.'[78] Nina was a little unusual in not having enough to occupy her; Christina was more typical in describing the daily round of washing and cleaning, shopping and feeding but when asked to describe a typical day her response was revealing: 'I don't really know. I don't seem to do anything. The time just goes. I go out everyday shopping. I make myself go out. Because otherwise I'd just sit there and rot.'[79]

Feminist research and writing on the issue of women's distress confirmed what had already been articulated in the media but where it departed from popular discourse was in its analysis of the causes and its recipe for change. The women's movement interpreted women's unhappiness as rooted in women's oppression and sought to mobilize women's feelings to do 'political work'.[80] Feminist writers argued that women's poor mental health was an inevitable casualty of domesticity, that women were trapped by the 'conflict of values' between women's and society's expectations of their lives and the demands of family life and that the medical response was to readjust women to the patriarchal structures that caused their ill health in the first place, either by means of psychological therapies that reinforced dominant structures and attitudes or by means of drugs which similarly were designed to help women accept gender norms.[81] In this case the understanding that the personal was political was deployed to develop new approaches to mental health care rooted in women's experience rather than a medical response to reported symptoms. While debate in the pages of the feminist press reinforced and expanded women's emotional repertoire by offering a more politically inflected discourse, grassroots action by the women's movement was located in consciousness-raising groups (established on 'the premise that "sharing private

[76] See https://apni.org/history/. The Aberdeen *Press and Journal* 9 April 1985 reported on a local initiative in that city. On MAMA see Crook, *Postnatal Depression* (forthcoming).

[77] Oakley, *Here to Maternity*, p.157.

[78] Oakley, *Here to Maternity*, p.156.

[79] Oakley, *Here to Maternity*, p.239.

[80] Crook, 'The Women's Liberation Movement', p.1154.

[81] For examples, Agnes Miles, *Women and Mental Illness: The Social Concept of Female Neurosis* (1988); Phyllis Chesler, *Women and Madness* (London: Harcourt Brace Jovanovich, 1972).

suffering" could be healing and emphasized personal experience as a path to political struggle'), self-help therapy, and locally based therapeutic provision.[82] And it was to be self help, an organizational strategy for effecting change, that was to be so important for women, both feminists and even more so for those who were 'not self-consciously feminist' in the 1960s.

Spaces for Screaming

Women had found their emotional range. A combination of press and broadcast media interest and academic research had legitimized women speaking about their negative feelings on marriage and motherhood. Here was the expressive turn manifested in the collective cry of relief of women who now understood that their feelings were not abnormal, that it was OK to admit to being unhappy, that they were not alone and they could do something about it. Their exasperated and sometimes desperate cries for recognition and help began to appear in a range of written communications from letters to newspapers and magazines, personal letters to one another, and in the publications of women's self-help organizations. It is here that we can hear the cries of frustration with the boredom, isolation, and sheer day-to-day banality of being a housewife and mother and the conflicts so many women experienced between the person they had been and the person they had become.

But it was in the 1960s, often described as the 'do-it-yourself' decade, when women began to help themselves on a collective and nationwide level. With the aid of the 'Mainly for Women' page of *The Guardian* newspaper, a raft of self-help organizations started to meet women's needs for social contact and practical support, the largest and most prominent being the National Housewives Register (NHR) and the Pre-School Playgroups Association (PPA). Founded in 1960 and 1961, respectively, they quickly grew from the kitchen table to become national organizations with thousands of members. They offered safe spaces where women could meet face-to-face and communicate in personal correspondence and through newsletters and other forms of publication. These networks of like-minded women who wanted to be wives and mothers but did not want the dilution of identity that seemed to come with those roles, facilitated safe and non-judgmental spaces where women could admit to their frailties, confess to their 'failures' and disclose their emotional condition to others who would understand.

The National Housewives Register was established in direct response to the dilemma experienced by so many women caught in the conflict between their own expectations and those of society. The catalyst was Betty Jerman's letter

[82] Crook, 'The Women's Liberation Movement', p.1158.

published in *The Guardian* in 1960 in which she wrote about the dulling effects of suburbia on the young mothers who were moving there in droves. Although Jerman appeared to agree with those who regarded the new housing estate as a prime incubator of female neurosis, in fact she urged women to act: 'They stay here all day. They set the tone. Many of them look back with regret to the days when they worked in an office. Their work kept them alert. Home and child-minding can have a blunting effect on a woman's mind. But only she can sharpen it.'[83] And act they did. A young mother, Maureen Nicol, saw Jerman's call to arms and set about establishing a national register—a list initially put together at her kitchen table—of 'housebound wives with liberal interests and a desire to remain individuals'. Nicol described the NHR as 'a great groundswell of lively-minded, reasonably educated mothers, torn from family and friends by mobile husbands... largely solving their feelings of mental stagnation and loneliness by getting together and expanding their own lives.'[84]

> The majority of members are 'bound' in that they are restricted to a routine probably more confining that anything they have hitherto encountered. Intelligent women with small children under school age, who have held interesting, stimulating and responsible jobs, now find their lives centred around the home as never before. They take a pride in their homes and families, accepting the restrictions and responsibilities inherent in their situation, but they find themselves mentally frustrated with the curtailment of their personal freedom.[85]

The NHR initially couched its raison d'être in terms of providing a safety valve and opportunity to keep the mind active for educated women who were adjusting to being full time home-makers after being active in the workplace. And whilst the language of neurosis and mental health was used quite freely, NHR was careful not to link women's domestic role per se with neurotic symptoms. As Nicol explained in a talk in 1962:

> I would like to make a personal plea. It is to ask you to try and maintain your own individual identity in spite of demands of children and home. There is always so much to do, I know only too well it is easy never to quite finish reading that article on the Common Market, and never to really make up your mind on the rights and wrongs of the Campaign for Nuclear Disarmament, or even what to tell your children about religion and your belief or disbelief in God. I do think

[83] Betty Jerman, 'Squeezed in like sardines in suburbia', *The Guardian*, 19 February 1960.
[84] Maureen Nicol cited in Jerman, *Lively-Minded Women*, p.29.
[85] LSE, Women's Library: 5/NWR/1/16—Survey Reports 1966.

> [it] vitally important that women, and particularly mothers read, discuss and decide about the important things happening around us now.[86]

Sustaining mental alertness and an interest in the wider world, through NHR's model of meetings of local groups who would research and discuss topics to the exclusion of baby-talk and domestic complaints, was conceptualized as necessary for women as mothers and for themselves. To be contented (and good) mothers, women needed to keep their brains active. And certainly this formula worked for many members like Chris White who recalled that when she joined the Bolton group 'I seemed to belong and for these evenings at least I was not just Cliff's wife or James' mum. At last I could come to terms with being a housewife because I could still be me as well.'[87] Some groups engaged more directly with their own predicament. One 'had a discussion about Gavron's Captive Wives (sic) which we had read about in the newspapers. We wanted to find some practical suggestions for combating the feeling of being a captive wife.'[88]

The NHR provided a safety valve through its organizational format: local groups of women who met in one another's houses, organized in regional networks under the umbrella of a national committee which produced a newsletter. Likewise, the Pre-School Playgroups Association which, although employing a national advisor, was in essence a parent-led organization at the local level, at least in its early years.[89] These kinds of organizations—which also included the National Childbirth Trust, the Association for Post-Natal Illness and Welfare of Children in Hospital amongst others, were run on a shoestring and necessitated personal contact and an informal mode of communication at national and local level. Joining a local group allowed women to meet others in a similar situation and compare notes. One Welsh correspondent to the 1966 NHR Newsletter articulated the feelings of many. '[T]ime after time I've heard comments like: "I think I'm going round the bend/up the wall/crazy"; "I'm in such a rut"; "I've been in a steady decline for ages"; "thank god someone else feels the same"; "I never see a soul"; "I can't seem to meet people"; "no-one to talk to"; and so on and so on.'[90] The language of neurosis and mental illness was not included in the official image NHR wished to project—it preferred to represent its members as intelligent women, not 'cabbages' and perhaps associated this more with working-class women who were not its desired constituency. However, members frequently

[86] LSE, Women's Library: 5/NWR/1/5: Cheshire group c.1960. Notes by Maureen Nicol for a talk given to Manchester group in 1962.

[87] LSE, Women's Library: 5/NWR/5/3 Maureen Nicol—Letter from Chris White, 17 February 1994.

[88] LSE, Women's Library: NHR Autumn Newsletter, 1966.

[89] This changed in the 1980s after a financial scandal when it became a professionally run rather than volunteer-run organization. See Jill Faux, 'The impact of change' in Ann Henderson (Ed.), *Insights from the Playgroup Movement: Equality and Autonomy in a Voluntary Organisation* (Stoke-on-Trent: Trentham Books, 2011), pp.141–62.

[90] LSE, Women's Library: NHR Spring Newsletter, 1966.

referred to their own encounters with psychiatric problems in both jovial and serious ways. The NHR 'certainly kept me away from the tranquillizers when I felt embedded in nappies' recalled Jane Godwin.[91] And Hilary Bushill claimed the Register

> was instrumental, nineteen years ago, in preventing me from doing serious damage to my daughter. By giving me space of my own in my then very stressful life and the opportunity to have intelligent conversation with other sympathetic women with whom I shared a wide variety of interests, I gained the composure to deal with my daughter's difficult behaviour in a more acceptable manner than the one I had often contemplated.[92]

Far more commonly, boredom, the lack of adult conversation, the daily grind of cooking and cleaning drove women 'round the bend'. 'It is high time there was a more sympathetic approach to women who are very good mothers in many ways and in some ways better than average, but who are just incapable of spending 95% of their time engulfed in domesticity' wrote a member from Farnborough. 'It took a severe nervous breakdown, 4 months in hospital and several months psychotherapy to make me see the folly of trying to conform...I had to accept that I am not Societies Ideal Mother [sic].'[93] Similarly Helena Wood, a member from Bishop Auckland shared her feelings about being a full-time mother:

> I have been obliged to have psychiatric treatment, but the only 'cure' is for me to get work—part time. Because of the lack of nurseries, I am obliged to take antidepressants, waste my GP's time once a week and my psychiatrist's once a month. I have been shocked to discover how many women are in the same unnecessary mess. We would be better for our children as part-time mums than as full-time lunatics.[94]

The Pre-School Playgroup movement, unlike NHR, was ostensibly set up to provide pre-school children with social contact and supervised play but the desperate need for play provision was as much in the women's interests as their children's. In 1961 Belle Tutaev, the mother of a small child who had recently moved to London, wrote to *The Guardian* on the subject of 'Do-it-Yourself Nurseries'. Responding to the absence of pre-school provision, Belle started a campaign—the campaign for Nursery Education—but when this failed to have an impact she

[91] LSE, Women's Library: 5/NWR/5/3: Maureen Nicol. Testimonial from Jane Godwin.
[92] LSE, Women's Library: 5/NWR/5/3: Maureen Nicol. Testimonial from Hilary Bushill.
[93] LSE, Women's Library: NHR Newsletter, Spring 1966.
[94] LSE, Women's Library: NHR Newsletter, Autumn 1966.

set up her own playgroup in a Marylebone church hall. Her letter was a call to arms to 'mothers and teachers who would like to create their own solutions to their problems'.[95] When she received 150 letters in response, the Pre-School Playgroups Association was born. However, it was mothers who gained the most from volunteering as playgroup helpers and like their sisters in NHR, they vented their feelings about stay-at-home motherhood in the organization's publications.

Under the headline 'Sobbing in a Locked Room' in the first issue of PPA's newsletter *Playgroup News*, Moya Codling who started a playgroup with her neighbours, initially meeting in their own homes in Bracknell new town before moving to a local community hall, expressed the feelings of many women in the same boat:

> You will know how lonely mums can be if you have ever locked the bathroom door and just sobbed. Have you ever rushed out of the house to run anywhere, just to come back again at the end of the garden path?... Have you ever thrown the sugar bowl at the piano or the nappies out of the kitchen window and two minutes later picked them up and washed them for the nine hundredth and ninety-ninth time?[96]

Or as another contributor to the PPA's *Contact* magazine put it: 'We can't concentrate full-time on Andy Pandy and semolina—that way lies madness.'[97] Indeed, Brenda Crowe, the PPAs energetic national advisor was evangelical about the value of playgroups to mothers. 'I'm sure that I shouldn't be saying it' she wrote in 1969, 'but I can't help feeling that mothers need playgroups as much as the children do.'[98] She acknowledged the various needs of mothers, from distraction from the monotony of everyday routine at home to the opportunity to share their frustration and guilt for those who found it 'more difficult to adapt to a maternal role'.[99] Both organizations, as Betty Jerman, progenitor of NHR acknowledged, met needs well beyond their purported remit.

> Pat Baker can laugh now about when her son Mark made Mum some coffee by pouring coffee powder, sugar and water into her washing machine... But her voice reflects the desperation of that time... having just moved into a strange neighbourhood in SE London she knew no-one, she was 'going mad' and Mark's speech was backward. Out shopping one day she saw a notice about an attempt to open a playgroup with mothers participating and put her name down fast. Now... Mark is a different child... Pat is different too. Before her marriage she

[95] *The Guardian*, August 1961.
[96] UCL, IoE: PLA, PPA 16/1-3—*Playgroup News*, issue 1, 1969.
[97] UCL, IoE: PLA/PPA 6/1—Memories (Juliet Baxter).
[98] UCL, IoE: PLA/PPA 1/1- Comparison Report, 1967–9, p.1.
[99] UCL, IoE: PLA/PPA/4/6—Brenda Crowe, 'Parent Involvement' in Parents in Playgroups (c.1971).

was a personal secretary and with the help of that experience she is now assistant and secretary to the playgroup. She has to present logical arguments to the local Council in defence of the playgroup's grant... She used to 'keep herself to herself' but now she is outgoing... once she thought a playgroup was where you parked your children and went to work... 'It is a kind of therapy' she says, 'for the mothers as well as the children.'[100]

Figure 6.1 'Mother's Homework' by Juliet Baxter in the Pre-School Playgroup magazine *Contact*, September 1974.

[100] National Library of Scotland (NLS): SPPA Lothians Playgroup News, 1974–77.

Both organizations provided a safe space for women to admit they were lonely and struggling in their new role though it was undoubtedly easier for NHR and PPA members—overwhelmingly educated and middle-class—to go public with their inadequacies than less privileged women whose 'failures' were more often the subject of criticism and which could precipitate state interventions. 'It is not only the women who have some form of higher education who are frustrated mentally' observed a member from the Amersham group. 'The high percentage of neurotics one meets amongst the apparently happy little housewives is quite frightening. I include non-members of NHR of course. Those of us who meet through NHR meetings and "natter" or discuss *anything at all* do have the opportunity to recognize our own fears and inadequacies.'[101]

Outside the group meetings and the Newsletter, NHR also facilitated personal connections between office holders who were located around the country and thus communicated primarily by letter. These communications became a means of sharing common experiences of guilt and the inability to live up to perceived standards. In 1965 Sheila Partington, a recent member and soon to be a local organizer in Norwich, and Lesley Taylor, the NHR's national organizer, exchanged a series of letters purportedly dealing with various NHR matters. Sheila had recently moved to East Anglia from London and found herself living a very different life. Formerly a journalist for *The Guardian* she was a graduate with a wide range of interests but these had all been 'modified by the rapacious appetites of the children for my time'.[102] The communications between Sheila and Lesley were to manage national committee issues but Sheila's *modus operandi* was to always include some chatty details of her everyday life, thus establishing a common language between the two women. '[E]xcuse the ee Cummings look my letter has suddenly taken on the baby is teething frantically just now—the elder is just plain teething—and I have him on my knee helping' was her penultimate comment in a typed letter concerning newsletter production, which was then followed by some handwritten concluding remarks: 'Have you read the feminine mystique by betty friedan that someone mentioned in the newsletter. Oh dear. The gasman long-awaited has appeared: also the baker and the dustmen. Must go.'[103]

A few months later Sheila's letter to Lesley once again rolled personal observations about her inability to be the perfect housekeeper into a letter about NHR business (and indicated that Lesley employed the epistolic sharing strategy too):

> I hope all goes well with the wee one—and that her family is getting some sleep. I've hardly dared look again at your phrase about normal housework getting

[101] LSE, Women's Library: NHR Newsletter, Spring 1966—report on Special Group Report: Worthing, Lancing and Littlehampton.

[102] LSE, Women's Library: 5/NWR/1/15—Correspondence 1969–1972, Letter from Sheila Partington in Norwich to Lesley Taylor, National Organiser, 29 October 1964.

[103] LSE, Women's Library: 5/NWR/1/15—Correspondence 1969–1972, Sheila Partington to Lesley Taylor, 15 February 1965.

> done quite easily. I must be just the world's worst housekeeper—my two take all my time and the housework gets scrambled in around the edges. Or is this the scientific approach?...I'm sure there is a worthwhile piece to be written about this—so many women who were efficient and good at their jobs and enjoyed coping find themselves absolutely floored by the effort to try and get everything domestic done as efficiently—and pursued by the guilty feeling that they should be able to.[104]

Women used the Register's communication channels—newsletters, personal letters, and no doubt meetings too—to vent, to let off steam, to make contact with other women using a shared language. They could do this because they were assured that others would be experiencing the same and would refrain from being judgemental.

Self-help organizations such as NHR and PPA were dominated by those who had the luxury of time and the expectations of the educated. And for all their talk of 'going mad' and climbing the walls, the majority accepted that their place was at home while the children were small. With the exception of those who developed recognized conditions such as post-natal depression or agoraphobia and required medication or other medical interventions, these women could write and speak about the frustrations of domestic life in ways that referenced the discourse of neurosis precisely because they had an outlet and could envisage a life beyond the home. Involvement in self-help organizations eased the isolation and mental stagnation that many experienced when their children were very young and for many provided a route back into education and employment.

Neither the PPA or the NHR provided a vent for working-class women's isolation and frustration, or at least not initially. Both relied on volunteers who had access to time, support, and confidence. Working-class women were far more likely to consider returning to work to escape the 'small world' of the home, to regain some of their independence and to bring in a much needed income.[105] In any case NHR modelled itself as an organization meeting the needs of women who had had careers and who were now crying out for mental stimulation. 'Intelligent women' not 'cake-icers' summed up the demographic they were seeking to recruit. 'As we live in a rather "non-U" area it is difficult to make contacts' wrote a Lewisham member to the NHR Newsletter in 1966. Her solution was to obtain the addresses of those who received delivery of *The Guardian* for leafletting.[106] And a Northwich member approached her newsagent to ask if a NHR leaflet could be delivered with copies of *She* and *Nova*: 'the liveliest magazines and

[104] LSE, Women's Library: 5/NWR/1/15 Correspondence 1969–1972, Sheila Partington to Lesley Taylor, 22 April 1965.

[105] MRC, NSHD: Frequent Job Changers Survey: cases 130–020 and 102–029.

[106] LSE, Women's Library: NHR Newsletter, Spring 1966.

in our group the most read'.[107] Members assiduously challenged any insinuation that NHR was merely an 'organization which enabled women to get away from it all and have a natter'.[108] Or as National Organizer Brenda Prys-Jones wrote to her successor Lesley Taylor:

> I also had the problem of making it plain, tactfully, if possible, that we exist to provide friendship for intelligent women. There had at one time been some rather off target publicity by mis-guided members which had resulted in the formation of 'toddlers' clubs for young mums. All sorts of (to put it crudely) 'undesirables' were applying. I tried to stop this trend by suggesting that our organizers direct such people to other clubs in the area.[109]

Given this attitude, it is not surprising that NHR members tended to come from professional and semi-professional occupations prior to having children. A survey of members in 1966 identified 19 per cent were graduates and 50 per cent had undergone some professional training. The majority of members were '"bound" in that they are restricted to a routine probably more confining than anything they have hitherto encountered'. These were women who did not reject their role as wives and mothers; they simply wanted space for themselves.[110]

Nothing had changed seven years on when the average NHR member was described as '30–39 years old and has 2.9 children half of whom are at school. She has lived in her area for 6–20 years, has professional training and has a paid job.'[111] The profiles of the women who became NHR national organizers or members of the national committee confirms this description. Maureen Nicol, founder and first national organizer, followed her husband to Uganda in 1967 but on returning to the UK a few years later she 'turned her energies towards the clearing of footpaths, building of bridges and stiles and founded the Kenilworth Footpath Preservation Society; being a super energetic women Maureen is also chairman of Kenilworth WEA, a CAB [Citizens' Advice Bureau] counsellor in Coventry...works for the tiny Labour party branch in Kenilworth and still a keen NHR member; she says she worries a lot and is wearily climbing on to the nuclear disarmament bandwagon again.'[112] Serial voluntary work was not unusual amongst this cohort and for some this led to

[107] LSE, Women's Library: NHR Newsletter, Autumn 1966.

[108] LSE, Women's Library: NHR Newsletter, Autumn 1967.

[109] LSE, Women's Library: 5/NWR/1/15—Correspondence 1969–1972, Brenda Prys-Jones to Lesley Taylor, 18 August 1964.

[110] LSE, Women's Library: 5/NWR/1/16—Survey Reports 1966—1st survey 1966 (published March 1967) conducted by Congleton WEA course on Sociology 1966–7, University of Manchester Extramural Department.

[111] LSE, Women's Library: 5/NWR/1/16—Survey Reports 1966—Analysis of National Questionnaire of June 1973.

[112] LSE, Women's Library: 5/NWR/5/3—Profile of Maureen Nicol.

new careers and opportunities. For these women NHR acted initially as a support network and then as a springboard to other things, be they community work or employment.

Self-Help or Just Help?

Working-class women certainly shared many of the same feelings of their middle-class peers with respect to the frustrations and boredom of caring for young children and running a home. But they had the added stresses of inadequate housing and lack of support, including from partners. Gavron observed that while working-class women were more prepared for motherhood than middle-class wives, when confronted with the reality 'there was an atmosphere of confusion and muddling through' 'and their ability to keep their head above water as mothers appeared considerably less than that of their middle-class counterparts'.[113] The evidence from Gavron's sample indicated that 'although the middle-class mother may encounter psychological difficulties concerning her role as an individual with her first baby, she very soon makes a deliberate effort to assert her own rights as an individual. The working-class mother who sees motherhood as inevitable is in fact less prepared for the ties of children and is less able to cope with the isolation that follows.'[114] Gavron was alert to the difficulties besetting the working-class mothers in her study. 'Bad housing, lack of play facilities, lack of nursery schools, lack of babysitters, reduced contact with their extended family, and reduced earning capacities' coupled with a more home-centred leisure dominated by the television all contributed to these women's isolation from social contact and support and their reporting of nervous strain.[115] This was certainly the situation on Scottish housing estates a decade later where the Scottish PPA conducted an analysis of playgroup provision. Such was the poverty of the environment comprising poor housing, isolation, absence of safe space for children to play and families 'unable or unwilling to provide any support and the husbands or co-habitees feel little obligation to the children', that 'the mothers' desperate needs override those of the children. The mothers have a need to come and be calmed down.'[116] In some playgroups it was said 'there is the seeming apathy and indifference on the part of the mothers, and in others the needs of the mothers to talk about their problems and their lives seem equal to their children's need to play.'[117]

Not only were the mothers trapped, unable to escape their responsibilities 'even for a hair wash and set', but they were also anxious about their children.[118]

[113] Gavron, *Captive Wife*, pp.81–2.
[114] Gavron, *Captive Wife*, p.89. [115] Gavron *Captive Wife*, pp.82, 89.
[116] UCL, IoE: PPA 2/28—Playgroups in Areas of Need, pp.7, 13.
[117] UCL, IoE: PPA 2/28—Playgroups in Areas of Need, p.13.
[118] Gavron, *Captive Wife*, p.89.

The particular concerns of mothers of pre-school children living in high flats had been aired in a number of studies. Mothers' stress was exacerbated by the high flats environment: noise carried easily through the thin walls and up and down voids in the buildings and there were few if any safe spaces for children to play. Mothers were constantly on edge trying to keep their children quiet and they worried about their children's lack of socialization with others, hindering their development.[119]

The public conversation about 'miserable wives' and guilty mothers focused predominantly on the experiences of educated middle-class women who were better able to articulate their feelings to one another, to medical professionals and through the media. The founding of self-help organizations was a concrete outcome of this openness. But the working-class women living in private rented accommodation or in high flats did not, on the whole, read the *Guardian* or *Nova* and if they considered joining the NHR—after all some did express their anxieties about staying at home and becoming a 'cabbage'[120]—the NHR's *modus operandi*, meeting in one another's homes, researching 'intellectual' topics for discussion, was hardly conducive to inclusivity. Even by the 1980s, despite the change of name to The National Women's Register, its profile had changed little. 'The NHR does tend to be somewhat middle class', reported the *Lincolnshire Echo*. 'There are very few young mums from tower bloc territory among their ranks which puzzles members. "We really don't know why they don't join us" said one official.'[121]

The reasons were clear. The self-help discourse which urged women to engage more with their community and to help themselves simply did not recognize the everyday realities of many women who lacked their advantages. This response published in a newspaper to a letter from a woman who bemoaned her limited existence with two children under five and 'no adult life of my own', sums up the distance that existed between the self-help advocates and women who had few resources.

> You do not have to live in a cage. You can open the door and come out, but no-one else can open it for you...I do understand how exhausting two under fives can be and you probably feel too tired to make the effort to make your life more interesting, but other mothers have succeeded, so do have a go. Take these suggestions one at a time in any order. Start your elder child at a playgroup; talk to other mums about your 'cage' and learn how some of them have emerged from

[119] Pearl Jephcott, *Homes in High Flats* (Edinburgh: Oliver & Boyd, 1971); Elizabeth Gittus, *Flats, Families and the Under-Fives* (London: Routledge, 1976); Joan Maizels, *Two to Five in High Flats. An Enquiry into Play Provision for Children Ages Two to Five Living in High Flats* (London: Housing Centre Trust, 1961).

[120] MRC, NSHD: Frequent Job Changers Survey—case 208-036.

[121] LSE, Women's Library: 5/NWR/4/1/31—Lincolnshire 1971–1997: *Lincolnshire Echo*, 24 February 1982.

> theirs for part of each day; join a keep fit class in the day time if possible; ask about baby sitters if you have no friend or relative to leave the children with; ask your husband to give you one night off a week; join a club like the National Housewives Register where subjects like babies and housework are taboo—or just go off and visit a friend.[122]

NHR was no solution for working-class women whose economic and material circumstances were such that they required help themselves. The difficulties such women confronted were exposed when initiatives to establish pre-school playgroups in urban areas of deprivation foundered or at best struggled, in part because this self-help initiative, like the NHR, was built around the needs and capacities of educated women with time and money. In Birmingham, social workers were said to be 'struck by the number of young mothers who eventually get round to voicing their very real fear of madness' but efforts to establish playgroups in the inner city had already foundered in the face of the financial and cultural challenges posed by mothers unable to pay or to 'cope with this kind of situation' and children lacking the advantages of those who usually populated playgroups. Upon trying to establish a group 'in the deprived part of town' after being 'sick of being told that we only start Playgroups where we are not really needed', this PPA activist discovered 'she was more allergic than she thought she would be to children who smelt and whose noses were all over their faces'.[123]

One such ill-fated attempt to counter the isolation of young mothers in a socially deprived part of Glasgow was conducted by Pearl Jephcott's high flats research team. Jephcott had a track record in this regard, having worked with the Save the Children Fund to set up outdoor playgroups in Notting Hill, London in the 1960s with the aim not only of improving the lives of the children but also of helping the mothers 'to be more resourceful', especially those of West Indian and West African heritage whose mothering practices had been pathologized for not conforming to white cultural norms.[124] However, she struggled to recruit Black mothers to playgroups. By the time Jephcott moved to Glasgow in the mid 1960s, the Pre-School Playgroups association was already well established across the UK though its presence in areas of social need was very limited. Only two out of 49 high-rise estates in Glasgow had playgroups by 1968; indeed it was not until the 1970s that the Scottish PPA accelerated its efforts to reach mothers and children in these areas.

[122] LSE, Women's Library: 5/NWR/4/1/31 Lincolnshire 1971–1997—unidentified newspaper cutting dated 8 April 1986.

[123] UCL, IoE: PLA-PPA—Brenda Crowe, Birmingham report, November 1967.

[124] Pearl Jephcott, *A Troubled Area: Notes on Notting Hill* (London: Faber, 1964); Helen McCarthy, 'Pearl Jephcott and the politics of gender, class and race in post-war Britain', *Women's History Review* 28:5 (2019), pp.779–93, here 784–8. See also Bailkin, *Aftermath of Empire*, pp.188–95.

The Royston experiment, whereby Jephcott and her research team worked with mothers to set up a regular group for young children on the high-rise estate, also foundered in the face of a gap between expectations and capabilities. It was observed that the 'mothers had less knowledge and were less articulate than would really have been necessary for the project to continue without support' and, according to the researcher, 'were not very flexible in their thinking…if one scheme was frustrated seemed unable to pick up the threads and work out the alternatives'.[125] Her observation inadvertently revealed a gap in understanding of the lives of these women. Little had changed a few years later when the Scottish PPA reported on efforts to establish playgroups in areas of deprivation across Scotland. 'Many mothers and toddlers arrive in a state of depression, fatigue and even despair…the group of adults can appear tired and inactive meeting after meeting.'[126]

Elsewhere playgroup provision in areas of need was less reliant on mothers' active participation and was supported financially. In Edinburgh the Corporation provided a grant to a voluntary agency, the Voluntary Health Workers' Association, to run 36 play centres in the city, seven in estates containing high flats, and in London the GLC similarly offered grant aid to a range of voluntary groups such as Save the Children as well as running its own One o'clock Clubs.[127] The critical element in the success of these initiatives was funding for premises and more especially, paid play workers or supervisors in order that the groups were not entirely dependent on mother helpers. An experiment in Glasgow in 1968 was said to be 'causing problems' on account of paying a supervisor for one term only. 'If the supervisor is withdrawn as intended, the group will collapse.'[128] While mothers in these areas were desperate for their children to have the opportunity to play with others of the same age group, the mothers also needed support and social contact. The pre-school playgroup model rested on understandings about child development and activities, guided by mother helpers, were designed to meet children's developmental stages. Central to the PPA's raison d'être was the distinction between 'play' and 'Play', the latter incorporating structured activity designed to stimulate and guide children's development, creativity, and motor skills. This required that the helpers were prepared to engage with play pedagogy. It became clear however, that while facilitators became frustrated with some mothers treating the playgroup as somewhere to leave the children so they could have a break from them, this is precisely what many mothers did

[125] UGA, DC 127/16/4: Valerie Somerville, 'Charles Street Playgroup', dissertation, pp.20, 27.

[126] IoE, PLA, PPA 2/28: Jennifer Overton, *Stepping Stone Projects. The First Three Years 1979–1981* (1981), p.12.

[127] IoE, PLA, PPA 1–4: Crowe area report, Scotland 1968; Caroline Moorehead, 'Playgroups for (Non-Working) Mothers', *Times Education Supplement*, 7 May 1971.

[128] IoE, PLA, PPA 1–4: Crowe area report, Scotland 1968 (Glasgow).

need. The assumption by the early PPA activists that parental involvement would yield benefits in terms of increasing their self-confidence and personal skills rested on a flawed understanding of the situation of many women in less affluent areas. To be fair, the PPA's national advisor Brenda Crowe, was well aware that the self-help model did not adapt well to areas characterized by economic and social deprivation where mothers' capacity was compromised by a range of factors: their need to work, their lack of experience, and their own need for support.

The PPA learned from its early efforts to engage with areas of need and by the early 1970s playgroups were delivering an 'invaluable service' in deprived parts of Glasgow but still 'Many were in need of help and support, however, because the problems the mothers were encountering were such that even the more sophisticated groups would have difficulty coping with them'.[129] Certainly the mothers benefited in terms of expanding their social contact. 'It has improved my own confidence in meeting people and I have also made more friends than I would have thought possible' reported one and another remarked: 'Made me feel less isolated in the high flats through twice weekly contact with other mothers.'[130]

Playgroups could go some way to alleviating some of the loneliness and stress experienced by working-class mothers by providing a point of social contact and some relief from one-to-one care of the children for a few hours. And there is some evidence to suggest that in some areas working-class mothers used playgroups to prepare their children for school, though this is not in evidence in the Scottish case.[131] But whereas their middle-class counterparts used the PPA, and NHR to a lesser extent, as a bridge to a return to work or the opportunity to learn a new set of skills as well as a social network for letting off steam, working-class women were more likely to use playgroups as respite while their children were young before a return to un- or semi-skilled work. The argument that involvement in PPA created 'employment-like' commitments for the mothers of young children which could then initiate a career owing to gains in self-confidence and self-esteem rings true for women like Cynthia who we met at the beginning of this chapter and a good number of her contemporaries who discovered in the PPA a structured pathway to a career in social work or early years provision. But self help was not a long-term solution for women experiencing isolation, anxiety, or depression and with few resources or support. For them there was no community of feeling.

[129] NLS: E. Rae Paul, *Playgroups in an Industrial City* (Scottish PPA, Glasgow, 1974), p.6.

[130] E. Rae Paul, *Playgroups in an Industrial City*, p.26.

[131] Angela Davis, *Pre-School Childcare in England: 1939–2010: Theory, Practice and Experience* (Manchester: Manchester University Press, 2015), pp.170–1.

Conclusions

In a wide sense, the 1960s liberated women's feelings. While it may be the case that this cohort of women were more likely than previous generations to experience a spectrum of negative feelings contingent on losing their identity to their social role as wives and mothers, it is certainly true that now women felt freer to be honest and open about how they felt. The 'conspiracy of silence' around motherhood was being broken, not just by feminists but by social and medical researchers, the media, and most importantly, by women themselves, whether self-describing as feminists or not. They began to see themselves in the media and encountered more sympathetic doctors. Social researchers took them seriously and allowed them to speak for themselves. The expressive culture of the time encouraged talking and candour, and legitimized more emotional openness and a vernacular which women could use to describe how they felt. And finally, some amongst this cohort with social confidence used the media and their own educational and social capital to effect change. All of these elements were necessary to foster the early construction of an environment, a community of feeling, in which women could admit to emotions that hitherto had been largely suppressed. Women were emerging as active agents in the alleviation of those feelings.

Neither the National Housewives Register nor the Pre-School Playgroups Association were avowedly feminist. They never explicitly or publicly offered a critique of the institutions such as marriage or of the economic and social conditions that underpinned women's distress, especially when they were young mothers. Neither did they explicitly criticize men (at least not in public pronouncements) or propose that fathers might take on a more active role in the home though within PPA they did increasingly recognize and welcome fathers' growing involvement with their children's development.[132] They recognized the tensions experienced by many women when they found themselves trapped between their own aspirations and expectations and the conditions of domesticity. But for the most part these organizations existed to alleviate women's feelings of physical and intellectual isolation and to provide first a safety valve, then a stepping-stone to new friendship networks and in the case of PPA, the acquisition of new knowledge and skills via the extensive training on offer. They did this successfully for women who already had educational and social advantages, who had little to lose by admitting their vulnerabilities and who had the resources to make the transition from isolated wife and mother to networked and socially capable member of the community. There is no evidence that either organization explicitly addressed the psychological symptoms reported by so many women and which

[132] For example, NLS: Scottish Pre-School Playgroups Association, AGM 1977: 'You too can be a father helper.' The following year fathers were invited to attend the AGM for a session on 'Fathers and pre-school children'.

they were set up to alleviate; however, as we have seen, PPA was alert to the position of mothers in deprived areas and understood that their problems were far more deep seated than playgroup provision could solve. Mental health issues were aired in public and in personal correspondence but most often using vernacular language and a jokey tone. No doubt women benefited from being able to let off steam in this way and to admit to feelings they might have refrained from being open about with family or a doctor, but the do-it-yourself movement placed emphasis on practical efforts to counter women's distress rather than analysing its causes.

7
Liberating the Domestic Self

Introduction

This chapter follows our cohort of women as they negotiated an untrodden path. Ann Oakley summed up their position in 1974 when she wrote, in *Housewife*, 'Today…the birth of the first child, and not marriage itself, is the major transforming event in a woman's life.'[1] Marriage in their twenties and children soon after, coupled with an expectation and, for many, a desire that they would not return to the labour market at least until the children were at school, meant that women of all social classes were looking for social contact and stimulation during this period of their lives. Public debate predominantly focused on whether and how married women and mothers could return to paid work. This had been ongoing since the 1950s, although few advocated that the mothers of young children should re-enter the labour market. It was not until the later 1970s and feminist demands for 24-hour childcare that the idea of the dual role—whereby women picked up their career after a period for child rearing—was seriously questioned. Thus, in the 1960s and 1970s, women found themselves in limbo, unable or unwilling to return to work while children were small, often content to prioritize motherhood over work for a period and generally of a mind that staying at home with their pre-school children was beneficial. But they were also searching for opportunities to make social contact with like-minded women, to get out of the house, engage the brain, and for some, to begin to chart a way back to the world of work. The story of this chapter is one of our cohort forging a distinctive bridge between the 'old regime' of delaying return to work until children were at school and sometimes much later, and the 'new regime' of working through child rearing. The limbo was not wasted.

The self-help organizations discussed in the previous chapter are a key part of this story. They spanned home and work, offering a safe environment in which to gain confidence, skills, and experience. We have already seen how the emergence of the do-it-yourself movement was a response to the ennui and frustration of mainly middle-class stay-at-home mothers, easing isolation and providing a space to deploy existing skills and learn new ones. Organizations like the Preschool Playgroups and National Housewives Register and on a smaller, more

[1] Oakley, *Housewife*, p.114.

Feminist Lives: Women, Feelings, and the Self in Post-War Britain. Lynn Abrams, Oxford University Press.
 DOI: 10.1093/oso/9780192896995.003.0007

local scale, the Working Association of Mothers (WAM), provided frustrated women with a 'space to scream', an outlet for the boredom and lack of social contact experienced by mothers of young children. But voluntary organizations also acted as stepping-stones, giving many women, not just those with financial or time privileges, the confidence to transform their lives, not only in respect of self-development through further training, education, and participation in civil society in either a voluntary or paid capacity, but also in terms of their personal growth.

Pre-school Playgroups, National Housewives Register, and the National Childbirth Trust along with a plethora of other organizations mostly focused on improving the lives of women and children and disadvantaged groups, were more than empathetic communities.[2] As they grew they established local, regional, and national structures with all the bureaucratic and administrative paraphernalia required to maintain and drive forward a complex organization. All three organizations created national networks whose local branches facilitated integration into new communities amongst this mobile and capable generation. They all published newsletters and magazines which maintained and sustained the community through imparting and sharing information. And NCT and PPA established training for their volunteers which created long-term commitment. Women could engage on many levels and via a number of strategies which included various kinds of training, accepting leadership roles at local and national level, sitting on committees, working with local authorities and government and in the longer term, using the confidence and skills they had acquired to enter further or higher education, to embark on a new career, or to make changes in their personal lives. In short they offered women opportunities to achieve personal growth while putting their children first.

First then, this chapter examines the decision-making process undertaken by women who had been working until they embarked upon a family and argues that, notwithstanding economic pressures, many women were genuine in their desire to be at home while children were very young while intending to return to the labour market when the children were older. Second, it examines the strategies employed by women to manage this period in which they became detached from their work identity but were committed to being good enough mothers. Focusing on women's engagement with the self-help organizations, the chapter shows how these helped women to square the circle—to maintain a connection with the social world, to feel socially useful, undertaking 'work-like' activity but not compromising their parenting role. Finally it assesses the claims

[2] Other DIY groups included: The Welfare of Children in Hospital, Association for Improvement in Maternity Services (AIMS), National Council for the Single Woman and her Dependents, Invalids at Home, Disablement Income Group, Association for the Prevention of Addiction. All of these were initiated by a letter to *The Guardian* newspaper. *The Guardian*, 13 May 1968.

of these organizations and some of their members that they were instrumental in fomenting not just greater self-confidence in women but that they facilitated self-actualization, hence challenging the privileging of paid work as the primary site for self-realization.

It is important to recognize that few mothers questioned the assumption that staying at home was the best thing for their children though their ability to do so varied. Whilst the popularization of the writings of John Bowlby, Donald Winnicott, and others whose theories of maternal deprivation and instinctive parenting—or mothering—achieved considerable reach and certainly shaped many public pronouncements on patterns of maternal care amongst working-class and especially ethnic minority mothers, historians have identified a range of responses.[3] Middle-class women were more likely to consume parenting literature and to have the resources to put attachment theory into practice.[4] Working-class mothers, on the other hand, lacked the same economic resources. Some certainly absorbed 'Bowlbyism', manifested in their negative attitudes towards nurseries and yet Cowan emphasizes the flexibility and adaptability of parents who did what they felt was 'right for their child'.[5] This varied enormously with the use of childminders, playgroups, and informal forms of childcare utilized as cultural and economic circumstances allowed. And as Smith Wilson and Paterson argue, this group was at the forefront of redefining good mothering by pioneering the bi-modal pattern, that is returning to the labour market when children were older.[6] It is likely that other factors weighed just as heavily on women's decisions. On the positive side, for those couples in favourable economic circumstances, a second wage was not a financial necessity. Many of the younger women interviewed for the Pahls' study of managers' wives were financially comfortable and regarded a return to the labour market largely as a route to self-fulfilment.[7] On the negative, poor childcare provision, the burden of housework, the gendered division of labour in the home, husbands' opposition, limited availability of shift or part-time work, and practical impediments to easy travel to the workplace when most women did not drive or have access to a car, all created obstacles to even considering a return to the labour market when children were of school age. A 1964 study of graduate women in work identified four requirements to allow a woman to reconcile paid work with 'the housewives' lot': paid help, labour-saving household equipment, a car, and a cooperative family alongside determination.[8]

[3] On responses to South Asian and West Indian and African childcare practices see Bailkin, *Afterlife of Empire*, pp.187–95.

[4] Thomson, *Lost Freedom*, pp.79–105.

[5] David Cowan, 'Modern' Parenting and the Uses of Childcare Advice in Post-war England, *Social History* 43:3 (2018), pp.332–55.

[6] Smith Wilson, 'A New Look at the Affluent Worker', p. 207; Laura Paterson, 'Women and Paid Work in Industrial Britain', PhD thesis, University of Dundee, 2014, pp.245–6.

[7] Pahl and Pahl, *Managers*.

[8] *The Guardian*, 29 Sept. 1966: review of Arregger (Ed.), *Graduate Mothers at Work*.

But graduate women in the 1960s were in a small minority. Women in less favourable economic circumstances found ways to earn a living without these props. Working mothers employed a range of strategies, what Paterson and Worth have termed 'organizational labour', which was often hidden and invariably required considerable effort.[9] Yet both contemporary and retrospective accounts of that time contain positive sentiments about stay-at-home motherhood (contrasting with the pejorative appellation 'housewife'). This is not surprising in itself, but sufficient to force a serious consideration of the decision to stay at home that takes women's words as authentic expressions of their feelings rather than post-dated justifications. When women, both at the time and in retrospective interview, say that they found satisfaction and enjoyment in their role as primary carers for their young children, we must take them seriously whilst recognizing the contexts in which they made the decision and in which they retrospectively accounted for it.

It is important, however, to note that a model of non-earning motherhood was not universal. Amongst some Black and ethnic-minority communities, full-time work was not incompatible with and often intrinsic to mothering. Higher rates of employment have been recorded for this group compared with white women since the 1970s and 'good mothering' was closely tied to women's ability to provide for their family.[10] One strategy, especially in the south Asian community, was for women to undertake homework, predominantly for the textile industry though this was intensive work and poorly paid.[11] A not dissimilar attitude has been identified amongst white working-class mothers for whom wage-earning was central to their sense of self though this group was more likely to delay the return to the workplace until children started school.[12]

In what follows we explore the trajectories of our cohort of women as they worked out how to negotiate their way through the post-war reconfiguring of women's life cycles. Women who were 'pulled in two between the desire to be a good mother and the longing to realize the self' found they had to help themselves.[13] Existing women's organizations designed to meet the needs of women in an earlier era had matured with their membership rather than changing their offer to recruit younger women. And there was little local provision of daytime activities which women could attend with or without young children. Today's plethora of parent-and-toddler groups, exercise classes, and provision of sports

[9] Laura Paterson and Eve Worth, '"How is She Going to Manage with the Children?" Organizational Labour, Working and Mothering in Britain, c.1960–190', *Past and Present*, Supplement 15 (2020), pp.318–43.

[10] Tracey Reynolds, *Caribbean Mothers: Identity and Experience in the UK* (London, 2005), pp.97–103.

[11] Din, 'British-Pakistani Homeworkers'; Annie Phizacklea and Carol Wolkowitz, *Homeworking Women: Gender, Racism and Class at Work* (London: Sage, 1995), pp.45–68.

[12] Laura Paterson, '"I didn't feel like my own person": paid work in women's narratives of self and working motherhood', 1950–1980, *Contemporary British History* 33:3, (2019), pp.405–26, here 419.

[13] IoE, PLA PPA 1–4: Crowe report, Birmingham, p.4.

centres and part-time educational provision throws into stark relief the barren landscape that confronted many young mothers at this time. Returning to paid work was rarely an option while children were of pre-school age and childcare provision was hard to come by. Whether one lived on a new housing estate, in a leafy suburb or in a high-rise flat, opportunities to pursue personal growth and find a space to rediscover the self were limited. In this situation, some women took the initiative to create an environment in which the self could be realized on their own terms.

Stay-at-Home Mothers

The decision whether or not to stay at home while the children were small was, for most new mothers, not a difficult one to make given the obstacles to combining paid work and motherhood. Women of this cohort expected that this would be their trajectory; that is they would continue to work after marriage but that they would leave employment to start a family, possibly returning when the children were older though responses to a survey in 1961 demonstrated that only 50 per cent expected to do so.[14] When asked at the age of 16 what she hoped for by the age of 25, this girl was clear: 'To be married, possibly with children. If this happened I would not work'.[15] Another in unskilled work reported that she and all of her work colleagues 'are all longing to leave and stay at home'.[16] A teacher who had married in her twenties remarked that she and her husband were 'making the most of two salaries at the moment living comfortably as we realize life will be difficult when we have to cope on one salary', presumably looking forward to starting a family. Two years later, at the age of 25 she was head of the art department at a girls' grammar school and expected at 35 to be 'housewife and mother—possibly some part-time teaching'.[17] Not all looked on this prospect with joy; some were resigned. 'Housework!' was the response of a teacher asked what job she expected to be doing at the age of 35. '[will have to] Resign post [in order to do housework]'. She expected the change to be 'drastic'.[18] This demonstrates the widespread understanding and, for some, resignation, that when a woman married and had children she made a transition from the single life focused on the self, to a family life which involved compromise and sacrifice.

Work that had been experienced by some women as self-fulfilment was, once children arrived, presented as a selfish activity that detracted from family life.

[14] Joyce Joseph, 'A Research Note on Attitudes to Work and Marriage of Six Hundred Adolescent Girls', *The British Journal of Sociology* 12:2 (1961), pp.176–83, 179.

[15] MRC, NSHD: Sample 10—Personal questionnaire 1962.

[16] MRC, NSHD: Persistent Job Changers Study, 010011.

[17] MRC, NSHD: Sample 31—Personal questionnaire 1970.

[18] MRC, NSHD: Sample 15—Personal questionnaire 1971.

It could be returned to when the children no longer required their mother's full attention. For women who had been encouraged to pursue a career, who had enjoyed independence and who had also flung themselves into marriage and home-making, motherhood could be a rude awakening and present the first significant bump in the road of their life so far. Pregnancy and motherhood interrupted career progression. Lorna, who had been a dental nurse before she had her first child, was planning on doing an Open University degree 'and then I got pregnant with [son] and after having [son] it was impossible, so I didn't. And I felt as though I'd missed an opportunity there.' Instead, she took a number of short-term jobs—as a dinner-lady and a receptionist—before running a bed-and-breakfast business in her own home, work that she could fit in around her family responsibilities. In interview many years later she reflected:

> I would have probably studied more. But I felt quite fulfilled with what I had. I felt, up to my 40s really I was always aware of the lack of education and then something hit me and I suddenly thought, I accepted life and I thought 'no, I know what I'm capable of' and I just accepted and I stopped worrying about lack of qualifications and accepting me for what I was. And I didn't find it a problem.[19]

The majority of women in the 1960s and 1970s gave up paid work shortly before having their first child and did not return to it until children were of school age or older. Only 19 per cent of working women in 1961 had children under five.[20] Those who did return to the labour market quickly while their children were still small generally did so for financial or professional reasons. Sara returned to her job as a legal secretary in London six months after the birth of her child, employing a childminder. Although this was fairly unusual amongst this cohort of women she remarked: 'At the time I just did it, don't think I thought about it, just did it cause I needed the money.'[21] Maureen, who had been a typist for a bank before she left to have her first child, did a cleaning job in the early mornings when the child was still quite young and staffed the cloakroom at the local ice rink because 'financially we were really up against it'. She described the complicated logistics, the 'organizational labour' required to enable her to do this:

> And I worked there I think one evening a week in the cloakroom. So [husband] would come home from work, we'd have tea, I didn't drive, we had a car seat in the car for [child], so he'd drive me to Richmond, I'd do my job and I'd get the bus back. Other than that, I do early morning cleaning, so there was Nella Hall around the corner from us, so I'd start work at, what time was it, five, half five in the morning, be home in time to take [child] to school. So that's the sort of jobs

[19] UKDA, SN 850818: M56.
[20] Paterson, 'I didn't feel like my own person', p.407.
[21] UKDA, SN 850818: M42.

> I did until [husband] was ill, and I didn't want to go back to the bank but I did and I stayed there till I was 50.[22]

But there were also very many obstacles to women returning to work when their children were small. In the first place, before 1975, women had no statutory right to return to a job after giving birth. But added to this, it was the social expectation that a woman would withdraw from the workplace to focus on her under-fives and women felt the pressure to conform as well as being pushed by their employers in some cases and also constrained by husbands. Maureen recounted an occasion when she applied for a job when her child was still very young. The man who interviewed her 'got quite stroppy and he was saying "Well what will you do with your child during the holidays?" and I said "Well my husband could look after my daughter" "Well have you asked your husband? Is he amenable to this?" and I remember thinking at the time "Bloody hell, who do you think you are?"'[23] In the previous chapter we met Cynthia who recounted having to give up her job in journalism when she became pregnant, highlighting the persistence of structural sexism in some workplaces in this period, but for many, staying in work or returning after a period of maternity leave simply was not an option when childcare was so limited despite the financial pressures experienced by some couples. Amongst the women interviewed for the Pahls' study were several whose husbands opposed them working, including Mr Manston who went into a huff and 'got out the Hoover' when he perceived that his wife was not keeping on top of the housework. However, others were grudgingly more accepting of their wives' desires to explore returning to the workplace: Mr Eastwell said he would not 'consider it an affront to his virility if she did go out to work'.[24] Maureen, who eventually returned to secretarial work, was lucky that her husband was willing and able to undertake the childcare when she worked. When asked to reflect on why she did not return to a job she enjoyed as a conference organizer, despite a stated intention to do so, Gillian explained that although she and her husband 'desperately needed the money', the circumstances conspired to prevent her. In addition to travel difficulties—she didn't drive—she had no childcare. She would have been unhappy leaving her child with a stranger and the couple had moved house to be on 'neutral territory' between her mother and mother-in-law. Gillian eventually returned to part-time work when her second child was four years old.[25]

Notwithstanding the very real practical constraints and psychological pressures upon women, Wendy's assertion that 'I might not have been a very good

[22] UKDA, SN 850818: M61. On the concept of 'organizational labour' see Paterson and Worth, 'How is she going to manage', p.319.
[23] UKDA, SN 850818: M61.
[24] UKDA, SN 853296: Interview with Mrs Manston; interview with Mr Eastwell p.26.
[25] UKDA, SN 850818: M48.

housewife, I might not have been a very good mother but I've done the right thing' needs to be taken seriously.[26] The desire to be at home with the children was genuinely felt, both at the time and even more strongly in retrospect in many cases, especially in the case of interviews carried out in women's later life when their own daughters' and daughters-in-law were grappling with the home-work balance dilemma. The stress they observed in the lives of the next generation of working mothers was contrasted with the relative simplicity of their own when being a stay-at-home mother was the convention. Angela, a teacher, married at 25 and continued to work full time, remarking that her husband 'never thought that his wife should be a housewife. He always believed in everybody having their own life.' But when their first child arrived seven years later Angela was clear that she 'wanted to have his upbringing and not pass it on to someone else, you know go to nurseries'.[27] Angela had moved away from her family to follow her husband's job and was living in rural part of the country with little or no availability of childcare. Her plight was increasingly common amongst this mobile generation. But Angela's views were also influenced by observing the day nurseries used by women factory workers when she was undertaking her teacher-training. 'They had babies whose mums worked in factories because it was necessary then when they didn't have the money. And they used to put these babies in just from a month old and they were there until the mother came at 5 o'clock.'[28]

Yet some women made the positive choice to stay at home and discovered their 'vocation'.[29] Lorna had her first child relatively late, at the age of 28. She explained that 'I didn't work because, um, I didn't want to go back…And I loved being at home, I loved being a mother, and our son was only born sixteen months after so it was lovely. I really, really enjoyed motherhood.' Moreover, while this couple were not wealthy they were able to manage on one salary: 'And I didn't have to work. We didn't have much financially, we made our own wine and we didn't have many things but we were very happy and it was lovely. It was really nice.'[30] And Veronica who had been a teacher explained that she took to being at home 'like a duck to water'. I was perfectly happy to be at home and had decided…to give up, I'd actually given up school.'[31] The first few years at home as a family she described as 'momentous'. When she did eventually return to work it was accidental. A chance encounter at her children's nursery school led to her being asked to go in to play the guitar for the nursery class, a temporary role that led to her returning as a supply teacher. It was an arrangement that fitted in with her children's needs as she explained:

[26] UKDA, SN 850818: M31. [27] Interview with Angela. [28] Interview with Angela.

[29] Ingham, *Now We Are Thirty* includes a number of accounts of stay-at-home motherhood as a positive choice, pp.191–4.

[30] UKDA, SN 850818: M56. [31] UKDA, SN 850818: M26.

> Well about six weeks later I was still there but [my] other child was in the nursery and so [headteacher] said 'they can stay in the nursery in the afternoon'... And then the job there ended and I got a job at [school] and that was, first of all a day a week then two days a week, then three days a week, point eight of a week until in the end they said to me 'Now either you take a full-time job or it won't be there'. But by then they were well settled in school and so I took it.[32]

Twenty-six years later she was still there.

Women of this cohort were on the cusp between two life course models; it was they who, in their twenties and thirties, made the first tentative steps towards a new pattern of work and family, negotiating a path through the prioritizing of childcare and family whilst not losing the self-identity they had established through work and marriage. Rosemary was one of those women who was establishing a career in occupational therapy. As a young woman she had been to college, travelled, and become independent. She married aged 25 in 1971 and was shocked when, at the wedding, one of her mother's friends asked '"and will you be carrying on working?" And I went "pardon? Well yes. What would I do if I didn't?"' Rosemary regarded this as an extraordinary exchange for the time, encapsulating the generation gap between herself and her mother who 'dropped work like a hot brick and had absolutely no intention of ever going back'. But when Rosemary had her children she initially stayed at home. She explained that 'the social pressure was not to work if you could afford not to'. She joined the National Housewives Register as one of the 'well educated women who were Mums, and who were at home and didn't really want to let their brains completely shrivel and [who] probably all intended to go back to work at some stage'. However, when the family moved to the far north of Scotland when the children were still small, Rosemary returned to work for a few hours a week to help out the overstretched occupational therapy service there. And in the absence of any childcare provision Rosemary utilized the local playgroup to enable her to work part time: 'I think I did six hours a week actually, to start with. So I left her at play group, went and did two hours work, came back and picked her up went home and we had dinner. It was perfect, absolutely perfect yeh. Yes, there wasn't organized childcare, then.'[33] By the early 1960s part-time work in female-dominated professions such as teaching and health-related occupations was becoming commonplace as graduate and women were encouraged back to the labour market to meet a chronic labour shortage.[34]

Rosemary's experience was typical of women for whom their identity as a professional in the workplace and as a mother were not mutually exclusive. While social expectations and structural constraints played a part in her decision to

[32] UKDA, SN 850818: M26. [33] Interview with Rosemary.

[34] McCarthy, *Double Lives*, pp.263–9.

withdraw from the labour market for a time, the circumstances that drew her back more quickly than she might have expected forced her to redefine for herself what it meant to be a good mother. Her involvement in the National Housewives Register and then the playgroup helped her to manage the tension in psychological and practical ways at the time, but in interview some 40 years later, Rosemary was also able to reflect on how she managed the conflicting demands and expectations. As she explained, the social pressure as much as the material and psychological circumstances of real life shaped her actions:

> I do think that however much you intellectualize things, you shouldn't underestimate the power of sort of society pressure actually, and I do think we go along with that a lot...So I mean I would intellectualize that I was going to stay home and look after my children because why do you have children to hand them over to somebody else to bring them up. I don't understand why anybody would do that, so it's my job now to stay at home until they go to school, which is what I did, and then I started to go back to work, part time. But, from a feminism point of view that didn't really impinge I don't think, on what I did. But... I was married to a civil engineer who worked very long hours, so in terms of household things I would say that I rationalized it that I ended up doing most of the work because he worked such incredibly long hours, so I could rationalize that.[35]

In order to manage the two parts of her life—as a mother and a professional health worker—Rosemary, like so many mothers of young children, found practical ways of meeting the demands of both and satisfying both parts of her identity. NHR provided her with intellectual stimulation and social contact: 'it took you right away from babies and nappies and husbands and food and, you know, you were using your brain. It was good, it was very good.'[36] The playgroup provided part-time childcare until her children could attend school. Moreover, in reflecting many years later on how she had rationalized the decision to withdraw from the labour market and then turning the problem around and finding a positive in what to her, in retrospect, was an unsatisfactory or incoherent account, Rosemary rescued the autonomous self in the narrative.

Women in less skilled jobs may have been keener to give up work upon motherhood but had fewer choices when their earnings were more critical to the household finances. However, Paterson argues that working-class women's identity was more likely to be centred on wage earning and the sacrifices made to support the family.[37] For this group, access to work when children were still young was eased somewhat by the growth in part-time and shift work, especially

[35] Interview with Rosemary.
[36] Interview with Rosemary.
[37] Paterson, 'I didn't feel like my own person', p.419.

in the manufacturing sector. Evening shifts were introduced during the Second World War as a means of mobilizing married women and some industries retained what became known as the 'housewives' shift—6 p.m. to 10 p.m.[38] New towns acted as the crucible of change in this regard.[39] In Stevenage, one of the first wave of English new towns, it was said that firms were increasingly reliant on part-time female workers but because the factories were two miles away from the housing in the town, employers were offering 'special shift systems for working mothers'. Kodak operated what it called the 'granny shift' from 6 p.m. to 10 p.m. 'which enables mothers to work and leave grandmother in charge of the family', avoiding the so-called 'latch-key problem' when critics of working mothers focused on children being left to let themselves into an empty house on returning home from school. The Mentmore factory in Stevenage which produced pens and stationery, provided a creche.[40] In East Kilbride in Scotland, the Laird Portch clothing factory did the same.[41] Workers with fewer skills, however, were likely to experience a more fractured return to work than their professional and semi-professional counterparts, with limited opportunities to receive training or promotion and perhaps a greater propensity to emphasize their satisfaction with motherhood as their primary career. Karen gave up a job in a bakery when she had her first child, returned to the labour market as a classroom assistant when her second went to school, and ended her working life as supervisor for a cleaning company until she had to give it up owing to ill health. When asked whether motherhood had impacted her working life she responded:

> It has... yeah, I think to me if you're gonna be... I'd probably get shouted at if I said this but I was brought up that if you're a mother that's your job, that's your career... you choose a career or motherhood and I don't... it's not I'm putting people off, if you want a career and motherhood it's fine but for me motherhood was everything, was my career... now I look back and I think it would have been nice to have had a career but then I've had the children and they've had me so that's it... yeah.[42]

Wives of manual workers were more likely to be working in the 1960s than the wives of professional men. They did so for the money, to be able to afford a more comfortable domestic lifestyle and to support their aspirations for their children.

[38] Paterson, 'Women and Paid Work', pp.61–2.

[39] See Jo Foord, 'Conflicting Lives: Women's Work in Planned Communities', PhD thesis, University of Kent, 1990; Jane Lewis and Jo Foord, 'New Towns and New Gender Relations in Old Industrial Regions: Women's Employment in Peterlee and East Kilbride', *Built Environment* 10:1 (1984), pp. 42–52.

[40] 'Working mothers force planners to think again', *The Guardian*, 15 Aug. 1961.

[41] *East Kilbride: The People's Story* (East Kilbride, 2015) mentions the nursery at the textile factory, Laird Portch.

[42] UKDA, SN 850818: 063.

They also worked for the sociability it provided and, in some cases, the self-satisfaction and confidence they derived from it.[43] Even boring and repetitive work could 'give women an individuality many of them lack at home' discovered a study of stress in the workplace.[44] But educated and economically more comfortable married women found other ways of staving off loneliness whilst gaining in confidence and taking baby-steps back to the world of work for those who aspired to it. Forming, joining and volunteering in one of the burgeoning self-help groups met all of those needs for many thousands of women and which enabled them to walk the tightrope between motherhood and career, professional identity and conventional femininity.

Stepping Stones

The self-help revolution of the 1960s, as we have seen, provided women climbing the walls with boredom and frustration with an empathetic community of the like-minded. These organizations quickly began to offer their members more than stimulating conversation or a place to leave the children for a couple of hours. They were distinctive for members' active engagement and, in the case of pre-school playgroups in particular, the ambition to provide women with an opportunity to stretch themselves beyond the walls of the home.

The Observer journalist Dilys Rowe rather acerbically and a little unfairly recounted the experience of a recent arrival to a Wiltshire village looking for a social circle. She considered the Women's Institute until she realized that if she attended a talk by the NSPCC inspector 'she would have to witness (if not contribute to) a display of flower arrangements made in thimbles and mounted in matchboxes'. Rowe correctly noted that these longstanding women's organizations lacked spontaneity and the ability or willingness at local level to change.[45] At national level, as Beaumont has established, the more traditional groups like the WI, Townswomen's Guild, and Mothers' Union were active in campaigning on issues affecting women of all ages, recognizing the changing role of women in modern society, rejecting the traditional ideology of domesticity and acknowledging that 'being a good housewife also meant being a good citizen'.[46] Whilst continuing to represent the interests of housewives they also concerned themselves with the issues encountered by working mothers and campaigned on

[43] Paterson, 'I didn't feel like my own person', pp.411–12; McCarthy, *Double Lives*, pp.237–40.

[44] 'Keeping a finger on the button', *The Guardian*, 17 March 1978.

[45] Dilys Rowe, 'The Beetle Drive Belt', *The Observer*, 29 Oct. 1961.

[46] Beaumont, *Housewives and Citizens*, p.192; Beaumont, 'What Is a Wife'? Reconstructing Domesticity in Post-war Britain before The Feminine Mystique', *History of Women in the Americas* 3 (2015), https://journals.sas.ac.uk/hwa/article/view/2186.

divorce reform, widows' earnings and family planning.[47] Yet local groups were less adaptable, continuing, for the most part, to cater to the needs of an older demographic with a focus on home-making.[48] The new organizations, on the other hand, explicitly sought to fulfil the post-war generation's social, intellectual, and emotional needs. The fact that the PPA, NHR, and a host of local initiatives such as the WAM in London and the Home Counties, the Family Club in Birmingham, and the Cornelians in Edinburgh, were founded and run by precisely the women for whom they were intended meant they understood women needed more than diverting talks by food demonstrators and a raffle.[49]

Rowe's characterization of the old-fashioned and self-satisfied offer of traditional women's organizations may seem harsh, but for women who had given up jobs, an afternoon watching a Tupperware demonstration was not likely to provide the stimulation needed. Mrs Ickham who had been a nurse before marriage, children and a move to a house in the country following her husband's work, was keen to escape the boredom of home but the local Young Wives club was not an attractive option: 'I said "Not yet". It's probably a revolt against the way I was brought up. My mother was involved in the Women's Institute and the Young Wives and I had enough of it then... I'd rather have outside interests more on my husband's level, so I don't get bogged down with the family, kids and domesticity.'[50] Young Wives' Clubs, affiliated to the churches, were in precipitous decline through the 1960s. One such group in Norwich, founded in 1957, was already struggling for new members just a few years on. Attempts to grow—lifting the age limit from 40 to 45 and then abandoning it altogether, leafleting a new housing estate and distributing their programme of events to the local playgroup—all failed to address the decline.[51] One reason may have been the character of their activities. In 1969 they heard talks on wallpapers, religion and the older child, medieval Norwich, spring flower arranging and Shelter and were entertained and informed by a demonstration on the Bamix food mixer. Another reason was almost certainly the secularizing trend amongst women who no longer affiliated themselves to a church. The dissolution of female piety in the 1960s and younger women's rejection of Christian models of female identity centred on the family and home, had repercussions for faith-based organizations like Young Wives and

[47] Beaumont, *Housewives and Citizens*, pp.190–210.

[48] See, for example, the Housewives' Clubs which were run under the aegis of the National Association of Women's Clubs in the 1950s. NLS: 'Clubs for Housewives', 1953. On activity at national level see Catriona Beaumont, 'Beyond Women's Liberation. Intergenerational Female Activism in England, 1960s–1980s', Inaugural lecture, 12 Oct. 2022. https://www.youtube.com/watch?v=4eB_2Jm3yqI and Beaumont, 'What *Do* Women Want? Housewives' Associations, Activism and Changing Representations of Women in the 1950s', *Women's History Review* 26:1 (2017), pp.147–62, 158.

[49] NLS: 'Clubs for Housewives', 1953. The Cornelians was founded by Anne Scott following her letter to *The Scotsman* in 1960. It affiliated to NHR in 1963. See Jerman, *Lively-Minded Women*, p.102.

[50] UKDA, SN 853296: Interview with Mrs Ickham, p.3.

[51] Norfolk Record Office (NRO): FC 79/420 Young Wives' Club (Heartsease Lane Methodist Young Wives Club)—Annual General Meeting Minutes, Jun. 1957–Sept. 1978.

the Mothers' Union who aged with their members.[52] Membership of this Norwich group haemorrhaged. In 1978 those few remaining agreed to wind up: 'it was the only thing left to do'.[53]

If the constituency Young Wives hoped to attract were joining anything at all it was more likely to be one of the new self-help groups which eschewed the domestic and embraced the potential of their members for self-development. Local groups of the National Housewives Register required members to undertake research to prompt informed discussion. The Pre-School Playgroups Association went much further in incorporating mothers as volunteer mother-helpers and thereafter provided opportunities for training and advancement within the organization. And all the self-help organizations were run by a band of volunteers raising funds, making practical arrangements, organizing conferences, establishing training, liaising with local authorities and so on. Some described this kind of activity as 'work-like'. For others, like Brenda Crowe, the indefatigable national organizer of the PPA, it was 'real women's lib because you liberate yourself by doing something for yourself'.[54]

Jennifer was one of those who embraced Crowe's philosophy. She had been a music teacher but when a move to another part of the country prompted her to give up her career and start a family, she and a neighbour started a nursery club, anticipating the nationwide pre-school playgroup movement by months. Jennifer described herself as 'somebody who can start something' and this moment as being 'on this crest of the wave. And there really wasn't any opposition. There was only like, enthusiasm.' After forming a branch of the PPA in 1963 Jennifer became a paid playgroup organizer two years later, progressing to the role of training and development officer for the west of Scotland and then development worker for the Scottish playgroup association Stepping Stones. Eventually Jennifer resigned to undertake further training in child development and worked for the Scottish Institute for Human Relations. The initial impetus for Jennifer's involvement in the playgroup initiative was loneliness and a feeling that being a mother 'didn't satisfy the whole of me', but her engagement with the practical and theoretical challenges of establishing the playgroup movement was personally transformative.

> So everybody was new and there was wild excitement about playgroups which were sort of embedded into little halls throughout Cumbernauld. And so it really was a quite amazing experience being so involved in something that was so lively. I met all these women, you know more and more and more women, all of whom were desperately keen to do something. And so I think I was at the sort

[52] Callum G. Brown, *The Death of Christian Britain. Understanding Secularisation 1800–2000* (London: Routledge, 2009), pp.175–80.

[53] NRO: FC 79/424—Secretary's correspondence and papers (mainly with local businesses, associations and institutions re arrangement of visits and talks), 1969 programme.

[54] *The Times*, 5 May 1971.

> of crest of a wave and I just was at the point in time when women were waking up, blinking their eyes, and seeing there's more to life than looking after children. It wasn't that they didn't want their children, but there was more to life and they were feeling it. They were feeling it rather than keeping it in and having to be, you know…And of course it turned into an open door to take teacher training, to go to university…All of these things were possible. It was like a door opening.[55]

For Jennifer, involvement in the playgroup movement was immersive and creative. Her account vividly portrays how she and other women felt and the exhilaration of acting on those feelings. It opened doors to new experiences, new skills, and ultimately for Jenny, a deep engagement in the psychology of child development. Hierarchy was rejected in favour of parental participation and learning by doing. Hands-on training was preferred to 'somebody speaking and giving a lecture and so on' and there were 'loads and loads of discussion groups'. The contrast with the more traditional women's organizations could not have been more stark. These underlying principles were designed to open training to allcomers and to instil confidence in parents who may have had little or no post-school education. In this way the door was pushed ajar for those who wished to take the next step. And many did.

Jennifer was a self-confessed do-er. The self-help organizations were founded by women, for women, in response to the frustration, loneliness and lack of intellectual stimulation experienced by a generation who were struggling with isolation from their peers and the mundanity of home in contrast with the lives they had left behind. And those who 'did' were in possession of the skills and confidence to make things happen. Elizabeth Belcher remarked that 'The [PPA Foundation] course was my lifeline…and it was such a relief to find myself in a group of "do-ers"'.[56] Rita Miller recalled that 'each time I was offered a new PPA job I felt, I can't do that, and did it'.[57] And the do-ers tended to be serial joiners. Catherine, a graduate who worked in a research capacity for a drug company before she had children, tried all manner of women's groups in the late 1970s including: the National Association of University Women (profile of members too old), Business & Professional Women's Club (ditto), a variety of church groups including Young Wives (sat on the committee), Mothers and Toddlers, the NCT, NHR, and Girl Guides. In later life she was and is still active in the National Women's Register and found the University of the Third Age (u3a) to be a similarly valuable environment for social and intellectual exchange.[58]

55 Interview with Jennifer.

56 IoE, PLA, PPA 6/1: Memories—Elizabeth Belcher.

57 IoE, PLA, PPA 6/1: Memories—Rita Miller.

58 Personal correspondence with Catherine, National Women's Register, 2021.

Janette agreed that she too, was the kind of person who got involved: 'But I mean blimey, I was in Guiding, NCT, NWR and PTA at school.'[59] Initially she joined the National Childbirth Trust for friendship and support when she was at home with a young baby. Janette explained that her NCT group was very close; so close in fact that they breast-fed each other's babies: 'You know, if you were baby sitting and the baby was howling. How do you shut it up, plug it in. Well I had one friend in particular, we were quite open and quite happy to do that.' Her own problems with breastfeeding her daughter led her to a breastfeeding counselling training course. She became a NCT breast-feeding counsellor in London and then, when she moved to Scotland, was quickly welcomed into the NCT family there where she took up the counselling again until she got sick of 'cracked nipples'. Involvement in NCT provided Janette with a network of friends who supported her when she was struggling with her first child and it then facilitated her integration into a new city when she moved to follow her husband's job. NCT ante-natal classes had a similar function (see Figure 7.1). In Edinburgh she joined a young mothers' club after discovering the University Ladies' Club, where her husband worked, to be full of 'stuffy old bags'. The mothers' club on the other hand, was 'great fun! That was fantastic and I got put on the exec.... so I'd deliberately unbutton my braces at the top of my dungarees and breastfeed my baby. Well why not!'[60]

These organizations met women's social and practical needs but they also fulfilled a desire for personal growth or self-actualization. Maslow's concept of 'the full realization of one's potential' was, according to Betty Friedan, incompatible with the lives of many women. Housewives, she argued, were unable to achieve personal growth as self-actualization was only attainable via the pursuit of activities outside the home.[61] Friedan's interpretation has been widely questioned, not least in the British context where 'traditional' women's organizations had, since the inter-war years, argued that women could combine marriage, motherhood, and public life.[62] The new voluntary organizations such as PPA, NCT, and NHR did not explicitly use the language of self-actualization, and they rejected the assumption that the home was necessarily a barrier to women realizing their potential. Indeed, although they did not celebrate or fetishize the home, they did accept and condone that many women would spend some years, especially when their children were small, in a home-focused role. But the significance of these organizations is much greater than their role in keeping women's brains ticking over and providing an outlet for women's frustration. NHR was seen as providing 'an essential link between careers past and future, by giving us the opportunity to

[59] Interview with Janette. [60] Interview with Janette.

[61] Friedan, *Feminine Mystique*, pp.253–73.

[62] See Caitriona Beaumont, 'What Is a Wife? Reconstructing Domesticity in Post-war Britain before *The Feminine Mystique*', *History of Women in the Americas* 3 (September 2015), pp.61–76.

Figure 7.1 Erna Wright, National Childbirth Trust antenatal class, undated.

be ourselves for a few precious hours—a selfish need but a desperate one for those rapidly sinking in an endless sea of domestic chores'.[63] Active participation in NHR or PPA could also be part of a reorientation of roles in the home as women's absence, at conferences, committee meetings or social events, forced husbands to recognize the importance of their wives' involvement and to step up to the housework or childcare, if only on an occasional basis. Josephine recalled how women in her NHR group had battles with their husbands over their attendance at events: 'Go to these conferences and "oh how great, not to have to cook a meal" and to leave the children, it was so difficult to find someone to look after them, or "get my husband to do it" or "I'll have to get back early because he can't do it in a Sunday night, he has to go to", that sort of thing.'[64] For some individual women NHR provided a space in which they could reconnect with their former selves and an environment in which to think about the future. Kathleen, who had been a draughtswoman before she had children, described having a 'black hole' in her life once she left her job 'so having sort of, you know, a meeting where you could discuss, I don't know... suicide, or a book group or divorce or any current issue of the day, you know... miners' strikes, um, you know, anything... And then later on, as NWR progressed, women of my age were then talking about going back to work, you know, further education, that sort of thing.[65]

[63] LSE, Women's Library: NHR Spring Newsletter 1967.
[64] Interview with Josephine.
[65] Interview with Kathleen.

As a self-help organization NHR relied on its members to maintain it as it grew exponentially. By the 1970s, with a membership in the thousands, running NHR was an operation involving hundreds of women as area organizers or national committee members. And many of them used that knowledge as a stepping-stone to further education (especially the Open University) and to careers in the voluntary sector. Josephine established a branch of the NHR in her small town in rural Scotland as a means of meeting like-minded women. Married to a farmer she nevertheless knew that her generation had 'more of a life than our mothers had, and we're going to make more of it'. She started to attend the national conferences where she met the incumbent national committee members and recalled:

> and I was just so excited for me to be in a hall full of lively-minded women, you know, all talking, and discussing and making decisions, and committees. We didn't go for committees a lot, but you know, making decisions, and that I think I just found so interesting, and meeting people and then being able to write to them, or something, after that. And I, they asked for volunteers and I said I was interested in it and then I got a phone call saying 'do you want to do it?' you know, and I didn't quite know what I was letting myself in for, none of us did! (Laughter)

Josephine had not experienced post-secondary education but she had attended grammar school which stood her in good stead when advising new start-up groups.

> And that was...I loved it because people would come and say you know, 'there's no group here and I'm terrified and I don't know how to do it' there was a lot of lack of confidence, lack of ability, I'd been to a grammar school and, you know, we'd learnt—maybe...I think I'd been to a good grammar school—and learnt debating and setting up our own groups, you know, like—different groups that you'd set up and I must have got some confidence there, I wasn't a great scholar, and other people just seemed as though...a lot of women just had no confidence at all—'how do I do it?' you know and 'I daren't' and of course you know 'I can't do that, my husband won't approve' or 'I'll have to ask my husband' (chuckling).[66]

At this time NHR consisted of more than 5000 groups with 20,000 members around the country. On an annual honorarium of £250, Josephine helped to draw up a new constitution and engage with the Charity Commission. She articulated the newness of this kind of activity by contrasting her involvement with her mother's membership of a more traditional women's organization, the Townswomen's Guild (TWG). Josephine's mother, who had left school at 14, described her

[66] Interview with Josephine.

involvement in the TWG as 'an education' but Josephine contrasted it with her own engagement with the NHR: 'she really got a lot out of it, but it was, you know, on trips going around a factory—They'd go—and get a lecture and come away again, whereas we were about sorting out, putting the world to rights, yes, putting the world to rights quite a lot.' 'It is highly significant for me', wrote Josephine, 'that the development of NHR had sown in my mind the realization that women, on marriage, need not spend their days homemaking, entertaining and going to the Townswomen's Guild twice a month . . . But that intellectual activities . . . could and should develop as an integral part of daily living.'[67]

Active involvement in NHR was a springboard for Josephine to became more deeply engaged in women's issues in her locality. She helped to establish a playgroup and worked as a paid advisor at a local Action Centre providing advice and counselling to the homeless, victims of domestic abuse and those with addiction problems. She explained that it was involvement in the NHR that enabled her to take on this work: 'that was, again, another whole world was opening up to me, but I got the confidence . . . I'd have found it somewhere I was sure, that confidence, but the National Housewives Register gave me the confidence that I could do things. I could stand in front of an audience of 2, 3, 4, I think probably 500 and talk to them, you know, and run meetings and things like that.' In Beaumont's words, she learned the 'vocabulary of democracy'.[68] And like many women of her generation, that confidence boost alongside an active engagement in social issues propelled her back into education. 'It was that that set me off. "If I can do this then I can do Open University". But I shall never forget that first day when you open the OU books and there's a sort of "read this and these are the questions" you know, and I sort of "can I do it, can I do it?" . . . the house was empty and I read it and I could answer the questions.'[69]

The journey did not end here for Josephine. The transformation of her life occurred in two dimensions—the professional and the personal. Her degree and her work experience in the Action Centre gave her the self-confidence and the skills to apply for a full-time job in London working for the Quaker International Centre. She moved south with two children and combined work with studying for an MA which in turn enabled her to teach for the Open University. She eventually moved to Glasgow to help establish a Centre for Women's Health. In parallel, the experience and knowledge she gathered over the years of active engagement starting with a small branch of the National Housewives Register gave her the confidence to leave her husband.

Josephine narrated a story of personal growth and self-actualization which was echoed by many other women—the 'do-ers'—who found their active involvement in self-help organizations was instrumental in enabling them to take control of

[67] Josephine Jaffray in Jerman, *Lively Minded Women*, p.113.
[68] Beaumont, 'Beyond Women's Liberation'.
[69] Interview with Josephine.

their lives. 'Looking back I am amazed at what I learned and what I achieved through my involvement with the [PPA]' wrote Dawn Collins, recalling many years of activity at local and county level. She identified a number of experiences as 'important milestones in my growth and development' which included professional training, committee work, attending national AGMs, and chairing her local PPA committee.[70] The PPA offered more than social interaction and committee work. While some of the same frustrations of 'housebound mothers' allied to the absence of pre-school nursery or playschool provision gave rise to the PPA, it quickly became a multi-faceted organization combining a network of local playgroups meeting in church halls and community centres up and down the country with a commitment to parental—predominantly mothers'—participation (the volunteer rota was critical to the running of local groups), comprehensive training provision and political and civic engagement. In this sense PPA straddled the personal and the political in more concrete ways than any of the other self-help organizations of the post-war era.

Unlike NHR, the PPA and especially its charismatic national organizer Brenda Crowe, who had a background as a nursery school teacher and child guidance remedial worker, explicitly acknowledged the role of the organization in meeting the needs of mothers, not just for social contact but for self-development.[71] Linnet McMahon, a parent co-founder of a village playgroup in 1968 who went on to become a playgroup course tutor concurred: 'What mothers were doing was, like their children, learning through play, in the sense that they were able to try things out—or try new ways of being—in an emotionally facilitating environment where it felt safe, where it was alright to make mistakes. In the process they created something new or became someone different. They were developing a sense of autonomy and identity.'[72] The PPA quickly expanded in size and purpose from DIY and home-based playgroups to a national network with funding from local and national government and a structured training regime—following a pattern established by the New Zealand playgroup movement some years earlier. It was this structure that provided many women with a pathway to personal growth.

Catalyst for Change

Champions of playgroups over nurseries and other forms of childcare provision emphasized that playgroups enabled women to 'grow in their capacity to bear authority with responsibility'. 'The parent-run playgroup', argued a consultant psychiatrist at the PPA's AGM in 1972, 'is a growth situation for children and their

[70] IoE, PLA, PPA 6/1: Memories—Dawn Collins.

[71] PLA/PPA/4/6: Brenda Crowe, 'Parent Involvement' in *Parents in Playgroups* (c.1971).

[72] Linnet McMahon, 'The significance of play for children and adults', in Henderson (Ed.), *Insights*, pp.32–3.

mothers together'.[73] In the initial stages the 'playgroup pioneers' shared good practice and planned activities with neighbouring groups but quite quickly the demand for courses came from parents, especially the helpers, who wanted to learn more about child development through play. Initially the courses took the form of informal meetings or workshops, often led by a group member who had some experience or knowledge of child development. The philosophy of the PPA was that learning was a shared enterprise with parent-helpers and supervisors learning together with the emphasis on acknowledging and valuing each individual's experience. 'Our job as tutors is not to try to force professional standards on mothers to "bring them up to scratch", stated Brenda Crowe. 'We must help them to grow.'[74] But quite quickly courses run by tutors, were instituted for parents, play leaders, supervisors, and committee members.

At the core of PPA's approach to the involvement of parents and to training was the 'moving on' philosophy, the belief that through involvement in the organization women could gain skills and progress in their own learning (see Figure 7.2). Jennifer described how, in Scotland, they 'started off with courses for parents. They were organized by the playgroup and then there were courses for play leaders...There were 3 levels of courses...We took play leaders right up to the door. You know, the door going on to do something else afterwards and then they were courses for Area Organizers.'[75] In a survey of active parents some 50 years on from their involvement, it was concluded that 'moving on offered a variety of pathways for mothers whose energy, imagination, creativity and abilities had often been limited by an unfulfilling experience of school or by the home environment, or who had cut short stimulating work experience to start a family, and felt the loss'.[76] The PPA was a multi-layered, bureaucratic organization, providing numerous opportunities for participation in committee work at local, regional or national level, for paid work as a play leader or supervisor, as tutors, area organizers and national officers. Amongst the 134 surveyed, 30 women remained with the organization for 10 years and more than half for 20 to 30 years.[77] Involvement could be life changing. Respondents spoke of gaining confidence and skills and finding a sense of purpose. 'PPA turned my life around in terms of education and learning' wrote one who had left grammar school with one 'O' level. 'PPA changed my life and helped me to discover the person I truly had the capacity to become.'[78] The language of self-actualization employed here was typical of those women for whom the PPA enabled a step-change in terms of their self-esteem.

[73] IoE, PLA, PPA 1/3: AGM 1972: Max Paterson, 'Parents matter most'.

[74] Brenda Crowe cited in Sue Griffin, 'Learning on PPA courses' in Henderson (Ed.). Henderson (ed.), *Insights*, p.48.

[75] Interview with Jennifer.

[76] Sheila Shinman, 'Moving on' in Henderson (ed.), *Insights*, p.98.

[77] Shinman, 'Moving on', p.105.

[78] Shinman, 'Moving on', p.110.

The experience of Mary Fawcett was not typical but her trajectory does illustrate how the PPA's structure and philosophy could become, as she described it, 'a catalyst' for change.[79] Fawcett had trained as an early years teacher but, in 1965, she found herself a 'mother and housewife' in a strange city but with 'time for commitment'. Having started up a playgroup with a group of like-minded women, they established a parent committee. The PPA assisted with a constitution and soon Mary was assisting the PPA's Area Organizer to support the fledgling movement across the city of Bristol. Despite her teaching experience Mary recalled 'being amazed that I could stand up and talk to parents for almost an hour without hesitation or repetition'. A city branch of the Pre-School Playgroups Association was formed which engaged Mary in more meetings and conferences. As the movement grew, training was needed. Mary set up and led a year-long Foundation course for playgroup staff with over 20 women attending weekly for a year. For Mary personally, the experience of tutoring and practising 'non-directive teaching' led to a dramatic change in her approach. Teaching parents, she discovered, had to be about 'facilitating their already rich thinking', a bottom-up approach that drew on the recognition of women's informal skills and experience, something that characterized PPA courses in the early years.[80] In 1975 Mary returned to formal education and was able to use her five years teaching experience as a playgroup tutor to access a degree course. PPA had an antipathy to qualifications in its early years, preferring to emphasize learning and confidence, but this meant that those who wished to move on to more formal education had nothing to verify their skills.[81] While still a student she was appointed to a lecturer in early years education, and after several years was appointed to the role of Director of Early Childhood Studies at the University of Bristol. Mary Fawcett was indebted to playgroups which she described as having had 'profound consequences' for her life for 40 years. What she had learned through her involvement with the PPA 'went far beyond' her teacher training and not only enabled her to expand her horizons but changed her thinking.

Fawcett's trajectory was only unusual in the seniority she achieved. Active involvement in the PPA could lead to careers or volunteering in related fields, notably teaching and lecturing in further education, work in the social care sector and paid or voluntary work across a range of health and social services at a time when work in these fields was offering women a wide range of opportunities.[82] While some who took this route had experience in early years care and education, others discovered a thirst for knowledge about child development or an aptitude for administration and policy making. Others, after years of voluntary roles, were

[79] IoE, PLA PPA 6/1: Memories—Mary Fawcett.

[80] Later courses were run by colleges etc. and became more top-down and formalized.

[81] Maude Henderson, *Cogs and Spindles: Some Impressions of the Playgroup Movement* (London: PPA, 1978). pp.71–2.

[82] Shinman, 'Moving on', pp.113–14.

appointed to paid PPA posts.[83] Progression through the PPA structures offered new careers, while for others PPA involvement acted as a springboard to other opportunities. Muriel Goulden, who had been a secretary before having her children, was a founder member of her local PPA branch and quickly took advantage of its courses. In 1974, needing to find paid work when her marriage broke down, she was appointed a Social Service Worker, remarking that 'it was the first time they had appointed anyone whose only qualifications were certificate of attendance from various PPA courses'.[84] Training under the auspices of the WEA and the Open University as PPA expanded its training portfolio, offered routes to qualifications in the education and social care fields at a time when access to such opportunities were facilitated by access to local education authority grants.[85]

Experience with running the National Housewives Register was less immediately transferable as training was not part of this organization's remit. Jerman observed in her 1980 history of the organization that no office holders regarded the role as a career stepping-stone, though she did ask the question as to how an employer would interpret service to NHR on a CV.[86] Confidence was not a paper qualification. Nonetheless, examples abound of members who ascribed their later accomplishments—personal and career—to the confidence gained from NHR activity. Quita Brown, who joined as a young mother in 1976, recalled 20 years later that 'formulating arguments for debate or even just being stimulated by a lively discussion' had been beneficial and as a direct result 'of gaining confidence in my abilities through membership of NHR' she applied to become a magistrate. 'I am sure' she wrote, 'I would not have taken that step if I had not had the experience of belonging to NHR being "only a housewife", with no obvious qualifications for such a demanding job.' In 1989 she was appointed to the bench.[87] A roll call of former NHR national organizers revealed trajectories that included a lot of voluntary work, a return to education and work with third sector organizations or local authority services.[88] For Lesley Taylor, on demitting the post of national organizer of NHR she 'took stock and began to plan for a future alone from the springboard of confidence and a new self awareness'. Running NHR had helped Lesley to 'forget domestic cares and gave me stability and awareness of other people's problems'. When her marriage broke down, she launched herself into a psychology degree.[89] She remarried, divorced for a second time, and became an education welfare officer, at that point reverting to her maiden name 'not because

[83] See, for example, Janet McAllister, 'What Did PPA Do for Me (and my Family)?' in *Memories of the Playgroup Movement in Wales 1961–1987*, (2008), p.42.

[84] IoE, PLA: PPA 6/1: Memories—Muriel Goulden.

[85] Henderson, *Cogs and Spindles*, p.74.

[86] Jerman, *Lively-Minded Women*, p.196.

[87] LSE, Women's Library, 5/NWR/5/3: Maureen Nicol: Letters relating to nomination of Nicol for an honour. 1994.

[88] Jerman, *Lively Minded Women*, pp.198–201.

[89] Jerman, *Lively Minded Women*, pp.56–64.

I am a women's libber . . . but because through the Register I came to believe that . . . above all else, women must retain their identities'.[90]

Those who credited these organizations with transformative powers were apt to be rather evangelical about their impact, including for those women who came to playgroups with less experience and even less confidence than Mary Fawcett. The claim by PPA for example, that many 'just mums' grew as parents is uncontroversial, but to insist that the opportunities bestowed by PPA involvement on mothers who had left school 'without qualifications or ambitions to widen their horizons' contributed to personal growth and development, needs closer examination.[91] One who made such claims was Barbara Keeley, one of the pioneer activists who established a playgroup in Leighton Buzzard in 1962. Just a year later she was treasurer on the PPA National Executive Committee and she continued to play a key role in the organization at local, regional and national levels until 1979 when she embarked on research to consider the impact of pre-school provision on the mothers of young children.[92] Keeley had a degree, had worked in medical research and as a teacher in West Africa and Malaya before settling down in the UK in 1955. She had four children between 1955 and 1967 and it was during what she described as her 'mobile child rearing time' that playgroups became her work or what she would have termed 'employment like'.[93] It was Keeley's contention that involvement with the playgroup movement and other pre-school groups acted as an introduction to 'a career-like sequence of development'.[94] Furthermore she argued that women would not have reached the same potential had they 'returned to the subordinate paid employment that they would have expected to take'.[95] She cites the example of 'Carol' who left school at 16, found employment as a dental nurse and then married and had three children which precipitated a period of depression. Becoming a parent-volunteer at the playgroup led to her becoming secretary of her local PPA, a tutor for playgroup courses followed by work in a private nursery and then a home visitor for a local authority-run nursery school. Carol said, 'Without the playgroup and tutoring experience I wouldn't have stood a chance—but then I wouldn't have had the confidence to apply anyhow!'[96]

Although Keeley's arguments mirrored many of the positions taken by Brenda Crowe, in particular the claim that playgroups provided mothers with the opportunity to gain satisfaction from their children and to increase their confidence and self-esteem by taking responsibility within the playgroup structures, Keeley

[90] Jerman, *Lively Minded Women*, p.200.
[91] This claim is made in Shinman, 'Moving on', p.117.
[92] IoE, PLA, PPA 6/1: Memories—Barbara Keely.
[93] IoE, PLA, PPA 4/46: Barbara Keeley, 'The effect of pre-school provision on the mothers of young children', MSc thesis, Cranfield Institute of Technology, 1981, p.76.
[94] Keeley, 'The effect of pre-school provision', p.70.
[95] Keeley, 'The effect of pre-school provision', p.76.
[96] Keeley, 'The effect of pre-school provision', pp.72–3.

went further in equating playgroup involvement with paid work. It was the distinctiveness of the playgroup, its dependence on volunteer parents, that provided the launch-pad for women to develop their potential. 'In the informal, flexible, non-statutory playgroup system, they had worked according to their real ability… unrestricted by lack of qualifications, learning on the job as their interests grew and widened.'[97] Keeley's research was informed by Maslow's model of the hierarchy of needs. In using the language of self-actualization she suggested that, in opposition to Friedan and many feminists, women did not need to participate in the paid workforce to achieve fulfilment. Indeed, women's 'employment-like' commitment to the pre-school playgroup movement was, in her judgement, more valuable in terms of women's self-esteem than paid work. Keeley's somewhat controversial position was that state-run childcare produced what she called 'simulated childlessness so that the course of [women's] lives can proceed without let or hindrance' and the deskilling of child-rearers. For her, and for the mothers she interviewed, childcare was a job and any dissatisfaction they felt at being at home full time could be offset by enhancing their enjoyment of their children.[98]

Others, especially those who progressed through the organization taking on increasing responsibility, took a similar view. Anne John who was a key member of the movement in Wales in the 1970s and 1980s, described it as 'a profession in its own right'. She went on to articulate a position that was shared across the playgroup community: 'It gave women an opportunity to express their views, to change thinking in society at large and, at the same time, give children the best start in life.'[99] John was expressing a widely held view amongst playgroup parents (and amongst many women of this generation): that under-fives were best served by their mothers staying at home but those same mothers needed stimulation, the opportunity to learn for their children's benefit but also for their own self development. Although playgroup women were not 'in it for themselves', its advocates argued that involvement was enriching for children and parents. In the words of one, 'I have found myself again as a person in my own right'.[100] For Keeley it was this dimension that distinguished the playgroup movement from the state-run childcare sector which, in her view made 'no contribution to the higher needs of the women' on account of it being run by professionals. The ethos of playgroups on the other hand, permitted 'self-actualization, fulfilment and personal growth'.[101]

But self-actualization did not always pay the bills and she failed to consider that women's 'higher needs' might just as well have been served by employment. Keeley was somewhat blind to the economic ramifications of a woman choosing

[97] Keeley, 'The effect of pre-school provision', p.76.

[98] Keeley, 'The effect of pre-school provision', pp.116–17.

[99] Anne John, 'The Pre-School Playgroups Association—How It Influenced my Life, my Family and my Thinking', in *Memories of the Playgroup Movement in Wales 1961–1987* (Aberystwyth, 2008), p.99.

[100] Ann Henderson, 'Introduction' in Henderson (ed.), *Insights*, p.xv.

[101] Keeley, 'The effect of pre-school provision', p.114.

Figure 7.2 Cover Illustration from *After Playgroup What Next*? Pre-School Playgroups Association Publication, 1979.

to undertake voluntary work with a playgroup as opposed to paid work, nor indeed the social pressures on mothers of young children to stay at home or the barriers to their engaging in the labour market. She was critical of campaigns like Wages for Housework which focused on the financial reward for work at the expense of the psychological aspects.[102] While the PPA did not adopt this position, it was clear about the value to women of active engagement with children's development, and never really engaged with the kind of thinking that made a case for valuing childcare in macro-economic terms. In fact few mothers in paid work made use of playgroups and a significant proportion of those who did re-enter the labour market after having children—36 per cent—were employed in work at a lower grade than their occupation before they had their first child.[103]

Challenges of 'Do-It-Yourself'

The career trajectory fostered by self-help groups was more easily navigated by women with a background of post-school education or training. PPA was conscious that its mode of operation which required time, money (to hire halls and buy equipment), and connections could not be easily replicated in 'deprived' areas where, it was said, mothers possessed little get-up-and-go or indeed understanding of what a playgroup could offer their children, let alone themselves. On a visit to Birmingham in 1968 Brenda Crowe observed that 'playgroups can't be a solution' in deprived areas where mothers possessed less social capital and where many were in part-time employment.[104] So, acknowledging that it had 'got stuck with the middle class tag', PPA engaged with working-class communities in both old and new urban areas where the need for pre-school facilities of all kinds, from playgroups to nurseries, was much more acute and where women's isolation could hinder their access to other services.[105]

The difficulty of applying the self-help philosophy when it left the leafy suburbs was writ large in Glasgow, a city which, in the 1960s and 70s, had rehoused hundreds of thousands of people on new council housing estates, in high flats, two new towns and far-flung overspill communities, where deprivation limited the ability of many mothers to engage with such initiatives. The first playgroup in the city with parental participation was the University of Glasgow Nursery Playgroup founded in 1966, but although the intention had been to include a cross-section of children from different social backgrounds, the fees and probably its location

[102] Keeley, 'The effect of pre-school provision', p.99.

[103] Heather Joshi and P.R. Andrew Hinde, 'Employment after Childbearing in Post-War Britain: Cohort-Study Evidence on Contrasts Within and Across Generations', *European Sociological Review* 9:3 (1993), pp.203–27, here p.221.

[104] IoE, PLA/PPA 1-4: Crowe area report, Birmingham, February 1968.

[105] IoE, PLA/PPA 5/4: *Contact*, 1964.

in the relatively well-to-do West End meant it remained predominantly middle class.[106] This playgroup had its own premises but beyond the privileged environs of the University there was a shortage of suitable accommodation for playgroups or indeed a lack of appropriate indoor or outdoor space for pre-school children to play safely. The PPA had established a playgroup in a high flat in the city with a paid supervisor for just one term in acknowledgement of the inability of local mothers to manage it on their own. But once the supervisor was withdrawn Brenda Crowe recognized this playgroup had no future, echoing the identical observations of social researcher Pearl Jephcott whose efforts to establish a playgroup in a high-rise estate foundered, as we saw in the previous chapter.[107] While the spokesperson for the Scottish PPA wrote of 'the seeming apathy and indifference on the part of the mothers' in some playgroups and their 'unreliability' for the rota of helpers, she also acknowledged that 'the needs of mothers to talk about their problems and their lives seem equal to their children's need to play'.[108] 'Mothers needed a place to be for themselves', observed Brenda Crowe, 'and needed time and help to take ownership of the playgroup'.[109]

When the Scottish PPA published a report on playgroups in so-called areas of need in 1977 they discovered that the majority had been initiated by outside agencies, usually social workers, and were grant aided. The do-it-yourself philosophy that had worked so well for more affluent areas did not translate easily to communities where women faced numerous challenges: poor-quality housing, poor economic circumstances, and often unsupported by other family members. In these conditions the PPA's philosophy of the central importance of voluntary parental involvement (in practice this meant mothers) was seriously challenged. Some worked part time, some were 'unreliable' and others were reluctant to become involved, regarding the group as a social work department initiative.[110] The study authors remained optimistic, however, recommending that more emphasis in these playgroups needed to be on mothers learning alongside their children and in workshops and meetings in order to bolster the mothers' confidence. The report optimistically remarked: 'Through learning there is growth of confidence in one's abilities, and this can then be used to take both learning and experience further.'[111] There was some progress in levels of mothers' involvement but less in respect of them taking the training courses which were such an

[106] E. Rae Paul, *Playgroups in an Industrial City* (Scottish PPA, Glasgow, 1974), p.5.

[107] B. Hazley, V. Wright, L. Abrams, and A. Kearns, 'People and their Homes Rather than Housing in the Usual Sense'? Locating the Tenant's Voice in Homes in High Flats'. *Women's History Review* 28:5 (2019), pp.728–45.

[108] IoE, PLA/PPA 2/28: Scottish Pre-School Playgroups Association, *Playgroups in Areas of Need* (1977), p.13.

[109] Brenda Crowe, *The Playgroup Movement* (London: George Allen & Unwin, 1973), p.25.

[110] IoE, PLA/PPA 2/28: Scottish Pre-School Playgroups Association, *Playgroups in Areas of Need* (1977).

[111] Ibid., p.15.

important stepping-stone for women in less trying circumstances. However, the report did lead to the Stepping Stones project which explicitly recognized the challenges faced by families in areas of deprivation. On one estate half the mothers were single parents and most families were living on benefits. In response the local PPA developed a raft of additional activities including running a toy library, a parents' lunch club, and even drugs counselling.[112] And eventually a new approach was taken whereby family centres were established in houses provided by the council with their own project leaders, a precursor of the Sure Start programme of the 1990s.

It is not easy to see how the women discussed in this report and elsewhere in the PPAs work with 'deprived' communities, could achieve the growth in confidence and self-esteem through involvement with playgroups so commonly reported by more affluent women.[113] But champions of playgroups were adamant that they were not just a middle-class luxury. Kay Carmichael, an influential Scottish social policy advisor from the University of Glasgow, was one such, advocating in 1976 that: 'The playgroup movement has taught many women to be themselves, it has enabled them to go on growing out of one stage into another, and to realize they have something to offer to the community, which raises their self-respect, dignity and sense of responsibility.'[114] And mothers did appreciate the benefits of attending with their children. In a survey of 50 Glasgow playgroups in 1974, 34 per cent of mothers responded that the playgroup gave them time for themselves and 20 per cent had made friends through the playgroup. One commented that: 'I have also found that the playgroup has helped me greatly in my social life as I didn't get out very often, but now I get to bus runs, fashion parties and women's clubs.'[115] Only one saw no benefit at all.[116]

The voluntary principle of PPA which underpinned parental involvement was always difficult to implement in working-class areas which meant that playgroups soon folded without outside support.[117] And working mothers, it was increasingly acknowledged, didn't need playgroups; rather they needed day-care where they could leave the children while they worked. Amongst those working mothers were Black and ethnic minority women who practised a rather different model of motherhood whereby paid work was not inimical to good mothering. Many made use of unregistered childminders in the absence of local authority nursery care

[112] Meg Burford, 'Playgroups in the community', in Henderson (Ed.), *Insights*, p.89.

[113] See Abrams et al., 'Isolated and dependent'.

[114] Scottish PPA Newsletter, Nov. 1976.

[115] Paul, *Playgroups in an Industrial City*, p.27.

[116] Paul, *Playgroups in an Industrial City*, p.19.

[117] See *Playgroups in Areas of Need* (1977) and Janet Finch, 'The Deceit of Self Help: Preschool Playgroups and Working-Class Mothers', *Journal of Social Policy* 13:1 (1984), pp.1–20. The PPA was not blind to the problem. On a visit to Birmingham in 1968 Brenda Crowe was confronted with the realities of a 'deprived' area where mothers required nurseries and nursery schools with trained staff rather than playgroups. IoE, PLA/PPA 1–4: Area Report, Birmingham, February 1968.

which prompted concerns about the quality of care received by the children.[118] In Manchester in the 1970s, playgroups in Hulme and Moss Side offered childcare to release mothers for time to be themselves, freeing them from the 'emotional labour' of mothering for a while, but also enabling them to attend retraining schemes. In this respect, these organizations enabled Black women's participation in the labour market, though as White indicates, this could be at the expense of exacerbating the double burden and intensifying racialized inequality.[119]

By the end of the decade the working mother increasingly became the object of attention from women's groups. The growth in the number of married women in employment, increasing from 27 per cent of mothers in 1961 to almost 50 per cent 20 years later, was a result of a number of factors.[120] Part-time and shift work in the manufacturing industries accommodated women with children who could work the daytime or twilight shift without being noticeably absent from family life. In the professional labour market, especially in teaching, nursing, and the growing para-medical sector, steps were taken to encourage married women to return to work, reflecting a growing recognition that educated women's training was being wasted. Consumer demand for greater material comfort and enjoyment for the whole family pushed married women back to work as did a growth in house purchase. And the working mother was increasingly visible in public discourse from the BBC to the quality press and women's magazines.[121] These addressed how to enable graduate women to return to the labour market, how to make life easier for women factory workers so they could fulfil their family responsibilities and, by the 1970s, inequalities in the workplace.[122] By the 1970s and 1980s, the mood music changed. In the context of rising male unemployment, more married women were entering the labour market and for working mothers playgroups offered diminishing benefits. Jennifer commented: 'Scottish people would agree that the mothers were... wanting to go back to work and they wanted to put their children into somewhere where they could go back to work.

[118] See Brian Jackson and Sonia Jackson, *Childminder. A Study in Action Research* (London: Routledge & Kegan Paul, 1979); Sonia Jackson, *The Illegal Child-Minders. A Report on the Growth of Unregistered Child-Minding and the West Indian Community* (Cambridge: Priority Area Children, 1971).

[119] Jessica White, 'Child-centred Matriarch or Mother Among Other Things? Race and the Construction of Working-class Motherhood in Late Twentieth-century Britain', *Twentieth Century British History* (2022), pp.14–15.

[120] Paterson, 'I didn't feel like my own person', p.407.

[121] See Elizabeth Gundrey, *Jobs for Mothers* (London: Zenith, 1967).

[122] Examples: 'Working mothers force planners to think again', *The Guardian*, 15 Aug. 1961; 'Work Bureau will help to win back to offices women of 35-plus', *The Guardian*, 2 March 1966; 'Women Talking', *The Guardian*, 5 August 1963 which mentions regular BBC broadcast every Friday appealing for women to return to teaching. BBC Written Archives Centre: R51-1025-1: Woman's Hour Minutes, 5 Jan. 1960—meet with Viola Klein to discuss her report on women at work; R51-1016-6: discussion of advertising a new radio series run by Education Department—'second start' to help keep women teachers currently at home in touch with developments in schools, 1964. 'Here's what happened to women in our search'—Alma Birk launched her careers advisory service for *Nova* 3 years ago—she helped hundreds of women back to work—Today we tell you what they think', *Nova*, April 1970.

And so the era sort of semi closed, or sort of cracked it almost completely.'[123] Or as a former national adviser to the PPA put it: 'the supply of unwaged, undereducated women who started and supported playgroups and ended up running them either as voluntary or lowly paid play-leaders or as trustees was diminishing.'[124] Childcare 'was becoming an essential service for some parents instead of an optional adventure.'[125]

In this environment a variety of women's groups including the Working Association of Mothers (WAM) and women's liberation recognized the shortcomings of the playgroup model, preferring to argue for 24-hour nurseries and childcare provision over playgroups which would enable women to take on paid work. WAM had started out in 1969 as a women's self-help co-operative, catering to the needs of isolated women primarily in south-west London through facilitating social contact for mothers and play provision via its PLAYWAM initiative (see Figure 7.3). But for Diana Priestley, its founder, the difficulties of mothers accessing part-time or flexible work had always been high on the agenda and by 1971 WAM's scope included universal nursery education, out-of-school provision for children, further education and training opportunities for mothers and 'flexible working hours which give mothers freedom of choice.'[126]

Figure 7.3 Working Association of Mothers publicity material, undated, c.1970.

[123] Interview with Jennifer.

[124] Jill Faux, 'The impact of change' in Henderson (Ed.), *Insights*, p.145.

[125] Ibid., p.146.

[126] LSE, Women's Library: 5WAM—unidentified newspaper cutting, September 1971.

The original self-help organizations were forced to adapt to the changing circumstances. As PPA developed into an organization providing a statutory service, in receipt of state funding and tied to delivery contracts, it began to lose its original raison d'être in respect of what it believed mothers needed. Barbara Keeley's vision of PPA providing an alternative to employment was overtaken by these changes in women's working patterns, in particular the increase of married women returning to education, training, and employment, especially in the growing health and social care sectors as the welfare state expanded. The 1970s, it has been argued, were a turning point for higher education participation amongst women and a golden age of social mobility as women re-evaluated their lives and took advantage of the opportunities on offer to eschew mundane and poorly paid work for professional and semi-professional jobs.[127] Working in the pre-school playgroup sector was folded into the wider growth of care and service-sector jobs and by the 1980s the playgroup movement was forced to professionalize and as one activist described it, played the 'government's tune', losing in the process its bottom-up structure.[128] The PPA that activists celebrated as enabling and adaptable, became a hierarchical organization as opposed to a movement. In 1995 PPA became the Pre-school Learning Alliance.

The National Housewives Register was also forced to adapt. By the late 1970s the membership was ageing, prompting a mild identity crisis.[129] The national committee struggled to recruit its officers, partly owing to the competition of paid work.[130] A change of name in 1988 to National Women's Register reflected the shifting profile of members such as Lesley Easterman, elected to the national committee in 1982, 'busy mother of two, part-time speech therapist, counsellor for Bolton branch of National Childbirth Trust'.[131] NHR continued to insist it occupied a niche between the 'Tupperware scene' where women 'greet meetings like a gateau contest' and protesting feminists because 'we don't want to protest about anything in particular'.[132] But in rejecting taking a stance on the major women's issues of the day, NHR may have condemned itself to a period of stagnation in terms of its membership profile and with an ageing membership it was perhaps less motivated to engage with debates on equal pay, reproductive rights, gender-based violence and so on which were the subject of debate and campaigning by the more traditional women's organizations albeit at the executive rather than the grass-roots level.[133] Moreover, despite establishing a number

[127] Worth, *Welfare State Generation*, pp.67–8.

[128] Faux, 'The impact of change', p.152.

[129] LSE, Women's Library, 5/NWR/1/2: National Housewives Register Annual General Meeting (Conference) Minutes, 1976–84—Manchester Conference 1978.

[130] Jerman, *Lively Minded Women*, pp.195–6.

[131] LSE, Women's Library, 5/NWR/4/1/29: Lancashire, *Bolton Evening News*, 27 July 1982.

[132] LSE, Women's Library: 5/NWR/4/21/33: Merseyside 1968–1990, *The Reporter*, 19 April 1985—St Helen's.

[133] Caitriona Beaumont, 'What *Do* Women Want? Housewives' Associations, Activism and Changing Representations of Women in the 1950s', *Women's History Review* 26:1 (2017), pp.147–62.

of branches overseas, NHRs profile was overwhelmingly white.[134] Unlike the PPA which did acknowledge the need for playgroup provision in multi-ethnic communities and worked with the Association for Multi-Racial Playgroups recognizing that seeing themselves as 'crusaders taking the light to the unenlightened' was unproductive, NHR had little presence in areas where migrant communities settled in numbers.[135] Even the international groups were comprised largely of British women who had followed their husbands' work. The South African group, for example, was founded by a British expat who exported her experience with NHR from Suffolk. Although the group was 'open to all', members were predominantly immigrants.[136] In Zimbabwe a more concerted effort to attract members beyond the white ex pat community had failed because 'the majority of African women who would be interested in joining...are either professional women holding down full-time jobs or heavily committed politically'.[137]

Back to Work

For all the efforts by the do-it-yourself organizations to provide women with intellectual and purposeful activity whilst their children were small and they were 'housebound', it remains the case that this period witnessed a transformation in the employment landscape as wage-earning wives and mothers became normalized rather than a social problem.[138] Pearl Jephcott researching women workers in Bermondsey in the 1950s where more than half of all married women were in employment, remarked upon the psychological need women had for work outside the home alongside the financial benefits. It was 'meeting deep seated needs which are now felt by women in general in our society'.[139] To some extent the emergence of the self-help groups was evidence of this need going unmet. However, as McCarthy and others have pointed out, although working motherhood became 'increasingly ordinary' in the 1950s and especially the 1960s and 1970s, 'it was a narrowly conformist kind of ordinariness' which still required mothers of young children to stay at home and which offered little assistance to those mothers who had to earn an income or chose to continue working.[140] Social expectations, alongside an absence of childcare, limited the choice of mothers across the socio-economic spectrum. It is hard not to conclude that

[134] No information on the ethnicity of members is available from the archival record and efforts to obtain current data has been unsuccessful.

[135] IoE: PLA-PPA 1–4: file 2—Themed report on Churches, March 1968. PPA worked with the Association of Multi-racial playgroups. See IoE, 1 PLA/PPA/1/4: Brenda Crowe's papers as presented to the NEC and reports from Bristol, Cambridge and reports from Bristol, Cambridge and Leeds, 1968. PLA/PPA FAW1: 'A Good Start with Camden's Playgroup', *Times Educational Supplement*, 8 Nov. 1968.

[136] Jerman, *Lively Minded Women*, pp.187–8.

[137] Jerman, *Lively Minded Women*, p.189.

[138] McCarthy, *Double Lives*, p.230.

[139] Jephcott cited by McCarthy, *Double Lives*, p.230.

[140] McCarthy, *Double Lives*, p.231.

self-help organizations like the PPA and NHR plugged a gap for women who had the expectation that they would return to work and the financial comfort that permitted them to remain out of the labour market. Even WAM which had established an employment agency to match members with suitable flexible work, struggled to survive beyond its status as a social network.[141] Its founder resigned after just two years citing the 'immense strain' of the role and the need to find paid employment.[142]

Not all women had the desire or the opportunity to be involved in such groups. For some, work and motherhood existed on a continuum with no breaks. Grace had ambitions at school to be an actress or work with animals but with no encouragement from her parents or her school she embarked on the typical career journey of girls who left school at the leaving age: a short period as a veterinary nurse followed by receptionist and a job in a supermarket. She had her first child at 19 and three more in subsequent years, but throughout this time she was working: as a cleaner when she was near destitute after the break up of her first marriage, in a variety of roles with a major retailer, as a teaching assistant and finally back to being a veterinary nurse at the age of 55 and this time undertaking the formal training to qualify.[143] This work pattern is commonplace amongst working-class women with no post-school training. She worked because she needed the money.

It would be a mistake, then, to exaggerate the significance of self-help groups at this moment in women's lives at the expense of their participation in the labour market. Hazel's trajectory is instructive. Having looked forward to giving up work when she had her first child, she and a friend started a mother-and-toddler group because she 'just felt that women needed to get together'. On moving to a village she did the same again but at the same time began to run her own holiday-let business while her children were small. Another move saw her finding work in retail and then a part-time job as a home help for social services at which point her husband was convicted of a crime. 'That was it then, I had to get a career... so then I started to do some training and re-educate myself.' Hazel developed a career for herself in mental health services, ending up as a manager. She did not need a self-help group to aid her personal development. As Hazel explained, it was motherhood that made her 'more determined'. 'I think motherhood, I found a strength in it.' Having a child made her more assertive 'and that was when I sort of realized, oh there has been some movement then and actually that if you want something you've got to go and get it'.[144] Hazel found a balance. 'I'm glad I had time off with my baby... I'm glad I took that time out really, really glad because I know I made a difference being there with her.'[145]

[141] LSE, Women's Library: 5WAM/1: WAM Newsletter, Summer 1970. WAM was unable to find funding to support a national network, unlike NHR and PPA.

[142] LSE, Women's Library: 5WAM/1: WAM Newsletter, September 1971.

[143] UKDA, SN 850818: 049.

[144] UKDA, SN 850818: M65.

[145] UKDA, SN 850818: M65.

The focus on married women's participation in employment as a route to self-fulfilment reflects the position taken by some feminists who argued that the self could only be fully realized outside the home. Others within the Women's Liberation Movement who adopted the socialist-feminist stance saw the workplace as the site of class-consciousness raising via trade union membership, though activism in this space often clashed with the more instrumental aims of female workers who some feminists characterized as 'apathetic'.[146] As the narratives of the wives of managers discussed in Chapter 5 illustrated, paid work was often seen as the route out of a restrictive and unfulfilling domesticity though rarely did women see the two as mutually exclusive. In her analysis of working-class women and self-identity, Paterson has argued that wage earning was intimately related to women's sense of responsibility to the family and did not negate their identity as a 'good' mother.[147] Indeed, women's relational self-positioning in interviews (as individuals situated in relation to others) posits a more nuanced account of the complex thought processes, both at the time and in retrospect, that informed their decision-making. Most mothers were tugged in two directions. Penny Tanner, a librarian with one child and another expected, worked part-time but like many women in her position, had mixed feelings of guilt alongside the knowledge that she needed to work for her own mental wellbeing: 'I have got the choice, and I don't know if it's good.' She continued: 'It seems to me that I can't feel envy about bits of [her son's] life that don't include me when I have consciously decided to exclude him from bits of mine, which I have done by going to work and not being like the old-fashioned mother that stays at home.'[148] Penny's dilemma, how to preserve and nurture that part of the self that was separate from her identity as a mother, was felt across this generation of women.

Conclusions

The transition generation encountered a clash between the societal expectations of mothers of a previous era and their own needs, expectations, and ambitions. The majority of new mothers accepted they would stay at home while their children were small, but they were not prepared for the isolation, lack of social purpose beyond child-rearing, and the intellectual stagnation. The do-it-yourself organizations allowed these women to service the self, to attend to their own growth and development whilst not compromising on their role as primary carers. Attending an NHR meeting, volunteering at a playgroup or becoming more deeply involved as a play leader, regional organizer or NCT breastfeeding

[146] See Moss, *Women, Workplace Protest and Political Identity*, especially Chapter 4.
[147] Paterson, I didn't feel like my own person', pp.415–19.
[148] Oakley, *Social Support and Motherhood*, pp.203–4.

counsellor, gave these women a pathway to a new friendship network, greater confidence and skills in negotiation, public speaking, running committees, and organizing events. Some undertook training and obtained expertise in children's play, child development or, in the case of NCT, breastfeeding or antenatal care. Many used it as a springboard to active engagement in related spheres, to further training and education or paid work. But importantly, active participation in a self-help organization was regarded as complementary to childcare and family life in contrast with paid work. Indeed all of these organizations offered women guilt-free membership, positioning themselves as intermediaries or safety valves or as conduits to a life post the stay-at-home stage which would allow women to balance motherhood, family life, and paid work. Thus, women who accepted or embraced staying at home for a few years and who expressed the belief that it was in their children's best interests, could do so without being criticized for neglecting their family.

For most women participation in these organizations was not on a par with paid work. It was part time and voluntary; it could be fitted in around other responsibilities and in the case of PPA especially, was child-centred. Volunteers were told that the more they understood about child development and the PPA's play-centred approach, the better parents they would be. And while NHR's raison d'être was to provide a child-free space in the sense that domestic concerns were not to be discussed at meetings, members were clear that participation in NHR allowed them to breathe; the break from baby talk and toddler tantrums was essential if they were to be good mothers. Husbands understood this too. In some partnerships, household roles had to be adjusted to accommodate the woman's absence from home and by the 1970s there was greater involvement from fathers in their children's care.[149] For other women, although their participation was not equivalent to a paid job it was, in their minds at least, 'work-like' and as the biographical sketches above have made clear, active engagement did assist some to commence a journey back into the labour market and in some cases a change of career.

The focus by contemporary researchers, feminist commentators and recent historians on paid work as the primary, or at least equal site, alongside the family of women's identity has largely effaced the significance of the do-it-yourself organizations in this period. The feminist critique in particular, which treated these groups as a mere prelude to women's liberation activism and which regarded them as 'helping mothers to do "their" work more happily', rather underplays the significance of the movement in a moment of transition when most women were effecting that change through finding new ways to live their lives rather than

[149] The founder of WAM, Diana Priestley, reported that her husband wanted to take an active part in bringing up their children. LSE, Women's Library: 5WAM—*Richmond & Twickenham Times*—undated c. 1969.

formulating critiques of societal structures. By giving voice to the many thousands of women who found something of value in groups that responded to their feelings and met their needs for friendship, intellectual stimulation, and life experience beyond the home, we have a fuller picture of how women effected change through their agency to form and sustain networks that bridged home and work, personal, and political. But they also draw attention to lives which make little sense without recognizing women's engagement in voluntarism. If we look at the transition generation over the long term it is clear that paid work is not necessarily the only or primary place where modern selves were made. If we agree that the making of the modern self was contingent upon 'choice, fulfilment, self-discovery and self-realization', then these concepts or experiences were to be found in many spaces and for women for whom work and family jostled in their minds and their lives, involvement in an organization that was neither work nor domestic or family care could be liberating.[150]

Women's testimonies about the place of self-help organizations in their lives are powerful precisely because they often occupy a pivotal moment and place. The friendships made sustained women at a critical moment when they were attempting to manage the conflict between motherhood and selfhood. Some credited their involvement with one of the groups with getting them through a personal crisis. And they acted as a stepping-stone to change, giving women greater self-confidence and, in some cases, valuable experience and training to launch new careers. Although it is incontrovertible that self-help was predominantly a white and middle-class phenomenon, its impact spread wider than this self-selecting group of doers. Women of all socio-economic backgrounds recognized the impact of participation and it is they, speaking about the change they saw in themselves, who make the point most effectively: 'See me! I used to be deid!' exclaimed a working-class Scot who attributed her growth in confidence to involvement with PPA.[151]

[150] Langhamer, 'Love, Selfhood and Authenticity', p.278.
[151] IoE, PLA/PPA 1/3: AGM 1972. Speech by Max Paterson, p.21.

8
Caring for the Self

The Feminist Spectrum

In 1972, in her final column for *The Guardian's* women's page, Mary Stott summarized some of the changes charted by that newspaper over the course of 15 years. The concerns that featured in the 'Mainly for Women' column in the early 1960s—discontentment and intellectual stagnation amongst graduate wives, the conflict between home and work, the difficulty of managing a home without help, and the guilt of working mothers—had largely dissipated. Although the discontented housewife had not gone away, by 1972 she had 'calmed down'. Working mothers were now commonplace. 'Nearly all the heat has gone out of the "to work or not to work" debate; the social pressures have lightened. There has been a great and welcome, lessening of guilt feelings.'[1] *The Guardian* took some credit in helping to translate 'ideas into words [which] stimulate action' in the shape of the do-it-yourself organizations. Ten years later, in an article celebrating 20 years of the National Housewives Register, Stott urged social historians to take serious note of this organization and its sister self-help groups. Their existence, she argued, was evidence of an 'assertion of women's purposeful independence' and demonstrated that the climate was ripe for the consciousness-raising of the Seventies. They were 'a bridge between two phases of a lively-minded woman's career' and a model of women's networking which, she suggested, women's liberation might do well to emulate.[2]

Stott was correct in her summation of the changes that had occurred in women's lives over the course of her tenure, but she was apt to exaggerate the significance of the do-it-yourself movement that, in her words, sprang like 'spontaneous combustion' from the pages of her newspaper. There is no doubt, as previous chapters have demonstrated, that these organizations were one of the conduits via which women charted a route out of domesticity and back to a semblance of a self that they recognized and with which they felt comfortable. The life narratives of those who assumed key roles in these organizations as well as rank-and-file members are testament to their place in translating feelings into action. They provided a space between motherhood and the outside world

[1] Mary Stott, *The Guardian*, 5 Jan. 1972.

[2] Mary Stott, 'Maureen Nicol was there long before Germaine Greer and Simone de Beauvoir', *The Guardian* 14 Jan. 1982.

Feminist Lives: Women, Feelings, and the Self in Post-War Britain. Lynn Abrams, Oxford University Press.
 DOI: 10.1093/oso/9780192896995.003.0008

of work or voluntarism. In that space women could express themselves freely, they found an empathetic community, and they could begin to explore how to care for the self as well as caring for others. The do-it-yourself organizations then, were one route away from the self-sacrifice of their mothers' generation and towards the self-care of the transition generation.

The do-it-yourself revolution did not emerge from nowhere. The spontaneous combustion was nothing of the sort. The women who founded these groups from the bottom-up had grown up with an incipient sense of entitlement: to a better education than their mothers, to a wider choice of careers, to the exercise of personal choice in clothes, travel, and entertainment and increasingly in personal relationships. Marriage was regarded as a continuation of this quest for self-realization, a space in which to mature and grow, a necessary step to gain independence and family life with the expectation that it would be both emotionally fulfilling and mutually supportive. By the late 1960s a new kind of female self had been forged which was self-propelling. There was no turning back. When this generation experienced the ideological and physical constraints that accompanied motherhood, they drew on their access to social, economic, and emotional capital to reclaim the 'individualistic, agentic self'.[3] That capital was not exclusively a middle-class privilege, but women from working-class and Black and ethnic minority backgrounds travelled a parallel road at a different speed. It is notable that in the 1970s, community organizing within some Black communities replicated some of the features of the women's self-help groups of the 1960s and that, after marrying young, working-class women were able to prioritize their own needs at an age when a return to education or training did not feel like such a leap.[4] The emergence of courses in women's studies at higher education institutions in the 1980s and 1990s was one way in which those needs were satiated alongside access to the Open University and study and training at Further Education colleges. By the 1980s there were several points of convergence across class and race and ethnicity in terms of proportions of married women in work and the decreasing importance of self-help groups for younger married women.

Mary Stott's challenge to the Women's Liberation Movement to emulate the practices of the do-it-yourself movement likely fell on deaf ears, but the place of feminism and the WLM in the story told in this book is significant in several respects. The efforts of organizations like the National Housewives Register to distance themselves from 'women's lib' and, conversely, the dismissive attitude of some feminists towards organizations that they said merely assuaged the discontent of housewives without challenging fundamental sexual inequality, suggests

[3] Val Gillies, *Marginalised Mothers: Exploring Working Class Experiences of Parenting* (London: Routledge, 2007), p.76.

[4] White, 'Child-centred matriarch'; Reynolds, *Caribbean Mothers*; Paterson, 'I didn't feel like my own person'.

an unbreachable chasm between them. And hitherto, those who have documented the history of women's liberation—activists and historians—have reinforced the division. The accounts of some of the prominent players in women's liberation pay homage to distant feminist predecessors but are largely silent on the kinds of grass-roots activism that didn't look like women's liberation to them. Or they fail to include the do-it-yourself activism focused on family and children within the scope of the new alternative politics.[5] Playgroups and women's discussion groups did not meet the criteria of 'rebellion' in such accounts. Histories of women's liberation also tend to ignore evidence of collective efforts to change lives before the advent of WLM. And they have paid limited attention to the everyday feminism enacted by women of this generation in their efforts to challenge societal expectations and structural barriers to them achieving self-realization.[6] One of the reasons for the effacement of the achievements of organizations deemed not feminist enough by those documenting the history of WLM is generational; once more the daughters were seeking to distinguish themselves from their mothers by casting the latter as outmoded and conservative in their views on women's role.

Certainly, at the time, women's liberation activists could see no connection to the traditional women's organizations like the Women's Institute and Townswomen's Guild. Sheila Rowbotham described how a talk she delivered to a Guild group was met with 'blank bemusement'. Yet she was alert to the value of community-based organizing outwith the state and understood that women's everyday life could be the basis of a new politics.[7] And some feminists acknowledged that organizations like PPA and NCT were motivated by some of the same grievances as the WLM. Moreover, some of the solutions suggested and implemented were not dissimilar.[8] The consciousness-raising enacted by WLM groups seemed, writes Rowbotham, 'to offer an alternative type of politics open to all women'. Their value and potential lay in their ability to turn 'private hurts' into 'collective expression' and then to translate that into effecting material changes.[9] Experience and activity were what shaped WLM, and this is precisely what drove the women's self-help groups of the 1960s and 1970s too. Rather than viewing each mode of activism within its own silo, it is more productive to take a wider perspective on this era. It is clear that women's groups across the spectrum were part of an upsurge in grass-roots or community or voluntary activism, implementing change in a range of domains from health to childcare. The bubbling up of local nursery and play provision, including pre-school playgroups, one o'clock clubs, Black women's co-operatives, community nurseries, and adventure playgrounds,

[5] For example, Rowbotham, *Daring to Hope*, p.6.

[6] Though Margaretta Jolly does consider 'feminist everyday life' in *Sisterhood and After: An Oral History of the Women's Liberation Movement, 1968–Present* (Oxford: Oxford University Press, 2019), pp.121–58. See also Sutcliffe-Braithwaite and Thomlinson, 'Vernacular discourses'.

[7] Rowbotham, *Daring to Hope*, pp. 20, 94, 122, 128.

[8] Wilson, *Only Halfway to Paradise*, p.184.

[9] Rowbotham, *Daring to Hope*, pp.16–17.

is one example of parallel and complementary initiatives addressing the same problem and proffering similar solutions albeit with differing underlying ideological positions.[10]

What this demonstrates is that the Women's Liberation Movement was part of a much longer and wider process of change in post-war Britain and less the catalyst it is wont to be portrayed. Women's liberation is, at least in memoirs, often positioned within the larger radical moment of the 1960s and 1970s, alongside leftist and radical political groupings. Yet across the UK women's liberation took on a variety of guises with their foci of activity aligned to the profile of local membership and local issues affecting women.[11] And feminism, broadly understood, was already embedded in British life, through the scores of national and local women's organizations from the longstanding groups like the Women's Institute and the National Council of Women, to the Mothers' Union, Young Wives Clubs, University Women's Clubs and the newcomers like NHR and PPA with membership in the hundreds of thousands. As Beaumont has shown, even those organizations with the most traditional image embraced and addressed many hard-core issues facing women in the 1960s and 1970s such as 'battered wives', child benefit, homelessness, and the menopause.[12] Even the Women's Fellowship of the Methodist Church in London made provision for unmarried mothers by providing flatlets and a day nursery 'where babies can be cared for while their mothers are at work'.[13]

Do-it-yourself activists could be equally dismissive of women's liberation. They tended to equate feminism with the WLM, flippantly using terminology such as 'bra-burners' and 'women's libbers' to distinguish themselves from what some perceived as a radical, man-hating movement. But this meant that they were reluctant to identify with the elements of WLM philosophy or provision which sat comfortably within a broader conception of feminism that encompassed a wide range of issues and political positions. It is possible that some of these negative statements about 'women's lib' reflected an ignorance of what women's liberation really stood for and a conflation of the more separatist activities and campaigns of the WLM with feminism more broadly. Organizations like NHR, PPA, and others were not the precursors of women's liberation, but they did reflect a much more general belief amongst women of all social classes in gender equality and the right of women to pursue self-fulfilment, whether that be through work or voluntary activity or through responsibilities in the home.

[10] Rowbotham acknowledges all of these as 'communal approaches to caring for children' within context of 'radical community politics' but leaves aside their significance for mothers. *Daring to Hope*, p.189.

[11] Emily Flaherty, 'The Women's Liberation Movement in Britain, 1968–84: Locality and Organisation in Feminist Politics', PhD, University of Glasgow, 2017.

[12] Caitriona Beaumont has identified 120 national organizations for women in 1964. 'Bridging the gap'.

[13] NRO: File FC 79/424—Secretary's correspondence and papers, 1967, 1970–1974. Bulletin of Women's Fellowship, winter 1973.

The PPA's national organizer Brenda Crowe's claim that playgroups were the 'real women's lib' exemplifies this attitude. Whilst the do-it-yourself organizations may not have addressed inequality in the home or gender-based violence head on, they helped to normalize a discourse on gender equality and in some respects effected change through grass-roots activity. The PPA undoubtedly shifted the debate around childcare by insisting on the benefits for mothers as well as children. At the level of family dynamics PPA was part of the movement to engage fathers with their children's development. And women's involvement in anything that took them away from the home required compromise concerning care of the household while they were absent, preparing the ground for further manifestations of women's independence.

More significantly, this generation of women have absorbed the primary underlying tenets of feminism, evident in their personal testimony. In interview, those who had no connection with women's liberation, found questions about feminism disconcerting, often regarding it as a test, yet their accounts were informed and shaped by a belief in gender equality on their own terms. Feminism for many of these women was perceived as doctrinal and intellectual.[14] Their personal testimony, on the other hand, evinced authoritative accounts in which they are the heroes of the story. It was not only educated women who had the facility to do this. The lone mothers of Chapter 4 interviewed by Marsden spoke about lives that appeared to lack autonomy or independence and yet their accounts evinced both on their own terms. In Chapter 6, the testimonies of Sadie Innes and Eileen Parr claim autonomy through taking control of their own lives and their own narratives. The 'coherence system', to use Linde's term, of a belief in gender equality and the pervasive acceptance of an everyday feminism, was a narrative strategy that enabled women from all backgrounds, to present self-validating narratives embedded in the material circumstances of their lives.[15] Susan, for example, had never been actively engaged in organized feminism but she situated her life experiences within an interpretive framework made possible by the discursive culture of feminism. Susan had a working-class upbringing, was denied university, spent a period working as a bi-lingual secretary in Geneva before a life-changing move to the Middle East with her Iraqi husband. Upon returning to the UK with a family and admitting that she had lost her self-confidence, Susan charted a route back to her former confident self via the Open University and the National Women's Register. In interview she was able to articulate a life story that encapsulates the experience of inequality, an understanding of what underpinned that and, crucially, an acceptance in later life of the value and validity of life

[14] See Abrams, 'Talking about feminism'.

[15] Linde, *Life Stories: the Creation of Coherence* (Oxford, 1993). See also Abrams, 'Liberating the Female Self'; Sutcliffe-Braithwaite and Thomlinson, 'Vernacular Discourses'.

experiences and decisions.[16] Susan described herself as having had 'many womanhoods'. It was a sentiment with which many of my interviewees would concur.

Self-Care

Those womanhoods represent different points on a spectrum: at one end sits self-fulfilment, independence, and autonomy and at the other, self-sacrifice, dependence, and feelings of a life unfulfilled. The former state may thrive more easily outside the patriarchal structures that contain and determine women's choices. Creativity and integrity may find more space to develop in 'formless, inchoate' spaces.[17] Somewhere on this spectrum sits the concept and practice of self-care, of consciously attending to one's own wellbeing. It is a concept that emerged as important during the course of writing this book. The latter stages were conducted in the wake of the Covid-19 pandemic, a time when caring for the self and others' mental and physical health achieved prominence in media discourse and personal practice. We started this book with the argument that one of the things that distinguishes this generation of women from that of their mothers is the ability to put themselves first, to privilege their own feelings in determining action, rather than bowing to a sense of duty or convention. However, the rejection of self-sacrifice does not imply a life driven solely by individual self-fulfilment as the liberal, rationalist model of autonomy tends to suggest. An autonomous fulfilled life depends upon healthy relations with others where women's roles as wives, mothers, daughters, siblings, workers, and friends incorporate service to others in a productive way.[18]

The practices usually associated with self-actualization in the 1960s and 1970s, such as consciousness-raising, psychotherapy, some forms of political activism, and even drug taking, conceptually exist outside the conventional everyday of marriage, housework, paid work, and childcare. 'Traditional' roles and institutions were seen by some feminists as inhibitors of self-actualization rather than spaces where the self could be fulfilled.[19] This means that years of women's lives were potentially devoid of self-care as they serviced the needs of their families. Yet, this cohort of women who had experienced their teenage and young womanhood years pursuing social and, in some cases, sexual self-fulfilment, and who anticipated marriage to be fulfilling in different ways, found practical means of

[16] For an extended discussion of Susan's narrative see Abrams, 'Heroes of Their Own Life Stories', pp.9–12.

[17] Rachel Cusk, *Aftermath: on Marriage and Separation* (London: Faber and Faber, 2012), p.5.

[18] See M. Freedman, 'Autonomy and Social Relationships: Rethinking the Feminist Critique' in D. Teitjens Meyers (Ed.), *Feminists Rethink the Self* (Boulder, CO: Westview Press, 1997), 40–61, and Catriona Mackenzie and Natalie Stoljar eds., *Relational Autonomy: Feminist Perspectives on Autonomy, Agency and the Social Self* (Oxford: Oxford University Press, 2000).

[19] For example, Oakley, *Housewife*.

pursuing autonomy which intersected rather than conflicted with their everyday lives. And as often as not, this was an autonomy that was dependent upon mutually constitutive social connections, especially with other women, in self-help groups relating to children and the family or in the workplace, especially in female-dominated education and health and social care settings. They created nourishing empathetic communities that allowed them to express their feelings in a safe space.

Hitherto, self-care has been understood historically as a feminist political act to counter, in particular, patriarchal health practices which tended to treat women's bodies as inherently sick and which denied women autonomy over their bodies, particularly in the area of reproductive rights. Carole recalled that when she went to have a coil fitted in 1976 after her second child was born, her husband had to provide written permission.[20] The contraceptive pill was not prescribed to single women until 1968, seven years after it became available to married women. It was in this context that self-help was developed by the Women's Liberation Movement as an ideology and a set of practices around healthcare, first of all in the United States and subsequently exported elsewhere, with the objective of 'reclaiming one's health, sexuality and reproductive power'.[21]

At the heart of the feminist alternative health movement was the Boston Women's Health Book Collective's *Our Bodies Ourselves*, available commercially from 1973, a book written in an accessible format to 'serve as a model for women to learn about themselves, communicate their findings with doctors, and challenge the medical establishment to change and improve the care that women receive'.[22] *Our Bodies Ourselves* was inspired by women of the transition generation who had been raised to 'be nice to everyone', whose identities had been squashed by dominant 'cultural notions of femininity' but who, through honest discussions with each other had rediscovered themselves. That rediscovery involved a celebration of what made them women and an embrace of their feminine qualities.[23] Many were married and had children but they were searching for a 'space to discover who we were, separate from these primary relationships, so that we could become autonomous adult people as well as have important relationships with others'.[24] The space they created was free from patriarchal boundaries—it was autonomous, self-organized, and incredibly productive. The change the book inspired, 'inviting women to use their own experiences as resources for producing situated, critical knowledge about their bodies and

[20] Interview with Carole.

[21] Maud Bracke, 'Our Bodies Ourselves: The Transnational Connections of 1970s Italian and Roman Feminism', *Journal of Contemporary History* 50:3 (2015), pp.560–80, here p.566.

[22] See https://www.ourbodiesourselves.org/our-story/.

[23] Boston Women's Health Book Collective, *Our Bodies Ourselves. A Health Book By and For Women* (London: Penguin, 1978), p.15.

[24] https://www.ourbodiesourselves.org/wp-content/uploads/2020/03/OurChangingSenseofSelf.pdf. p.5.

health' was the outcome of women acting on their feelings and understanding that taking care of the self was a relational or collective project. Care was an emotional act.

Self-care was not solely a feminist endeavour however. The feelings expressed in consciousness-raising and other collective forums that mobilized women's liberation activists to establish mental health provision as well as a wide range of other initiatives at a local level, from women's centres to action on reproductive rights, followed on from the Sixties do-it-yourself activism. Although the latter did not employ a feminist critique by and large, it was an early attempt to direct personal anguish into political action. All the women's self-help groups discussed in this book understood that women, a group often conditioned to care for others before themselves, needed to practise self-care if they were to effectively undertake that care for others. Self-sacrifice was not a long-term option.

Feminist Voices

This book has privileged women's own versions of their lives as the primary driver of the narrative and analyses of their accounts through the prisms of the self and emotions or feelings. Their stories reveal an emotional revolution. Women of this generation liberated their feelings, making themselves visible to one another; they found ways of speaking about their feelings, translating them into action and in the process they sought and sometimes found self-fulfilment or self-actualization. This is one of the reasons why this generation is able to narrate their lives with themselves at the centre of the story. They tell feminographies: life narratives that acknowledge the validity of women's own interpretation of experience, that understand the structural and ideological causes of that experience and that demonstrate action contingent on that understanding. These are consciously or unconsciously feminist narratives, 'testimonials to a belief in a set of fundamental principles which have the purpose of reaffirming the narrator's self-identification as a feminist and sustaining the discursive narrative for posterity'.[25] Their accounts are the consequence of women of the transition generation seizing agency over their destiny. Unlike their mothers' generation who are often portrayed as self-sacrificing, subordinating their feelings to their duty towards others, the women who take centre stage in this book understand that they are heroes of their own life stories.

This is not a homogeneous story however. The women of this generation reach this understanding at different moments in their life histories and through different processes and experiences. Those who enjoyed a period of tertiary education

[25] Abrams, 'Talking about feminism', p.84.

or who moved away from home for training or work, were more likely to experience self-realization in their twenties. Pam's recounting of the story of calling off her engagement, giving up her safe teaching job and moving to Spain and Suzanna's rejection of marriage to men she didn't love, both fit this typology. By contrast, Eileen's recounting of an abusive marriage in which she reclaimed control of the narrative in the interview some 30 years later, is an example of a woman who took much longer to find the self-confidence and the language to put herself and her interpretation of what happened, first. It was a college course in women's studies later in life that enabled Eileen to understand and interpret her experiences and to forge a new path on her own terms. And for Diane it was a failed marriage that turbo-charged her determination to be 'smart and independent' in order not to be so emotionally reliant on another person. When her second marriage ran into trouble in the 1980s and her husband reneged on his promise to assist with the childcare while she worked, she had a reservoir of self-determination to draw on. She said: 'I'm just so determined not to give this job up because it was only then I realized that my identity had gone and for once I was in the shop I was me and not [the children's] mum or [husband's] wife.'[26]

The language of personal growth was not often explicitly employed by voluntary organizations or women themselves in the 1960s and 1970s, but retrospective accounts are rich with the discourse of self-actualization and self-care, albeit expressed in everyday or vernacular terms. This reflects the normalization of the personal growth and development narrative in popular culture, but also an understanding that what they experienced in their twenties and thirties can now be understood within a framework of a journey towards greater gender equality. This ability to re-evaluate a life through a feminist lens is especially evident amongst working-class women who took advantage of opportunities to return to education as mature students in the 1970s and 1980s. The majority did so to gain qualifications and improve their employment prospects, especially in the public sector, coinciding with the establishment of women's studies courses in higher education institutions in the 1980s. Women of this generation placed a high value on education throughout their life course, regarding it as transformative for personal development.[27] Eileen returned to study as a mature student in her 50s. She recognized that her gender studies course had helped her understand what had happened to her, that her husband's abuse was not her fault and that 'there are other sides to things'. She found people she could talk to there in contrast with her best friend from her home community who 'only sees things as she sees them in her life'.[28] But the epiphanic moment for Eileen occurred while she was attending a course on domestic violence as part of her job as a housing officer. She vividly described the moment of realization:

[26] UKDA, SN 5190: Interview with Diane Brown.
[27] Worth, *Welfare State Generation*, pp.68–73, 149.
[28] UKDA, SN 5190: Interview with Eileen Parr, p.32.

> Yes, oh, fancy having to fuckin' be here, we were all muttering and having a cup of tea and a biscuit, oh, right, we're ready to start. We all sat down and this thing came up on the screen, and I sat there reading it, panic [..] I thought I was going to die, I thought, that's me, d'you know what I mean, it was all there, it was as if, [pants] I couldn't breathe, I started to sweat, and I had to get out, d'you know what I mean, and obviously there's people there who are aware that this could happen, 'cause they took me out and nobody, I mean, there was one other woman there who had, you know, who got affected as well, um, but, and it weren't till that moment that I realized that I had been a victim of domestic violence for 30-odd years, you know what I mean, and I think that was the worst thing that's ever happened to me, of all the dreadful things that have happened in my life, that was the worst.
>
> *The realization that that label fitted you?*
>
> Yeah.[29]

At the time she was interviewed in 2002, Eileen was in a new relationship, but on her own terms, having told her new partner that 'there are limits, and he's got to learn my limits...so that we...trust each other and everything, you know'. Eileen concluded the interview by saying that 'this last two years of my life have been more productive in terms of self-fulfilment and everything than the whole, the rest of it put together'. It had taken Eileen three decades to reach that point.

Eileen now put herself first. The growth in women's take-up of complementary and alternative therapies, body practices from weight-watchers to yoga and pilates as well as various manifestations of new-age spirituality, reflect this generation's embrace of expressive individualism albeit not at the expense of the care they still provide for others.[30] Gina's biography, written when she was nearing 70, encapsulates this dichotomy. When she left school in 1966 Gina attended university before embarking on a career in television. Marriage and two children followed. But Gina's life narrative emphasized her multi-faceted interests and activities encompassing body practices, community activism, and personal fulfilment—a rich amalgam of care for others and care for herself:

> I have been many things—a garden designer, Relate counsellor, lecturer, media trainer, reiki healer, an environmental campaigner and latterly a social entrepreneur. I have founded two successful community groups...I also teach people about nutrition and health and have an international business supporting

[29] UKDA, SN 5190: Interview with Eileen Parr, p.31.

[30] Suzanne Newcombe, 'Stretching for Health and Well-Being: Yoga and Women in Britain, 1960–1980', *Asian Medicine* 3 (2007), pp. 37–63; Katrina-Louise Mosely, 'Slimming One's Way to a Better Self? Weight Loss Clubs and Women in Britain, 1967–1990' *Twentieth Century British History* 31: 4 (2020), pp.427–53; Paul Heelas and Linda Woodhead, *The Spiritual Revolution: Why Religion Is Giving Way to Spirituality* (Oxford: Blackwell, 2005).

> customers and team members round the world. Had breast cancer 5 years ago…I have published books of poetry and ghost stories…I make and sell art, and have written a new Christmas carol. I travel. A current project is about Goddesses… Recently I have become interested in shamanism.[31]

The legacy of the self-help and self-care project initiated by the post-war generation in the 1960s is to be seen in the prevalence of alternative modes of self-care practised by these women in later life. Organizations like the National Women's Register which offers 'lively conversation' and fun via 342 local groups throughout the UK at the time of writing, and the University of the Third Age offer women, now in their seventies and eighties, companionship and opportunities for self-development.[32]

Becoming Visible

The post-war decades, the era prior to the emergence of the Women's Liberation Movement and women's liberation, are a watershed moment for women in Britain. It was then that this generation began to chart a new modern female life course which encompassed paid work and family, care for others, and self-care. This book has listened to women's own interpretations of those lives, some narrated in retrospect and others contemporaneously, providing a woman-centred view of how they negotiated a path between change and opportunity on the one hand, and convention and social expectation on the other hand. By attending to women's feelings, expressed at the time and recalled subsequently, we can see the moments of crisis and epiphany, and better understand the meaning of experiences. This approach shifts the focus from what historians and contemporary observers have tended to deem significant to women's own interpretations.

The post-war generation of women is a generation visible to itself. Fuelled by the conditions in which they grew up and were educated, which facilitated experimentation with relationships and identities, these women permitted themselves to express how they felt to one another which in turn ignited a social movement of women's groups and local and national activism. By speaking about their feelings they turned the expressive revolution into an emotional revolution, acknowledging their feelings and finding strength in community to act on them. For some, the do-it-yourself organizations provided an empathetic community which validated their feelings and enabled them to find their feet, boosting confidence,

[31] 'Gina' in 'South Hampstead High School Potted Histories of School Leavers 1966', (2016).
[32] https://nwr.org.uk/ (accessed 14 September 2022).

enabling networks and acting as a stepping-stone to the next stage whether that be a return to education or training or employment. They rejected the self-sacrifice and regret many witnessed in their mothers' generation in favour of a more balanced lifestyle which combined care for others with care for the self. This was a significant shift. Women had long been expected to sacrifice their own needs and desires to the demands and expectations of others: husbands, brothers, children, the elderly, and patients in the female-dominated care sector. Achieving a better balance between individual self-fulfilment and servicing the needs of others, whether that be through motherhood, home-making or paid work, was a process characterized by struggle and trial and error. But they understood that in order to be contented and fulfilled they needed to find space for the self.

This is a relational history as well as an emotional history. Women made themselves and their feelings visible to one another. In personal correspondence, the pages of newsletters and magazines, in sitting rooms and village halls, and even in conversation with academic researchers, they made their feelings count. The empathetic community of other women validated feelings that may have been discounted by husbands or even mothers. The 'you've made your bed, now lie in it' response from the older generation and a lack of understanding on the part of some husbands to their wives' unhappiness meant that women had to seek support amongst other women who did understand. This book has focused on the self-help movement in this regard. Organizations like NHR, PPA, NCT, and others offered an outlet for feelings that were hard to express elsewhere and then they also directed those feelings into activity to relieve the isolation and provide confidence building, intellectual stimulation, practical experience, and skills. The workplace also fulfilled this function and for others there will have been other spaces which nurtured women's selves: politics, education, sport. This was a collective response to feelings of guilt, of stagnation and loneliness. It was not, in the early stages at least, an intellectual critique of women's position although, as we have seen, some activists did position the do-it-yourself movement within a longer and broader feminist trajectory albeit without the direct challenge to patriarchal structures or thinking. Neither did these groups explicitly argue for an equality agenda, largely because they accepted and wished to see valued women's qualities as mothers and had an uninformed understanding of what women's liberation stood for. But the binary analysis which situates this self-help movement against women's liberation misses an opportunity to give feminism its rightful and important place in British post-war history. Feminism appears in many guises, not least in the ways in which women claimed the right to do things differently and how they understood, interpreted, and narrated that claim. The presence of feminism as a broad set of beliefs about equality of opportunity and treatment pervades the testimony of this generation. They lived feminist lives.

Coda

The generation at the heart of this book saw, and still sees itself 50 years later, as distinctive and one of the ways in which they mark that difference is by situating their choices, opportunities, and experiences in relation to their mothers' and their daughters' lives. In the personal testimony of this generation, mothers—either collectively or more often, individually—represent a life and a lifestyle rejected, the complexities and realities of their lives effaced by daughters who felt the need to validate their own decisions. But this is a self-reflective generation who, in later life, can empathize with their mothers' position having recognized that elements of their life had been replicated in their own. 'I knew', writes Rachel Cusk, 'that once upon a time [my mother] had had her own reality, had lived as it were, in real time.'[33] Caroline's story of the red stockings which brought Chapter 2 to a close, encapsulates a shift in perspective of the narrator from the daughter who needed to rebel against the constraints she associated with her parents' generation, to the mature woman and mother who can now read that incident with more emotional intelligence. Caroline's mother's reaction to her wearing red stockings in church was understood as an emotional reaction that stemmed from her own frustration at missing out on the life that her daughter was now leading.[34] Anne, who had reacted to viscerally in her teens to what her mother represented, came to a rapprochement with her in later life based on their shared experience of motherhood.[35]

Part of the re-evaluation of their lives carried out by this generation is also conducted in relation to the lives of young women today. For those who have daughters and grand-daughters, there is little envy or resentment of their wider opportunities. Rather, the post-war generation see themselves as fortunate in being able to have 'had it all' or close to all, as they interpret it, in particular staying at home while children were small and only returning to employment when they chose to do so. In informal conversations when the recorder was turned off, a number of interviewees talked to me about their concern for their daughters and daughters-in-law who were pulled in two directions by home and work. They were proud of what the next generation had achieved as and for women but regretful for what had been lost along the way. And yet, whereas some historians see the transition generation as disappointed and unfulfilled in later life, 'searching for ways to exercise their agency', having lost their work identities, the women at the heart of this book regard themselves as lucky to have benefited from the opportunities and freedoms of the post-war decades without the pressure to be superwomen.[36] In generating their stories they make sense of the disconnectedness of a woman's life and redeem a coherent self from the compartmentalized or multiple womanhoods they have lived.

[33] Cusk, *Aftermath*, p.11.

[34] Interview with Caroline.

[35] Interview with Anne.

[36] Worth, *Welfare State Generation*, p.152.

Bibliography

Primary Sources

Archives

BBC Written Archives Centre

Woman's Hour Files
R51/774/1 Report on Woman's Hour Listeners in Distress Referred to Welfare Organisations during 1960
R51/1016/4 Woman's Hour 1961
R51/1016/5: Woman's Hour Correspondence
R51/1016/6 Woman's Hour 1964

British Library

Sisterhood and After: An Oral History of the Women's Liberation Movement https://www.bl.uk/sisterhood

Glasgow Women's Library

Scottish Women's Liberation Movement Workshop: Edinburgh 2009—witness testimony.

Medical Research Council, University College London

National Survey of Health and Development: 1946 birth cohort study. MRC NSHD 1946–2005 Data. MRC Unit for Lifelong Health and Ageing at UCL. http://dx.doi.org/10.5522/NSHD/Q101
wiki: https://skylark.ucl.ac.uk
metadata browser: https://skylark.ucl.ac.uk/Skylark
Student Study Transcripts (1965)
Persistent Job Changers' Survey (1968)

National Library of Scotland

Scottish Pre-School Playgroups Association Papers

Norfolk Record Office

FC 79/420, 79/424: Young Wives' Club (Heartsease Lane Methodist Young Wives Club), 1957–78

SO 226/9, 226/10: National Council of Women Norfolk and Norwich Branch, 1958–71.

UK Data Archive, University of Essex

Hockey, J., Robinson, V., and Meah, A., *Cross-Generational Investigation of the Making of Heterosexual Relationships, 1912–2003*. Colchester, Essex: UK Data Archive, October 2005. SN: 5190, http://dx.doi.org/10.5255/UKDA-SN-5190-1

Lawson, A., *Adultery: An Analysis of Love and Betrayal, 1920–1983* [computer file]. Colchester, Essex: UK Data Archive [distributor], November 2004. SN: 4858, http://dx.doi.org/10.5255/UKDA-SN-4858-2

Marsden, D., *Mothers Alone: Poverty and the Fatherless Family, 1955–1966* [computer file]. Colchester, Essex: UK Data Archive [distributor], February 2005. SN: 5072

Pahl, R. (2018). *Managers and their Wives: A Study of Career and Family Relationships in the Middle Class, 1965–1967.* [data collection]. UK Data Service. SN: 853296

Todd, S. and Young, H., *Coventry and Liverpool Lives Oral History Collection, c.1945–1970* [computer file]. Colchester, Essex: UK Data Archive [distributor], May 2014. SN: 7485 http://dx.doi.org/10.5255/UKDA-SN-7485-1

Wallace, C.D., Pahl, R.E. (2019). Social and Political Implications of Household Work Strategies, 1978–1983. [data collection]. UK Data Service. SN: 4876, http://doi.org/10.5255/UKDA-SN-4876-1

Wiggins, M. (2013). Looking Back on Becoming a Mother: Longitudinal Perspectives on Maternity Care and the Transition to Motherhood. [data collection]. UK Data Service. SN: 850818, DOI: 10.5255/UKDA-SN-850818

Institute of Education Archive, University College London

Pre-School Playgroup Association Papers

PLA/PPA/1/1: Brenda Crowe 1st National Advisor Papers, 1967–74

PLA/PPA/1/3: National Executive Committee Papers, 1963–92

PLA/PPA/1/4: Brenda Crowe Papers as First National Adviser for the PPA, 1967–70

PLA/PPA/1/29: Brenda Crowe Reports 1972–77

PLA/PPA/2/8: Scottish Association Material, 1967–74

PLA/PPA/2/9: Scottish PPA

PLA/PPA/2/28: Scottish Association's Annual Reports and Newsletters

PLA/PPA/2/67: Birmingham Playgroups, 1973–74

PLA/PPA/4/6: Brenda Crowe, 'Parent Involvement' in Parents in Playgroups (c.1971).

PLA/PPA/4/25: Booklet 'Why playgroups', c.1970

PLA/PPA/4/46: Masters dissertation by Barbara Keeley

PLA/PPA/4/58: Publications, 1968–92

PLA/PPA/4/62: Publicity Materials

PLA/PPA/5/4: *Contact* magazine

PLA/PPA/6/1: Playgroup Memories and Reminiscences, 1960–2011

PLA/PPA 16/1–3: *Playgroup News*, issue 1, 1969

PPA FAW/1–3: Newscutting Books, 1966–1976

University of Glasgow Archives and Special Collections

Homes in High Flats papers
DC 127/16/4: Valerie Somerville, 'Charles Street Playgroup', dissertation.

Wellcome Collection

National Childbirth Trust Papers
SA/NCT PP/GDR/F/12: National Childbirth Trust Newsletters and Publications
SA/NCT/A/1/1/2: Landmarks/Documents of historical interest
SA/NCT/H/4/4: Conferences, papers and reports
SA/NCT/J/2/2/1: Copies of NCT Journal 'New Generation' 1967–1968
SA/PAT/C/42 : Miscellaneous correspondence and papers

Women's Library, London School of Economics,

National Housewives Register Papers
NHR Newsletters 1963–84
5/NWR/1/2: Constitution 2 1974–5
5/NWR/1/5: Cheshire group c.1960
5/NWR/1/14: Survival Correspondence 1996–7
5/NWR/1/15: Correspondence 1969–1972
5/NWR/1/16: National Group 1976 onwards
5/NWR/1/18: Survey Forms 1970
5/NWR/1/21: Advice and Information Leaflets 1980s
5/NWR/3/5: International Conference 1980–
5/NWR/4/1: Press cuttings from the regional groups
5/NWR/4/4/1: Promotional Material
5/NWR/5/2: National Organiser 1960–
5/NWR/5/3: Maureen Nicol

Working Association of Mothers Papers
5WAM/1–8: Working Association of Mothers, 1969–80: Correspondence, newsletters, press cuttings

Private Collections

* indicates pseudonym
Private papers of Suzanna*
Private papers of Cynthia
South Hampstead High School Potted Histories of School Leavers 1966 (2016).

Oral History Interviews

All interviews were conducted by the author unless otherwise stated.
* indicates pseudonym.

Name	Date of birth	Primary places of residence
Jennifer	1930	England, Scotland

Jan*	1934	England, Scotland
Frances*	1937	England, Scotland
Dorothy*	1939	England, Scotland
Rhian*	1940	Wales, England, Scotland
Cynthia	1940	England
Sandra*	1941	England, Scotland
Lorraine*	1941	Scotland, Sudan
Ruth*	1941	England, Canada
Sally*	1943	England, Scotland
Caroline*	1943	India, England, Scotland
Betty*	1944	Scotland
Susan*	1944	England, Iraq, Scotland
Pam*	1945	England, Scotland
Kathleen*	1946	England, Scotland
Diana	1946	England, Scotland
Shirley*	1946	Scotland
Rosemary*	1946	England, Scotland
Anne H.	1947	England
Suzanna*	1948	England, Scotland
Jane*	1948	England, Scotland
Janette*	1948	England, Scotland
Deborah	1949	England, Scotland
Linda*	1949	England, Canada
Carole*	1949	England, Scotland

Humanist Lives (private collection)

Anne Auchterlonie 1942 Scotland (Interviewed by Callum G. Brown)

Housing and Everyday Life (University of Glasgow Archives and Special Collections)

John and Carol c.1947 Scotland (Interviewed by Valerie Wright)

Personal Correspondence

Correspondence from Suzanna to the author, September 2021
Correspondence from Anne to the author, August 2021

Newspapers and Magazines

Cosmopolitan
Drapers' Record
The Guardian
Modern Woman
Nova
The Observer
Petticoat
Press and Journal

Published Primary Sources

Abrams, Mark, *The Teenage Consumer* (London: The London Press Exchange, 1959).

Abrams, Mark, *Teenage Consumer Spending in 1959* (London: The London Press Exchange, 1961).
Bakewell, Joan, *The Centre Of The Bed: An Autobiography* (London: Sceptre, 2019).
Barber, Lynn, *An Education* (London: Penguin, 2009).
Barrett, R.E., 'Suburban Neurosis Up To Date', *The Lancet* 271 no.7017 (1958).
Beyfus, Drusilla, *The English Marriage* (Littlehampton: Littlehampton Book Services Ltd, 1968).
Black, Brian and Sonia Black, *Childminder: A Study in Action Research* (London: Routledge & Kegan Paul, 1979).
Boston Women's Health Book Collective, *Our Bodies Ourselves. A Health Book By and For Women* (London: Penguin, 1978).
Bray, Judith, Joan Conway, Marjorie Dykins, Leontia Slay, Ivy Webster, and Wendy Hawkins, *Memories of the Playgroup Movement in Wales 1961–1987* (Aberystwyth: Wales Pre-School Playgroups Association, 2008).
Coleman, S.D., *Mental Health and Social Adjustment in a New Town: An Exploratory Study in East Kilbride* (University of Glasgow, 1965).
Ker Conway, Jill, *The Road from Coorain* (New York: Vintage, 1989).
Coote, Anna and Beatrix Campbell, *Sweet Freedom. The Struggle for Women's Liberation* (London: Picador, 1982).
Crowe, Brenda, *The Playgroup Movement* (London: George Allen & Unwin, 1973).
Dunn, Nell, *Up the Junction* (orig.1963, London: Virago, 2013).
Dunn, Nell, *Talking to Women* (London: Pan, 1966).
Dunn, Nell, *Poor Cow* (orig, 1967, London: Virago, 2013).
Frazer Lamb, Patrizia and Kathryn Joyce Hohlwein, *Touchstones: Letters Between Two Women 1953–1964* (Boston, MA: G.K.Hall, 1983).
Friedan, Betty, *The Feminine Mystique* (London: Victor Gollancz, 1963).
Galloway, Janet, *All Made Up* (London: Granta, 2012).
Gavron, Hannah, *The Captive Wife: Conflicts of Housebound Mothers* (London: Routledge & Kegan Paul, 1966).
Gilroy, Beryl, *Black Teacher* (London: Faber & Faber, 2021).
Gittus, Elizabeth, *Flats, Families and the Under-Fives* (London: Routledge, 1976).
Gundrey, Elizabeth, *Jobs for Mothers* (London: Zenith, 1967).
Harman, Harriet. *A Woman's Work* (London: Penguin 2018).
Heron, Liz, *Truth, Dare or Promise: Girls Growing Up in the Fifties* (London: Virago, 1985).
Hubback, Judith, *Wives Who Went to College* (London: William Heinemann, 1957).
Jackson, Brian and Sylvia Jackson, *Childminder. A Study in Action Research* (London: Routledge & Kegan Paul, 1979).
Jackson, Sonia, *The Illegal Child-Minders. A Report on the Growth of Unregistered Child-Minding and the West Indian Community* (Cambridge: Priority Area Children, 1971).
Jephcott, Pearl, *Some Young People* (London: George Allen and Unwin, 1954).
Jephcott, Pearl, *Married Women Working* (London: Allen and Unwin, 1962).
Jephcott, Pearl, *A Troubled Area: Notes on Notting Hill* (London: Faber, 1964).
Jephcott, Pearl, *Homes in High Flats* (Edinburgh: Oliver & Boyd, 1971).
Joseph, Joyce, 'A Research Note on Attitudes to Work and Marriage of Six Hundred Adolescent Girls', *The British Journal of Sociology* 12:2 (1961), pp.176–83.
Maitland, Sara (Ed.), *Very Heaven. Looking Back at the 1960s* (London: Virago, 1988).
Maizels, Joan, *Two to Five in High Flats. An Enquiry into Play Provision for Children Ages Two to Five Living in High Flats* (London: Housing Centre Trust, 1961).
Maizels, Joan, *Adolescent Needs and the Transition from School to Work* (London: Athlone Press, 1970).

Marsden, Dennis, *Mothers' Alone: Poverty and the Fatherless Family* (London: Allen Lane, 1969).

McCrindle, Jean and Sheila Rowbotham, *Dutiful Daughters: Women Talk About their Lives* (London: Viking, 1977).

Penelope Mortimer, *About Time Too, 1940–1978* (London: Phoenix, 1994), p.52.

Murray, Jenni, *Memoirs Of A Not So Dutiful Daughter* (London: Transworld, 2009).

Myrdal, Alva and Viola Klein, *Women's Two Roles* (London: Routledge, 1968).

Oakley, Ann, *Housewife* (Harmondsworth: Penguin, 1974).

Oakley, Ann, *Becoming a Mother* (London: Pelican, 1979).

Oakley, Ann, *Here to Maternity: Becoming a Mother* (Harmondsworth: Penguin, 1986).

Pahl, J.M and R.E. Pahl, *Managers and Their Wives: A Study of Career and Family Relationships in the Middle Class* (Harmondsworth: Penguin, 1971).

Paul, E. Rae, *Playgroups in an Industrial City* (Glasgow: Scottish PPA, 1974).

Quant, Mary, *Quant by Quant: the Autobiography of Mary Quant* (orig.1966, London: V&A, 2018).

Roberts, A.H., 'Housebound Housewives: A Follow-Up Study of a Phobic Anxiety State', *British Journal of Psychiatry* 110 no.465 (1964), pp.191–7.

Rowbotham, Sheila, *Women's Liberation and the New Politics*, (London: Spokesman Books, 2020; orig. 1971).

Rowbotham, Sheila, *Threads through Time: Writings on History and Autobiography* (London: Penguin, 1999).

Rowbotham, Sheila, *Promise of a Dream: Remembering the Sixties* (London: Allen Lane, 2000).

Rowbotham, Sheila, *Daring to Hope: My Life in the 1970s* (London: Verso, 2021).

Sage, Lorna, *Bad Blood: A Memoir* (London: William Morrow & Co,. 2002).

Sharpe, Sue, *'Just Like a Girl': How Girls Learn to Be Women* (Harmondsworth: Penguin, 1976).

Stone, Robert, *Prime Green: Remembering the Sixties* (New York: Harper Collins, 2008).

Street-Porter, Janet, *Fall Out. A Memoir of Friends Made and Friends Unmade* (London: Headline, 2007).

Summerskill, Edith, *Letters to my Daughter* (London: Heinemann, 1957).

Taylor, Stephen, 'The suburban neurosis', *The Lancet* 231, 5978 (1938).

Veness, Thelma, *School Leavers: Their Aspirations and Expectations* (London: Methuen, 1962).

Walters, Julie, *That's Another Story. The Autobiography* (London: Weidenfeld & Nicolson, 2008).

Zweig, Ferdynand, *Women's Life and Labour* (London: Victor Gollancz 1952), p.18.

Secondary Sources

Published

Abrams, Lynn, 'Mothers and Daughters: Negotiating the Discourse on the "Good Woman" in 1950s and 1960s Britain' in N. Christie and M. Gauvreau (Eds), *The Sixties and Beyond: Dechristianisation in North America and Western Europe, 1945–2000* (Toronto: University of Toronto Press, 2013), pp.60–83.

Abrams, Lynn, 'Liberating the Female Self: Epiphanies, Conflict and Coherence in the Life Stories of Post-War British Women', *Social History*, 39:1 (2014), pp.14–35.

Abrams, Lynn, *Oral History Theory* (London: Routledge, 2016).

Abrams, Lynn, 'A Wartime Family Romance: Narratives of Masculinity and Intimacy During World War Two' in L. Abrams and E. Ewan (Eds), *Nine Centuries of Man: Masculinities in Scottish History* (Edinburgh: Edinburgh University Press 2017), pp.160–79.

Abrams, Lynn, 'Heroes of Their Own Life Stories: Narrating the Female Self in the Feminist Age', *Cultural and Social History* 16:2 (2019), pp.205–24.

Abrams, Lynn, 'The Self and Self-Help: Women Pursuing Autonomy in Post-War Britain', *Transactions of the Royal Historical Society* 29 (2019), pp.201–21.

Abrams, Lynn, 'Talking about Feminism: Reconciling Fragmented Narratives with the Feminist Research Frame', in K. Srigley, S. Zembrzycki, and F. Iacovetta (Eds), *Beyond Women' Words: Feminisms and the Practices of Oral History in the Twenty-First Century* (New York: Routledge, 2019), pp.81–94.

Abrams, Lynn, Linda Fleming, Barry Hazley, Valerie Wright, and Ade Kearns, 'Isolated and Dependent: Women and Children in High-Rise Social Housing in Post-War Glasgow', *Women's History Review* 28:5 (2019), pp.794–813.

Abrams, Lynn, Ade Kearns, Barry Hazley, and Valerie Wright, *Glasgow: High-Rise Homes, Estates and Communities in the Post-War Period* (London: Routledge, 2020).

Ahmed, Sarah, *The Cultural Politics of Emotion* (Edinburgh: Edinburgh University Press, 2014).

Aiston, Sarah, 'A Maternal Identity? The Family Lives of British Women Graduates Pre- and Post-1945', *History of Education* 34:4 (2005), pp.407–26.

Allen, Sheila and Carol Wolkowitz, *Homeworking: Myths and Realities* (London: Macmillan Education, 1987).

Almond, Kevin and Elaine Evans, 'A Regional Study of Women's Emotional Attachments to the Consumption and Making of Ordinary Clothing, Drawing on Archives in Leeds, West Yorkshire, 1939–1979', *Costume*, 56.1 (2022), pp.74–100.

Arnold-Foster, Agnes and Alison Moulds (Eds), *Feelings and Work in Modern History: Emotional Labour and Emotions About Labour* (London: Bloomsbury, 2022).

Attfield, Judith, 'Inside Pram Town: A Case Study of Harlow House Interiors, 1951–1961' in Judith Attfield and Pat Kirkham (Eds), *A View from the Interior: Feminism, Women and Design* (London: Women's Press, 1995).

Attfield, Judith, *Bringing Modernity Home. Writings on Popular Design and Material Culture* (Manchester: Manchester University Press, 2007).

August, Andrew, 'Gender and 1960s Youth Culture: The Rolling Stones and the New Woman', *Contemporary British History* 23:1 (2009), pp.79–100.

Aytoun, Slvia, 'A Love Hate Relationship with Couture', *Costume* 39:1 (2005).

Bailey, Beth, *Sex in the Heartland* (Cambridge, MA: Harvard University Press, 1999).

Bailkin, Jordanna, *The Afterlife of Empire* (Berkeley, CA: University of California Press, 2012).

Beaumont, Caitriona, *Housewives and Citizens: Domesticity and the Women's Movement in England, 1928–64* (Manchester: Manchester University Press, 2013).

Beaumont, Caitriona, 'What *Do* Women Want? Housewives' Associations, Activism and Changing Representations of Women in the 1950s', *Women's History Review* 26:1 (2017), pp.147–62.

Bracke, Maud Anne, *Women and the Reinvention of the Political. Feminism in Italy, 1968–1983* (London: Routledge, 2014).

Bracke, Maud Anne, 'Our Bodies Ourselves: The Transnational Connections of 1970s Italian and Roman Feminism', *Journal of Contemporary History* 50:3 (2015), pp.560–80.

Brayfield, Celia, *Rebel Writers. The Accidental Feminists* (London: Bloomsbury, 2019).

Brewitt Taylor, Sam, 'Christianity and the Invention of the Sexual Revolution in Britain, 1963–1967', *Historical Journal* 60:2 (2017), pp.519–46.

Brooke, Stephen, '"Slumming" in Swinging London?', *Cultural and Social History* 9:3 (2012), pp.429–49.

Brooke, Stephen, '"A Certain Amount of Mush": Love, Romance, Celluloid and Wax in the Mid-twentieth Century', in Alana Harris and Tim Willen Jones (Eds), *Love and Romance in Britain, 1918–1970* (Basingstoke: Palgrave Macmillan, 2015), pp.81–99.

Brown, Callum G., *The Death of Christian Britain: Understanding Secularisation 1800–2000* (London: Routledge, 2001).

Brown, Callum G., 'Sex, Religion, and the Single Woman c.1950–75: The Importance of a 'Short' Sexual Revolution to the English Religious Crisis of the Sixties', *Twentieth Century British History* 22:2 (2011), pp.189–215.

Brown, Callum G., *Religion and The Demographic Revolution: Women and Secularisation in Canada, Ireland, UK and USA since the 1960s* (London: Boydell, 2012).

Brown, Callum G., *Becoming Atheist: Humanism and the Secular West* (London: Bloomsbury, 2017).

Browne, Sarah F., 'Women, Religion and the Turn to Feminism. Experiences of Women's Liberation Activists in Britain in the Seventies' in Nancy Christie and Michael Gauvreau (Eds), *The Sixties and Beyond: Dechristianisation in North America and Western Europe, 1945–2000* (Toronto: University of Toronto Press, 2013), pp.84–97.

Browne, Victoria, 'Backlash, Repetition, Untimeliness: The Temporal Dynamics of Feminist Politics', *Hypatia* 28:4 (2013), pp.905–20.

Bryan, Beverley, Stella Dadzie and Suzanne Scafe, *Heart of the Race: Black Women's Lives in Britain* (London, Verso, 2018).

Bryant, Joanne and Toni Schofield, 'Feminine Sexual Subjectivities: Bodies, Agency and Life History', *Sexualities* 10:3 (2007), pp.321–40.

Buckley, Cheryl, 'On the Margins: Theorizing the History and Significance of Making and Designing Clothes at Home', *Journal of Design History* 11.2 (1998), pp.151–71.

Bunkle, Phillida, 'The 1944 Education Act and Second Wave Feminism', *Women's History Review* 25:5 (2016), pp.791–811.

Burman, Barbara, 'Home-sewing and "Fashions for All", 1908–1937', *Costume* 28:1 (1994), pp.71–80.

Chamberlain, Mary, 'The Global Self: Narratives of Caribbean Migrant Women', in Tess Coslett, Celia Lury, and Penny Summerfield (Eds), *Feminism and Autobiography: Texts, Theories, Methods* (London: Routledge, 2000), pp.154–66.

Chamberlain Mary, *Narratives of Exile and Return* (London: Routledge, 2017).

Charnock, Hannah, 'Teenage Girls, Female Friendship and the Making of the Sexual Revolution in England, 1950–1980', *The Historical Journal* 63:4 (2020), pp.1032–53.

Cherry, N., 'Women and Work Stress: Evidence from the 1946 Birth Cohort', *Ergonomics* 27 (1984), pp.519–26.

Chesler, Phyllis, *Women and Madness* (London: Harcourt Brace Jovanovich, 1972).

Cohen, Deborah, *Family Secrets: The Things We Tried to Hide* (London: Penguin, 2014).

Collins, Marcus, *Modern Love: An Intimate History of Men and Women in Twentieth Century Britain* (London: Atlantic Books, 2003).

Collins, Marcus, *The Beatles and Sixties Britain* (Cambridge: Cambridge University Press, 2022).

Conekin, Becky E., Frank Mort, Chris Waters (Eds), *Moments of Modernity? Reconstructing Britain 1945–1964* (London: Rivers Oram, 1999).

Cook, Hera, *The Long Sexual Revolution: English Women, Sex and Contraception 1800–1975* (Oxford: Oxford University Press, 2004).

Cook, Hera, 'From Controlling Emotion to Expressing Feelings in Mid-Twentieth-Century England', *Journal of Social History* 47:3 (2014), pp.627–46.

Cook, Hera, 'Nova 1965–1970: Love, Masculinity and Feminism, But Not As We Know It', in Alana Harris and Timothy Willen Jones (Eds), *Love and Romance in Britain, 1918–1970* (Basingstoke: Palgrave Macmillan, 2015), p.225–44.

Cooke, Rachel, *Her Brilliant Career. Ten Extraordinary Women of the Fifties* (London: Virago, 2014).

Cowan, David, 'Modern Parenting and the Uses of Childcare Advice in Post-war England', *Social History* 43:3 (2018), pp.332–55.

Cox, Pamela, *Gender, Justice and Welfare: Bad Girls in Britain, 1900–1950* (Basingstoke: Palgrave, 2003).

Crook, Sarah, 'The Women's Liberation Movement, Activism and Therapy at the Grassroots, 1968–1985', *Women's History Review* 27:7 (2018), pp.1152–68.

Crook, Sarah, *Postnatal Depression in Post-war Britain: Women, Motherhood and Social Change* (forthcoming).

Cruikshank, Julie, *The Social Life of Stories: Narrative and Knowledge in the Yukon Territory* (Lincoln, NE: University of Nebraska Press, 2000).

Cusk, Rachel, *Aftermath: On Marriage and Separation* (London: Faber and Faber, 2012).

Cvetkovich, Ann (Ed.), *An Archive of Feelings: Trauma, Sexuality, and Lesbian Public Cultures* (Durham, NC: Duke University Press, 2003).

Davis, Angela, *Modern Motherhood. Women and Family in England, 1945–2000* (Manchester: Manchester University Press, 2012).

Davis, Angela, *Pre-school Childcare in England, 1939-2020* (Manchester: Manchester University Press, 2015).

Delap, Lucy, 'Feminist Bookshops, Reading Cultures and the Women's Liberation Movement in Great Britain, c.1974–2000', *History Workshop Journal* 81 (2016), pp.171–96.

Din, Aleena, 'British-Pakistani Homeworkers and Activist Campaigns, 1962–2002', *Women's History Review* (online 2022).

Diski, Jenni, *The Sixties* (London: Profile Books, 2009).

Drabble, Margaret, *The Millstone* (London: Weidenfeld & Nicolson, 1965).

Dyhouse, Carol, *No Distinction of Sex: Women in British Universities, 1870–1939* (London: UCL Press, 1995).

Dyhouse, Carol, 'Graduates, Mothers and Graduate Mothers: Family Investment in Higher Education in Twentieth-Century England', *Gender and Education* 14:4 (2002). pp.325–36.

Elliott, Jane and Jon Lawrence, 'Narrative, Time and Intimacy in Social Research: Linda and Jim Revisited' in Graham Crow and Jamie Ellis (Eds), *Revisiting Divisions of Labour. The Impacts and Legacies of a Modern Sociological Classic* (Manchester: Manchester University Press, 2017), pp.189–204.

Finch, Janet, 'The Deceit of Self Help: Preschool Playgroups and Working-Class Mothers', *Journal of Social Policy* 13:1 (1984), pp.1–20.

Fink, Janet and Penny Tinkler, 'Teetering on the Edge: Portraits of Innocence, Risk and Young Female Sexualities in 1950s and 1960s British Cinema', *Women's History Review* 26:1 (2017), pp.9–25.

Fowler, David, *Youth Culture in Modern Britain c.1920–c.1970: from Ivory Tower to Global Movement—A New History* (London: Bloomsbury, 2008).

Freedman, M., 'Autonomy and Social Relationships: Rethinking the Feminist Critique', in D. Teitjens Meyers (Ed.), *Feminists Rethink the Self* (Boulder, CO: Westview Press, 1997), pp.40–61.

Friday, Nancy, *My Mother Myself: The Daughter's Search for Identity* (orig. 1977. London: Harper Collins, 1994).

Frisch, Michael, *A Shared Authority. Essays on the Craft and Meaning of Public and Oral History* (New York: SUNY, 1990).

Gavron, Jeremy, *A Woman on the Edge of Time: A Son Investigates His Trailblazing Mother's Young Suicide* (London: Experiment, 2016).

Giddens, Anthony, *Modernity and Self-Identity. Self and Society in the Late Modern Age* (Cambridge: Polity, 1991).

Giddens, Anthony, *The Transformation of Intimacy: Sexuality, Love, and Eroticism in Modern Societies* (London: Polity, 1993).

Gildea, Robert, Mark James and Annette Warring (Eds), *Europe's 1968: Voices of Revolt* (Oxford: Oxford University Press, 2013).

Giles, Judy, '"Playing Hard to Get": Working-class Women, Sexuality and Respectability in Britain, 1918–40', *Women's History Review* 1:2 (1992), pp.239–55.

Giles, Judy, '"You Meet 'em and That's it": Working-class Women's Refusal of Romance Between the Wars in Britain', in Lynne Pearce and Jackie Stacey (Eds), *Romance Revisited* (London: Lawrence & Wishart, 1995), pp.279–92.

Gillies, Val, *Marginalised Mothers: Exploring Working Class Experiences of Parenting* (London: Routledge, 2007).

Gillis, John, *A World of Their Own Making: A History of Myth and Ritual in Family Life* (Oxford: Oxford University Press, 1997).

Gluck, Sherna Berger, 'What's So Special About Women?' in S.H. Armitage with P. Hart and K. Weathermon (Eds), *Women's Oral History* (Lincoln, NE: University of Nebraska Press, 2002).

Gluck Sherna Berger and Daphne Patai (Eds), *Women's Words: The Feminist Practice of Oral History* (London: Routledge, 1991).

Grant, Linda, *Sexing the Millennium: Political History of the Sexual Revolution* (London: Harper Collins, 1993).

Green, Jonathan, *All Dressed Up: The Sixties and the Counterculture* (London: Pimlico, 1999).

Guy, Alison and Maura Banim, 'Personal Collections: Women's Clothing Use and Identity', *Journal of Gender Studies* 9.3 (2000), pp.313–27.

Haggett, Ali, *Desperate Housewives, Neuroses and the Domestic Environment 1945–1970* (London: Pickering & Chatto, 2012).

Halbert, Jade, 'Just like the King's Road, Only Nearer: Scotland's Boutique Bonanza', *Costume* 56:1 (2022), pp.101–24.

Hamlett, Jane, 'Mothering in the Archives: Care and the Creation of Family Papers and Photographs in Twentieth Century Southern England', *Past & Present* 246, Supplement 15 (2020), pp.186–214.

Handley, Susannah, *Nylon: the Manmade Fashion Revolution* (London: Bloomsbury, 1999).

Hazley, Barry, *Life History and the Irish Migrant Experience in Post-War England: Myth, Memory and Emotional Adaptation* (Manchester: Manchester University Press, 2020).

Hazley, Barry, Valerie Wright, Lynn Abrams, and Ade Kearns, 'People and Their Homes Rather than Housing in the Usual Sense'? Locating the Tenant's Voice in Homes in High Flats', *Women's History Review* 28:5 (2019), pp.728–45.

Heelas, Paul and Linda Woodhead, *The Spiritual Revolution: Why Religion Is Giving Way to Spirituality* (Oxford: Blackwell, 2005).

Held, Lisa and Alexandra Rutherford, 'Can't a Mother Sing the Blues? Postpartum Depression and the Construction of Motherhood in Late 20th-Century America', *History of Psychology* 15:2 (2012), pp.107–23.

Henderson, Ann (Ed.), *Insights from the Playgroup Movement: Equality and Autonomy in a Voluntary Organisation* (Stoke-on-Trent: Trentham Books, 2011).

Henderson, Maude, *Cogs and Spindles: Some Impressions of the Playgroup Movement* (London: PPA, 1978).

Hinton, James, *Nine Wartime Lives: Mass Observation and the Making of the Modern Self* (Oxford: Oxford University Press, 2010).

Hockey, Jenny, Angela Meah, and Victoria Robinson, *Mundane Heterosexualities: from Theory to Practice* (London: Palgrave Macmillan, 2007).

Holmes, Katie, 'Does it Matter if he Cried? Recording Emotion and the Australian Generations Oral History Project', *The Oral History Review* 44:1 (2017), pp.56–76.

Hughes, Celia, *Young Lives on the Left: Sixties Activism and the Liberation of the Self* (Manchester: Manchester University Press, 2015).

Ingham, Mary, *Now We Are Thirty: Women of the Breakthrough Generation* (London: Eyre Methuen, 1981).

Jackson, Louise A., 'The Coffee Club Menace: Policing Youth, Leisure and Sexuality in Post-war Manchester', *Cultural and Social History* 5:3 (2008), pp.289–308.

Jackson, Louise A. with Angela Bartie, *Policing Youth: Britain 1945–70* (Manchester: Manchester University Press, 2014).

Jamieson, Lynn, *Intimacy: Personal Relationships in Modern Society* (London: Polity, 1997).

Jennings, Rebecca, *Tom-Boys and Bachelor Girls. A Lesbian History of Post-War Britain, 1945–71* (Manchester: Manchester University Press, 2007).

Jerman, Betty, *The Lively-Minded Women: The First Twenty Years of the National Housewives Register* (London: Heinemann, 1981).

Jolly, Margaretta, *Sisterhood and After: An Oral History of the UK Women's Liberation Movement, 1968-Present* (Oxford: Oxford University Press, 2019).

Kirby, Jill, *Feeling the Strain. A Cultural History of Stress in Twentieth Century Britain* (Manchester: Manchester University Press, 2019).

Knott, Sarah, *Mother: An Unconventional History* (London: Penguin, 2019).

Kristjansson, Kristjan, *The Self and its Emotions* (Cambridge: Cambridge University Press, 2010).

Kynaston, David, *Modernity Britain. Book One: Opening the Box 1957–59* (London: Bloomsbury, 2013).

Kynaston, David, *Modernity Britain, Book Two: A Shake of the Dice 1959–62* (London: Bloomsbury, 2014).

Laite, Julia, *Common Prostitutes and Ordinary Citizens: Commercial Sex in London, 1850–1960* (Basingstoke: Palgrave Macmillan, 2011).

Langhamer, Claire, 'Love and Courtship in Mid-Twentieth Century England', *The Historical Journal* 50:1 (2007), pp.173–96.

Langhamer, Claire, 'Love, Selfhood and Authenticity in Post-War Britain', *Cultural and Social History* 9:2 (2012), pp.277–97.

Langhamer, Claire, *The English in Love: the Intimate Story of an Emotional Revolution* (Oxford: Oxford University Press, 2014).

Lawler, Steph, 'Getting Out and Getting Away: Women's Narratives of Class Mobility', *Feminist Review* 63:1 (1999), pp.3–24.

Lawler, Steph, *Mothering the Self: Mothers, Daughters, Subjects* (London: Routledge, 2000).

Lawrence, Jon, *Me, Me, Me: the Search for Community in Post-War England* (Oxford: Oxford University Press, 2019).

Lawrence, Jon, 'On Historians' Re-use of Social Science Archives', *Twentieth-Century British History* 33:3 (2022), pp.432–44.

Lawson, Annette, *Adultery: An Analysis of Love and Betrayal* (London: Wiley-Blackwell, 1989).

Lessing, Doris, *The Golden Notebook* (London: Simon & Schuster, 1962).

Levy, Shawn, *Ready, Steady, Go. Swinging London and the Invention of Cool* (London: Fourth Estate, 2002).

Lewis, Jane, *Women in Britain since 1945: Family, Work and the State in the Post-war Years* (Oxford: Blackwell, 1992).

Lewis, Jane and Jo Foord, 'New Towns and New Gender Relations in Old Industrial Regions: Women's Employment in Peterlee and East Kilbride', *Built Environment* 10:1 (1984), pp.42–52.

Light, Alison, *A Radical Romance: A Memoir of Love, Grief and Consolation* (London: Fig Tree, 2019).

Linde, Charlotte, *Life Stories: The Creation of Coherence* (Oxford: Oxford University Press, 1993).

Macdonald, Charlotte, 'Body and Self: Learning to be Modern in 1920s–1930s Britain', *Women's History Review* 22:2 (2013), pp.267–79.

Mackenzie, C. and N. Stoljar (Eds), *Relational Autonomy: Feminist Perspectives on Autonomy, Agency and the Social Self* (Oxford: Oxford University Press, 2000).

Macrae, Eilidh, *Exercise in the Female Life-Cycle in Britain, 1930–1970* (Basingstoke: Palgrave, 2016).

Mahood, Linda, *Thumbing a Ride: Hitchhikers, Hostels and Counterculture in Canada* (Vancouver: UBC Press, 2018).

Mandler, Peter, 'Educating the Nation I: Schools', *Transactions of the Royal Historical Society*, Sixth series, 24 (2014), pp.5–28.

Mandler, Peter, 'Educating the Nation III: Social Mobility', *Transactions of the Royal Historical Society* 26 (2016), pp.1–23.

Mandler, Peter, *The Crisis of the Meritocracy. Britain's Transition to Mass Education since the Second World War* (Oxford: Oxford University Press, 2020).

Mandler, Peter, 'Briefing paper: parents'. https://sesc.hist.cam.ac.uk/wp-content/uploads/2018/09/Briefing-Paper-Parents.pdf

Martin, Bernice, *A Sociology of Contemporary Cultural Change* (Oxford: Oxford University Press, 1981).

Marwick, Arthur, *The Sixties: Cultural Revolution in Britain, France, Italy and the United States, c.1958–c.1974* (Oxford: Oxford University Press, 1998).

Marwick, Arthur, *History of Britain in the Swinging Sixties* (London: Little Brown, 2006).

Maslow, Abraham, 'A Theory of Human Motivation', *Psychological Review* 50 (1943), pp.370–96.

Maslow, Abraham, *Towards a Psychology of Being* (New York: 1968).

McCarthy, Helen, *Women of the World: the Rise of the Female Diplomat* (London: Bloomsbury, 2014).

McCarthy, Helen, 'Social Science and Married Women's Employment in Post-War Britain', *Past and Present* 233:1 (2016), pp.269–305.

McCarthy, Helen, 'Women, Marriage and Paid Work in Post-War Britain', *Women's History Review* 26:1 (2017), pp.46–61.

McCarthy, Helen, *Double Lives: A History of Working Motherhood* (London: Bloomsbury, 2020).

McCarthy, Helen, 'Career, Family and Emotional Work: Graduate Mothers in 1960s Britain', *Past & Present*, Supplement 15 (2020), pp.296–317.

McLeod, Hugh, *The Religious Crisis of the 1960s* (Oxford: Oxford University Press, 2007), pp.215–31.

McRobbie, Angela, *Feminism and Youth Culture* (Basingstoke: Macmillan, 2000).

Miles, Agnes, *Women and Mental Illness: The Social Concept of Female Neurosis* (London: Wheatsheaf, 1988).

Mills, Helena, 'Using the Personal to Critique the Popular: Women's Memories of 1960s Youth', *Contemporary British History*, 30:4 (2016), pp.463–83.

Mitchell, Gillian, 'Reassessing "the Generation Gap": Bill Haley's 1957 Tour of Britain, Inter-Generational Relations and Attitudes to Rock 'N' Roll in the Late 1950s', *Twentieth Century British History* 24:4 (2013), pp.573–605.

Mort, Frank, *Capital Affairs: London and the Making of the Permissive Society* (New Haven, CT: Yale University Press, 2010).

Mortimer, Penelope, *The Pumpkin Eater* (Harmondsworth: Penguin, 1962).

Mortimer, Penelope, *Daddy's Gone-a-Hunting* (orig. 1958; London: Persephone Books, 2008).
Mosely, Katrine-Louise, 'Slimming One's Way to a Better Self? Weight Loss Clubs and Women in Britain, 1967–1990', *Twentieth Century British History* 31: 4, (2020), pp.427–53.
Moskowitz, Eva, '"It's Good to Blow Your Top": Women's Magazines and a Discourse of Discontent, 1945–1965', *Journal of Women's History* 8:3 (1996), pp.66–98.
Moss, Jonathan, *Women, Workplace Protest and Political Identity in England, 1968–1985* (Manchester: Manchester University Press, 2019).
Newcombe, Suzanne, 'Stretching for Health and Well-Being: Yoga and Women in Britain, 1960–1980', *Asian Medicine* 3 (2007), pp.37–63.
Nicholson, Virginia, *Perfect Wives in Ideal Homes. The Story of Women in the 1950s* (London, Viking, 2015), pp.290–1.
Nicholson, Virginia, *How Was it for You? Women, Sex, Love and Power in the 1960s* (London: Penguin, 2019).
Noakes, Lucy, *Dying for the Nation: Death, Grief and Bereavement in Second World War Britain.* (Manchester: Manchester University Press, 2020).
Oakley, Ann, *Women Confined: Towards a Sociology of Childbirth* (Oxford: Wiley-Blackwell, 1979).
Oakley, Ann, 'Interviewing women: A Contradiction in Terms?' in H. Roberts (Ed.), *Doing Feminist Research.* (London: Routledge and Kegan Paul, 1981), pp.30–61.
Oakley, Ann, *Experiments in Knowing: Gender and Method in the Social Sciences* (Cambridge: Polity Press, 2000).
Oakley, Ann, 'Interviewing Women Again: Power, Time and the Gift', *Sociology* 50:1 (2015), pp.195–213.
Oakley, Ann, *Social Support and Motherhood. The Natural History of a Research Project* (London: Policy Pres, 2019).
Osgerby, Bill, *Youth in Britain since 1945* (Oxford: Blackwell, 1998).
Owram, Doug, *Born at the Right Time: A History of the Baby-Boom Generation* (Toronto: University of Toronto Press, 1996).
Pascoe-Leahy, Carla, *Becoming a Mother: an Australian History* (Manchester: Manchester University Press, 2023).
Passerini, Luisa, 'A Memory for Women's History: Problems of Method and Interpretation', *Social Science History* 16:4 (1992), pp.669–92.
Passerini, Luisa, *Autobiography of a Generation: Italy 1968* (Middletown, CT: Wesleyan University Press, 1996).
Paterson, Laura and Eve Worth, '"How is She Going to Manage with the Children?" Organizational Labour, Working and Mothering in Britain, c.1960–190', *Past & Present,* Supplement 15 (2020), pp.318–43.
Pearson, Helen, *The Life Project* (Harmondsworth: Penguin, 2016).
Personal Narratives Group (Eds), *Interpreting Women's Lives: Feminist Theory and Personal Narratives* (Bloomington, IN: Indiana University Press, 1989).
Phizacklea, Annie and Carol Wolkowitz, *Homeworking Women: Gender, Racism and Class at Work* (London: Sage, 1995).
Pierce, Rachel M., 'Marriage in the Fifties', *The Sociological Review* 11:2 (1963), pp.215–40.
Ramsden, E., 'Surveying the Meritocracy: The Problems of Intelligence and Mobility in the Studies of the Population Investigation Committee', *Studies in History and Philosophy of Biological and Biomedical Sciences* 47 (2014), pp.130–41.
Reid Banks, Lynn, *The L-Shaped Room* (London: Chatto & Windus,1960).
Renshaw, Daniel, 'The Violent Frontline: Space, Ethnicity and Confronting the State in Edwardian Spitalfields and 1980s Brixton', *Contemporary British History* 32 (2018), pp.231–52.

Reynolds, Tracey, *Caribbean Mothers. Identity and Experience in the UK* (London: Tufnell Press, 2005).

Robinson, Lucy, *Gay Men and the Left in Post-War Britain: How the Personal Got Political* (Manchester: Manchester University Press, 2007).

Robinson, Victoria, Jenny Hockey, and Angela Meah, '"What I Used to Do...On My Mother's Settee": Spatial and Emotional Aspects of Heterosexuality in England', *Gender, Place & Culture* 11:3 (2004), pp.417–35.

Rose, Nikolas, *Governing the Soul: The Shaping of the Private Self* (London: Routledge, 1989).

Rose, Nikolas, 'Assembling the Modern Self', in Roy Porter (Ed.), *Rewriting the Self: Histories from the Middle Ages to the Present* (London: Routledge, 1992).

Rosenwein, Barbara H., *Emotional Communities in the Early Middle Ages* (Ithaca, NY: Cornell University Press, 2006).

Sandbrook, Dominic, *Never Had it So Good: A History of Britain from Suez to the Beatles* (London: Little Brown, 2005).

Sandbrook, Dominic, *White Heat: A History of Britain in the Swinging Sixties* (London: Little Brown, 2006).

Savage, Mike, *Identities and Social Change in Britain since 1940: The Politics of Method* (Oxford: Oxford University Press, 2010).

Scheer, Monique, 'Are Emotions a Kind of Practice? (And is that what makes them have a history)? A Bourdieuean Approach to Studying Emotion', *History and Theory* 51 (2012), pp.193–220.

Schofield, Michael, *The Sexual Behaviour of Young People* (London: Longmans, Green & Co., 1965).

Shapira, M., *The War Inside: Psychoanalysis, Total War, and the Making of the Democratic Self in Post-war Britain* (Cambridge: Cambridge University Press, 2013).

Smith Wilson, Dolly, 'A New Look at the Affluent Worker: The Good Working Mother in Post-War Britain', *Twentieth Century British History* 26:3 (2015), pp.424–49.

Spanabel Emery, Joy, *A History of the Paper Pattern Industry: the Home Dressmaking Fashion Revolution* (London: Bloomsbury, 2014).

Steedman, Carolyn, *Landscape for a Good Woman* (London: Virago, 1986).

Steedman, Carolyn, 'Writing the Self: The End of the Scholarship Girl', in Jim McGuigan (Ed.), *Cultural Methodologies* (London: Sage, 1997), pp.106–25.

Strimpel, Zoe, *Seeking Love in Modern Britain: Gender, Dating and the Rise of the 'Single'* (London: Bloomsbury, 2020).

Summerfield, Penny, 'Dis/composing the Subject: Intersubjectivities in Oral History', in Tess Cosslett, Celia Lury, and Penny Summerfield (Eds), *Feminism and Autobiography* (London: Routledge, 2000), pp.91–106.

Summerfield, Penny, 'Culture and Composure: Creating Narratives of the Gendered Self in Oral History Interviews', *Cultural and Social History* 1:1 (2004), pp.65–93.

Sutcliffe-Braithwaite, Florence and Natalie Thomlinson, 'Vernacular Discourses of Gender Equality in the Post-war British Working Class', *Past & Present* 254, Issue 1 (2022), pp.277–313.

Szreter, Simon and Kate Fisher, *Sex Before the Sexual Revolution: Intimate Life in England, 1918–1963* (Cambridge: Cambridge University Press, 2010).

Taylor, Barbara, *The Last Asylum. A Memoir of Madness in our Times* (London: Penguin, 2014).

Taylor, Charles, *A Secular Age* (Cambridge, MA: Harvard University Press, 2007).

Taylor, Chloe, *The Culture of Confession from Augustine to Foucault: A Genealogy of the 'Confessing Animal'* (New York: Routledge, 2008).

Taylor, D. J., *The Lost Girls: Love, War and Literature, 1939–51* (London: Constable, 2019).

Thane, Pat, 'Girton Graduates: Earning and Learning, 1920s–1980s', *Women's History Review* 13:3 (2004), pp.347–61.

Thompson, Paul, Ken Plummer and Neli Demireva, *Pioneering Social Research* (Policy Press, online, 2021), pp.146–7.

Thomson, Mathew, *Psychological Subjects: Identity, Culture and Health in Twentieth Century Britain* (Oxford: Oxford University Press, 2006).

Thomson, Mathew, *Lost Freedom: The Landscape of the Child and the British Postwar Settlement* (Oxford: Oxford University Press, 2013).

Tinkler, Penny, *Constructing Girlhood: Popular Magazines For Girls Growing Up In England, 1920–1950* (London: Routledge, 1995).

Tinkler, Penny, 'Are You Really Living?' If Not, 'Get With It!', *Cultural and Social History* 11:4 (2014), pp.597–619.

Tinkler, Penny, 'Going Places or Out of Place? Representations of Mobile Girls and Young Women in Late-1950s and 1960s Britain', *Twentieth Century British History*, 32:2 (2020), pp.1–26.

Tinkler, Penny, Resto Cruz, and Laura Fenton, 'Recomposing Persons: Scavenging and Storytelling in a Birth Cohort Archive', *History of the Human Sciences* 34:3/4 (2021), pp.266–89.

Todd, Selina, *Young Women, Work and Family 1918–1950* (Oxford: Oxford University Press, 2005).

Todd, Selina, *The People: The Rise and Fall of the Working Class* (London: John Murray, 2014).

Todd, Selina, *Tastes of Honey. The Making of Shelagh Delaney and a Cultural Revolution* (London: Chatto & Windus, 2019).

Todd, Selina and Hilary Young, 'Baby-Boomers to "Beanstalkers": Making the Modern Teenager in Post-War Britain', *Cultural and Social History* 9:3 (2012), pp.451–67.

Tulloch, Carol, 'Style—Fashion—Dress: From Black to Post-Black', *Fashion Theory* 14:3 (2010), pp.273–303.

Tulloch, Carol, *The Birth of Cool. Style Narratives of the African Diaspora* (London: Bloomsbury, 2021).

Wadsworth, M., Kuh, D., Richards, M., and Hardy, R. (2005) 'Cohort Profile: The 1946 National Birth Cohort (MRC National Survey of Health and Development)', *International Journal of Epidemiology* 35:1 (2005), pp.49–54.

Wallis, R., 'Self-telling, Identity and Dress in Lifestyle Migration Memoirs', *Area* 51 (2019), pp.736–42.

Waters, Chris, 'Disorders of the Mind, Disorders of the Body Social', in Conekin et al. (Eds), *Moments of Modernity* (London: River Oram, 1999), pp.13–51.

Webb, Clive, 'Special Relationships: Mixed-race Couples in Post-war Britain and the United States', *Women's History Review* 26:1 (2017), pp.110–29.

Weeks, Jeffrey, *The World We Have Won: the Remaking of Erotic and Intimate Life* (London: Routledge, 2007).

Wellings, Kaye, *Sexual Behaviour in Britain: The National Survey of Sexual Attitudes and Lifestyles* (Harmondsworth: Penguin, 1994).

White, Cynthia L., *Women's Magazines 1693–1968* (London: Michael Joseph, 1970).

White, Jessica, 'Black Women's Groups, Life Narratives, and the Construction of the Self in Late Twentieth Century Britain', *The Historical Journal* 65:3 (2021), pp.1–21.

White, Jessica, 'Child-centred Matriarch or Mother Among Other Things? Race and the Construction of Working-class Motherhood in Late Twentieth-century Britain', *Twentieth Century British History* (2022), pp.1–24.

Wight, Daniel, *Workers not Wasters: Masculine Respectability, Consumption and Employment in Central Scotland* (Edinburgh: Edinburgh University Press, 1993).

Wills, Clair, *Lovers and Strangers:An Immigrant History of Post-war Britain* (London: Penguin, 2017).
Wilson, Amrit, *Finding a Voice. Asian Women in Britain* (London: Daraja Press, 2018).
Wilson, Elizabeth, *Only Halfway to Paradise: Women in Post-war Britain: 1945–68* (London: Tavistock Publications, 1980).
Wilson, Elizabeth, *Adorned in Dreams: Fashion and Modernity* (London: I.B.Taurus, 2009).
Worth, Eve, *The Welfare-State Generation. Women, Agency and Class in Britain since 1945* (London: Bloomsbury, 2021).
Worth, Rachel, 'Fashioning the Clothing Product: Technology and Design at Marks & Spencer', *Textile History* 30:2 (1999), pp.234–50.
Worth, Rachel, *Fashioning for the People: A History of Clothing at Marks & Spencer* (Oxford: Berg, 2007).
Yates, Nigel, *Love Now, Pay Later: Sex and Religion in the Fifties and Sixties* (London: SPCK, 2010).

Unpublished

Beard, Alice, 'Nova Magazine, 1965–1975: a History', PhD thesis, University of London, 2013.
Beaumont, Catriona, 'Beyond Women's Liberation. Intergenerational Female Activism in England, 1960s-1980s', Inaugural lecture, 12 Oct. 2022. https://www.youtube.com/watch?v=4eB_2Jm3yqI
Charnock, Hannah, 'Girlhood, Sexuality and Identity in England, 1950–1980', PhD thesis, University of Exeter, 2017.
Donaldson, Anni, 'An Oral History of Domestic Abuse in Scotland, 1945–1992', PhD, University of Strathclyde, 1992.
Flaherty, Emily, 'The Women's Liberation Movement in Britain 1968–1984: Locality and Organisation in Feminist Politics', PhD, University of Glasgow, 2017.
Foord, Jo, 'Conflicting Lives: Women's Work in Planned Communities', PhD thesis, University of Kent, 1990.
Halbert, Jade, 'Marion Donaldson and the Business of British Fashion, 1966–1999', PhD thesis, University of Glasgow, 2017.
Lynch, Charlie, 'Scotland and the Sexual Revolution c. 1957–1975: Religion, Intimacy and Popular Culture', PhD, University of Glasgow, 2019.
Paterson, Laura, 'Women and Paid Work in Industrial Britain', PhD thesis, University of Dundee, 2014.
Tooth Murphy, Amy, 'Reading the Lives Between the Lines: Lesbian Literature and Oral History in Post-War Britain', PhD, University of Glasgow, 2012.

Index